# PEREGRINE PSALMS

*A New Translation
from the Original Hebrew
and Set to
the Ancient
Peregrine Tone*

REV. JOSEPH L. PONESSA, SSD

# PEREGRINE PSALMS

*A New Translation
from the Original Hebrew
and Set to
the Ancient
Peregrine Tone*

REV. JOSEPH L. PONESSA, SSD

EMMAUS
ROAD
PUBLISHING
Steubenville, Ohio
www.emmausroad.org

EMMAUS
ROAD
PUBLISHING

Emmaus Road Publishing
1468 Parkview Circle
Steubenville, Ohio 43952

Library of Congress Control Number: 2015940959
ISBN: 978-1-941447-19-2

This is an original translation. The author is not relying on another English edition. The source for the Hebrew text is the *Biblia Hebraica Stuttgartensis*, and the Dead Sea Scroll references are from the Qumran Psalm Scroll, both of which are listed in the bibliography.

Cover design and layout by Mairead Cameron

*Nihil Obstat*
Rev. Jose Valliparambil, STD, Glasgow MT
7 May 2012

*Imprimatur*
Most Rev Michael William Warfel, DD, Great Falls-Billings MT
4 July 2012

The *nihil obstat* and *imprimatur* are official declarations that a work is considered to be free from doctrinal or moral error. It is not implied that those who have granted the same agree with the content, opinions, or statements expressed.

*Consultants*
Most Rev. Johannes Liesen, SSD, Breda (Netherlands)
Most Rev. Donald Trautman, SSL STD, retired
†Rev. Jay D. Dobbin, STD PhD, Great Falls-Billings MT
Rev. Denis Fournier OSB, PhD, Assumption Abbey ND
Rev. Augustine DeNoble OSB, MLS, Mount Angel Abbey OR
and especially
†Rev. Martin Fisher, BMus BSMus, Great Falls-Billings MT

*Financial Backing*
The Estate of Rev. Martin Fisher
Anita M. Tschida, Tucson AZ
Jackline M. Cox, Billings MT

# TABLE OF CONTENTS

# INTRODUCTION

"The psalms are songs. And a song is not a song unless it is sung."
(Father Lucien Deiss, 1974)

Many nations had poet kings, but ancient Israël is probably unique in having a poet as founder of the royal house. According to Scripture the young David sang psalms while in hiding, and the elderly David wrote many psalms and encouraged others to do so. With this example before them, the Hebrews became a highly poetical people. They sang psalms in their temple and in their homes, and were famed for their songs even as exiles in Babylon:

"There our captors asked us for words of song,
and our wardens for joyful song: 'Oh, sing to us a song of Ziön!'"
(Psalm 137:3)

The Hebrews wrote down the texts of many of their songs, some of which were collected in the Book of Psalms. At first only the consonants were written, while both the vowels and their tonal values remained in the sphere of oral tradition. Finally in the eighth century AD, scholars of the Masoretic school wrote down the vowels for the first time, but the cantillation marks that they put into the text remain obscure.

Christians claimed the Book of Psalms as the prayerbook of the Church, and in both cathedral and monastery the Psalms have been chanted for nearly two millennia. The first book of annotated music is the tenth-century *Liber cantatorium* (Cod.Sang.359) produced and preserved at the Abbey of Sankt-Gallen in Switzerland. Most of the materials in that volume, however, are much older. Already by late antiquity, the Greek and Latin rites had begun to employ eight chanting modes in a well-developed system.

The corpus of Gregorian chant contains one mode that stands outside the eight-mode system and has been identified as an ancient Hebrew melody. Eric Werner (*The Sacred Bridge*, 1959, p. 466) found that Yemenite Jews sing Psalm 114 to *tonus peregrinus*, the "pilgrim tone" on which that psalm is sung in Sunday Vespers of the Roman Office (*Liber usualis*, 117). Such wide geographical dispersal is a sign of great antiquity in musicology as in other sciences such as those of linguistics and genetics. Geographically, the central point between Rome and Yemen is Jerusalem.

Tonus peregrinus differs from the other eight Gregorian modes by being the only chant in the collection with two tonics—the first line of each verse is one step higher (La) than the second (Sol). Thus the music itself wanders, or goes on pilgrimage, and possesses a pleasing variety. Tonus peregrinus can provides a pattern to convey the innate musicality of the text.

Heretofore, translators have allowed the immediate context to dictate the translation of phrases, but the Hebrews, like other ancient peoples, used recurring phrases in their poetry. Phrases that fall repeatedly at the end of a line receive the same chant notes each time the verse is sung. Such text phrases become musical leitmotifs as well. The theological phrase "Hallelu-Yah," for example, occurs twenty-one times, always at the beginning or the end of a psalm. The anthropological phrase "children of Adam," for another example, appears twenty times and at the very end of a verse sixteen times, where it is always sung on the same notes:

> "All around, the unjust people are on parade,
> as if exalting the follies of *the childrèn óf Àdam*." (Psalm 12:9)

Such phrases often become lost in translation. One published translation, for example, renders "children of Adam" in five different ways —"children of men" (11:4 et al.), "sons of men" (12:2/9, 58:2), "human race" (21:11), "human prey" (57:5) or "low people" (49:3). Proliferation of such alternative renderings can only cloud over the resonances in the poetic text.

Theological terminology went the other direction, however, toward greater simplification. From the time of the Septuagint onwards, translators reduced three different Hebrew terms to "God" (*'el, 'eloah, 'elohiym*) and four terms to "LORD" (*'adon, 'adoniym, yhwh, yah*). Reduction of seven Hebrew terms to two reveals a suppression of vocabulary. The Psalms hold many more names and titles of God than have been transmitted. These theological phrases are among the most important, because this is sacred poetry. The goals of transparency and consistency would seem to necessitate restoring the nomenclature of the divine.

> "O Divine One, let me sing to you a song made new!"
> (Psalm 144:9)

The reader should note that The KJV/RSV tradition versifies differently than others. As a consequence the Interpreter's Bible commentary gives something like 1(2) or 10(11) for all the references; Anchor Bible, on the other hand, just ignores the RSV numbering. The Vatican document Liturgiam authenticam (2001) says that the *Nova Vulgata* translation is supposed to be the model for Catholic editions. Therefore, I have used their versification system, which is more universal.

# ONE

Psalm 1 introduces the virtuous individual, contrasted with the unjust mob. *'Iysh* is a man of substance, desirable as a spouse. Elsewhere, *'iysh* and *'adam* are nobleman and commoner (49:3, 62:10), *'iysh* and *'iyshah* are a husband and his wife (128:3). Standing at the head of the collection, then, is a psalm that proposes the authenticity of the individual. Though the Hebrews were a tribal people, they invented the notion of personhood, along with the Greeks and at about the same time. The identity of a person comes in part from social bonds, but even more from within.

1:1a **Blêssedness bèlongs to thát man \***
     *following* **no advice fròm únjust peòple,**          *78:10*

> **Blessedness** appears twenty-six times in the psalms, and is a "plural of the abstract." Singular *'asher* means **blessing**, plural *'ashriym* takes the construct form *'ashrey-*). **Blessedness belongs to that man** (*'ashrey ha'iysh* 1:1; *'ashrey 'iysh* 112:1) refers to a man of rank, who may be a nobleman (49:3, 62:10) or a husband (128:1).

> MUSICAL NOTE
> *Tonus Peregrinus* has a figure of La-Ti on the first syllable, shown here by circumflex accent ("blêssedness"). The first line has tonic of La, until a grave accent inflects downward to Sol. The line terminates with Ti, La, Sól, (unaccented Sol if needed, ) Fa and an asterisk (\*).

> The second line drops down to the tonic of Sol, until the concluding syllables on Re, Fá, Fa, elided Mi/Re always on the penultima, and Re always on the ultima.

1:1b **stânding with no sinnèrs on the páthway, \***
     **sitting with no scoffèrs ín sèssion,**
1:2   **bût delighting in** *the Torah of thè Font of Béing* **\***
     **and musing on his Toràh,** *dáy ànd night,*          *22:3*

> **Torah of the Font of Being** (*torath yhwh* 1:2, 19:8, 119:1). Torah means "teaching," not "law." Christian theology often contrasts law and gospel, but Benedict XVI made a fine parallel between the Torah of Moses and the Torah of the Messiah (the Gospel).

1

The complete divine nomenclature revealed to Moses at the burning bush was *FONT OF BEING, Divine One of your fathers, Divine One of Abraham, Divine One of Isaac, Divine One of Jacob* (*yhwh 'elohey 'ebotam 'elohey 'abraham 'elohey yitshaq 'elohey ya'aqob* Ex 3:5). On one end it was abbreviated *Divine One of Jacob* (*'elohey ya'aqob* 20:2, 46:8/12, 75:10, 76:7, 81:2/5, 84:9, 94:7) and on the other end *FONT OF BEING* (*yhwh,* which constitutes the opening word of twenty psalms: 3/6/7/11/15/21/23/24/27/38/88/93/97/99/120/131/139/141), then just to *BEING* (*yah* 68:5/19, 77:12, 89:9, 94:7/12, 102:19, 115:17/18, 118:5/ 14/17/18/19, 130:3, 135:4, 150:6). The revelation to Moses makes clear the meaning of the Name: "I Am Who Am," the font and origin of all being (compare liturgical phrases *fons et origo, caritatis fons et origo bonitatis, fons omnis sanctitatis, fontem vitae*).

**1:3**     **bêing *like a tree*, planted by *water-filled streàms,* †
**whose fruit ripens *in seasòn* but whose leáves fade not, ***
**and which thrives, hòwéver tènded.**                    *145:15*

*Like a tree* (*ke'ets*), here and in Jeremiah 17:8, introduces an extended simile, or parable. This is the first of many plant similes in the Book of the Psalms. The plants need to be accompanied by water images like ***water-filled streams*** (*palgey mayim* 1:3, 119:136).

MUSICAL NOTE
Verse 3 comprises three lines. In *Tonus Peregrinus*, the first line of three is prefatory, and is chanted on the tonic of La, until the inflected syllable goes down one note, to Sol. This kind of line ends in a dagger mark (†). The last two lines are chanted as in verse 1.

**1:4**     **Nòt so are thè unjust peóple, ***
**but rather *like the chaff*, blown àboút by wind.**

Verse 4 contains the second plant simile, ***like the chaff*** (*kammots* 1:4), which appears elsewhere as ***like chaff*** (*kemots* 35:5). Here it contrasts with the simile ***like a tree*** in the preceding verse. Similar contrasting similes are found in Chapter 17 of Jeremiah.

**1:5**     ***Thêrefore* unjust people stand nòt *at the júdgment,* ***     *25:8, 25:9*
**or sinners in concìl wíth the jùst ones.**
**1:6**     **Fôr the FONT OF BEING shows thè path to júst ones, ***
**but *the path of unjùst peóple* ìs nil.**                    *146:9*

# TWO

NEW TESTAMENT — Verses 1–2 in Acts 4:25–26
Verse 7 in Acts 13:33
Verse 9 in Rev 2:27, 12:5, 19:15
LITURGY OF HOURS — Office of Readings on Sunday I

The author of Psalm 2 never speaks in the first person, but perhaps refers to himself in the third person as "messiah" (verse 2), "king" (6) and "son" (7 and 12). The word "son" appears twice, first in Hebrew (*ben*, 7) and later in Aramaic (*bar*, 12). God orders the lesser, Aramaic-speaking kings to submit to the authority of his designated, Hebrew-speaking king. This is a psalm for enthronement, and at such times the kingdom was often vulnerable.

2:1   **Fôr what reasòn did the géntiles rant, ***
     **and natiòns múrmur ìn vain?**

2:2   ***Eârthly kings* rose up and togethèr princes plótted, ***
     **against FONT OF BEING and against his ànoíntèd one!**

> ***Earthly kings*** (*malkey 'arets* 2:2, 76:13, 89:28, 138:4, 148:11) in verse 2 and ***earthly judges*** (*shoftey 'arets*) in verse 10 bookend Psalm 2 and stand in parallel in Psalm 148:10/11. Whether anointed as king or acclaimed as judge, earthly rulers hold their authority only by sufferance of the divine monarch, and they contradict their mandate by putting themselves in opposition to the rule of heaven.

2:3   **"Ôh, let ùs burst their bóndage ***
     **and cast fròm ús their chaìrs!"**

2:4   ***Ône Seated in thè Skies* is laúghing! ***
     **Adonay is dèrídìng them!**

> ***Seated in the Skies*** (*yosheb basshamayim* 2:4; *hayyosheb basshamayim* 123:1) is a participial divine appellative, like ***Seated upon the Cherubim*** (*yosheb kerubiym* 80:2, 99:1), ***Seated in Ziön*** (*yosheb tsiyyon* 9:12), ***Rider on the Clouds*** (*rokeb ba'arabot* 68:5) and ***Rider in the Heaven of Heavens in the East*** (*rokeb bishmey shemey qedem* 68:34). Here it stands in parallel with the divine title ***Adonay*** (*'adonay*), the "plural of majesty" of Master or Lord (*'adon*), with a first-person suffix (*-ay*). This word came to be pronounced in synagogue in place of the Tetragrammaton, but it has its own proper place in the text as well.

2:5 Thên he cònfronts them ín his wrath, *
and in his angèr rébùkes them:

2:6 "Fôr I have placed à king of my own *
on Ziön, my *mount òf hóliness.*"  43:3

2:7 Lêt me recount the law the Font òf Being tóld me, *
"My Son are you! I have this day bègóttèn you!

2:8 Âsk for this fròm me, †
and I will give gentìles as your héritage, *
and for your takìng, *énds òf land,*

*Ends of land* ('*afsey-'arets* 2:8, 22:28, 59:14, 72:8; *kol 'afsey-'arets* 67:8, 98:3), like synonymous idiom **limits of land** (*qatsweh-'erets* 46:10, 48:11, 61:3, 65:6, 135:7) can mean either the extent of the Holy Land or the edge of the continent. The latter is favored in **from the river to ends of land** (*minnahar 'ad-'afsey-'arets* 72:8), where the Jordan is the western boundary of tributary territory.

2:9 for you to shepherd them wìth iron ás a staff, *
to shatter them *like shards* òf á kìlnman."  31:13

2:10 Ând now, O kìngs, attain wísdom; *
come, *earthly judgès,* tó the knòwledge!

The distinction between **earthly kings** (*malkey 'arets*) in verse 2 and **earthly judges** (*shoftey 'arets* 2:10, 148:11) here indicates that the Hebrews knew that some of their neighbors (like the Egyptians) had crowned kings and others (like the Athenians) had elected leaders.

2:11 Sêrve the Font of Beìng with atténtion *
and revel with trembling as you èmbráce thè Son,

2:12 lêst he be angered and you lose thè way, †
for his anger ignites *as ìf in a móment.* *
*Blessedness belongs to all takìng réfuge ìn him!*

*As if in a moment* (*kime'at* 2:12, 73:2, 81:5, 94:17, 105:12, 119:87) combines the comparative particle *ki-* with the adverb *me'at. Me'at* is an adverb meaning "but a little," the antonym of *me'od* "quite a lot."

*Blessedness* ('*ashriym*) *belongs to all who revere the Font of Being* (*kol yire'yhwh* 128:1), *to all who take refuge in him* (*kol hosey bo* 2:12; *kol hahosiym bo* 18:31, 34:23, 2 Sam 22:31). These blessings are not limited to the chosen people but are extended to any and all who revere and take refuge in the God of Israël.

# THREE

Psalm 3 begins a set of thirty-nine psalms, all but one of which are surtitled "of David." This subset seems to have been assimilated whole into the final collection. Psalm Three is also the first of twenty psalms to begin with the Divine Name, in two groupings at the start and at the end of the collection. For the fifty psalms that lie between, the Name appears only rarely.

3:1    (A Mizmor of David, as he fled from before the face of Absalom, his son.)

The King James / Revised Standard family of translations assign no verse number to the ancient psalm titles. Consequently, they have verse numbers that are frequently one less than other editions. This volume follows the numeration of Nova Vulgata Editio, which accords with the vast majority of editions.

3:2    **Ô Font of Being,** *how màny are* **foés to me!** *
**Many are risìng úp agaìnst me!**

*How many* (*ma rabbu*) appears twice in the Psalms (3:2 and 104:24). *Rabbu* is the verb derived from the adjective *rab*, meaning "great" in singular and "many" in plural, as in the next verse. By contrast, the adjective *gadol* means "great" in singular but "great ones" in plural.

3:3    *Mâny àre saying* **tó my soul:** *
**"Oh,** *for him there is no salvation* **ìn thé Divìne One!"**

*Many are saying* (*rabbiym 'omriym* 3:3, 4:7) refers to those spreading despair. Participle *rabbiym* seems to multiply threats—**bullocks manifold** (*pariym rabbiym* 22:13) and **waters manifold** (*mayim rabbiym* 18:17, 29:3, 32:6, 77:20, 93:4, 107:23, 144:7). The main verb, however, can multiply pleasant things—**their grain and their grape are manifold** (*deganam wethiyrosham rabbu* 4:8).

*For him there is no salvation* (*'eyn yeshu'athah lo* 3:3; *she'eyn lo teshu'ah* 146:3) is another defeatist expression like the following:
—**There is no Divine One** (*'eyn 'elohiym* 10:4)
—**There is no rescuer** (*'eyn-matssiyl* 7:3, 50:22, 71:11)
—**There is no helper** (*'eyn-'ozer* 22:12, 72:12, 107:12, Is 63:5)
—**There is no savior** (*'eyn-moshiya'* 18:42, 2 Sam 22:42, Deut 22:27, 28:29/31, Judg 12:3, Is 47:15, Hos 13:4).

5

*Divine One* (*'elohiym*) is the "plural of majesty" of the elative divine appellative *'eloah*, often appearing with a personal suffix as *my Divine One* (*'elohay*), *our Divine One* (*'eloheynu*), *your Divine One* (*'eloheyka*). The Septuagint used the single word *theos* to translate three Hebrew words—*'el, 'eloah* and *'elohiym*.

3:4    **Bût You, Font of Being, are à shield aboút me, ***
**My Glory, and the liftìng óf my head.**

*My Glory* (*kebodiy* 3:4, 16:9, 57:9) is a divine appellative, perhaps an abbreviation of **God of Glory** (*'el hakkabod* 29:3) or **King of Glory** (*melek hakkabod* 24:7/8/9/10).

3:5    *Wîth my voice* **I call to thè Font of Béing, ***
**and he answers me from his *mount òf hóliness*.**       *43:3*

*With my voice* (*qoliy* 3:5, 142:2) might also be interpreted "with the voice" or "vocally." In that case, the ending would be considered not the first person singular possessive, but an ancient Hebrew adverbial case ending.

3:6    **Dôwn I lày, and I wént to sleep; ***
**I awoke, for the Font of Beìng sústaìns me,**
3:7    **ûndismayed though a people by thè tens of thoúsands ***
**all around bè sét agaìnst me.**
3:8    **Rîse up, Font of Being! Save mè, my Divíne One! ***
**So strike on the jaw all my rivals! *Dèfång* the ùnjust!**

*Defang* (*shinney resha'iym shibbarta* 3:8; *heras-shinneymo befiymo* 58:7), or literally "smash the teeth" sounds like a harsh prayer. However, if the enemies were preparing to bite and tear at one's flesh, pulling the teeth would render them incapable of the harm intended.

3:9    **Tô the Font of Being belòngs the salvátion; ***
**upon your peoplè bé your blèssings.**

# FOUR

NEW TESTAMENT — Verse 5 at Ephesians 4:26
LITURGY OF HOURS — Saturday Night Prayer (Compline)

Psalm 4 seems to take place in a time of siege (verse 2). During prolonged siege supplies run out, and people do go to bed hungry (5). Grain and grape (8) refer to the crops; sacrifices (6) refer to thank oblations after the harvest.

4:1  (For the Director, *with strumming chords. A Mizmor of David.*)

> *With strumming chords* (*binegiynot*) tells the musicians how they are to accompany a psalm. The noun occurs mainly in the titles (4:1, 6:1, 54:1, 55:1, 61:1, 67:1, 76:1) but once in a psalm text: ***strumming chords for those imbibing drink*** (*negiynot shothey shekar* 69:13).

4:2  **Whên I call, answer me, my Divìne One of Jústice! \***
**During the siege, you released me! Pity me ànd heár my plea!**

> *During the siege* (*battsar* 4:2; *batssarah* 81:8; *batssaratha* 120:1; *betsarah* 91:15; *be'et tsarah* 37:39; *le'ittot batssarah* 9:10, 10:1, *le'et tsar* Job 38:23); *from the siege* (*mitssar* 32:7). When a city is being besieged, the inhabitants are confined to the narrow space between the walls, and those who confine them are the besiegers outside. Sieges are always times of great distress, even in a bulwark city (*'iyr matsor* 31:22, 60:11), with strong walls and good provisions. Always with a sense of great constraint, the word *tsar* or *tsarah* means:
> (a) something narrow, like a **narrow place** (*maqom tsar* Num 22:26, 2 Kings 6:1, Is 49:20) or a **narrow pit** (*be'er tsarah* Prov 23:27)
> (b) distress, like the besieging of a city or of a soul, or
> (c) the besieging foe who inflicts distress.

4:3  *Sôns of rank*, **how long will my Glòry be pút to shame? \***
**You love vanity! Yoù seék beguìlement!**

> *Sons of rank* (*beney 'iysh* 4:3) are those who were born with a silver spoon in their mouths and whose value system is not sound. In two other verses (49:3 and 62:10) they are contrasted with children of the common people (*beney 'adam;* see note at 11:4). These terms refer to social class, of course, not to age category.

4:4  **Sô know that the FONT OF BEING favòrs his devóted one; \***
**the FONT OF BEING listens when Ì cáll tò him.**

7

4:5 **Trêmble, and do nòt give yoursélf to sin; ***
**speak in your hearts** *on the place where yoù lié*, **and bè calm.**

> *On the place where you lie* (*'al mishkabkem* 4:5; *'al-mishkebotham* 149:5;
> *'al mishkabo* 36:5) paraphrases the term for bed (*'eres*):
> —*my bed* (*'arsiy* 6:7)
> —*on his sickbed* (*'al-'eres deway* 41:4), "on his bed of illnesses"
> —*on my bed of cushions* (*'al-'eres yetsu'ay* 132:3).

4:6 *Ôffer the oblàtions of* **jústice, ***
**and trust in thè** F**ÓNT OF** B**ÈING.**

> *Offer the oblations* (*zibhu zibhey* 4:6, 27:6, 107:22, 116:17) is "internal
> accusative," when the verb takes a direct object that derives from the same
> root. Some other examples are:
> —*sing a song* (*shiyru shiyr* 33:3, 96:1, 98:1, 149:1)
> —*want a want* (*wayyith'awwu ta'awah* 106:14, Prov 21:26)
> —*pursue a suit* (*riybah ribiy* 43:1, 119:154; . . . *ribeka* 74:22)
> —*do a deed* (*po'al pa'alta* 44:2).

4:7 *Mâny are saying,* **"Oh, who wìll show us whát is good? ***     *3:3*
**Lift upon us** *the light of your Face*, **Ò** F**ÓNT OF** B**ÈING!"**

> *The light of your Face* (*'or paneyka* 4:7, 44:4, 89:16) reappears once with
> another cognate noun (*me'or paneyka* 90:8). It is more than *a light of*
> *flame* (*'or 'esh* 78:14), such as guided the people through the desert; it
> is *the light of life* (*'or hahayyim* 56:14), like the rays of light that shone
> around the face of Moses.

4:8 **Înto my heàrt you have pút more joy ***
**than when their grain and their grape àre mánifold.**

4:9 **Whên Shalom is complete, Ì will reclíne and sleep, ***
**for you alone,** F**ONT OF** B**EING, settle me** *in a place of sècúrìty*.

> *In a place of security* (*labetah*) is connected twice with "to dwell" (4:9,
> 16:9), and once with "to lead" (78:53). The latter gives the best sense of the
> phrase: "He led them *to a place of security* (*labetah*) lest they should fear
> as the sea engulfed their enemies" (78:53).

## FIVE

NEW TESTAMENT — Verse 10 at Rom 3:13
LITURGY OF HOURS — Lauds of Monday I

Psalm 5 refers to the temple (verse 8) and thus indicates that the psalm is post-Davidic, because the temple was built by David's son, Solomon. Perhaps the title "of David" meant not that the historical king was the author of the psalm, but that the psalm was composed in a style like that of David. The shadow of the poet-king fell upon every subsequent Hebrew poet.

5:1    (For the Director, with wind instruments.
       A Mizmor of David.)

5:2    **Tô the things I declare lend Ear, Ò Font of Béing! ***
       **Understand hòw Í am síghing!**

5:3    **Âttune to the call of my beseechìng, †**
       *my King ànd my Divíne One,* ***
       **for to you I pray, Ò Fónt of Bèing!**

> ***My King and my Divine One*** (*malkiy we'elohay* 5:3, 84:4; *malkiy 'elohiym* 44:5; *'elohiym malkiy* 74:12) conjoins a political term with a theological one, appropriating language from the human order for application to the divine. God is sovereign of both orders.

5:4    *Ât dawn,* **may yoù listen tó my call; ***
       *at dawn,* **I reach out tò yoú, ànd wait,**

> ***At dawn*** (*boqer* 5:4a/b; *babboqer* 88:14, 90:5/6/14, 92:3), the sun rises (104:22) and the flowers bloom (90:6), animals and people are released from sleep (90:5), eastbound prayers rise up from the temple and from every home (88:14), and the heir of Adam goes out to his work (104:23). It is a time for mercy (see 90:14).

5:5    *Nôr surely* **are you a god pleàsed with injústice, ***         9:19
       *nor* **does evil àbíde withìn you,**

> This is the first apparition of the term ***god*** ('*el*), base word for the deity in the Semitic languages. Built up from this term are more elaborate ***godhead*** ('*eloah*) and ***the Divine One*** ('*elohiym*). Although not as common as ***Divine One*** or ***Most High*** ('*elyon*) in the psalms, it joins with them in compound phrases ***God-Divine One*** ('*el 'elohiym* 50:1, 84:8) and ***God-Most High*** ('*el 'elyon* 78:35).

9

**5:6**    **nôr can foolish peoplè stand befóre your Eyes; \***
**you detest all *doèrs óf èvil*;**

> **Doers of evil** (*po'eley 'awen* 5:6, 6:9, 14:4, 28:3, 36:13, 53:5, 59:3, 64:3, 92:8/10, 94:4/16, 101:8, 125:5, 141:4/9) and those **indulging in vice** (*po'alu 'awlah* 37:1; *po'elu 'awlah* 119:3) and **doing foul deeds** (*'olot tif'alut* 58:3) stand against the one **doing justice** (*po'el tsedek* 15:2) and the **Doer of Saving Deeds** (*po'al yeshu'ot* 74:12).

**5:7**    **yoû make nil *speakèrs of beguílement*, \***
**a *man of bloodshed* and deceit, loathing thè FÓNT OF BÈING.**

> **Speakers of beguilement** (*dobrey kazab* 5:7, 58:4; *debar-kazab* Prov 30:8) are like **those who speak wantonly** (*dobrey sheqer* 64:12) and the **speakers of idle things** (*dobrey sheqariym* 101:7). Though they may be **speaking Shalom** (*dobrey shalom*) among their friends, they have evil in their hearts (28:3). They stand over against the **speaker of truth** (*dober 'emeth* 15:2).

> **A man of bloodshed** (*'iysh damiym* 5:7) is singular only here. The **men of bloodshed** (*'anshey damiym* 26:9, 55:24, 59:3, 139:19) are those of high station, associated with the shedding of innocent blood, especially through human sacrifice. Twice the phrase expands as here to **a man of bloodshed and deceit** (*'iysh damiym umirmah* 5:7; *'anshey damiym umirmay* 55:24).

**5:8**    **Bût I, *by your great mercy*, càn enter yoúr house; \***
**I bow to the temple of your glory, ìn áwe òf you.**

> **By your great mercy** (*berob hasdeka* 5:8, 69:14). Mercy does not admit of degrees; one either has mercy or one does not. "The quality of mercy is not strained," as Shakespeare wrote in the *Merchant of Venice*. So **great mercy** (*rob hasdeyka*) is not relative but absolute.

**5:9**    **Ô FONT OF BEING, lead me by your *just deèds*; †**        *143:1*
**because òf *those who gláre at me*, \***
**make level your paths bèfóre my face.**

> **Those who glare at me** (*shoreray* 5:9, 27:11, 54:7, 59:11; *shuray* 92:12). *Shorray* is masculine plural participle (*shorriym*) with a first-person singular ending (*-iy*), like *Adonay* (my Lordship), *Elohay* (my Divine One), *Shadday* (my God of the Field), *son'ay* (those who hate me), *'oybay* (my enemies), *kappay* (my palms), *'oznay* (my ears), etc.

5:10  **Fôr nothing *in their mouths* is steadfàst;** †
 **their insides are rubble, theìr throat an *ópen tomb*;** *     *Jer 5:16*
 **they flattèr wíth their tongues.**

*In their mouths* (*befiyhem* 5:10, 49:14, 59:8, 78:30/36, 135:17; *befiw* 62:5) the idols have no breath, enemies foam, people commit perjury and cattle are fattened for slaughter. When the psalmist speaks in the first person,

however, *in my mouth* (*befiy* 34:2, 40:4, 89:2, 109:30; *befiw* 38:15) is praise-craft with which to make known God's fidelity.

5:11  **Cônvict them, O Divine Òne;** †
 **let them fall *by theìr own devíces*;** *
 **in their great rebellions banish them, for rèséntìng you.**

Those who have glared at the psalmist will fall *by their own devices* (*mimmo 'tsotheyhem* 5:11; *bemo 'tsotheyhem* 81:13), taking the bad *counsel* (*'atsah* 1:1) that they themselves have given.

5:12  **Bût let them rejoice, all who trust ìn you;** †
 *eternally* **let them sing, às you protéct them,** *
 **and let them exult in you, whò lóve yoùr Name.**

*Eternally* (*le'olam*) is a well-fixed temporal phrase, describing the expanse connecting the present time to the limitless future. This most frequent of several synonymous phrases occurs at least twenty-eight times in the Book of Psalms (5:12, 15:5, 30:7/13, 31:2, 37:18/27, 41:13, 49:9, 71:1, 72:17/19, 78:69, 89:53, 92:9, 102:13, 103:9, 105:8, 117:2, 119:89/98/111/142/144/152, 135:13, 138:8, 146:10). The same idea is found roughly in the following variations:
—*eternally* (*'olam* 9:8, 125:1)
—*for ever and an age* (*le'olam wa'ed* 9:6, 45:18, 119:44, 145:1/2/21)
—*ever and an age* (*'olam wa'ed* 10:16, 21:5, 45:7, 48:15, 52:10, 104:5)
—*for an age, for an eternity* (*la'ad le'olam* 111:8, 148:6)
—*for an eternity* (*'ad-'olam* 18:51, 48:9)
—*for eternity* (*'ad-ha'olam* 28:9, 133:4).

5:13  **Hôw you bless a just òne, FONT OF BÉING!** *
 **Like a buckler, with favòr yoú cròwn him.**

NEW TESTAMENT — Verse 9 at Mt 7:23 and Lk 13:27
LITURGY OF HOURS — Office of Readings on Monday I

Psalms 6 and 38 begin with exactly the same verse, but the other psalmist is preoccupied with guilt and this one with illness. Death knocks on his door (6). Doers of wickedness hover nearby (9), waiting to claim his property. This psalmist only hints at his guilt but it is enough to earn this a place among the seven Penitential Psalms (6, 32, 38, 51, 102, 130 and 143).

6:1    (For the Director *with strings.*                                      *4:1*
       *Upon the octave.* A Mizmor of David.)

> Cardinal numeral **eight** is *shemonah*, and ordinal numeral **eighth** is *sheminiy*. Two psalms are titled **upon the eighths** (*'al hashemiyniyth* 6:1, 12:1). This phrase could mean, in declining order of probability:
> —the tune is to use an interval of eight notes, or an octave
> —the psalm is for the eight-day festivals of Passover and Booths
> —the psalm is to be played upon an eight-stringed harp
> —the name of the melody is "Upon the Eighths."

6:2 = 38:2
       **Ô FONT OF BEING, nor in your ànger chastíse me, ***
       **nor in yoùr wráth corrèct me,**
6:3    **Pîty me, FONT OF BEING! Hòw weary àm I! ***
       **Heal me, FONT OF BEING! How shakèn áre my bones!**
6:4    **Môst shakèn also ís my soul, ***
       **and you, FONT ÒF BÉING, hòw long ... ?**
6:5    **Côme *back*, O FONT OF BEÌNG! Set my soúl free! ***
       **Make me safe for the sake òf yoúr mèrcy.**

> **Font of Being, how long? Come back, Font of Being!** (*yhwh 'ad-matay shubah yhwh* 6:5). The bones and soul of this psalmist were shaken, and now his speech is rattled, too. By the end of Psalm 6, the enemies are the ones who will be rattled. The author of Psalm 90 uses some of the same words, but has more composure in his mode of expression (*shubah yhwh 'ad-matay* 90:13).

6:6    **Fôr in the Death there is no rècalling óf you. ***
       **In Sheöl, who can gìve laúd tò you?**

6:7 Grôwn wearied wìth groaning ám I. *
I weep all night on my couch; with tears I bèdéw my bed.

6:8 Wâsted from thè strain is my eye, *
swollen from àll my distrèsses.

The human eye has been **wasted from the strain** (*'asheshah mikka'as*; *'asheshah beka'as* 31:10), become swollen (6:8), eclipsed (69:4), dimmed (69:24, 88:10) or filled with tears (116:8, 119:136), and the eyelids has become folded (77:5). The divine Eye has beheld our progress (139:16), perceives who are the steadfast (17:2), and keeps sentinel over us like the dilation of the pupil of an Eye (17:8).

6:9 Tûrn from me, all *dòers of évil*, *                                    5:6
for FONT OF BEING hears the soùnd óf my weèping.

6:10 Fônt OF BEING hears mè pray for píty. *
FONT OF BEING àccépts my plea.

6:11 Shâmed and most shaken àre all my rívals; *
shamed again altògéther àre they.

NEW TESTAMENT — Verse 10 at Rev 2:23
LITURGY OF HOURS — Midday Prayer on Monday I

Foes pursue the author of Psalm 7, but by the end they are in full flight before God, who can read "hearts and selves," literally "hearts and kidneys" (verse 10). The psalmist has begun in danger, but by the end nonchalantly strums his strings. The survivor is the one left singing after the battle.

7:1 (A Shiggayon of David,
which he sang to the FONT OF BEING because of Cush the Benjaminite.)

7:2 **Ô FONT OF BEING! My Divine Òne!** †
*In you have Ì taken réfuge!* *
**Save me from all** *who hunt for mè*, **ánd releàse me,**

A number of sanctuary cities were designated throughout the land, at which people could escape vengeance. At the top of five psalms, the psalmist declares that he has taken refuge in God:
—*In you have I taken refuge* (*beka hasiythiy* 7:2, 31:2, 71:1)
—*I have taken refuge in you* (*hasiythiy bak* 16:1)
—*In the FONT OF BEING I took refuge* (*beyhwh hasiythiy* 11:1).

*Those who hunt for me* (*rodfay* 7:2, 31:16, 35:3, 57:4, 119:84/150), *who hunt for my soul* (*yirdof nafshiy* 7:6, *doresh lenafshiy* 143:3), are those *pursuing harm for me* (*dorshey ra'athiy* 38:13) or *seeking harm for me* (*mebaqshey ra'athiy* 38:13, 71:13/24).

7:3 **lêst one could feed** *like à lion* **át my throat,** *
**mauling while** *no rescuèr woúld thère be.*

*Like a lion* (*ke'aryeh* 7:3, 10:9, 17:12) is first of a number of animal comparisons in the psalms—lion, bird, deer, dove, eagle, and sheep. Metaphors (without "like") are concentrated in Psalm 22—worm, bullock, lion, hound, and ox. At times there are literal animals, too, as the lion cubs (104:21) and raven chicks (147:9) beg for their food.

*There is no rescuer* (*'eyn-matssiyl* 7:3, 50:22, 71:11) is a defeatist statement that belongs to the same pattern as:
—*There is no Divine One* (*'eyn 'elohiym* 10:4)
—*There is no helper* (*'eyn-'ozer* 22:12, 72:12, 107:12, Is 63:5)
—*There is no savior* (*'eyn-moshiya'* 18:42, 2 Sam 22:42, Deut 22:27, 28:29/31, Judg 12:3, Is 47:15, Hos 13:4).

7:4　Ô FONT OF BEING, Divine One! Ìf I had dóne this thing, *
　　　if guilt were ùpón my palms,
7:5　îf I had deàlt badly wíth my friend, *
　　　or punished my foe bèyónd reàson,
7:6 see 143:3
　　　thên a fiend could *hunt for my soùl,* †　　　　　　　*7:2*
　　　and overtake and tramplè to the groúnd my life, *
　　　and my glory would lie ùpón thè dust.
7:7　Rîse up, O FONT OF BEING, in yoùr wrath! †
　　　Arise against the àttack of my foes *
　　　and awaken, my God, tò gíve jùdgment!
7:8　Thên let an assembly of nations gàther aboút you,
　　　and over them may you prèsíde àgain.
7:9　Lêt the FONT OF BEING discern among peoplès. †
　　　Judge me, FONT OF BEING, *as befìts what is júst to me,* *
　　　and as befits *the integrìty* withìn me.

This psalmist invites God to judge *as befits what is just to me* (*ketsidqiy* 7:9, 18:21/25, 2 Sam 22:21/25) but later in the same psalm praises God *as befits what is just to him* (*ketsidko* 7:18). This psalmist knows that the virtue of religion (giving God his due) is a subcategory of the virtue of justice (giving all their due).

The virtue of humility is recognizing where one stands before God, so the psalmist does not violate humility by speaking *as befits the integrity within me* (*kethummiy* 7:9; *bethummiy* 26:1/11, 41:13). A later psalmist also speaks of his *integrity of heart* (*thom lebabiy* 101:2) and another of David's *integrity of heart* (*thom lebabo* 78:72).

7:10　Kîndly stop the evil of unjust peoplè, †
　　　and estàblish the júst one; *
　　　for the Divine Just One probes *hearts ànd sélves withìn.*

*Hearts and selves within* (*libbot ukelayot* 7:10; *kilyothay welibbiy* 26:2) are literally hearts and kidneys. The ancient peoples practiced a form of superstition called "haruscopy," reading of sheep livers; the Akkadians put together a vast literature of liver omens, such as "if there are seven gall bladders, you will be king of the universe." The Book of Revelation concurs that God is the true interpreter of kidneys and hearts (Rev 2:23).

15

7:11 Â shield for me is the Mòst High Divíne One, *
Savior of *thè steádfast-heàrted.*

**Steadfast-hearted** (*yishrey leb* 7:11, 11:2, 32:11, 36:11, 64:11, 94:15, 97:11; *yosher lebab* 119:7). The adjective *yosher* means to be equitable and fair. Heart is the seat of mind in Hebrew anthropology, and so the phrase means "straight thinking" or "fair minded." The phrase is so important that it stands at the very end of two psalms (32:11, 64:11).

7:12 Ône who is Divine jùdges with jústice, *
and God is zealoùs *évery day.*

**Every day** (*bekol yom* 7:12, 145:2) is distributive like its synonym *day by day* (*yom yom* 61:9, 68:20, Prov 8:30/34) and they both have twenty-four hours as a standard. The phrase *day and night* (*yomam walaylah* 1:2, 22:3, 32:4, 42:4, 55:11) uses a variable ratio, with the daylight hours being longer in the summer and shorter in the winter.

7:13 Shoûld one not repent, he wìll sharpen hís blade, *
aim his war-bow ànd steády it,
7:14 ând for himself hè readies toóls of death, *
his arrows which he makes fòr thé tòrching.
7:15 Tô attention! Someòne conceives málice, *
and gestates trouble, and dèlívers fàlschood,
7:16 whô has marked à hole and dúg it, *
but he will fall into thè pít hè made;
7:17 hîs mischief will còme back upón his head, *
and on his scalp his own àbúse wìll fall.
7:18 Î laud the FONT OF BEING *as befìts what is júst to him,* *       *7:9*
and play chords to *the Name* "FONT ÒF BÉING, Mòst High!"

**The Name "FONT OF BEING"** (*shem yhwh* 7:18, 25:11, 83:17, 102:16/22, 113:1/2/3, 116:4/13/17, 118:10/11/12/26, 119:55, 122:4, 124:8, 129:8, 135:1, 143:11 and 148:5/13) occurs twenty-three times. It can also be rendered *the Name of the FONT OF BEING.*

**FONT OF BEING Most High** (*yhwh 'elyon* 7:18, 47:3, 97:9) is a divine appellative of a pattern with:
—**Divine One Most High** (*'elohiym 'elyon* 57:3, 78:56)
—**God Most High** (*'el 'elyon* 78:35).

16

NEW TESTAMENT — Verse 3 at Mt 21:16
Verses 5–8 at Heb 2:6–8 / Verse 7 at 1 Cor 15:27 and Eph 1:22
LITURGY OF HOURS — Lauds on Saturday II

The name "FONT OF BEING" appears twice in Psalm 8, in the first and last verses, in the poetical device known as "inclusion" or "framing." For this psalmist human nature is the finest tribute to God in all the cosmos.

8:1     (For the Director, *upon the Gittith.* A Mizmor of David.)

**Upon the Gittith** (*'al-haggittiyth*), meaning unknown, appears in the titles of three psalms (8:1, 81:1, 84:1).

8:2a/b = 8:10
**Ô FONT OF BÈING, our Ádonay! \***
**How splendid is your Name *ìn áll thè land,* \***

**All the land** (*kol ha'arets* 8:2/10, 45:17, 47:3/8, 48:3, 57:12, 66:1, 72:19, 83:19, 96:1/9, 97:5/9, 98:4, 101:1, 105:7, 108:6) is either all the Holy Land or all the Earth. Addressed with a plural imperative (66:1, 98:4, 100:1), it means "all the people of the land."

8:2c/3a
**whîch your majesty èxalts *abóve the skies,* \***
**by the mouth of infànts ánd of nùrselings.**

**Above the skies** (*'al hasshamayim* 8:2, 57:6, 113:4; *'al shamayim* 57:12, 108:8; *me'al hasshamayim* 148:4) may seem paradoxical, like "before the beginning." Hebrew cosmology saw strata in the sky, as **in the Heaven of Heavens in the East** (*bishmey shemey qedem* 68:34). God's throne is in highest heaven, above sun and moon.

8:3b/c
**Yoû founded a stronghold on àccount of yoúr foes, \***
**to silence *a fiend and a seekèr óf vèngeance.***

**A fiend and a seeker of vengeance** (*'oyeb umithnaqqem* 8:3, 44:17) are not necessarily the same. A fiend, whether demonic or human, seeks to victimize me; a seeker of vengeance perceives himself as victimized by me, and seeks the repayment of a debt of justice.

8:4 Fôr I behold your skiès that your Fíngers made, *
moon and stars that yoù pút ìn place.

8:5 Whât is man? Yet yoù keep him ín mind! *
Or a *son of Adam*? Yet yoù cáre fòr him!

*Son of Adam* (*ben 'adam*) occurs in the singular three times, always masculine. The sense is pejorative once (146:3), neutral once (8:5) and positive once (80:18). Luke uses the phrase to describe Jesus as *Son of Adam, Son of God* (Lk 3:38). The plural *children of Adam* (*beney 'adam*; see note at 11:4) is much more common in the psalms.

8:6 Yoû left him less lackìng than the ángels, *
and with glory and honòr yoú cròwn him.

8:7 Yoû give him command over *thè works of yoúr Hands*; *
you arrayed all things *bèneáth hìs feet*:

*Works of your Hands* (*ma'asey yadeyka* 8:7, 92:5, 102:26, 138:8, 143:5; *ma'asey yadaw* 19:2, 28:5, 111:7; *ma'asey kappaw* 9:17, 128:2) redound to the glory of the Divine One. By contrast, human makers become like what they make.

*Beneath his feet* (*tahat raglaw* 8:7, 18:1/39 and 47:4) is similar to *before his feet* (*leraglaw* 110:1). The king sat and courtiers stood, but defeated enemies and tributary kings knelt to kiss the royal feet. Stripped of descriptive imagery, the phrase is reducible to *beneath me* (*tahtay* 18:40/48, 144:2, 2 Sam 22:40/48).

8:8 shcêp and thè oxen, áll of them, *
and animals too of thè coúntryside,

8:9 bîrds of the sky ànd fishes óf the sea, *
traveling pathwàys óf thè seas.

8:10 = 8:2a/b
Ô FONT OF BÈING, our Ádonay! *
How splendid is your Name ìn *áll thè land*!

8:2

# NINE

NEW TESTAMENT — Verse 9 at Acts 17:31
LITURGY OF HOURS — Office of Readings on Monday I

Psalms 9 and 10 originally formed a single psalm, as in the Septuagint. The proof that the Septuagint arrangement is correct is that the original composition had an alphabetical structure. The psalm break occurs right in the middle of the alphabet. Psalm 9 preserves more of the original acrostic, lacking only two lines, while Psalm 10 preserves only the *Lamedh* line and the four last lines. There are eight such acrostic psalms (9/10, 25, 34, 37, 111, 112, 119 and 145) and several elsewhere in the Bible, most notably the first four chapters of the Book of Lamentations.

9:1   (For the Director, like "Death to the Lips." A Mizmor of David.)

9:2   *Aleph.*

**Lêt me laud the Font of Bèing *wholeheártedly,* ***
**taking account òf áll your màrvels!**

> *Wholeheartedly* (*bekol libbiy* 9:2, 119:10, 138:1; *bekol lebabiy* 86:12; *bekol lebab* 111:1; *bekol leb* 119:2/34/58/69/145) is a well-used phrase, found even in the great commandment of the Torah, to love God *with all your heart* (*bekol lebabka*, Deut 6:5).

9:3   **Lêt me rejoìce and delíght in you, ***
**playing chords to yoùr Náme, Mòst High!**

> Four psalms use the phrase **play chords to your Name** (*'ezammerah shimka* 9:3; *leshimka 'ezammerah* 18:50, 2 Sam 22:50; *yezammeru shimka* 66:4, *lezammer leshimka* 92:2). How can playing of strings connect to the Divine Name? One answer is that consonants YHWH had numerical values 10/5/6/5. The musical intervals between these numbers are an inverted fifth (major) and an inverted fourth (minor). These chords could have accompanied *Tonus Peregrinus*, which has two tonics, La (A) on the minor fourth and Sol (G) on the major fifth. With a minor chord of A/D and a major chord of G/D, the psalmists could accompany T.P. literally "to the Name."

9:4   *Beth.*

**Whîle my rivals fall bàck, let them stúmble, ***
**and become nil, from thè Fáce òf You.**

9:5 Îndeed: give me judgmènt and discérnment! *
Be seated on a bench, tò júdge with jùstice!

9:6 *Ghimel.*

Rêbuke gentiles! Make nìl the unjúst one! *
Erase their name *for evèr ánd àn age!*          *5:12*

9:7 Ân enemy *ever* drew blades, but you proòted their cíties; *
*the memory òf thém becàme nil.*          *34:17*

The phrase **For ever** (*lanetsah* 9:7/19, 10:11, 44:24, 49:10, 52:7, 68:17, 74:1/10/19, 77:9, 79:5, 89:47, 103:9; *'ad-netsah* 49:20, Job 34:36) employs a noun that means luster, legacy, and **lastingness** (*netsah* 13:2, 74:3). Here, luster of the blade causes the foe to draw it over and over, but the blade gives only a false glory that comes to nothing in the end.

9:8 Fôr the FONT OF BEING is *etèrnally seáted;* *
set up *for the judgmènt* ís hìs throne.          *25:9*

**Eternally Seated** (*le'olam yesheb* 9:8; *'olam yesheb* 125:1; *le'olam tesheb* 102:13) uses adverbial phrase **eternally** (*le'olam*, see 5:12) to modify a finite verb. It is not quite a divine appellative, because the verb is not a participle, but it relates closely to several appellatives:
—**Seated in the Skies** (*yosheb basshamayim* 2:4, 123:1)
—**Seated upon the Cherubim** (*yosheb kerubiym* 80:2, 99:1)
—**Seated in Ziön** (*yosheb tsiyyon* 9:12).

9:9 ând he rules thè world *with jústice;* *
he decides among natiòns *with faìrness,*

The phrase **with justice** (*betsedek* 9:9, 17:15, 65:6, 72:2) parallels the synonymous phrase **with fairness** (*bemeyshariym* 9:9, 96:10, 98:9) only here in Psalm 9. They could also be translated *justly* and *fairly*. Elsewhere **with justice** stands in parallel with another near synonym, **with judgment** (*bemishpot* 72:2, 112:5).

9:10 *Waw.*

ând for the oppressed the FONT OF BEÌNG was high réfuge, *
high refuge *at thè tímes òf siege.*          *4:2*

9:11 Thêy who know yoùr Name can trúst in you, *
for you forsake none who seek yoù, FÓNT OF BÈING.

9:12 *Zain.*

Plây chords for the FONT OF BEING, *seàted in Zíön;* *          *9:8*
tell his deeds àmóng the gèntiles.

Three synonyms exist for the non-Hebrew peoples:
—*among the gentiles* (*baggoyim* 9:12, 18:50, 22:29, 44:12, 79:10, 96:3/10, 106:27, 126:2, 149:7)
—*among the nations* (*bal'umiym* 44:15, 57:10, 108:4, 149:7)
—*among the peoples* (*ba'ammiym* 57:10, 77:15, 105:1, 108:4).

9:13 **Fôr he recalled how one soùght them with bloódshed; ***
**he did not forget the groanìng óf the lòwly.**

9:14 *Heth.*

**Pîty me, O FONT OF BEING! Bèhold my póverty! ***
**From *those who hate me*, lift me from *thè gátes òf death*,**

***Those who hate me*** (*son'ay* 9:14, 18:18/41, 69:15, 86:17, 118:7, 2 Sam 22:18/41) and ***those who hate you*** (*son'eyka* 21:9; *mesan'eyka* 83:3, 139:21) are usually one and the same people. The enemies of God hate the psalmist because he is known to worship God.

***Gates of death*** (*sha'arey maweth* 9:14, 107:18; Job 38:17) contrast with ***gates of Daughter Ziön*** (*sha'arey bath tsiyyon* 9:15; *sha'arey tsiyyon* 87:2) in the next verse. Corpses were carried out of the city through the gates of death, for burial outside the walls.

9:15 **fôr me to recite all your psalms in *gates òf Daughter Ziön!* ***
**Let me revel ìn yoúr salvàtion!**                                    *9:14*

9:16 *Teth.*

**Lêt the gentiles sink ìnto the pít they made, ***
**their feet be caught in thè nét thèy laid.**

9:17 **Fâmed is the FONT OF BEING fòr giving júdgment: ***
**let the unjust one be entangled by *thè wórk of hìs palms*.**

***Works of his Palms*** (*ma'asey kappaw* 9:17; *yegia' kappeyka* 128:2) is a variant of ***works of your Hands*** (*ma'asey yadeyka* 8:7, 92:5, 102:26, 138:8, 143:5) or ***works of his Hands*** (*ma'asey yadaw* 19:2, 28:5, 111:7). The palm is part of the hand, and so this idiom is in the figure of speech called *metonymy*, or "part for the whole."

9:18 *Yod.*

**Ûnjust peoplè turn to Shéöl, ***
**all gentiles forgettìng thé Divìne One.**

***All gentiles*** (*kol goyiym* 9:18, 59:9, 67:3, 72:11/17, 86:9, 113:4, 117:1) excludes Israël, but ***all the peoples*** (*kol ha'ammiym* 47:2, 49:2, 96:3, 97:6, 99:2) seems to include her. Israël is often *'am*, rarely *goy*.

***Forgetting the Divine One*** (*shokekey 'elohiym* 9:18) or ***forgetting the Godhead*** (*shokhey 'eloah* 50:22) or ***forgetting God*** (*shokeku 'el* 106:21; *shokhey 'el* Job 8:13) presumes people once knew and put that knowledge out of their minds. This is willful ignorance, not amnesia.

9:19 *Nôr surely* **will one in need be** *for èver* **forgótten,** *   *9:7*
**nor will hopes of lowly people come tò níl** *for àn age.*

*Nor surely . . . nor* (*kiy lo'. . . lo'* 5:5, 9:19, 16:10, 22:25, 44:4/7, 55:1, 75:7, 78:22, 94:14) is an unrecognized poetical construction in the psalms. An elaboration of the very common *nor . . . nor* (*lo'. . . lo'*), placement of the emphatic *surely* (*kiy*) at the beginning connects the double negative with the logical flow of what had gone before.

*For an age* (*la'ad* 9:19, 19:10, 21:7, 22:27, 37:29, 61:9, 111:3/8/10, 112:3/9, 148:6) employs one of the synonyms for eternity, along with *'olam*, *netsah* and *dor*. They avoid serving as the subject or object of a verb and instead cluster as objects of prepositions in adverbial phrases. Twice this phrase appears in the compound phrase *for an age, for eternity* (*la'ad le'olam* 111:8, 148:6).

9:20 **Rîse, O FONT OF BEING! Let nò human bé vain!** *
**Let gentiles be judged before thè Fáce òf You!**
9:21 **Ô FONT OF BEING, pùt some awe ínto them!** *
**Let the gentiles know thàt théy are hùman!**

**Psalm 10 — see introduction to Psalm 9.**
NEW TESTAMENT — Verse 7 at Rom 3:14
LITURGY OF HOURS — Office of Readings on Tuesday I

10:1 *Lamedh.*
Ô FONT OF BEING, why do you stánd in a fár-off place? *
hiding yourself *at thè tímes òf siege?*                                    *4:2*

10:2 Wîth pride, an unjust one pùrsues a lówly one; *
they will be caught in schemes thàt théy dèvised.

10:3 Fôr an unjust one boasts by the dèsires of hís soul, *
and blocking blessing, scorns thè FÓNT OF BÈING.

10:4 Ân unjust one befits his proud nòse: †
"Oh, he never follows through! *There ìs no Divíne One!"* *
These àre áll hìs thoughts.

An unjust one says, *There is no Divine One* (*'eyn 'elohiym* 10:4), but the
psalmist affirms, *There is a Divine One* (*yesh-'elohiym*, 58:12, 1 Sam
17:4). Here are further doubting statements:
—*There is no helper* (*'eyn-'ozer* 22:12, 72:12, 107:12, Is 63:5)
—*There is no rescuer* (*'eyn-matssiyl* 7:3, 50:22, 71:11)
—*There is no savior* (*'eyn-moshiya'* 18:42, 2 Sam 22:42, Deut
22:27, 28:29/31, Judg 12:3, Is 47:15, Hos 13:4).

10:5 Hîs ways are winding, ever on hìgh! †
Your judgments àre far from hís side! *
He scoffs àt áll hìs foes!

10:6 În his heart he says, "I will not stumble, àge after án age; *
I can curse something; that ìs nót ùnjust."

*In his heart he says* (*'amar belibbo* 10:6/11/13, 14:1, 53:3; *dober
bilebabo* 15:2; *bilbabiy* 13:3; *belibbiy* 66:18, 119:11; *'im lebabiy* 77:7;
*bilbabam* 28:3, 84:6; *belibbam* 35:25; *belibbotham* 125:4). Heart-speech
is the reasoning of the Hebrew mind residing there.

*Age after age* (*ledor wador* 10:6, 33:11, 49:12, 77:9, 79:13, 85:6, 89:2/5,
90:1, 102:13, 106:31, 119:90, 135:13, 146:10; *kemo dor wador* 61:7;
*bedor wa dor* 90:1; *'ad dor wador* 100:5). *This age* (*haddor zu* 12:8;
*ze dor* 24:6) is followed by the *next* (*dor 'ahron* 48:14, 78:6; *dor 'aher*,
109:13). *An age of ages* (*dor doriym* 72:5, *bedor doriym* 102:25, *ledor
doriym* Is 51:8) is 40x40, or 800 years.

10:7   Hîs mouth is filled with dèceit and wíth threat; *
      beneath his tongue lie troublè ánd màlice.

10:8   Hê occupies villages, in ambùsh; †
      in hidden places he would kill òne who is ínnocent; *
      his eyes seàrch oút a vìctim.

10:9   Hê waits in hiding *like a lion* in his thickèt; †     *7:3*
      he waits tò catch a lówly one. *
      He catches a lowly one, whom in his net hè drágs àway.

10:10  Ône is crushed; one fàlls, one collápses, *
      —in his clutchès áre the vìctims.

10:11  *În his heart he says*, "Gòd has forgótten; *     *10:6*
      he has covered his Face; nevèr doés hè see."

10:12  *Qoph.*
      *Rîse, O Font of Being*; Gòd, lift up yoúr Hand! *
      Do not forget thè lówly ones!

*Arise, O Font of Being* (*qumah yhwh* 10:12, 17:13, 21:14) seems based on the assumption that God is sleeping or reclining. The psalmist asks him to rise up for action. Many have risen up to oppose God (7:2), but the unjust will not rise at the judgment (1:5). This is the word for Resurrection and Easter in Christian Aramaic.

10:13  Fôr what does an unjust person *scòrn the Divíne One*? *
      *In his heart he says*, "He nevèr fóllòws through."     *10:6*

10:14  *Resh.*
      Yoû have seen trouble and beheld òffense, †
      and *in your Hand*, a victim can rèly upón you; *     *31:6*
      for an orphan, you are thè hélpfùl one.

10:15  *Shin.*
      Dîsarm the one who is ùnjust or wícked! *
      Prosecute his crime thoùgh úndisclosed!

10:16  Fônt of Being is king fòr *ever ánd an age*; *     *5:12*
      nil are gentìles fróm hìs land.

10:17  *Tau.*
      Heâr the desires of lowly people, Ò Font of Béing! *
      Shore up their hearts! Let yoùr Eárs be àttuned!

10:18  Gîve judgment for òne orphaned ór oppressed; *
      no longer let one be frightèned fróm thè land.

# ELEVEN

LITURGY OF HOURS — Vespers on Monday I

The author of Psalm 11 is hard pressed and feels unable to escape the unjust one (verse 1), who extends his evil-doing through archery and artillery (2), but the FONT OF BEING sees farther yet, even into their very souls (4), and they will not be able to escape the reach of the FONT OF BEING (6).

11:1   (For the Director. Of David.)
      *În the FONT OF BEING have Ì taken réfuge!* \*           *7:2*
      **Why say to my soul, "Fly, O bird, tò yoúr moùntain?"**

11:2   ***Tô attention!* The unjust aim a war-bòw!** †         *83:3*
      **They put their arròws to the bówstring,** \*
      **to target from shadow *thè steádfast-heàrted.***       *7:11*

11:3   **Whên the bàses are béing razed,** \*
      **even a just one—whàt cán hè do?**

11:4   **FÔNT OF BEING, whose glory is in the templè,** †
      **FONT OF BEING, whose seat ìs in the heávens,** \*
      **whose eyes see, whose brows probe *the childrèn óf Àdam.***

*Children of Adam* (*beney 'adam*) means "ordinary people" versus ***children of rank*** (*beney 'iysh* at 49:3), or the entire race when Adam has a definite article (*beney ha'adam* 33:13) or when ***all*** is used (*kol beney 'adam* 89:48). Without any of these markers, the sense goes toward the human race in general (11:4, 12:2/9, 14:2, 21:11, 31:20, 36:8, 53:3, 57:5, 58:2, 62:10, 66:5, 90:3, 107:8/15/21/31, 115:16).

11:5   **FÔNT OF BEING is just; he pròbes the unjúst one,** \*
      **who loves abuse and is spitefùl ín hìs soul.**

11:6   **Ôn unjust people hè rains down coáls of flame;** \*
      **sulfur and *searing wind* are the portiòn óf their cup.**

*Searing wind* (*ruah zil'afot* 11:6, 119:53, Lam 5:10). The adjective *zil'af* has a four-letter root, which is quite rare in Hebrew.

11:7   **Hôw just is the FONT OF BEING, lòver of júst deeds.** \*
      **Whoever is steadfast will bèhóld hìs Face.**

# TWELVE

The author of Psalm 12 stands in dismay of how people can flatter one another despite lack of mutual respect. The flatterer says one thing to a person's face and another elsewhere, and thus flattery is the false face of slander. There needs be a new kind of circumcision, of the lips (verse 4). The "children of Adam" (in their fallen state) are mentioned in both the first and last verses and thus form an "inclusion" or "framing."

12:1 (For the Director, *upon the octave.*           *6:1*
     A Mizmor of David.)

12:2 **Gîve safety, O Fᴏɴᴛ ᴏf Beìng! †**
**For vanished is the devoted one, gòne are the fáithful ones ***
**from among *the childrèn óf Àdam!***      *11:4*

12:3 **Thêy speak what is vaìn, each agaínst his friend; ***
**with a lip of flattery, heart agaìnst heárt thèy speak.**

12:4 **Fôɴᴛ ᴏf Being excises àll lips of fláttery, ***
**any tongue sayìng thíngs toò grand,**

12:5 **thôse saying, "Oh, by our tòngues we are máde strong; ***
**with our cutting lips, who could be mastèr óvèr us?"**

12:6 **"Àt plunder of the lowly, at groaning of needy peoplè, †**
**now do I arise," says thè Fᴏɴᴛ ᴏf Béing; ***
**"I will make safe whoevèr síghs fòr them."**

12:7 **Sâyings of the Fᴏɴᴛ ᴏf Beìng are pure sáyings, ***
**like silver molten in an oven from clay *sevèn-fóld* rèfined.**

The cardinal numeral **seven** is *sheba'* or *sib'ah* and ordinal numeral **seventh** is *shebiy'iy*. The devout psalmist praises God **seven times in the day** (*sheba' bayyom* 119:164), attends to the sayings of God like silver refined **seven-fold** and prays for retributive justice **seven-fold** (*shib'atayim* 12:7, 79:12).

12:8 **Yoû yourself, O Fᴏɴᴛ ᴏ̀f Being, guárd them; ***
**you preserve us fròm thís age àlways.**

12:9 **Âll around, the unjust peòple are ón parade, ***
**as if exalting the follies of *the childrèn óf Àdam.***     *11:4*

# THIRTEEN

Psalm 13 begins with the question word "how long," which begins each of the first four lines, in the figure of speech called *anaphora*. The psalm starts out as a four-fold rhetorical question (verses 2/3), continues as a prayer (4/5) and concludes with an affirmation of faith in God's mercy and salvation (6). Salvation is a concrete expression of mercy, distinct but inseparable. Mercy is a frequent theme in the psalms, often in companionship with some other quality in the figure of *hendiadys*, "one through two." The companions are redemption (Ps 130:7), goodness (23:6), judgment (101:1), salvation (13:6, 85:8, 119:41), tenderness (51:3, 103:4), justice (36:11, 103:17), fidelity (89:2/3/25/29/34/50, 92:3, 98:3, 100:5), and truth (25:10, 40:11/12, 57:4/11, 61:8, 85:11, 86:15, 89:15, 108:5, 115:1, 117:2 and 138:2).

13:1 (For the Director. A Mizmor of David.)

13:2 **Hôw long, FONT OF BEÌNG? †**
*For ever* **wìll you forgét me? \***          *9:7*
**How long will** *you hide the Face òf Yoú fròm me*?

> *You hide the Face of You* (*tastiyr paneyka* 13:2, 88:15; *'al taster paneyka* 27:9, 102:3, 143:7; *lo'-histiyr panaw* 22:25) invites an absent God to be present. The same thing, stated positively, is *Shine the Face of You* (*ha'iyrah faneyka* 31:17; *ya'er fana* 67:2; *faneyka ha'er* 119:135)

13:3 **Hôw long must I put beams on my nèck, †**
**sorrowing** *ìn my heart* **daíly? \***          *10:6*
**How long will my enemy be liftèd óvèr me?**

13:4 **Gâze down! Answer me, my divìne FONT OF BÉING! \***
**Make my eyes shine, lest Ì sleép thè death,**

13:5 **lêst my rival say, "Oh, Ì can subdué him!" \***
**lest my foes revel àt hów I stùmble.**

13:6 **Bût I myself have trusted in your mèrcy! †**
**My heart revels ìn your salvátion. \***
**Let me sing to the FONT OF BEING how hè deált wìth me!**

## FOURTEEN

NEW TESTAMENT — Verses 1-3 at Rom 3:11-12
LITURGY OF HOURS — Midday Prayer on Tuesday I

Psalms 14 and 53 are the same except for one greatly different verse (14:5/6≠53:6). In this version of the psalm, Elohim appears three times and FONT OF BEING four times, in alternation—A/B/A/B/A/B/B.

(For the Director. Of David.)

14:1  **În his heart a fool says, "Oh, there ìs no Divíne One." ***     *10:6*
     **People are spoiled; they act badly; there is nò dóer òf good.**

14:2  **Frôm the sky the FONT OF BEING espies *chìldren of Ádam*, ***
     **to see if any have wisdom, seekìng thé Divìne One.**     *11:4*

14:3  **Âll have turned aside, altogèther corrúpted; ***
     **there is no doer of good, nòt évèn one.**

Between verses 3 and 4, the Alexandrian manuscripts have a gloss (not found in parallel Psalm 53), reprising the catena from Romans 3:13–18, which begins with verses 1b/2b/3 of this psalm. Could Paul have had that gloss before him in the manuscript he read?

14:4  **Dîd they not undèrstand, †**
     **all *doers of evil*, feedìng on my peóple?**     *5:6*
     **They fed on bread; they did not call thè FÓNT OF BÈING.**

14:5  **Thêre! With feàr they were fríghtened: ***
     **that the Divine One is with àn áge that ìs just.**

14:6  **Yoû were shamed by the plàns of a lówly one, ***
     **whose refuge is thè FÓNT OF BÈING.**

14:7  **Whô gives safety from the Ziön to Isràël? †**
     **As *the FONT OF BEING repeals the bondàge* of his peóple, ***
     **Jacob will revel, Isràél rèjoice.**

*He repeals the bondage* (*beshub . . . shebut* 14:7, 53:7; *shabta shebut* 85:2; *beshub . . . eth-shiybat* 126:1) is a juridical term for the paroling of prisoners (Deut 30:3). The psalmists apply it to the state of exile in which one after another of the tribes found themselves.

# FIFTEEN

EARLIEST MANUSCRIPT — Verse 5 in Nahal Hever Ps 15/16
LITURGY OF HOURS — Vespers on Monday I

Psalm 15 begins with a question; the rest is the answer. The answer comprises three positive injunctions (verse 2), three negative ones (3), three more positive (4) and three more negative (4/5). The number of positive imperatives is six, the number of negative six, for a total of twelve. The structure thus resembles the calling forth of blessings and curses from Mounts Gerizim and Ebal by the twelve tribes of Israël after their entrance into the promised land.

15:1 (A Mizmor of David.)

Ô Font of Being, *who* can àbide in yoúr tent? *    24:3
*Who* can dwell on your *mount òf hóliness,*

*Your mount of holiness* (*har qodsheka* 15:1, 43:3; *har qodshiy* 2:6, 3:5; *har qodsho* 48:2, 99:9; *harrey qodesh* 87:1) is Mount Moriah, where Abraham went to offer up his son Isaac, and where David brought the Ark and Solomon built the temple.

15:2 wâlking with integrity ànd doing jústice, *
and *in one's heart speakìng* whát ìs true,    10:6
15:3 wîth no slander on òne's tongue, †
doing no hàrm to one's cómrade, *
and raising no rebuke àgaínst òne's friend;
15:4 hâving contempt in one's eyes for vilenèss, †
but honoring those who revere thè Font of Béing; *
keeping an oath to one's disadvantage, withoùt bíttèrness;
15:5 nôt loaning out one's silver for profit, †
and taking no bribe àgainst the ínnocent *
—one doing these things *wìll néver stùmble.*    5:12, 112:6

The last verse echoes the Akkadian *Hymn to Shamash*: "He who does not accept a bribe but intercedes for the weak is well-pleasing to Shamash (the sun god) and enriches his life" (ANET 388).

# SIXTEEN

EARLIEST MANUSCRIPT — Title in Nahal Hever Ps 15/16
NEW TESTAMENT — Verses 8-11 at Acts 2:25-28 and 31
LITURGY OF HOURS — Thursday Night Prayer (Compline)

The earliest surviving manuscript of Psalm 16 is just the title verse from a fragment from the first or second century, found in the Cave of Letters at Nahal Hever by Yigael Yadin. It contains the tail end of Psalm 15 and the title of Psalm 16 as it appears in the Masoretic edition.

16:1      (A Michtam of David.)
**_Keêp sentinèl over mé_, O God, ***
**for *I have takèn réfuge ín you*.**

                                                       7:2

*Keep sentinel over me* (*shomreniy* 16:1, 17:8, 140:5, 141:9; *shomray nafshiy* 25:20, 86:2) is the verb that corresponds to the participial noun **sentinel** (*shomer*). Urban sentinels (*shomriym*) hold watch duties on the walls. There are at least six participial divine appellatives using that epithet:
—**Sentinel of Eternal Truth** (*shomer 'emeth le'olam* 146:6)
—**Sentinel of Israël** (*shomer yisra'el* 121:4)
—**Sentinel for Aliens** (*shomer eth-geriym* 146:9)
—**Sentinel for All Who Love Him** (*shomer et-kol-'ohbaw* 145:20)
—**Sentinel for Simple People** (*shomer petha'iym* 116:6)
—**Sentinel for You** (*shomreka* 121:3/5).

16:2    **Î said "O FONT ÒF BEING-Ádonay! ***
**You are my Good; nothìng ís abòve you.**

Two appellatives join as **FONT OF BEING Adonay** (*yhwh 'adonay* 16:2, 68:21, 109:21, 140:8, 141:8) or **Adonay FONT OF BEING** (*'adonay yhwh* 69:7, 71:5/16, 73:28). In the synagogue, FONT OF BEING eventually came to be read as *Adonay*. When the FONT OF BEING and *Adonay* are together, the reading is *Adonay, Adonay*.

16:3    **Ô holy ones in the lànd, and these spléndid ones ***
**—all my dèlíght is ìn them."**

16:4    **Mâny troubles have they who hasten to anothèr god; †**
**nor do I pour out theìr blood libátions, ***
**nor do I put their names ùpón my lips.**

30

16:5 Ô FONT OF BEING, my allottèd portion ánd my cup, *
you weight the dice ìn fávor òf me.

16:6 Sûrvey lines fell to me ìn lovely pláces; *
yes, for me a shinìng herìtage.

16:7 Î bless the FONT OF BÈING, who coúnsels me; *
even *during the nights* my innèr sélf corrècts me.

*During the nights* (*leylot* 16:7; *balleylot* 92:3, 134:1) perhaps has
distributive phrase *day by day* (*yom yom* 61:9, 68:20, Prov 8:30/34) as
daytime equivalent. Singular *in the night* (*ballaylah* 42:9, 77:7, 88:2,
119:55, 121:6, 136:9) corresponds to the daytime phrase *at the dawn*
(*boqer* 5:4a/b; *babboqer* 88:14, 90:5/6/14, 92:3).

16:8 Î put the FONT OF BEING *bèfore me álways,* *
indeed, at my right hand; *nòr dó I stùmble.*                    *112:6*

The psalmist says that anxiety (38:18) and sins (51:5) and the FONT OF
BEING (16:8) are *before me always* (*negdiy tamiyd*). God says, your
oblations are *before me always* (*lenegdiy tamiyd* 50:8).

16:9 Sô my heart is glad and revèls in *my Glóry*; *              *3:4*
my flesh too abides *in a place of sècúrìty,*                    *4:9*

16:10 *nôr surely* will you abandon my soùl into Shéöl, *
*nor* will you give your devoted one tò seé dècay.              *9:19*

16:11 Shôw me a path òf life, †
fullness of joys alòng with the Fáce of You, *
lovely things in yoùr Ríght Hand àlways.

# SEVENTEEN

— Midday Prayer of Wednesday I

The author of Psalm 17 is involved in litigation as an accused defendant. He swears that he is telling the truth (verse 1) and submits himself for cross-examination (3). At the half-way point, poetry starts to happen. The psalmist throws himself on the mercy of the court, asking God to accept him as the dilation of the pupil of his eye, and to shelter him under the shadow of his wings (8). These may be legal terms for engaging a defense attorney.

17:1 (A Prayer of David.)
**Lîsten directly, O Font of Being! Attùne to my sínging! \***
**Lend Ear to my plea, on undèceíving lips!**

17:2 *Frôm before the Face of Yoù comes my júdgment; \**
*your Eyes perceive whò áre the steádfast.*

**From before the Face of You** (*millefaneyka* 17:2) comes judgment but the psalmist begs not to be cast **from before the Face of You** (51:13). The phrase has two prefixes, *min-* and *le-*, which contradict each other. Thus the opposite is found by taking *min-* away, leaving **before the Face of You** (*lefaneyka* 19:15, 22:28/30, 41:13, 76:8, 79:11, 86:9, 88:3, 102:29, 119:170, 141:2, 143:2).

17:3 **Prôbe my heart; test àt night; exámine me! \***
**Nor shall you find me scheming, nor my moùth óffènding!**

17:4 **Fôr the actions of Adam, by thè word of yoúr lips \***
**I guard myself fròm thiévìng paths.**

17:5 **Î keep my pacès on your páthways, \***
**lest my feèt shoúld stùmble.**

17:6 **Î called out to you, for yoù answer mé, O God! \***
**Bend your Ear to me; heàr whát Î say.**

17:7 *Wôrk the marvèl of your Mércies, \**
**Savior of refugees from their foes wìth yoúr Rìght Hand.**

**Work the marvel of your Mercies** (*hafleh hesadeyka* 17:7; *hifliy' hasdo* 31:22). From the verb, the first word in this phrase, comes the noun, the second word in the phrase **Maker of Marvels** (*'oseh nifla'ot* 72:19, 86:10, 136:4; *'oseh pele'* 77:15).

17:8    **Keêp sentinel ovèr me †**
**like the *dilation of thè pupil óf an Eye*; \***
***in the shadow of your Wings*, gìve mé rèfuge.**

*Dilation of the pupil of an Eye* (*'iyshon bat-'ayin* 17:8) reads literally *dilation of the daughter of an Eye*, and expands upon somewhat more common *dilation of an eye* (*'iyshon 'ayin* Deut 32:10, Prov 7:2). The word *'iyshon* occurs only in one other place, *at dilation of night* (*be'iyshon laylah* Prov 7:9). Beautiful though it may be, the traditional "apple of the eye" is not the actual idiom.

*In the shadow of your Wings* (*betsel kenafeyka* 17:8, 36:8, 57:2, 63:8). Wings represent the divine quality of omnipresence, as Eyes are omniscience, Arms and Hands power, Hands and Palms care, Feet dominion, Nose wrath, and so forth. The idea of God having Wings has not entered the artistic imagination the way that divine Eyes, Arms, Hands, Palms and Feet have.

17:9    **frôm the face of unjust peoplè, who attáck me, \***
**of fiends at the neck, whò stránglè me,**

17:10  **thôse who are ènclosed by theír fat, \***
**whose mouths have spoken wìth haúghtìness.**

17:11  **Oûr own Assyrìàns now surroúnd me; \***
**their eyes are fixed to toss mè tó thè ground.**

17:12  **Ône seems *like à lion* húnting prey, \***        *7:3*
**or like a cub crouched ìn híding plàces.**

17:13  ***Rîse, O Font of Beìng! †***        *10:12*
**Confront him to his fàce! Bring him tó his knees! \***
**Free my soul by your blade fròm óne ùnjust,**

17:14a **frôm such people, by your Hand, Ò Font of Béing, \***
**from such people, for whom the world is their párt ìn life,**

17:14b **ând your bounty fills their bosoms, sàted with chíldren, \***
**and whose profits they leave tò their òffspring.**

17:15  **Lêt me glimpse *dirèctly* the Fáce of You, \***        *9:9*
**fulfilled by awakening to thè Líkeness òf You.**

NEW TESTAMENT — Verse 50 at Rom 15:9
LITURGY OF HOURS —
Office of Readings on Wednesday and Thursday I

Psalm 18 reappears as Chapter 22 of Second Samuel, where the text is located just before the death of David. The psalm thus becomes a global thanksgiving by David for relief from his enemies, of whom Saul was only the first (though he is the only one mentioned in the shared title). Second Samuel omits verse 2, and adds the following words after verse 3: "And my Refuge, my Savior! From violence you keep me safe."

18:1  (For the Director.
Of the servant of the FONT OF BEING, of David, when he said these words of song to the FONT OF BEING, on the day the FONT OF BEING delivered him from the palm of all his enemies, and from the hand of Saul, and he said:)

18:2  **Î have tendèr feelings fór you, ***
**FONT OF BEÌNG, Ó my Strength!**

18:3  **FÔNT OF BEING,** *my Bedrock and my Fortrèss,* †
**my freedom, my God, my Rock, in whòm I take réfuge, ***
**my shield and my horn of salvation, hìgh réfuge fòr me!**

In this psalm of a warrior poet, *my Bedrock and my Fortress* (*sal'iy umtsudatiy* 18:2, 31:4, 71:3) is a divine appellative about which other military vocabulary is clustered—strength, rock, shield, horn. A fortress can be built on bedrock, but more often on a rocky hilltop. The great fortress of Masada, for example, is not built on bedrock.

18:4  **Thoûgh mocked, I will call thè FONT OF BÉING, ***
**and from my rivàls bé màde safe.**

18:5  *Snâres of deàth have entángled me, ***
**and floods of Belìál engùlfed me.**

Snares of any kind are greatly to be avoided, but the worst are the *snares of death* (*hebley maweth* 18:5, 116:3; *mishberey maweth* 2 Sam 22:5), a phrase expanded in the next verse into *snares of Sheöl, traps of death* (*hebley she'ol, moqshey maweth* 18:6) and expanded in a later psalm into *snares of death and anguish of Sheöl* (*hebley maweth umetsarey she'ol* 116:3).

18:6 Snâres of Shèöl surroúnded me; *
traps of death cònfróntèd me.

18:7 Ín my need I call, "FONT OF BEING!" and implore my Gòd. †
From his tèmple, he héars my call *
and my beseeching comes to his Ears, bèfóre hìs Face.

In my need or distress is mine (tsar liy 18:7, 31:10, 66:14, 69:18,
2 Sam 22:7) and their need or distress was theirs (tsar lahem 106:44,
107:6/13/19/28) are phrases that combine the word for a military siege
with a possessive personal pronoun. As a consequence, this idiom always
speaks of basic human needs, such as food when hungry and life when
threatened by death.

18:8 Lând both buckled and shoòk, †
and bases of the mountains bùckled and trémbled, *
so ènráged wàs he!

Land shook (tir'ash ha'arets 18:8, 77:19, 2 Sam 22:8; hir'ashtah 'erets
60:4; 'erets ra'ashah 68:9). The Holy Land sits on the Great Rift Valley,
a canyon in the planet's crust and prone to earth tremors. One great
earthquake made such an impression that it was mentioned by two of
the prophets. Amos dates the beginning of his ministry two years before
that quake (Amos 1:1). Zechariah says that on the day of wrath the valley
between the two mountains of Jerusalem will be filled, "as it was filled up
by the earthquake in the days of King Uzziah" (Zech 14:5).

18:9 Smôke arose in his Nostrìl †
and flame from hìs Mouth consúmed them; *
live coals sèt thém blàzing.

18:10 Hê crossed thè sky and cáme down, *
and darkness was bèneáth hìs feet.

8:7

18:11 Hê mounted upon à Cherub ánd flew, *
and glided òn wíngs òf wind.

On wings of wind ('al-kanfey-ruah 18:11, 104:3, 2 Sam 22:11) is one of
the finest metaphors in all literature, because it depends upon an additional,
unspoken simile. The wind can have wings only if it is understood that the
wind is like a bird (ketsippor 124:7).

18:12 Hê donned darkness as his dìsguise aboút him, *
as his cover darkening waters in canòpiés òf clouds.

18:13 Hîs canopies crossed from thè splendor óf his side, *
hail ànd coáls òf flame.

18:14 Hê shook them in the skies, thè FONT OF BÉING, *
and the Most High sent his call—hail ànd coáls òf flame.

18:15 Hê tossed his àrrows to scátter them *
and lightning àt lárge to roùt them.

18:16 Seên were *watered gorges*, and uncovèred *bases óf land*, *
at your rebuke, FONT OF BEING, windblàst óf your Nòstril.

These *watered gorges* (*'efiyqey mayim* 18:16, 2 Sam 22:16) are a little deeper than those for which the doe deer long (42:2). These are rifts in the crust of the earth revealing *bases of land* (*mosdey 'arets* 18:16, 2 Sam 22:16; *mosdoth tebel* 82:5). The Great Rift Valley and the Grand Canyon of Arizona go down to the basement rock, under which there are no more strata.

18:17 Hê reaches from on high; hè takes ahóld of me; *
he lifts me from the *watèrs mánìfold*.

*Waters manifold* (*mayim rabbiym* 18:17, 29:3, 32:6, 77:20, 93:4, 107:23, 144:7) are threatening because they constitute a flood, *bullocks manifold* (*pariym rabbiym* 22:13) are threatening because they are capable of a stampede, and *speakers manifold* (*rabbiym 'omriym* 3:3, 4:7) are more threatening yet, because slander is worse than floods or stampedes.

18:18 Hê frees me from my mighty rival ànd *those who háte me* *
though they be strongèr thán Ì am.                          *9:14*

18:19 Thêy test me on my dày of calámity,
but the FONT OF BEING is à búttress fòr me,

18:20 ând he leads me *into thè open spáces*; *
he sets me free, for he dèlíghts ìn me.

The liberator lifts the urban *siege* (*tsar*) and releases the inhabitants *into the open spaces* (*lammerhab* 18:20, 2 Sam 22:20; *bammerhab* 31:9, 118:5, 119:45), where they can forage for water and food. The opposite of *narrow* (*tsar*) is *wide* (*rahab*). Just as any siege is narrow and closed, so the lifting of a siege is wide and open.

18:21 FÒNT OF BEING deals wìth me †
*as befits what is júst to me;* *
for my purity of hànds hé repàys me.                          *7:9*

36

18:22 Fôr I kept the ways of thè FONT OF BÉING, *
and did not stray fròm my Divìne One.

18:23 Fôr all his còmmands are át my side, *
and I discard not his dècreés fròm me.

18:24 Î have beèn blameless wíth him, *
and I am guardèd fróm my sin.

18:25 FÔNT OF BEING repays me *as befits what is júst to me,* *
for my purity of hands bèfóre hìs Eyes.                    *7:9*

18:26 Wîth a devoted one, yoù are devótion; *
with a blameless man, yoù háve nò blame,

18:27 Wîth a pure òne, you are púrity, *
but with one who schemes, yoù wíll gràpple.

18:28 Fôr to lowly peoplè you give sáfety, *
but with your Eyes you cast thè prídefùl down.

18:29 Fôr you light my lamp, Ò FONT OF BÉING; *
my Divine One lights thè dárkness fòr me.

18:30 Fôr with you I make ground agaìnst a battálion, *
and with my Divine One I surmount à bárrìcade.

18:31 *Îs not God* blameless in hìs way? †                    *18:48*
Proven is a statement of thè FONT OF BÉING,
who is a Shield to all *takìng réfuge ìn him.*           *2:12*

18:32 Fôr who is divine besides thè FONT OF BÉING? *
And who is a rock besìdes oúr Divìne One?

18:33 *Îs not God*, is he nòt helping mé with strength? *   *18:48*
For he makes my path tò bé withoùt blame—

18:34 gîving me feèt that are *deér-like*, *                *42:2*
for on the heights hè státìons me—

18:35 fôrming my hànds for the báttle, *
my forearms for a curvìng bów òf bronze,

18:36 ând you give me your shield of salvatiòn, †
and by your own Rìght Hand suppórt me, *
and by your aid yoù sét mè free.

18:37 Yoû widen my pàthway beneáth me *
that my anklès máy not stùmble.

18:38 Î hunt for my rivals ànd overtáke them, *
and return not until they àre óvèrcome.

18:39 Î crush them so thèy cannot ríse again; *
they collapse *bèneáth my feet,*                         *18:48*

18:40 ând you gird me wìth might for báttle; *
    you bend *beneath me* those whò róse agaìnst me,        *18:48*

18:41 ând you give me my rivals by thè nape of thé neck, *
    and I silènce *thóse who hàte me.*        *9:14*

18:42 Thêy beseech, but *nò savior wíll there be,* *
    to the FONT OF BEING, who will nòt ánswèr them.

> *There is no savior* ('*eyn-moshiya*' 18:42, 2 Sam 22:42, Deut 22:27,
> 28:29/31, Judg 12:3, Is 47:15, Hos 13:4) is another way of saying, *There
> is no salvation for him* ('*eyn yeshu'athah lo* 3:3; *she'eyn lo teshu'ah*
> 146:3). Some other defeatist expressions are:
> —*There is no rescuer* ('*eyn-matssiyl* 7:3, 50:22, 71:11)
> —*There is no helper* ('*eyn-'ozer* 22:12, 72:12, 107:12, Is 63:5)
> —*There is no Divine One* ('*eyn 'elohiym* 10:4).

18:43 Î have sìfted them *líke the dust,* *
    tossed them like dirt against thè fáce òf wind.

> *Like the dust* (*ke'afar*) stands in parallel in one psalm to the phrase *like
> dirt* (*ketiyt* 18:43, 2 Sam 22:43) and in another to *like sand of the seas*
> (*kehol yammiym* 78:27). These phrases are truly ominous, because of the
> destructive power of the desert sandstorm.

18:44 Yoû free me from the conflicts of peoplè; †
    you appoint me as heàd over géntiles. *
    A people *unknown tò mé* will sèrve me.

> *Unknown to me* (*lo'yada'tiy* 18:44, 35:11/15, 71:15, 81:6, 2 Sam 22:44)
> is a humble statement of limitation by the psalmist. Opposite of unknown
> is fabled, famous or *famed* (*noda'*):
> —*Famed is the Font of Being for giving judgment* (9:17)
> —*Her citadel is famed as a stronghold* (48:4)
> —*Famed in Judah is the Divine One* (76:2).

18:45 Tô heed with the eàr, they must heéd me; *
    sons of a foreign land sùbmít tò me.

18:46 Sôns of a foreìgn land capítulate, *
    and tremble fòrth fróm theìr camps.

18:47 Lông live the FONT OF BEING, ànd blest be my Rock, *
    and exalted *my Divine Òne óf Salvàtion!*

*My Divine One of Salvation* (*'elohey yish'iy* 18:47, 25:5, 27:9; *'elohey teshu'atiy* 51:16 *'elohey yeshu'atiy* 88:2; *'elohey yish'enu* 65:6, 79:9, 85:5; *'elohey yish'o* 24:5) belongs to a family of divine appellatives that includes *My Divine One of Justice* (*'elohey tsidqiy* 4:2) and *My Divine One of Mercy* (*'elohey hasdiy* 59:11/18).

### 18:48 *Îs not God* gìving redréss to me? *
### For *he subdues peoplès úndèr me.*

Three verses in this psalm and two in another begin with a rhetorical question, *Is not God . . .* (*ha-'el . . .* 18:31/33/48, 68:20/21):
—*Is not God blameless?* (*ha-'el tamiym* 18:31)
—*Is not God, is he not helpful?* (*ha-'el ham'azreniy* 18:33)
—*Is not God giving redress?* (*ha-'el noten neqamot* 18:48).

*He subdues peoples under me* (*yadber 'ammiym tahtay* 18:48, 2 Sam 22:48; *yadber 'ammiym tahteynu* 47:4; *haroded 'ammiy tahtay* 144:2). God is sovereign, and subjects people to his deputy, the king. A fuller version is *beneath his feet* (*tahat raglaw* 8:7, 18:1/39, 47:4).

### 18:49 Yoû deliver me from my rivàls; †
### yes, above those risen agaìnst me you líft me high; *
### *from a man of abuse* you dèlívèr me.

*From a man of abuse* (*me'iysh hamas* 18:49, 140:12, 2 Sam 22:49), that is, *from a man of abusive deeds* (*me'iysh hemasiym* 140:2/5), the psalmist prays for deliverance. The psalmist does not have a victim mentality; there is nothing of the masochist in him.

### 18:50 *Thêrefore* do I laud yoù †                                    *25:8*
### *among the gentiles,* Ô FONT OF BÉING, *
### and *plày chórds to yoùr Name!*                                    *9:12, 9:3*
### 18:51 Hê magnifies the victories of hìs king †
### and makes mercy fòr his anoínted one, *
### for David and for his Seedling *for an ètérnìty.*

*For an eternity* provides an open ending for several psalms (*'ad-'olam* 18:51, 2 Sam 22:51; *'ad-ha'olam* 28:9, 133:4).

## NINETEEN

NEW TESTAMENT — Verse 5 at Rom 10:18
LITURGY OF HOURS
Part One — Lauds on Monday II
Part Two — Midday Prayer on Monday I

Psalm 19 seems to be a combination of two pre-existing psalms, only loosely connected. The first half is a cosmology but uses juridical terms like "edict" and "summons" (verse 5). The whole cosmos is making a deposition.

19:1    (For the Director. A Mizmor of David.)

19:2    **Heâvens are telling of thè glory óf God, \***
      **and the sky-dome relates *thè wórks of hìs Hands.***       *8:7*

19:3    **Dây spins to à day the speáking, \***
      **and night shifts to à níght the knòwledge.**

19:4    **Thêre is no speaking; thère is no wórding; \***
      **there is no hearìng óf theìr call.**

19:5    **Înto *all the land* goes thcir summòns, †**       *8:2*
      **and their edict to the ènd of the cósmos, \***
      **where a tent bèlóngs to thè sun,**

19.6    **which *like a bridegroom* emergès from his chámber, \***
      **eager like a strong man for thè próving ground.**

    ***Like a bridegroom*** (*kehatan*) is a comparison found both here and in Isaiah (61:10). Here the referent is the radiant sun; in Isaiah the referent is God. The same Isaian verse gives also the corresponding comparison *like a bride* (*kakkallah*).

19:7    **Frôm ends of the skies he comes, ànd goes to theír ends, \***
      **and there is no hidìng fróm hìs heat.**

19:8a    **Pêrfect is the *Torah of thè* FONT OF BÉING,\***      *119:1*
      **to make thè soúl rèfreshed, \***

19:8b    **Fîrm is the decree of thè FONT OF BÉING, \***
      **to make thè símplè wise.**

19:9a    **Steâdfast are the precepts of thè FONT OF BÉING, \***
      **to make thè heárt jòyful. \***

19:9b    **Noûrishing is the command of thè FONT OF BÉING, \***
      **to make thè éyes shìne bright.**

19:10a **Cleânsing is** *awe for thè* FONT OF BÉING, *
**standìng fór àn age.** *

The virtuous people have *awe for the* FONT OF BEING (*yir'at yhwh* 19:10, 34:12, 111:10); sinners need more *dread of the Divine One* (*pahad 'elohiym* 36:2; *pahad yhwh* 1 Sam 11:7, Is 2:10/19/21).

*Standing for an age* (*'omedet la'ad* 19:10, 111:3/10, 112:3/9). Many construction projects of the ancient world, like the pyramids of Egypt or the bridges of Rome, have stood for ages. They left a physical legacy, the Hebrews a spiritual one.

19:10b **Truê are judgments of thè** FONT OF BÉING, *
**altogethèr júst àre they.**

19:11 **Prêcious are they,** *more than the gold òr the* **grand** *gílding*, *
**and sweeter** *than honey* **or raw honèy fróm thè hives.**

19:12 **Îndeed your servant takes à caution fróm them;** *
**there is grand reward ìn keépìng them.**

19:13 **Ône's own lapsès, who can fáthom?** *
**From things hiddèn, párdòn me.**

19:14 **Yêt restrain your servant from presumptiòns.** †
**Let thèm not contról me;** *
**then I will be wholly innocént óf gràve sin.**

19:15 **Lêt my mouth have words and my heart thoùghts** †
**pleasing** *bèfore the Fáce of You*, *                      *17:2*
FONT OF BEING, **my** *Rock* **ànd my Redeèming.**          *92:16*

*My heart-thoughts* (*hegyon libbiy* 19:15; *haguth libbiy* 49:4). Heart is the seat of intelligence in Hebrew anthropology; therefore the heart has its own logic, which provides the human being with a modus operandi. Speech reveals these heart-thoughts.

# TWENTY

LITURGY OF HOURS — Vespers on Tuesday I

Psalm 20 addresses people who need reassurances liturgical (3/4), military (6/8) and political (7/10). "Answer" forms an inclusion in the first and last verses, as well as in verse 7. God is addressed in 1–6, the king is addressed in 8–10; both are in third person in transitional verse 7.

20:1    (For the Director. A Mizmor of David.)

20:2    **Mây the Font of Being answer you** *on à day of dístress,* *
        **lift you high in the Name of the** *Divine Òne óf Jàcob.*

> *A day of distress* (*beyom tsarah* 20:2, 50:15; *beyom tsarathiy* 77:3, 86:7) or *a day of need* (*beyom tsar* 59:17, 102:3) is not yet *a day of evil* (*beyom ra'ah* 27:5, 41:2; *yomey ra'* 49:6, 94:13).

> *Divine One of Jacob* (*'elohey ya'aqob* 20:2, 46:8/12, 75:10, 76:7, 81:2/5, 84:9, 94:7) and *Divine One of Israël* (*'elohey yisra'el* 41:14, 59:6, 68:9, 69:7, 72:18, 106:48) are interchangeable.

20:3    **Mây he send you assistànce from the hóly place,** *
        **and from the Ziön mày hé suppòrt you.**

20:4    **Mây he be mìndful of áll your gifts,** *
        **and receive yoùr whóle oblàtions.**

20:5    **Âs befits your heàrt may he gíve to you,** *
        **and all your plans mày hé fùlfill.**

20:6    **Lêt us rejoice in your salvatiòn,** †
        **and wave banners in the Name òf our Divíne One.** *
        **May the Font of Being fulfill àll yoúr rèquests.**

20:7    **Nôw I know the Font of Being saved his anointèd one,** †
        **whom he answers from hìs skies of hóliness** *
        **with mighty saving deeds àt hís Rìght Hand.**

20:8    **Sôme rally in the chariot and sòme in the stállions,** *
        **but we in the Name of the Font of Being, oúr Divìne One.**

20:9    **Thêy are the ones whò swayed and stúmbled,** *
        **but we arose and find oùrsélves still stànding.**

20:10   **Ô Font of Beìng! Make the kíng safe!** *
        **Let him answer us on thè dáy wè call.**

# TWENTY-ONE

In the title of Psalm 21 (as well as in the titles of fifty-seven other psalms), the noun *Mizmor* probably indicates a song to be accompanied by harp or lyre. The base verb *zamar*, which means to play on a stringed instrument, appears in the last verse of the text itself. The last two verses of Psalm 21 cleverly compare the bow strings of the FONT OF BEING with the strings of the psalmist's musical instrument.

21:1    (For the Director. A Mizmor of David.)

21:2    **Ô FONT OF BEING, in your might thè king rejoíces, ***
        **and revels so greatly ìn yoúr salvàtion!**

21:3    **Whât his heart dèsired you gáve him, ***
        **and the wish of his lips you dìd nót dèny.**

21:4    **Râther, you welcomed him with blèssings of goódness; ***
        **you placed on his head à crówn òf gold.**

21:5    **Lîfe is thè thíng he ásked of you; ***
        **you gave him *length of days, evèr ánd àn age.***      *5:12*

*Length of days* (*'orek yomiym* 21:5, 91;15; *le'orek yomiym* 23:6, 93:5) indicates a duration that remains unspecified, but is of great length. The word *yom* has a secondary meaning of lifetime, and so this phrase could be "lengthy life" or even "a length of lifetimes."

21:6    **Hîs greatest glory ìs your salvátion; ***
        **you bestow *majesty and grandeùr* úpòn him.**

*Majesty and grandeur* (*hod wehadar* 21:6, 96:6, 104:1, 111:3) are like angels before the Face of God, like the cherubim in the holy place (96:6), like vestments which God wears (104:1); they are found in his deeds (111:3) and bestowed upon his king (21:6).

21:7    **Fôr you array him wìth blessings *fór an age, ***      *9:19*
        **allow him with joy to see thè Fáce òf You.**

21:8    **Fôr the king has trust in thè FONT OF BÉING ***
        **and with mercy from on high *hè doés not stùmble.***    *112:6*

21:9    **Yoûr hand will discovèr all your rívals; ***
        **your right hand will discovèr *thóse who hàte you.***    *9:14*

21:10    **Sêt them like a bonfire when you appeàr, FONT OF BÉING, \***
        **when their anger swallows them ànd fláme consùmes them.**

21:11    **Caûse their fruit tò vanish fróm the land, \***
        **and their seedlings from among *the childrèn óf Àdam.***     *11:4*

Compare a passage from the Akkadian *Hymn to Shamash*: "Those who do evil, their seed shall not endure" (ANET 389).

21:12    **Fôr they spread èvil agaínst you; \***
        **they form plans, which thèy cánnòt do,**

21:13    **bût you wìll have them sét back, \***
        **when you pull your bowstrìngs ín their fàces.**

21:14    ***Rîse, O FONT ÒF BEING, ín your might! \****     *10:12*
        **Let us *sing and plày chórds* to yoùr strength!**

***Let us sing and play chords*** (*nashiyrah unzammerah* 21:14) implies that this psalm is to be performed by an ensemble of singers and players of musical instruments. Elsewhere the psalmist accompanies himself as he sings (*'ashiyrah wa'azammerah* 27:6, 57:8, 108:2).

## TWENTY-TWO

NEW TESTAMENT — Verse 2 at Mt 27:46
Verse 8 at Lk 23:35 and Mt 27:39 / Verse 9 at Mt 27:43
Verse 19 at Jn 19:24 / Verse 23 at Heb 2:12
LITURGY OF HOURS — Midday Prayer on Friday III

The author of Psalm 22 compares himself and his foes to animals—worm (verse 7), bullock (13), lion (14/22), hound (17/21) and ox (22). At first he expresses despair but after verse 23 he finds hope. Matthew (27:46) quotes Jesus reciting the first verse from the cross (in Aramaic translation), and thus implies that Jesus recited the whole psalm, including the hopeful conclusion. The psalm is about snatching victory from the jaws of defeat.

22:1   (For the Director, like "A Doe at the Dawn." A Mizmor of David.)

22:2   **Ô God of mine! O God òf mine! †
Why hàve you forsáken me? \*
Far from safety, these are my wòrds óf grièving.**

22:3   **Ô my Divine One, I cry out _by dày,_ but you ánswer not, \*
and _by night,_ but Ì háve nò rest.**

_Day and night_ (_yomam welaylah_ 1:2, 22:3, 32:4, 42:4, 55:11). The word _yomam_ bears an ancient ending for "accusative of time." The usage survives also in the very common Arabic term _yawman._ Though in Hebrew usage night precedes day (Gen 1:), this phrase seems to represent a more ancient precedence for the day.

22:4   **Yêt you yoursèlf are the Hóly One, \*
enthroned in the praise-craft òf Ísràël.**

22:5   **În you, oùr forebears trústed; \*
they trustèd, ánd you freèd them.**

22:6   **Tô you they crièd and were sét free; \*
in you they put their trust, and thèy wére nòt shamed.**

22:7   **Bût I myself am à worm, and nó man, \*
a rebuke to Adam, a scorn tò thé peòple.**

22:8   **Âll those whò see me jeér at me; \*
they spit with the lip; thèy sháke thè head:**

22:9   **"Ôh, he trusts in the FONT OF BEÌNG! †
Who can deliver hìm? Who can freé him? \*
To whom can hè bé so pleàsing?"**

22:10    **Yêt you drew mè *from the bósom*; \***           *22:11*
          **at my mother's breasts, you taught mè hów tò trust.**

22:11    **Bêcause of you I càme *from the ténder place*; \***
          **from *my mother's bosom*, yoù áre my God.**

*From the bosom* (*mibbaten* 22:10, 58:4, 71:6; *mibbeten 'immiy* 22:11, 139:13) and *from the tender place* (*merahem* 22:11, 58:4, 110:3) stand in parallel both here and another place (58:4), but they are not synonyms. *Beten* is often incorrectly translated "womb." God promised David that *one of the fruit of his beten* (*mipperiy bitneka* 132:11; *periy habbaten* 127:3) would sit upon his throne. If David has a *beten*, then it is not a womb, but rather the bosom, and so by process of elimination *the tender place* (*rehem*) must be.

22:12    *Bê not aloof from me*, **for dìstress approáches, \***
          **for *no helpèr wíll thère be!***

God was not aloof on Mount Sinaï in giving the Israëlites a set of negative imperatives; the Israëlites were not aloof in directing some negative imperatives back to God in prayer:
—*Be not aloof* (*'al-tirhaq* 22:12/20, 35:22, 38:22, 71:12)
—*Forsake me not* (*'al-ta'azbeniy* 27:9, 38:22, 71:9/18, 119:8)
—*Be not deaf* (*'al-teherash* 28:1, 35:22, 39:13, 83:2, 109:1)
—*Hide not the Face of You* (*'al-taster faneyka* 69:18)
—*Delay not* (*'al-te'ahar* 40:18, 70:6, Dan 6:19).

*No helper will there be* (*'eyn-'ozer* 22:12, 72:12, 107:12, Is 63:5) is a defeatist statement, of a pattern with:
—*There is no rescuer* (*'eyn-matssiyl* 7:3, 50:22, 71:11)
—*There is no savior* (*'eyn-moshiya'* 18:42, 2 Sam 22:42, Deut 22:27, 28:29/31, Judg 12:3, Is 47:15, Hos 13:4).

22:13    **Sûrrounding me àre bullocks mánifold, \***
          **mighty bulls of Bashan, thàt ménàce me;**

22:14    **thêy are gapìng at me wíth their mouths, \***
          **like lions feedìng ánd roàring.**

22:15    **Lîke the waters I poured and disjoìnted were *áll my bones*. \***
          **My heart was *like the wax*, meltìng wíthìn me.**

*Like the waters* (*kammayim* 22:15, 79:3, 109:18; *kemo-mayim* 58:8) and *like the wax* (*kaddonag* 22:15, 97:5; *kehimmes donag* 68:3) are both images of dissolution. Waters flow and wax melts, but the psalmist would prefer to keep his solid form.

*All my bones* (*kol 'atsmothay* 22:15/18, 35:10). This psalmist has every bone out of joint (22:15) and is so thin he can count them (22:18). Another invites his bones to join in praising God (35:10).

22:16 **Shrûnken is my might lìke clay, †**
**as *my tongue clìngs to my pálate,* ***
**while you ready me for thè dúst òf death.**

*My tongue clings to my palate* (*leshoniy mudbaq milqohay* 22:16; *tidbaq-leshoniy lehikkiy* 137:6, Lam 4:4; *dabaq leshon yoneq 'el-hikko* Lam 4:4) as a result of dehydration. The psalmist has been trying to outrun the bulls (verse 13), lions (14) and hounds (17).

22:17 **Fôr surrounding me are thè hounds; †**
**a *council of scoùndrels* encírcle me, ***
**nipping at my hands ànd át my feet.**

Like a pack of wolves, enemies gather in *a council of scoundrels* (*'edat mere'iym* 22:17), *assembly of scoundrels* (*qehal mere'iym* 26:5) or *league of scoundrels* (*sod mere'iym* 64:3).

22:18 **Î can take àccount of *áll my bones*; ***         *22:15*
**they gape; thèy gáwk àt me.**

22:18 **Thêy divide my clòthing amóng them, ***
**but for my cloak thèy dróp thè dice.**

22:20 **Bût, O FONT OF BÈING, *be nót aloof!* ***         *22:12*
**O Strength of mine, *tò hélp me hàsten!***

*Hasten!* (*hushah*) is an imperative verb that lends urgency to a prepositional phrase which can either come before, as in *To help me hasten!* (*le'ezratiy hushah* 22:20, 40:14, 70:2, 71:12) or come after, as in *Hasten to help me!* (*hushah le'ezrati* 38:20).

22:21 **Dêlivèr from the bláde my soul, ***
**my only lìfe fróm the hoùnd's paw.**

22:22 **Mâke me safe from the moùth of a líon, ***
**and from the horns of oxèn ánswèr me.**

22:23 **Î will recite your Nàme to my bréthren, ***
**in the midst of assembly Ì wíll laùd you:**

22:24 **Yoû who revere the FONT OF BEING, laud hìm! †**
**All seedlings òf Jacob, hónor him! ***
**Stand in awe of him, all seedlings òf Ísràël!**

22:25 ***Nôr surely* did he scorn or spurn a low one's lowlìness, †**
***nor* did hè *hide his Fáce from him,* ***         *9:19, 13:2*
**but heard whèn hé besoùght him.**

22:26 **With your help, with my *praise-craft in à vast assémbly*, \***
**I will fulfill my vows alongside thòse whó revère him.**

The psalmist, who has been afflicted, declares his resolution to sing
***praise-craft in assembly*** (*tehillathiy beqahal* 22:26; *tehillatho biqehal*
149:1). This verse is the turning point of the psalm. The author intends
to announce his healing ***in a vast assembly*** (*beqahal rab* 22:26, 35:18,
40:10; *leqahal rab* 40:11). All the adult males were to gather before
the ark, or later before the temple, on the high holidays of Pentecost,
Passover, and Booths.

22:27 **Lôwly ones eat, and fed they laud thè FONT OF BÉING, \***
**you who seek him, long live yoùr heárts, *for àn age*!**    *9:19*

22:28 **Lêt *all ends of land* again recall thè FONT OF BÉING \***    *2:8*
**and all families of gentiles bow *before thè Fáce òf You*.**    *17:2*

22:29 **Fôr dominion belongs to thè FONT OF BÉING, \***
**and he is commander *amóng the gèntiles*.**    *9:12*

22:30 **Thêy feasted and worshipped, all with wealth ìn land; †**
**they will kneel *bèfore the Fáce of Him*, \***    *17:2*
**all go down to dust, where their soul nò lóngèr lives.**

22:31 **Tô the seedling let sèrvice be gíven; \***
**let this age be told òf Ádònay.**

22:32 **Thêy come and tell his justice to a peoplè yet to bé born: \***
***how hè hás àcted!***

***How he has acted*** (*kiy 'asah* 22:32), or ***how you have acted*** (*kiy 'attah
'asiyta* 39:10; *kiy 'asiyta* 52:11) is the message to be passed down
from generation to generation. Religion is based on what God has
done, though people have their own proper response.

# TWENTY-THREE

LITURGY OF HOURS — Midday Prayer on Sundays II and IV

Assyrian kings called themselves shepherds of their people, and so the language of Psalm 23 is royal as well as pastoral. This poetic masterpiece has several phrases joining two elements, one concrete and one abstract, in the poetical figure called metonymy: "pastures of green" (verse 2), "waters of rest" (2), "paths of justice" (3), "vale of deathly shadow" (4).

23:1 (A Mizmor of David.)
FÔNT OF BEING ìs shepherdíng me; *
I wìll nót be làcking.

23:2 Ȋn pastures òf green he láys me down; *
by waters òf rést he tènds me.

23:3 Tô my soul hè gives refréshment; *
he guides me in paths of justice *for thè sáke of hìs Name.*   *25:11*

23:4 Thoûgh I walk in a vale of *deathly shadow*, Ì fear no évil, *
for you are with me; your Rod and yoùr Stáff consòle me.

*Deathly shadow* (*tsalmaweth* 23:4, 44:20, 107:10/14, Jer 13:16) is a compound noun, combining *shadow* (*tsal*) and *death* (*maweth*). It descends like nightfall (Jer 13:16); through it one might have to walk (23:4), by it to be cloaked (44:20) and in which to dwell (107:10/14). Elsewhere, the expression expands to the epexegetical *darkness and deathly shadow* (*hoshek wetsalmaweth* 107:10/14).

23:5 Yoû spread before my face à table, neár my foes; *
you anoint my head with oil, from my cùp óf plènty.

23:6 Ȏnly goodness and mercy follow mè *all my dáys of life*; *
I dwell in the *house of the FONT OF BEING* fòr *léngth
òf days.*   *42:5, 21:5*

*All my days of life* (*kol yemey hayyay* 23:6, 27:4, 128:5, Prov 31:12) begin with *days of youth* (*yemey 'alumay* 89:46) and proceed through the *days of a human being* (*'enosh . . . yomaw* 103:15). Here days are like seasons or stages of life.

49

TEMPLE LITURGY — Sunday
NEW TESTAMENT — Verse 1 at 1 Cor 10:26
Verse 4 at Mt 5:8
LITURGY OF HOURS — Lauds on Tuesday I
Office of Readings on Sunday IV

Rabbinic sources indicate that Psalm 24 was recited in the temple on the first day of the week. Though some say the Jews acquired the week during their exile, not a single Babylonian document mentions the week as such.

24:1    (Of David. A Mizmor.)
**Tô Font of Being belongs the lànd *and what fílls it*, *
*a world and they whò dwéll withìn it.***

These four encyclopedic statements occur in the psalms:
***sea and what fills it*** (*hayyam umlo'o* 96:11, 98:7)
***land and what fills it*** (*ha'arets umelo'ah* 24:1)
***world and they who dwell in it*** (*tebel weyoshebey bah* 24:1, 98:7)
***world and what fills it*** (*tebel umelo'ah* 50:12, 89:12).
The term ***world*** (*tebel*) means the continental land mass, and thus is a close synonym for ***land*** (*'arets*). Creatures that dwell in the sea apparently are not included among those who dwell in the world.

24:2    **Fôr he has foundèd it upón the seas, *
and placed it on thè ríverways.**

24:3    ***Whô* may ascend the mount of thè Font of Béing? *
And *who* may stand in his place òf hóliness?**

***Who?... who?*** (*miy... miy* 15:1, 24:3, 60:11, 94:16, 108:13; *mimmiy ... mimmiy* 27:1). Doubling the interrogative word gives a searching quality, either catechetical or rhetorical.

24:4    **Ône whose palms are clean, *whòse heart has púrity*, *
whose soul is not given to vanity òr sweáring fàlsehood,**

***Whose heart has purity*** (*bar lebab* 24:4; *barey lebab* 73:1) is one who keeps his soul free of vanity (that is, of idol worship) and his lips free of giving false witness. ***Pure is the command of the Font of Being*** (*mitswat yhwh barah* 19:9), and one who keeps it is ***pure of hands*** (*bor yaday* 18:21/25).

24:5    **whô accepts blessing from thè Font of Béing \***
    **and justice from his _Divine Òne óf Salvàtion._**        _18:47_

24:6    **Thîs is the age òf those who fóllow him, \***
    **_those seeking the Face of You_, thè Óne of Jàcob.**

> **_Those seeking the Face of You_** (_mebaqshey paneyka_ 24:6; _'et-paneyka_
> _'ebaqqesh_ 27:8); **_seek the Face of Him_** (_baqshu fanaw_ 105:4). Those
> seeking the Face are seeking God. Thus **_the Face of You_** (_paneyka_) is
> simply an elaborate, emphatic way of saying **_You Yourself_** (_'attah_).

24:7    **Lîft, O gates, yoùr heads, †**
    **and be lifted, doorwàys of etérnity, \***
    **and may he enter às Kíng of Glòry!**

> **_Lift . . . your heads_** (_se'u . . . ro'sheykem_ 24:7/9). It is generally
> believed that the word **_head_** (_ro'sh_) here refers to the upper part of
> the gate, the actual lift mechanism. However, elsewhere the lifting
> of heads suggests selection of leaders (_nas'u ro'sh_ 83:3; _yariym ro'sh_
> 110:7), and that may be implied here as well. Protocol would certainly
> dictate that a delegation of urban leaders be present at the gates to
> meet the arriving King of Glory.

24:8    **Whô is this, the King of Glory? †**
    **Font of Bèìng, strong and míghty! \***
    **Font of Bèìng, stróng in bàttle!**

> **_Who is this?_** (_miy zeh_ 24:8, 25:12; _miy hu' zeh_ 24:10). This psalm is
> concerned with entrance requirements. The psalmist first asks twice
> who are the worshippers with rights to enter the temple (24:3) and then
> asks twice who is the divine King with the right to enter Jerusalem
> (24:8/10). The psalm is like a small catechism.

24:9    **Lîft, O gates, yoùr heads, †**
    **and lift the doorwàys of etérnity, \***
    **and may he enter, thè Kíng of Glòry!**

24:10   **Whô is he, thìs King of Glóry? \***
    **Font of Being, Sabaöth! He is thè Kíng of Glòry!**

# TWENTY-FIVE

LITURGY OF HOURS — Midday Prayer on Thursday I

Psalm 25 is second of eight acrostic psalms (9/10, 25, 34, 37, 111, 112, 119, 145). *Waw* and *Qoph* are missing (after verses 5/17), but two *Resh* verses and an extra *Pe* at the end make the verses equal the letters of the alphabet. The extra *Pe* verse mentions redemption (*peduth*), as at the end of Psalm 34.

25:1 (Of David.) *Aleph.*
**Tô you, thè FONT OF BÉING, \***
**I lift my soul tò my Divìne One.**

*To you, FONT OF BEING* (*'eleyka yhwh* 25:1, 28:1) are opening words here and again at Psalm 28, where the second verse expands the phrase to read *when I beseech you* (*beshaw'iy 'eleyka* 28:2, 31:23). This too, then, is probably a psalm of beseeching.

In the previous psalm the heads of the gates were lifted up (24:7/9); this psalmist says *I lift my soul* (*nafshiy 'essa'* 25:1, 86:4; *nasa'thiy nafshiy* 143:8). Other psalmists also lift their eyes (121:1, 123:1), their heads (83:3) and their palms (63:5, 119:48).

25:2 *Beth.*
**În you I trusted; nor lèt me be pút to shame; \***
**nor let my enemies gloàt óvèr me.**                              *30:2*

*Gloat over me* (*ya'altsu liy* 25:2; *simmahta liy* 30:2; *yismehu liy* 35:19/24, 38:17, 40:4, 52:8) implies all the behavior of triumphant enemies—shouting, singing, dancing, pillage, slaughter, and rape.

25:3 *Ghimel.*
**Îndeed! Let none whò wait for yoú be shamed; \***
**shamed be they who cònsórt with vaìn things.**
25:4 *Daleth.*
**Wâys of yours, FONT OF BÈING, make knówn to me; \***
**teach mè yoúr pàthways.**
25:5 *He.*
**Poînt me in your truth and teach mè, †**
**for you are my Divine Òne of Salvátion; \***                     *18:47*
**in you have I been hopìng áll thè day.**

*All the day* (*kol hayyom* 25:5, 32:3, 35:28, 37:26, 38:7/13, 42:4/11, 44:9/16/23, 52:3, 56:2/3/6, 71:8/15/24, 72:15, 73:14, 74:22, 86:3, 88:18, 89:17, 119:97) means either the daytime, or day plus night.

## 25:6 *Zain.*

**Keêp in mind your tender feelings, Ò FONT OF BÉING, *** 
**and your mercies, how they are *from ètérnìty*.**

*From eternity* (*me'olam* 25:6, 93:2) considers an infinite span that has no beginning. Expanded phrases *from eternity to eternity* (*me'olam 'ad-'olam* 90:2) and *from eternity and to eternity* (*me'olam we'ad-'olam* 103:17) consider an infinite span without beginning nor end.

## 25:7 *Heth.*

**Câll not to mind the sins of my youth or my rebelliòns; †** 
**as befits your mercy, bè mindful óf me, *** 
**for the sake of your goodnèss, FÓNT OF BÈING.**

*As befits your mercy* (*kehasdeka* 25:7) stands between a memory not desired (of his sins) and one desired (of him personally). Elsewhere the phrase stands in parallel with:
—*as befits your great tenderness* (*kerob rahmeyka* 51:3)
—*as befits your judgment* (*kemishpoteka* 119:149).
An expanded form of the phrase is:
—*as befits your mercy give me life* (*kehasdeka hayyeni* 119:88/159).

## 25:8 *Teth.*

**Goôd and steadfast is thè FONT OF BÉING; *** 
***therefore* he guides sinnèrs ón thè way.**

*Therefore* ('*al-ken*) appears thirteen times in the psalms, five at the head of a verse (1:5, 18:50, 46:3, 119:127/128) and eight in mid-verse (25:8, 42:7, 45:3/8/18, 110:7, 119:104/129). Dahood says that this "expresses the cause of things already stated" (*Psalms* I:271).

## 25:9 *Yod.*

**Hê directs lowly peoplè *in the júdgment*, *** 
**and teaches his way to thè lówly peòple.**

*At the judgment* (*bammishpot* 1:5 and 25:9), and related phrase *for the judgment* (*lammishpot* 9:8 and 76:10) are juridical terms for standing as the defendant in a trial.

25:10 *Coph.*

**Âll paths of the FONT OF BEING àre *mercy ánd truth* ***
**for those who keep his bond ànd hís dècrees.**

*Mercy and truth* (*hesed we'emeth* 25:10; *hasdeka wa'amitka* 40:11/12) may
seem like odd bedfellows, but they are greater than the skies (57:11, 108:5),
embrace one another (85:11) and are directed to the Divine Face (89:15), yet
they have been appointed our protectors (40:12) and companions (61:8), and
they show the path (25:10).

25:11 *Lamedh.*

**Fôr the sake of your Nàme, "FONT OF BÉING," ***
**forgive even my offense, thoùgh ít bè grave.**

*For the sake of your Name* (*lema'an shimka* 25:11, 31:4, 79:9, 143:11;
*lema'an shemeka* 109:21); *for the sake of his Name* (*lema'an shemo* 23:3,
106:8). God will honor his own Name by forgiving the psalmist.

25:12 *Mem.*

**Whô is this, the man who reveres thè FONT OF BÉING, ***                    *24:8*
**to whom he teaches thè wáy tò choose?**

25:13 *Nun.*

**Ône whose soul is dwèlling with goódness, ***
**and whose offspring *lày claím to thè land.***                             *37:9*

25:14 *Samech.*

**Leâgued is the FONT OF BEING with thòse who revére him, ***
**and to them he màkes knówn hìs bond.**

25:15 *Ain.*

**Êyes of mine are ever on thè FONT OF BÉING, ***
**that from the snare he mày freé my feet.**

25:16 *Pe.*

**Tûrn to me and tàke pity ón me, ***
**how lonely and hòw lów àm I.**

Shared by Psalms 25 and 86 are **Turn to me and take pity on me** (*peneh-
'elay wehonneniy* 25:16, 86:16), **I lift my soul** (*nafshiy 'essa'* 25:1, 86:4), **all
the day** (*kol hayyom* 25:5, 86:3), **mercy and truth** (*hesed we'emeth* 25:10,
86:15), **keep sentinel for my soul** (*shomrah nafshiy* 25:20, 86:2).

25:17 *Tsade.*
**Neêds of my heart àre of long stánding; \***
*from my anguìsh sét mè free.*

*From my anguish set me free* (*mimmetsuqotay hotsiy'eniy* 25:17). This psalmist tried to think of a word that started with the letter *Tsade*. His mind produced the first word **need** (*tsarah*), but along with its frequent companion, **anguish** (*tsuq*). Another psalm uses this phrase as a kind of responsory, with varying verbs:
—*mimmetsuqoteyhem yatsiylem* (**deliver them** 107:6)
—*mimmetsuqoteyhem yoshiy'em* (**set them free** 107:13/19)
—*mimmetsuqoteyhem yotsiy'em* (**rescue them** 107:28).

25:18 *Resh.*
**Bêhold my lowlinèss and my troúble, \***
**and take àwáy all my sins.**

25:19 *Resh.*
**Bêhold my rivals, hòw they are mánifold, \***
**and how they loathe me with àbúsive loàthing.**

*How they are manifold* (*kiy rabbu* 25:19, Is 22:9, Jer 14:7, 46:23) is just like saying *how many they are* (*ma rabbu* 3:2, 104:24). The contrary statement is *they became few* (*yihyu me'attiym* 109:8, Qohelet 5:1).

25:20 *Shin.*
*Keêp sentinel over my soùl, and delíver me; \**          *16:1*
**nor will I be shamed, for I hàve trústed ìn you.**

25:21 *Tau.*
**Întegrity and faìrness presérve me, \***
**for I hàve hóped ìn you.**

25:22 *Pe.*
**Gîve ransom, O Divìne One, to Ísraël, \***
**from all òf theír distrèsses.**

# TWENTY-SIX

The author of Psalm 26 bathes his hands (verse 6), as will another (73:13). This gesture elsewhere seems juridical (Mt 27:24), but here seems liturgical, because followed by the line "and I process about your oblation table." "With integrity" (verses 1/11) ends in long vowel "i," which resembles the first person singular genitive. In fact, however, it is an old case ending that disappeared in standard Hebrew but still exists in Arabic.

26:1　(Of David.)
**Jûdge me, Font of Being! For I wàlked *with intégrity*, \***　　7:9
**and trusted in the Font of Being; Ì wíll nòt stray.**

26:2　***Prôbe me*, Font of Bèing, and próve me; \***
**examine *my inner self and thìs heárt òf mine.***　　7:10

The psalmist says **Probe me** (*behananiy* 26:2, 139:23) and presents himself to God for an examination, like a patient appearing before a doctor. This Physician is a cardiovascular specialist.

26:3　**Îndeed, your mercy rèmains befóre my eyes, \***
**and I have walked wìthín yoùr truth.**

26:4　**Nôr did I dwell with persòns of beguílement, \***
**nor did I go in with people òf mystèry.**

26:5　**Î have shunned the *assèmbly of scoúndrels*, \***
**and dwell not wìth únjust peòple.**

Like a pack of wolves, enemies gather in ***a council of scoundrels*** (*'edat mere'iym* 22:17), ***assembly of scoundrels*** (*qehal mere'iym* 26:5) or ***league of scoundrels*** (*sod mere'iym* 64:3).

26:6　***Î wash my pàlms into cleánliness* \***
**and go about your oblation-tablè, Fónt of Bèing;**

A psalmist already ***clean of palms*** (*neqiy kappayim* 24:4), with an established ***state of cleanliness in his palms*** (*ubeniqqayon kappay* Gen 20:5), can declare ***I wash my palms into cleanliness*** (*'erhats beniqqayon kappay* 26:6, 73:13). This phrase may derive from a text for ritual purification in the temple.

26:7   **thât there bè heard *the soúnd of laud*, ***
**to recount all your marvèls, FÓNT OF BÈING.**

*The sound of laud* (*qol todah* 26:7) follows an idiomatic pattern shared by *the sound of song* (*qol rinnah* 47:2, 118:15), *the sound of song and laud* (*qol rinnah wetodah* 42:5), *the sound of my pleading* (*qol tahnunothay* 86:65; *qol tahnunay* 116:1, 130:2, 140:7), *sounding of your thunder* (*qol ra'amka* 77:19, 104:7) and *shofar sounding* (*qol shofar* 47:6, 98:6).

26:8   **Î love the àbode of yoúr house, ***
**and the place of dwellìng óf your Glòry.**

26:9   **Nôr together wìth sinners coúnt my soul, ***
**nor my life wìth *mén of bloòdshed*,**             5:7

26:10   **în whose hànds is conspíracy, ***
**and whose right hands àre filled wìth bribes.**

26:11   **Bût I wàlk *with intégrity*; ***             7:9
**redeem me and tàke píty òn me.**

26:12   **My foot is stàndìng *upón a plain*; ***
**in groups I bless thè FÓNT OF BÈING.**

*Upon a plain* (*bemiyshor* 26:12, Mal 2:6). The expression can also be translated *in integrity*. In this case, however, the subject is the psalmist's own foot, which needs to stand on physical ground

*In groups* uses a rare noun that apparently is sometimes masculine (*bemaqheliym* 26:12) and sometimes feminine (*bemaqhelot* 68:27). The word comes from the same triliteral root as the frequent noun *assembly* (*qahal*), which by the way is masculine as in the phrase *vast assembly* (*qahal rab*).

# TWENTY-SEVEN

LITURGY OF HOURS — Vespers on Wednesday I

Psalm 27 is the exact opposite of a penitential psalm, indeed it is a vehement protestation of innocence, in which the psalmist pleads not guilty to charges made against him, and begs that he not be excommunicated (verse 4).

27:1a   (Of David.)
    **Fônt of Being is light to me ànd safety tó me; \***
    *of whom* **shoùld Í be ìn awe?**         *24:3*

27:1b   **Fônt of Being is the strònghold of lífe to me; \***
    *of whom* **shoùld Í be ìn dread?**         *24:3*

27:2   **Whên scoundrels came near mè to consúme my flesh, \***
    **my foes and rivals of mine stumblèd ánd thèy fell.**

27:3   **Thoûgh an army camp against me, my heart be nót awed. \***
    **Though battle surge against me, evèn thén may Ì trust.**

27:4a   **Ône thing I asked the Font of Being, this Ì seek: †**
    **that I may dwell in the house of thè Font of Béing \***   *42:5*
    *all thè dáys of my life,*

*All the days of my life* (*kol yemey hayyay* 23:6, 27:4, 128:5, Prov 31:12), from the *days of youth* (*yemey 'alumay* 89:46) onward, stand threatened by the *day of evil* in the next verse.

27:4b   **tô behold the beauty of thè Font of Béing \***
    **and greet the dawn wìthín his tèmple.**

27:5   **Fôr he will guard me in his booth** *on à day of évil,* **\***
    **hide me in the secrecy of his tent, lift mè óntò rock,**

*On a day of evil* (*beyom ra'ah* 27:5, 41:2, *yomey ra'* 49:6, 94:13) is on a day of true catastrophe, not just *on a day of distress* (*beyom tsarah* 20:2, 50:15; *beyom tsarathiy* 77:3, 86:7).

27:6   **ând now my head is higher than my rivals about mè, †**
    **and in his tent I will** *offer òblations óf* **song; \***    *4:6*
    *I will sing and play chords* **for thè Font of Bèing.**   *21:14*

27:7   **Heâr, O Font of Being, thè voice with whích I cry, \***
    **and take pity on me, ànd ánswèr me!**

27:8     Tô you my heart sàys, "Let them seék his Face!" *
      I *seek the Face of You,* thè FÓNT OF BÈING.       *24:6*

27:9     *Nôr hide the Face of You from me,* †       *13:2*
      nor turn in anger from yoùr servant! Bé my help! *
      Nor leave me *nor forsake me, my Dìvíne Salvàtion.*       *18:47*

Several psalmists, feeling the need for God's presence, pray: *nor forsake me* ('*al-ta'azbeniy* 27:9, 38:22, 71:9/18, 119:8). One goes farther and says that God is absent from him: *You have forsaken me* ('*azabtaniy* 22:2).

27:10     Thoûgh my father or my mòther forsáke me, *
      may the FONT OF BEÌNG wélcòme me.

27:11     Teâch me your ways, FONT OF BEÌNG, †
      and guide mè on a lével path, *
      because of *those whò gláre àt me.*       *5:9*

27:12     Yôke me not to the neck of my foès, †
      for they have risèn up against me, *
      testifying falsely ànd breáthing àbuse.

27:13     Bê that as it may, I have à firm intèntion *
      to see the goodness of the FONT OF BEING in *à lánd òf life.*

The *land of life* ('*erets hayyim* 27:13, 52:7; '*erets ha-hayyiym* 142:6), also called the *lands of life* ('*artsot hahayyiym* 116:9, Is 38:11, Job 28:13), will be ruled by the *God of life* ('*el hay* 42:3; '*el hayyay,* 42:9). The opposite is the land of death. Yet the psalmist says (139:80), "Were I shrouded in Sheöl, I would behold you!"

27:14 see 31:25
      Waît for the FONT OF BEÌNG; †
      be firm ànd let your heárt be strong, *
      and wait for thè FÓNT OF BÈING.

# TWENTY-EIGHT

The author of Psalm 28 pleads before the inner sanctum (verses 1/2) against those who say *Shalom*, but do not mean it (3). After being heard, the author blesses the FONT OF BEING with the word *Baruch* (6). In the psalms, this word is used to bless the FONT OF BEING twelve times, Elohim five times, Adonay once, his Name once, people three times (115:15, 118:26, 128:4).

28:1    (Of David.)

*Tô you*, FONT OF BEING, **my Rock, Ì call:** †        *25:1*
*Nor be deaf* **to mè, nor be múte to me** *
**lest I be like** *those going down ìntó à pit.*

God expects his people to hear him, through his prophets; in return the people ask God to hearken to their prayers. Put positively, the imperative is **Listen!** (*shama'*); put negatively it is **Nor be deaf** (*'al-teherash* 28:1, 35:22, 39:13, 83:2, 109:1). Other prayers in the negative imperative form include:
—**Be not aloof** (*'al-tirhaq* 22:12/20, 35:22, 38:22, 71:12)
—**Forsake me not** (*'al-ta'azbeniy* 27:9, 38:22, 71:9/18, 119:8)
—**Hide not the Face of You** (*'al-taster faneyka* 69:18)
—**Delay not** (*'al-te'ahar* 40:18, 70:6, Dan 6:19).

**With those going down into a pit** (*'im-yordey bor* 28:2, 88:5, 143:7). The authors of Psalms 88 and 143 thought of Sheöl in their use of this phrase but nothing in this psalm suggests that. Prisoners like Joseph or Jeremiah were often held in pits.

28:2    **Heâr the sound of my plea,** *whèn I beseéch you,* *    *25:1*
        **when I lift my hands to yoùr ínner sànctum.**

28:3    **Câst me not with unjust people or** *doers of evìl,* †    *36:13*
        **saying Shàlom amóng their friends,** *
        **while** *in their heárts* **is èvil.**    *10:6*

28:4    **Pây them for their dealings and their evìl deeds.** †
        **As befits the** *works of their hands* **repáy them;** *    *8:7*
        **reward them with what befits thèm ín jùstice.**

28:5    **Fôr they discern not the deeds of the** FONT OF BEÌNG †
        **or** *thè works of hís Hands;* *    *8:7*
        **he will uproot them ànd nót rebuìld them.**

28:6     **Blêssed be thè FONT OF BÉING, ***
            **for he has heard thè soúnd of my plea.**

28:7     **FÔNT OF BEING is my strength and my shièld, †**
            **in whom my heart trusts, fòr I have beén helped, ***
            **and my heart leaps, and with my song Ì gíve hìm laud.**

28:8     **FÔNT OF BÈING is Stréngth for him, ***
            **and a Stronghold of Safety for his ànoíntèd one.**

28:9     **Mâke safe your people, ànd bless your héritage, ***
            **and shepherd them, and raise them up** *for ètérnìty.*

*For eternity* (*'ad-ha'olam* 28:9, 133:4; *'ad-'olam* 18:51, 48:9, 113:2, 2 Sam 22:51) brings several of the psalms to apt conclusion. See synonymous phrases listed at 5:12.

# TWENTY-NINE

JEWISH FEASTS — Feast of Tabernacles
NEW TESTAMENT — Verse 3 at Acts 7:2
LITURGY OF HOURS — Lauds on Monday I

The author of Psalm 29 enlists the forces of nature in the service of divine praise. Practitioners of other ancient religions worshipped the forces of nature as gods. The God of the Hebrews is not a force of nature himself. Nonetheless, the Hebrew God has personal command of everything in the physical universe— thunder (verse 4), forests (5), wild animals (6), lightning (7), desert places (8), and the flood (10). All doings of the FONT OF BEING, however, are oriented for the benefit of people (11).

29:1 see 96:7/8/9
(A Mizmor of David.)
**Gîve to FONT OF BEING, Ò *children óf gods*, ***
**give to FONT OF BEÌNG glóry ànd might!**

***Children of gods*** (*beney 'eliym* 29:1, 89:7) need not be thought of as divine offspring. "Children of" can mean those under some kind of influence, as in ***those doomed to death***, literally "children of the death penalty" (*beney themuthah* 79:11, 102:21).

29:2 **Gîve to FONT OF BEING thè glory óf his Name! ***
**Adore FONT OF BEING in robes òf hóliness!**

29:3 **Câlling of FONT OF BEING is *above the watèrways*! †**
**God of glory ìs in the thúnderbolts! ***
**FONT OF BEING is above *watèrs mánìfold!***          *18:17*

***Above the waterways*** (*'al-hammayim* 29:3, 74:13, 136:6). In Hebrew cosmology, there are waters above and waters below. The FONT OF BEING established the land above the lower waters (136:6) but his call comes from above the upper waters (29:3). From above, he demonstrated dominion over the waters at the Red Sea (74:13).

29:4 **Câlling of FONT OF BÈING is ín the might! ***
**Calling of FONT OF BEING is in thè májèsty!**

29:5    Câlling of FONT OF BEÌNG splits the cédar trees! *
FONT OF BEING splits the *cedars of thè Lébànon,*

*The cedars of Lebanon* (*'arzeh hallebanon* 29:5; *'arzeh lebanon* 104:16; *'erez ballebanon* 92:13) are scented pine-bearing evergreens on the mountains of Phoenicia. God himself planted them (104:16) but they are not to be used in pagan-style cult, because God can smash them with his lightning whenever he chooses to do so (29:5). They are used as one of the similes describing the just one (92:13). Solomon used them in constructing his temple and his palace.

29:6    sêtting them to dancìng: †
Lebanòn like a búll-calf, *
and Syrià líke an òx-calf.

29:7    Câlling of thè FONT OF BÉING *
strikes wìth blásts òf flame!

29:8    Câlling of FONT OF BEING sets to dàncing a wílderness! *
FONT OF BEING sets to dancing the wildèrnéss of Qàdesh!

29:9    Câlling of FONT OF BEING sets thè deer to fáwning *
and strips the forests, and in his templè áll say "Glòry!"

29:10   FÒNT OF BEING is seàted abóve the flood, *
and seated is FONT OF BEING as king for ètérnìty.

29:11   FÒNT OF BEING gives mìght to his peóple; *
FONT OF BEING blesses his peoplè wíth Shàlom.

# THIRTY

TEMPLE LITURGY — Dedication of the Temple
LITURGY OF HOURS — Vespers on Thursday I

The author of Psalm 30 was healed (verse 3) and spared descent into *She'ol*. That word appears sixteen times in the psalms, as a synonym for death (6:6, 18:6, 55:16, 89:49, 116:3) or netherworld (139:8), as a proper destiny of the unjust (9:8, 31:18, 49:15 twice, 55:16, 141:70) or universal destiny (89:49). The psalmists feel threatened by its proximity (18:6, 88:4, 116:3), but are grateful for being spared (16:10, 30:4, 49:16, 86:13). The Septuagint uses Greek term *Hades* as does the New Testament when quoting these passages (Ps 16:10 in Acts 2:27, 13:35) but elsewhere it uses *Gehenna*, from *Ge-Hinnom*, the Hinnom Valley, the garbage pit of Jerusalem. Jesus favors "where there is weeping and grinding of teeth" (Mt 8:12, etc.).

30:1   (From the Mizmor, A Song for the Dedication of the Temple. Of David.)

30:2   **Î *exalt you*, FONT OF BEING, fòr you have lífted me, ***
**and allowed my enemies *no gloatìng óvèr me.***

Each of the two adjectives for ***great*** has produced a derived verb:
—*ram* yielded **I exalt you** (*'eromimka* 30:2, 145:1, Is 25:1)
—*gadol* yielded **Let us magnìfy hìm** (*'egaddelennu* 69:31).

*Gloating over me* (*simmahta liy* 30:2; *yismehu liy* 35:19/24, 38:17, 40:4, 52:8; *ya'altsu liy* 25:2) implies all the behavior of triumphant enemies—shouting, singing, dancing, pillage, slaughter, and rape.

30:3   **Ô FONT OF BEING! Ò my Divíne One! ***
**I besought you and yoù máde mè well.**

30:4   **Ô FONT OF BEING, you raised my soùl up from Shéöl; ***
**you gave me life after my fall ìntó à pit.**

30:5   **Plây chords for the FONT OF BEING, Ô his devóted ones, ***
**and give laud, to keep in mind hìs hólìness.**

30:6   **Thoûgh a moment be his wrath, his favòr lasts a lífetime; ***
**one stays weeping at twilight, but singìng tóward thè dawn.**

*Toward the dawn* (*labboqer* 30:6, 49:15, 59:17, *labbeqariym* 73:14, 101:8; Is 33:2, Lam 3:23) is much like ***toward the sunset*** (*la'ereb* 59:7/15, 90:6; *'adey-'areb* 104:23). Both phrases look forward in time, to the end of night and to the end of day, respectively.

64

30:7    **Bût I mysèlf said in my ease, \***
      **"*I will not stumble, ètérnàlly!*"**          *112:6*

30:8    **Ô FONT OF BEÌNG, †**
      **in your pleasure, you made me like à mountain fórtress; \***
      **when *you hid the Face of You*, Ì gréw àfraid.**

*When you hid the Face of You* (*histarta faneyka* 30:8), this psalmist grew fearful, but in the garden it was Adam who hid his face from God (Gen 3:10). Another psalmist begs God to hide his Face from his sins (*haster faneyka* 51:11), but a third concurs with the first and asks God not to do so (*'al taster faneyka* 69:18).

30:9    **Tô you, FONT ÒF BEING, dó I cry, \***
      **and beg Adònáy for pìty.**

30:10   **Whât gain is there from my silent fallìng into á pit? \***
      **Can dust laud you? Can ìt téll yoùr truth?**

30:11   **Heâr, FONT OF BEING, and tàke pity ón me! \***
      **O FONT OF BEING, be à hélper tò me!**

30:12   **Yoû changed my grief intò dancing fór me; \***
      **you loosed my sackcloth and crowned mè wíth rejoìcing,**

30:13   **thât one can play chords to your Glòry, †**
      **and not be silènced, FONT OF BÉING! \***
      **My Divine One, I will laud you *ètérnàlly!***      *10:6*

# THIRTY-ONE

NEW TESTAMENT — Verse 6 at Lk 23:46
LITURGY OF HOURS — Wednesday Night Prayer (Compline)

A major theme of Psalm 31 are the "lips of falsehood" (19) and the "lips of flattery" (12:3/4). False lips speak perjury from one side of the mouth, flattery from the other.

31:1    (For the Director. A Mizmor of David.)

31:2 = 71:1/2a

    **Ȋn you, FONT OF BEING, have I taken refùge!** †    *7:2*
    **Let me not bè shamed *etérnally*; ***    *5:12*
    **by your justice dèlívèr me.**

31:3 = 71:2b

    **Bênd to me with your Ear! Swiftly free mè!** †
    **Become for me à mountain strónghold, ***
    **a house of fortresses tò keép mè safe.**

31:4 ⁻ 71:3a

    **Fôr *my Bedrock and my Fortress* are yoù,** †    *18:3*
    **and *for thè sake of yoúr Name* ***    *25:11*
    **you lead me ànd yoú tènd me.**

31:5    **Dêliver me from the snàre that they sét for me! ***
    **For you are tò mé a strònghold.**

31:6    **Ȋnto your Hànd I put my breath; ***
    **redeem me, FONT OF BEING, Ò Gód òf Truth.**

*Into your Hand* (*beyadeka* 10:14; *beyadka* 31:6/16). A victim should entrust himself (10:14), the psalmist his very breath (31:6) to God's power; one's entire lifetime takes place in the Hand of God (31:16).

31:7    **Ȋ have shunned *those keeping òbjects devoíd of breath*, ***
    **for I have trusted in thè FÓNT OF BÈING.**

*Those keeping objects devoid of breath* (*shomriym habley-shaw'* 31:7, Jon 2:9) are like the soldiers of Judas Maccabeus who wore amulets when they fell in battle.

31:8    **Lêt me revel and rejoìce in your mércy; ***
    **when you beheld my illness, you knew thè neéds of my soul,**

31:9 & and did not put me into the *hànd of an énemy.* *
You have set my feet *in thè ópen spàces.*                    *18:20*

> **Hand of an enemy** (*beyad 'oyeb* 31:9; *miyyad 'oyeb* 106:10). The psalmist
> begs not to be in an enemy's power. Synonyms include:
> —**hand of one unjust** (*yad rasha'* 140:5)
> —**hand of unjust people** (*yad-resha'iym* 36:12, 82:4, 97:10)
> —**hand of a hater** (*yad sone'* 106:10).

31:10 Pîty me, FONT OF BEÌNG, for *distréss is mine;* *              *18:7*
wasted from strain are my eye, soul ánd bosom.                  *6:8*

31:11 Fôr my life declines in trouble and my yeárs in síghing; *
my strength waned in illness, even my bònes wére wàsted.

31:12 Bêcause of all my foes I very much bècame †
disgrace to my neighbors, ànd dread to my friends; *
seeing me, thèy fleé fròm me.

31:13 Î am discarded from thè heart like óne dead, *
become *like shárds* of wrèckage.

> **Like shards** (*kikeliy* 2:9, 31:13) describes the smashing of enemies of the
> people in Psalm 2, but the smashing of the Psalmist himself in Psalm 31.
> Pots are prone to breakage, but potsherds are hard as rock.

31:14 Hôw many I heard saying, *"Òh, dread from áll sides!"* *
They conspired against me, plotting tò seíze my soul.

> **Dread from all sides** (*yagor missabib* 31:14; Jer 6:25, 20:3/10, 46:5,
> 49:29; Lam 2:22) was a taunt applied to Jeremiah by his foes. It connects
> this psalm with the final days of the kingdom.

31:15 Bût I have trusted in yoù, FONT OF BÉING; *
I said: *"My Dìvíne One àre you!"*

> **My Divine One are you!** (*'elohay 'attah* 31:15) or **You are God!** (*'attah
> 'el* 90:2; *'attah 'eliy* 89:27, *'eliy 'attah* 118:28, 140:7) responds to **The
> Divine, your Divine One am I** (*'elohiym 'eloheyka 'anokiy* 50:7) and **I
> am the FONT OF BEING, your Divine One** (*'anokiy yhwh 'eloheyka* 81:11,
> Ex 20:1, Lev 26:45, Deut 5:6).

31:16 *Within your Hand* are my seasòns; †                          *31:6*
free me from the hànd of my énemies *
and of *those whò húnt fòr me.*                                *7:2*

31:17 ***Shîne the Face of You ùpon your sérvant; ***
***save mè by your mèrcy.***                                    *109:26*

> **Shine the Face of You** (*ha'iyrah faneyka* 31:17; *ya'er fanaw* 67:2;
> *faneyka ha'er* 119:135) is the same as **Do not hide the Face of You**
> (*'al taster paneyka* 27:9, 102:3, 143:7; *lo'-histiyr panaw* 22:25; *tastiyr*
> *paneyka* 13:2, 88:15).

31:18 **Fônt of Being, let me not be shàmed, for I cálled to you; ***
**let the unjust be shamed, made silènt ín Shëöl.**

31:19 **Wrâpped in silence be *idle lips* thàt speak agaínst the just ***
**with insolence, wìth príde and scòffing.**

> **Idle lips** (*sifthey sheqer* 31:19, *sefath sheqer* 120:2) are outlets for the
> **idle tongue** (*leshon shaqer* 109:2, Prov 6:17, 12:19, 21:6, 26:28). The
> **speakers of idle things** (*dobrey sheqariym* 101:7) are skilled in making
> perjury pleasing to the ear.

31:20 **Whât great goodness you keep for those who revere yoù, †**
**which you put into action for those who tàke refuge ín you ***
**before *the childrèn óf Àdam*.**                              *11:4*

31:21 **Yoû hide them in secret, by the Face òf You, †**
**from intrìgues of a pérson; ***
**you guard them securely from thè wár òf tongues.**

31:22 **Blèssed be the Font of Beìng, †**
**for he *works the marvel of hìs mercy* fór me ***
**in à *búlwark cìty*.**                                        *17:7*

> **A bulwark city** (*'iyr matsor* 31:22, 60:11; *'iyr mibtsar* 108:11, 2 Kings
> 3:19, Jer 1:18) fulfills one of three requirements for a **city in which to
> dwell** (*'iyr moshab* 107:4/7/36)—good geography for defence, internal
> water sources and sufficient farming land in the vicinity.

31:23 **Bût I said as I fled, "I am cut òff from befóre your Eyes." ***
**Yet you heard my pleading call *when Ì soúght for you.***    *25:1*

31:24 **Lôve the Font of Being, all his devotèd ones, †**
**the faithful are preserved by thè Font of Béing, ***
**but he pays with a bonus those whò áct wìth pride.**

31:25 see 27:14
**Bê firm, ànd let your heárts be strong, ***
**all those awaiting thè Fónt of Bèing.**

# THIRTY-TWO

NEW TESTAMENT — Verses 1–2 at Rom 4:7–8
LITURGY OF HOURS — Vespers on Thursday I

Psalm 32 is the second of the seven penitential psalms (6, 32, 38, 51, 102, 130, and 143). Paul quotes the first two verses (Rom 4:6) and seems to identify with David, in that both are penitent (verse 5), but Paul's sin was more like that of his fellow tribesman Saul, who persecuted David.

32:1 (Of David. A Maskil.)
**Blêssedness belongs to being liftèd from rebéllion, ***
**to beìng cloáked fròm sin.**

32:2 ***Blêssedness belongs to Adàm's kind †***
**whom the FONT OF BEING holds tò be withoút guilt, ***
**and in whose breath ìs nó beguìlement!**

*Blessedness belongs to Adam's kind* ('*ashrey 'adam* 32:2, 84:6/13). *Blessedness* opens five psalms (1, 32, 41, 119, 128). In two of them it opens both the first and second verses (32:1/2, 119:1/2), providing an even more ample description of the blissful person.

32:3 **Fôr I have been rèduced to sílence; ***
**my bones weakened as I cried oùt *áll thè day*.**    *25:5*

32:4 **Fôr *day and night* your Hànd weighed upón me, ***    *22:3*
**pressing on my breast as in droughts òf súmmèrtime.**

32:5 **My sin I showed you, and my guilt I cloaked nòt; †**
**I said: "For I admit my rebellion to thè FONT OF BÉING," ***
**and you *lifted up thè guílt* of my sin.**

First rebellion was lifted (35:1) and then *guilt is lifted* (*nasa'tha 'awon* 35:5, 85:3). In all three of these verses the verb *to cloak* (*kasah*) parallels *to lift* (*nasa'*). The relationship between these two antonyms is most clear in Psalm 85, where the author uncloaks his guilt so that the FONT OF BEING may lift it away.

32:6 **Fôr this each devout one begs you, for à time of fínding: ***
**for flood *waters manifòld* nót to reàch him.**    *18:17*

32:7 **Yoû are my hiding place! *From thè siege* presérve me; ***    *4:2*
**may you ring me wìth sóngs of freèdom.**

32:8 Î counsel you and teach you *whìch way you should go,* *
let me guide yoù wíth my Eye.

*The way you should go* (*bederek zu telek* 32:8; *derek zu 'elek*, 143:8) is
the *way of the just* (*derek tsaddiqiym*, 1:6). The word *derek* is inherently
positive, because the root word means straight or true (in a directional
sense). The winding road is a *pathway that is not good* (*derek lo-tob*,
36:5; Prov 16:29).

32:9 Bê not like stallion, like mule, lackìng sense; †
bridle and bit bèdeck and rúle them, *
or they woùld nót come neàr you.

32:10 Mâny are the sorrows òf the unjúst one, *
but one trusting in the FONT OF BEING ìs rínged with mèrcy.

32:11 Rêjoice in the FONT OF BEING ànd revel, yoú just, *
and sing for joy, all of yoù *steádfast-heàrted.*

*7:11*

# THIRTY-THREE

EARLIEST MANUSCRIPT — 4QPs<sup>q</sup>


LITURGY OF HOURS — Lauds on Tuesday I

The preamble of Psalm 33 uses the musical terms "psalm" (1), "harp of ten strings" (2), "good music" and "signal cries" (3). This is a psalm about the FONT OF BEING, who is mentioned thirteen times in twenty-two verses.

33:1 **Sîng for joy, you just, in thè FONT OF BÉING, \***
**you steadfast people, wìth pleásing praìse-craft.**

33:2 **Laûd the FONT OF BEÌNG *with a lyre-bow*; \***
***on a harp of ten strìngs* pláy tò him.**

*A lyre-bow* (*kinnor* 33:2, 43:4, 49:5, 71:22, 92:4, 98:5, 147:7, 150:3) was an stringed instrument of moderate size easily carried from place to place. It was favored by wealthier shepherd boys.

*Harp of ten strings* (*nebel 'asor* 33:2, 144:9; *'aley 'asor wa 'aley nabel* 92:4) was a large instrument. It was not for use by shepherd boys, even wealthy ones, for it had to stay in one place, either the palace or the temple. Here it seems to be put to liturgical use.

33:3 **Sîng out tò him *a sóng made new*; \***
**make good music with à jóyfùl cry.**

*Sing out a song renewed* (*shiyru shiyr hadash* 33:3, 96:1, 98:1, 149:1; *shiyr hadash 'ashiyrah* 144:9) is an "internal accusative" construction. The noun *shiyr* derives from the verb *shiyr*. The internal construction is mitigated by addition of a third word.

33:4 **Fôr steadfast is the word of thè FONT OF BÉING, \***
**and all his deeds are done with Fìdélìty.**

33:5 **Lôving *Jùstice and Júdgment*, \***
**with the mercy of the FONT OF BEING, thè lánd ìs full.**

*Justice and judgment* (*tsedakah umishpot* 33:5; *tsedek umishpot* 89:15, 97:2; *mishpot utsedeqah* 99:4, *mishpot watsedeq* 119:121) are flip sides of a coin, but not identical. Justice fills the Right Hand of God (48:11); judgment is in his Mouth (105:5, 119:13).

33:6 **Ât the word of the FONT OF BÈING, the skiés were made, ***
**and all their array at thè breáth of hìs mouth,**

33:7 **gâthering into basins thè waters óf the sea, ***
**stowing them ìn deépèst vaults.**

33:8 **Lêt *all the land* revere thè FONT OF BÉING. ***        *8:2*
**Of him let them stand in awe, *all whò ín the wòrld dwell.***

*All who in the world dwell* (*yoshbey tebel* 33:8; *yoshbey haled* 49:2) include wildlife on the land (*haytho-'arets* 79:2) and birds of the sky ('*of hasshamayim* 79:2, 104:12), but apparently not the fishes of the sea (*degey hayyam* 8:9). God dwells everywhere, in heaven (2:4, 123:1) and in Jerusalem (9:12, 135:21).

33:9 **Fôr he spòke, and it cáme to pass; ***
**he commanded, ànd só ìt stood.**

33:10 **FÔNT OF BEING annuls thè plans of géntiles, ***
**blocks the purpòsés of peòples.**

33:11 **Plâns of the FONT OF BÈING for éver stand, ***
**intentions of his heart *for àge áfter àn age.***     *10:6*

33:12 **Blêssedness belongs to the natiòn †**
***whose Divine One is thè FONT OF BÉING, ***
**the people he chose for himself as à hérìtage!**

The nation *whose Divine One is the* FONT OF BEING ('*asher-yhwh 'elohaw* 33:12; *sheyhwh 'elohaw* 144:15) is, of course, Israël. Thus the divine appellatives include:
—FONT OF BEING, *Divine One of Israël* (41:14, 106:48)
—FONT OF BEING *from the Ziön* (110:2, 128:5, 134:3, 135:21).

*As a heritage* (*lenahelah*). This term can mean the land (136:21), which the people inherited from God, or the people (33:12), whom God inherited by the terms of the covenant.

33:13 **Frôm the skies looked down thè FONT OF BÉING; ***
**he beheld all *the childrèn óf Àdam.***     *11:4*

33:14 **Frôm the plàce of his dwélling ***
**he surveyed all whò dwéll in thè land:**

33:15 **Môlder of their heàrts intó one ***
**is the discerner òf áll their deeds.**

33:16 **Nô king is màde safe by greát strength, ***
**no strong man sèt freé through greát might.**

33:17 **Fruîtless is the stàllion for sáfety; ***
**even with his great strength, hè máy not èscape.**

33:18 **Bêhold the Eye of thè FONT OF BÉING ***
**is on those who revere him, waitìng fór his mèrcy,**

33:19 **tô deliver theìr souls from thé death, ***
**and in the famine tò gíve thèm life.**

33:20 **Oûr soul is in waiting for thè FONT OF BÉING; ***
*our help and oùr shiéld ìs He.*

God is literally ***our help*** (*'ezrenu*) and metaphorically ***our shield***
(*maginnenu*), in a responsory phrase found in two of the psalms
(33:20, 115:9/10/11).

33:21 **Îndeed, ìn him our heárt finds joy! ***
**Indeed, we have trusted in his *Name òf hólìness!***

***His Name of holiness*** (*shem qodsho* 33:21, 103:1, 105:3, 145:21;
*shem qodsheka* 106:47) is literally "the Name of his holiness." Semitic
grammar does not allow attaching a pronoun or a definite article to the
first word in such a series.

33:22 **Mây your mercy, FONT OF BEÌNG, be upón us, ***
**as wè waít fòr you.**

# THIRTY-FOUR

NEW TESTAMENT — Verse 9 at 1 Pet 2:3
LITURGY OF HOURS — Midday Prayer on Saturdays I and III

The author of Psalm 34 is a Levitical priest, who calls his order (verse 4) and invites them to partake in the ritual banquet (8). Then he invites young Levites to receive instruction (12) and articulates one of the paradigms of biblical ethics: "Turn from the evil and do good" (34:15, reprised at 37:27).

34:1 (Of David, when he feigned madness before Abimelech,
and he compelled him, and he departed.)

34:2 *Aleph.*

**Lêt me bless the Font of Being, *in every seáson*, ***      *145:15*
**with his praise-craft evèr *in my mouth*.**      *5:10*

34:3 *Beth.*

**În the Font of Bèing my soúl takes pride! ***
**The lowly wìll heár, and bè glad.**

34:4 *Ghimel.*

**Mâgnify the Font òf Being wíth me, ***
**and let us together èxált hìs Name.**

34:5 *Daleth.*

**Î sought the Font of Bèing, and he ánswered me, ***
**and from all my fears hè sét mè free.**

34:6 *He.*

**Thêy will gaze òn him and théy will shine, ***
**and their faces wìll nót bè shamed.**

34:7 *Zain.*

**Thîs lowly one called out, and thè Font of Béing heard, ***
**and *from all his dìstréss* he sàved him.**

*From all his distress* (*mikkol tsarothaw* 34:7; *mikkol tsarotham* 34:18; *mikkol tsarah* 54:9). *Distress* (*tsarah*) comes from the word *siege* (*tsar*) and retains the sense of constraint. One's *foes* (*tsariym*) are those who seek to restrict, assault, and destroy one's self.

34:8 *Heth.*

**Ân angel of the Font of Bèing †**
**embraces thòse who revére him, ***
**and dèlívèrs them.**

34:9 *Teth.*

**Tâste and see** *how good is thè* **FONT OF BÉING**; *
*blessedness belongs to the man* **who tàkes réfuge ìn him.**

*So good is the* FONT OF BEING (*kiy tob yhwh* 34:9, 100:5, 135:3, 145:9), along with the Name of the FONT OF BEING (52:11, 54:8) and the Mercy of the FONT OF BEING (106:1, 107:1, 109:21, 118:1/29, 136:1). The word *kiy* usually functions as subordinating conjunction *for* or *because*, but can also be a superlative adjective or adverb.

*Blessedness belongs to the man* (*'ashrey haggeber* 34:9, 40:5, 94:12, 127:5). The referent is masculine. Blisses are bestowed upon a man who was corrected and taught by the Torah (94:12), who takes refuge (34:9) and trusts in God (40:5).

34:10 *Yod.*

**Rêvere the** FONT OF BEÌNG, **O his hóly ones,** *
**for nothing is lacking to those whò révère him.**

34:11 *Coph.*

**Lîons have gròwn lean and húngry,** *
**but those seeking the** FONT OF BEING **lack fòr nó goòd thing.**

34:12 *Lamedh.*

**Côme, O childrèn, listen tó me;** *
**let me teach you** *awe for thè* FÓNT OF BÈING.                    *19:10*

34:13 *Mem.*

**Whô is the man, thè one who wánts life,** *
**yearning for days tò seé goòdness?**

34:14 *Nun.*

**Keêp your tòngue from the évil,** *
**and your lips fròm speáking fàlsehood.**

34:15 *Samech.*

**Tûrn from the èvil, and dó good;** *
**seek Shalom ànd fóllòw it.**

*Turn from the evil, and do good* (*sur mera' wa'aseh-tob* 34:12, 37:27). This verse links closely the two wisdom psalms, 34 and 37. Shalom is an important theme in both of them.

34:16 *Ain.*

**Êyes of the** FONT OF BEÌNG **are towárd the just,** *
**and his Ears towàrd theír beseèching.**

34:17 *Pe.*

**Âttention of the FONT OF BEING is on dòers of évil, ***
*to cut off memory of thèm fróm thè land.*

*To cut off memory of them from the land* (*lehakriyt me'erets zikram* 34:17; *weyakret me'erets zikram* 109:15; *'abad zikram* 9:7) is the imposition of intentional amnesia. Ancient kingdoms had the practice of striking criminals from the historical records. Pharaoh Tutmoses IV covered the inscriptions of his aunt, Hatshepsut, who had claimed the throne in her own name. The Romans practiced the *damnatio memoriae* (dooming of memory), by which the Emperor Caracalla destroyed all the images of his executed brother Geta. The genealogy of Jesus omits idolatrous kings of the House of David.

34:18 *Tsade.*

**Thêy cried out, and the FONT ÒF BEING lístened, ***
**and *from all their distress* hè sét thèm free.**                        *34:7*

34:19 *Qoph.*

**Neâr is the FONT OF BEING to *thè brokenheárted, ***
**and he makes safe those whòse breáth is crushed.**

*Brokenhearted* are "broken of heart" (*nishberey leb* 34:19; *nik'eh lebab* 109:16; *sheburey leb* 147:3) or "having a heart that is broken" (*leb nishbarah* 51:19). Since the Hebrews thought of the heart as the seat of intelligence, the brokenhearted were people who, assaulted by the adversities of life, had run out of solutions to their problems.

34:20 *Resh.*

**Mâny are the troublès of a júst one, ***
**but from all of them the FONT OF BEÌNG séts hìm free,**

34:21 *Shin.*

**keêping sentinèl over áll his bones, ***
**that not one of thèm máy be bròken.**

34:22 *Tau.*

**Êvil causes death fòr the unjúst one, ***
**and they incur guilt whò loáthe the jùst one.**

34:23 *Pe.*

**FÔNT OF BEING redeems the soùl of his sérvants, ***
**and they incur no guilt, *all who tàke réfuge ìn him.***          *2:12*

# THIRTY-FIVE

EARLIEST MANUSCRIPT — Verses 4-20 in 4QPs<sup>q</sup>
NEW TESTAMENT — Verse 19 at Jn 15:25
LITURGY OF HOURS — Office of Readings on Friday I

The author of Psalm 35 stumbles (verse 15) and limps (16), and has many fair-weather friends, for whom he offered prayers and fasting (13), and even mourned (14). He has done nothing to deserve their mistreatment, as he says twice in one verse (7). He is shocked to hear them mock him, as he quotes them twice (21/25). Like a playwright, the psalmist peppers the text with visual cues —wield spear (3), let fall (8), wear sackcloth (13), stumble (15), limp (16), gnash teeth (16), furrow brows (19), gape mouths (21).

35:1    (Of David.)
**Pûrsue, O FONT OF BEÌNG, *those pursuíng me*! ***
**Fight thòse fíghtìng me!**

*Pursue those who pursue me* (*riybah eth-yeriybay* 35:1; *riybah riybiy* 43:1, 119:154; *riybah riybeka* 74:22) and ***fight those who fight me*** (*leham et-lohamay* 35:1) are two instances of "internal accusative," when the verb takes a direct object that derives from the same root. Some other examples are:
—*sing a song* (*shiyru shiyr* 33:3, 96:1, 98:1, 149:1)
—*want a want* (*wayyith'awwu ta'awah* 106:14, Prov 21:26)
—*offer oblation* (*zibhu zebah* 4:6, 27:6, 107:22, 116:17).

35:2    **Tâke hold òf buckler ánd shield, ***
      **and arise wìth aíd fòr me!**

35:3    **Sô wield spear or axe to challènge *those who húnt for me*. ***
      **Say to my soul, "Your sàlvátion àm I."**          7:2

35:4    **Shâmed and disgraced bè they who *seék my soul*, ***    7:2
      **turned back and shamed be they plottìng hárm fòr me.**

35:5    **Lêt them become *like chàff toward the fáce of wind*, ***    1:4
      **and driven by the angel of thè FÓNT OF BÈÌNG.**

*Toward the face of wind* (*lifney-ruah* 35:5, 84:13) would be called in English a "head wind" as opposed to a "tail wind." The Hebrews apparently personified the wind as having bodily features like a face and wings (*kanfey-ruah* 18:11, 104:3).

35:6    **Lêt their pàthways be dárk and slick, \***
        **as the angel of the Font of Bèìng púrsuès them.**

35:7    **Fôr no cause they hid fòr me their nétting-pit; \***
        **for no cause they dug ìt fór my soul.**

35:8    **Lêt disaster unforeseen come to meet hìm, †**
        **and his netting that hè set entángle him; \***
        **into disaster—let him fàll íntò it.**

35:9    **Bût my soul will revel in thè Font of Béing, \***
        **will rejoice ìn hís salvàtion.**

35:10   **Lêt *all my bones* say, "O Font of Bèìng! †**         *22:15*
        ***Who, like you,* frees the lowly from òne stronger thán he, \***
        **and the *lowly and in need* from one dèspoílìng him?"**

***Who is like you?*** (*miy kamoka* 35:10, 71:19, 89:9; Ex 15:11a/b) is a rhetorical question, the clear answer to which is "no one." The name Michael means ***Who is like God?*** (*miy ka'el* Dan 10:13/21, 12:1). Two other questions that begin ***Who is like?*** are:
—***Who is like the Font of Being among the children of gods?*** (89:7)
—***Who is like our divine Font of Being?*** (113:5).

***Lowly and in need*** (*'aniy we'ebyon* 35:10, 37:15, 40:18, 70:6, 74:21, 86:1, 109:16/22, 116:16) is equivalent to the less common phrase ***poor and needy*** (*dal we'ebyon* 72:13, 82:4). Though each phrase has two terms, they describe a single person. Twice the psalmist refers to himself as ***lowly and in need*** (86:1, 109:22).

35:11   **Rîsen are àbusive wítnesses; \***
        **people *unknown to mè* quéstiòn me.**         *18:44*

35:12   **Thêy repay me with *èvil in pláce of good*, \***
        **to the sadnèss óf my soul.**

***Evil in place of good*** (*ra'ah tahath tobah* 35:12, 38:21, 109:5, Prov 17:13) is literally "evil beneath good." The same preposition is used for royal succession: ***In place of your fathers will be your sons*** (*tahath 'ebotheyka yihyu baneyka* 45:17).

35:13   **Bût when they were sick I *wore sàck*; †**
        **I made my soul hùmble through fásting \***
        **yet my prayer was turned back ùpón my lap.**

*I wore sack* (*lebushiy saq* 35:13, 69:12). Sackcloth was clothing for penitence, and the psalmist seems to have been doing penance for sins that his neighbors may have committed to bring on their illness.

35:14 Lîke a friend, like à brother tó me, *
I went about as one grieves a mother, in clothes of hùmílìty.

35:15 Bût at my fall they rejoiced and multìplied, †
multiplied against me, strikìng and *unknówn to me*, *    *18:44*
they maligned and they woùld nót bè still.

35:16 Whîle I was limping to bàkers of báked goods, *
they *gnashed theìr teéth* agaìnst me.

A sign of displeasure was *gnashing of teeth* (*haroq shinneymo* 35:16; *horeq shinnaw* 37:12; *shinnaw yaheroq*, 112:10). Jesus calls *Gehenna* a place for weeping and *gnashing of teeth* (*brugmos tôn odontôn* Mt 8:12, 13:42/50, 22:13, 24:51, 25:30; Lk 13:28).

35:17 Ô Adonay, how long will you look òn? †
Turn back my soùl from their fraúdulence, *
from the lions the òne lífe Ì have.

35:18 Thânks will I offer you in *à vast assémbly*; *    *22:26*
with people great in numbèr Í will laùd you.

35:19 Lêt them not *gloat over me, my enemiès for no reáson*, *    *30:2*
let them blink an eye, *who hate mè fór nò cause.*

*My enemies* (*'oybay*) and *those who hate me* (*son'ay*) both have the form of masculine plural participles (*'oybiym* and *son'iym*) with the first-person singular suffix (*-iy*). Cast in the same mold are *Adonay* (my Lordship), *Elohay* (my Divine One), *Shadday* (my Field God), *kappay* (my palms), *'oznay* (my ears), etc.

*For no reason* (*sheqer*) and *for no cause* (*hinnam*) are synonymous adjectives in parallel both here and elsewhere (35:19, 69:5). Yet another synonym is *beyond reason* (*reyqam*). Enemies come in two forms, those I deserve and those I do not. I would deserve them if I myself had provoked them, *if I had dealt badly with my friend or punished my foe beyond reason* (*reyqam* 7:5).

35:20 Sûrely they do not rèply with "Shálom!" *
but with false words they plot against thè meék of thè land.

35:21 Thêy have gàped their mouths át me; *
they say, "Oh, *a brother? A brother* have oùr éyes bèheld?"

*A brother? A brother?* (*he'ah he'ah*) was seemingly an expression of some currency, occurring in three psalms (35:21/25, 40:16, 70:4). Attaching the interrogative particle (*he-*) to the noun **brother** (*'ah*) has the effect of calling a fraternal bond into question. The first to do so was Cain, who asked, "Am I my brother's keeper?" (Gen 4:9).

35:22 **Loôk on, Ò Font of Béing!** *
    *Nor be deaf,* **Adonay,** *nor be àloóf fròm me.*      *28:1, 22:12*
35:23 **Âwaken and attènd to my júdgment,** *
    **to my contest, my Divine One ànd Ádònay.**
35:24 **Jûdge me as befits your justice, my divìne Font of Béing,** *
    **and** *let them gloat nòt óvèr me.*      *30:2*
35:25 **Lêt them** *within their hearts* **nòt ask,** †      *10:6*
    **"Oh, can this be** *à brother* **óf our souls?"** *      *35:21*
    **Let them not say, "We hàve swállòwed him."**
35:26 **Shâmed and all abashed be they who rejoice àt** *evil fór me,* *
    **clad in shame and disgrace be those màde greát abòve me.**

*Evil for me* (*ra'athiy* 35:26, 38:13, 40:15, 48:8, 70:13, 71:13/24) is what will happen *on the day of evil* (*beyom ra'ah* 27:5, 41:2; *yomey ra'* 49:6, 94:13).

35:27 see 40:17 = 70:5
    **Thêy sing and rejoice, delighting in what is just fòr me,** †
    **and those delighting in Shalom for hìs servant éver say,** *
    **"Great is thè Fónt of Bèing!"**
35:28 **Sô** *let my tongue rèpeat your jústice,* *
    *all thè dáy,* **your praìse-craft.**      *25:5*

*Let my tongue repeat your justice* (*leshon tehgeh tsidqeka* 35:28; *leshoniy tehgeh tsidqatheka* 71:24). The justice of God deserves to be noticed, to be discussed, to be mentioned again and again.

## THIRTY-SIX

NEW TESTAMENT — Verse 1 at Rom 3:18
LITURGY OF HOURS — Lauds on Wednesday I

Psalms 36 and 110 open with the prophetic word "oracle," but otherwise this psalm is not prophetic. The first verse has the uncommon phrase "fear (*pahad*) of God," which is real fear and not the awe in the frequent expression "respect (*yire'*) for God." *Pahad* takes God as object only in a few places (36:2, 119:120, 1 Sam 11:7, Is 2:10/19/21). "Heart" and "eyes" in verse 1 seem to have a first person singular suffix, but in fact have an ancient ablative ending. After the first four verses, the psalmist addresses God rather than the sinner. The psalm becomes a paean to divine mercy (11), as if to contrast the sinner's fear with the just person's confident trust.

36:1    (For the Director. Of the Servant of the FONT OF BEING, of David.)

36:2    **Ân oracle about sin, to one whose innèr heart is únjust, ***
**before whose eyes there is no *dread òf thé Divìne One,***

> ***Dread of the Divine One*** (*pahad 'elohiym* 36:2; *pahad yhwh* 1 Sam 11:7, Is 2:10/19/21) is true fear, and not respect as in ***awe for the FONT OF BEING*** (*yir'at yhwh* 19:10, 34:12, 111:10). The context dictates usage; the virtuous one has awe, but the sinner needs fear.

36:3    **whô so flatters himsèlf in his ówn eyes, ***
**lest he discover his guilt, lèst hé renoùnce it.**

36:4    **Wôrds of his mouth are dèceit and málice; ***
**he puts a stop to being wise, tò dóìng good.**

36:5    **Bâdly did he plan *on the place where he liès*; †**            *4:5*
**he takes his stand on à *way that ís not good*; ***
**he does not reject whàt ís èvil.**

> ***On a way that is not good*** (*bederek lo-tob* 36:5, Prov 16:29). The psalmist avoids calling any path bad, because the word *derek* is fundamentally positive. Its root verb means straight or true (in a directional sense). Of course, a straight road will go two ways, forwards and backwards.

36:6    **Ô FONT OF BEING, your mercy ìs in the heávens, ***
**your fidelity àbóve thè clouds!**

36:7   **Yoûr justice is like the mountains of Gòd, †**
**your judgment ìs like a *greát abyss!* \***
***Adam's kind and the cattle* you keep sàfe, FÓNT OF BÈING.**

**Great abyss** (*tehom rabbah* 36:7, Is 51:10, Amos 7:4; *tehomot rabbah* 78:15). An abyss is already something great by definition, but adding the adjective for great has a superlative effect.

**Adam's kind and the cattle** (*'adam ubehemah* 36:7) are all under the care of God. The expression takes on a more elegant form later, in the formula *from Adam to the cattle* (*me'adam 'ad-behemah* 135:8), as in the English saying "fit for neither man nor beast."

36:8   **Hôw precious is your mercy, O Divine Òne, †**
**that *the children of Adàm* can take réfuge \***
***in the shadòw óf yoùr Wings,***                     *11:4*
                                                        *17:8*
36:9   **Thêy share in thè stock of yoúr house, \***
**and at your stream of delights yoù gíve thèm drink.**
36:10  **Sûrely with you is à fountain óf life; \***
**in yoùr líght we seè light.**
36:11  **Yoû pour out your mercy to thòse who acknówledge you, \***
**and your justice to *thè steádfast-heàrted.***         *7:11*
36:12  **Nôr let the foot òf pride approách me, \***
**nor the *hand of unjùst peóple* toùch me.**

The psalmist prays to be delivered from the ***hand of unjust people*** (*yad-resha'iym* 6:12, 82:4, 97:10), from the hand of one unjust (*miyyad rasha'* 140:5), from the hand of Sheöl (*miyyad She'ol* 49:15 and 89:49), from the hands of sons of a foreign land (*miyyad beney nekar*, 144:7/11), from the hand of a hater (*miyyad sone'* 106:10), and from the hand of an enemy (*miyyad 'oyeb* 106:10).

36:13  **Thêre fallen are the *dòers of évil.* \***                     *5:6*
**They have stumbled and thèy cánnòt rise.**

NEW TESTAMENT — Verse 11 at Mt 5:5
LITURGY OF HOURS — Office of Readings on Tuesday II

Psalm 37 is an alphabetical psalm with two verses per letter, but for *Lamedh* and *Qoph*, which have only one verse each. Several phrases resonate with passages from the Sermon on the Mount (verse 11 is quoted at Mt 5:4).

37:1  (Of David.)
*Aleph.*
**Nôr let yourself be troùbled by scoúndrels, \***
**nor envy those who indúlge in vice.**                5:6

*Nor be troubled* (*'al tithar*) is the opening statement of the psalm, in which it occurs three times (37:1/7/8). This makes clear the author's intent to console the reader, who has seen the prosperity of *those who indulge in vice* (*po'eley 'awlah* 37:1; *po'elu 'awlah* 119:3), who commit *foul deeds* (*'olot* 58:3, 64:7).

37:2  **Fôr *like thè grass* they quíckly wilt, \***
**and like a vine òf greén thèy fade.**

*Like the grass* (*kehatsiyr* 37:2, 90:5, 103:15, 129:6) stands in a parallel with the synonyms *like a vine* (*keyereq* 37:2) and *like a blossom* (*ketsiyts* 103:15). These are not bad plant similes, such as *like the chaff* (*kammots* 1:4, 35:5), but are not very happy ones, because the small plants have such a short growing season. They are not *like a tree* (*ke'ets* 1:3, Jer 17:8), whether *like an olive tree* (*kezayt* 52:10, 128:3) or *like a palm tree* (*ketamar* 92:13) or *like a cedar tree* (*ke'erez ballebanon* 92:13), for these live a very long time and stay green year-round.

37:3  *Beth.*
**Trûst in the FONT OF BEING, ànd do what ís good; \***
**occupy the land, and be tendèd faithfùlly,**
37:4  **ând delight in thè FONT OF BÉING, \***
**and he will give you yoùr heárt's rèquest.**
37:5  *Ghimel.*
**Dêdicate to the FONT OF BÈING your páthway, \***
**and trust in him, ànd hé wìll act,**

37:6   ând he will release lìke light your jústice, *
and your judgmènt líke the noòntime.

37:7   *Daleth.*

Bê still before the FONT OF BEING, and wait fòr him; †
*be not troubled by* one who sùcceeds in hís way, *     *37:1*
by a man who puts schemìng ínto àction.

37:8   Hôld back ànger and cónquer wrath; *
*be not troubled* evèn wíth èvil.     *37:1*

37:9   *He.*

Fôr scoundrèls will be cút off, *
but they who await the FONT ÒF BÉING *claìm land.*     *37:34*

*To claim land* (*lareshet 'arets* 37:34) is a major theme in this psalm
(*yiyrshu-'arets* 37:9/11/22/29) and mentioned in another (*yiyrash-
'arets* 25:13). Land is the patrimony of the covenant. The very word
**heritage** (*nahlah*) means the Holy Land: "He made a heritage fall to
them by survey line" (78:55).

37:10   *Waw.*

Bût yet a little, and the ùnjust one wíll be gone; *
and you may search his place, *but there is nò móre òf him.*

To affirm the existence of something, one uses the verb *there is* (*yesh*)
as in *There is a Divine One* (*yesh-'elohiym* 58:12, 1 Sam 17:4). To
deny the existence of something, one uses the verb *there is not* (*'eyn*)
as in the following statements:
—*There is no more of him* (*we'eynennu* 37:10/36, 103:16)
—*There is no Divine One* (*'eyn 'elohiym* 10:4)
—*There is no helper* (*'eyn-'ozer* 22:12, 72:12, 107:12, Is 63:5)
—*There is no rescuer* (*'eyn-matssiyl* 7:3, 50:22, 71:11)
—*There is no savior* (*'eyn-moshiya'* 18:42, 2 Sam 22:42, Deut
22:27, 28:29/31, Judg 12:3, Is 47:15, Hos 13:4).

37:11   *Waw.*

Bût those who are lòwly will *claím land,* *     *37:9*
and delight ìn *gránd shàlom.*

Shalom is like mercy, indivisible and not admissible of degrees. There
is no such thing as small shalom. Like **great mercy** (*rob hasdeka* 5:8,
69:14), then, **grand shalom** (*rob shalom* 37:11, 72:7, 119:165) is not
relative but absolute.

37:12 *Zain.*
Ân unjust one broods àgainst the júst one, *
and *gnashes hìs teéth* àt him.                          *35:16*

37:13 Âdonày is deríding him, *
for he sees when hìs dáy wìll come.

37:14 *Heth.*
Ûnjust people drew a blade and aimed their war-bòws, †
to bring down òne *lowly ánd in need,* *          *35:10*
to slaughter those òf évèn path.

37:15 *Heth.*
Înto their own heàrts let their bláde go, *
and let their wàr-bóws be bròken.

37:16 *Teth.*
Bût a little is goòd for the júst one, *
more than the wealth of many whò áre ùnjust,

37:17 sînce arms of unjust peoplè will be bróken, *
but support for just ones is thè FÓNT OF BÈING.

37:18 *Yod.*
FÔNT OF BEING knows the days òf blameless peóple, *
and their heritage will endure *ètérnàlly.*          *5:12*

37:19 Thêy are not shàmed in an évil time, *
but in days òf fámine àre filled.

37:20 *Coph.*
Fôr the unjust are nil, and rivals of thè FONT OF BÉING, *
like splendid meadows they àre mówn, mown ìn smoke!

37:21 Ân unjust one may borròw but will nót repay, *
while a just one *feèls píty, ànd* gives.          *37:26*

37:22 *Lamedh.*                                              *37:9*
Fôr those blèssed by him *claím land,* *
but those doomed by hìm áre cùt off.

37:23 *Mem.*
By the FONT OF BEING are stèps of a man máde strong *
and his pathwày máde pleàsing.

37:24 Thoûgh he may tòtter, he doés not fall, *
for the FONT OF BEING is supportìve wíth hìs Hand.

37:25 *Nun.*
**Yoûng was *I*, then grew beàrded, yet néver saw \***
**a just one forsaken or his seedlìng béggìng bread.**

The aged author writes, **Young was I** (*na'ar hayiythiy* 37:25). A young man may struggle to keep to his path (119:9), but elderly Jesus ben-Sira writes that he began his quest for wisdom when ***I was a youth*** (*'eniy na'ar*, Sir 51:13 from 11QPsᵃ). When called by God, Jeremiah protested, ***I am a youth*** (*na'ar 'anokiy* Jer 1:6). God invites ***elders with youths*** (*zeqeyniym 'im-na'ariym* 148:12) to gather in worship.

37:26 **Âll the day he feèls pity ánd lends, \***                              *25:5*
**and his seedling will sèrve ás a blèssing.**

The Torah forbids usury, the lending of money at interest. The parable of the good steward suggests charging of commission fees were allowed. Even so, the biblical purpose for lending is not the making of profit but the expression of sympathy. ***He feels pity and lends*** (*honen umalweh* 37:26, 112:5).

37:27 *Samech.*
**Tûrn from the èvil, and dó good; \***                                        *34:12*
**and be dwelling ètérnàlly.**                                                *5:12*
37:28 *Ain.*
**Fôr the FONT OF BEING loves justìce, †**
**and abandons not his devoted ònes, ever képt safe, \***
**but a seedling of unjust peoplè ís cùt off.**
37:29 **Jûst peoplè will lay *claím to land*, \***                            *37:9*
**and dwell *for àn áge* upòn it.**                                           *9:19*
37:30 *Pe.*
**Moûth of a just one rèpeats the wísdom, \***
**and his tòngue speáks with jùdgment.**
37:31 **În his heart is the Torah òf his Divíne One; \***
**his footstèps dó not stùmble.**
37:32 *Tsade.*
**Ône unjust lies in waìt for the júst one, \***
**and seeks tò caúse hìs death;**

37:33    Fônt of Being will nòt leave him ín their hands, *
nor let them wrong him *àt hís indìctment.*

*At his indictment* (*behishhofto* 37:33, 109:7). This is the bringing of
charges and not yet the trial stage *at the judgment* (*bammishpot* 1:5
and 25:9) or *for the judgment* (*lammishpot* 9:8 and 76:10).

37:34    *Qoph.*
Waît for the Font of Being, and keep hìs way, †
and he will lift yoù up to *claim land*; *         *37:9*
when the unjust are cut off, thèn yoú wìll see.

37:35    *Res.*
Râmpant have I behèld the unjúst one, *
and spreading leaves like à nátìve bush,

37:36    bût he passed away, *and* behold *thère was nò móre of him,* *
and I searched for him, but he coùld nót bè found.     *37:10*

37:37    *Shin.*
Keêp sentinel over integrity, ànd behold cleárly *
how the hereafter belongs to à mán of Shàlom,

37:38    bût the rebèls are destróyed as one; *
the hereafter of unjust peoplè ís cùt off,

37:39    *Tau.*
bût safety of the just is from thè Font of Béing, *
their stronghold *in thè tímes undèr siege,*     *4:2*

37:40    ând the Font of Being helps them and delivèrs them, †
delivers them from unjust peòple, and sáves them, *
for they tàke réfuge ìn him.

# THIRTY-EIGHT

LITURGY OF HOURS — Office of Readings on Friday II

Psalm 38 is third of seven Penitential Psalms (6, 32, 38, 51, 102, 130, 143). Like the author of Psalm 6, this psalmist is both guilty and physically ill. The two psalms have exactly the same opening verse, from there on this psalmist is absorbed with his guilt. The first person pronoun occurs in every verse!

38:1   (A Mizmor of David. *For mindfulness.*)   *38:1, 70:1*

> *For mindfulness* (*lehazkiyr* 38:1, 70:1) stands in two titles, but they are not historical psalms. The psalmists are remembering their own lives. The author of Psalm 38 would surely remember if he borrowed his opening verse from Psalm 6, and the author of Psalm 70 if he borrowed his text wholesale from Psalm 40. Perhaps these titles were added by a sub-editor flagging repeated texts.

38:2 = 6:2

Ô Font of Being, nor in your ànger chastíse me, *
nor in yoùr wráth corrèct me,

38:3   thoûgh your àrrows may piérce me, *
and though you press upon mè wíth yoùr Hand.

38:4   Nôr is there health in my flesh in thè Face of yoúr wrath, *
nor Shalom in my bones, in thè fáce of my sin.

38:5   Fôr my offensès cover úp my head; *
as a weighty burden, thèy weígh upòn me.

38:6   My wounds fèster; they pútrefy, *
in thè fáce of my guilt.

38:7   Wrâcked am I, distùrbed *to the útmost*; *
*all the day* I roam aboút ìn grief.   *25:5*

> *To the utmost* (*'ad me'od* 38:7/9, 119:8/43/51/107). The adverb *greatly* (*me'od*) serves object of a preposition here, adding duration to the notion of intensity. The opposite of *greatly* (*me'od*) is *but a little* (*me'at*); the opposite of *to the utmost* (*'ad me'od*) must be something like *as if in a moment* (*kime'at* 2:12, 73:2, 81:5, 94:17, 105:12, 119:87), which abbreviates an instant of time.

38:8   Fôr my ìnsides are fílled with pain, *
and there is no heàlth ín my flesh.

88

| | |
|---|---|
| 38:9 | Nûmb have I grown and opprèssed *to the útmost*; * <br> from my heartàche, Í have crièd out. | 38:7 |
| 38:10 | Ô Adonay, all my yearnìng is befóre you, * <br> and my sighing is nòt hídden fròm you. | |
| 38:11 | My errant heartbeàt saps awáy my strength * <br> and the light of my eyes—even they àre nót wìth me. | |
| 38:12 | My dears and my neighbòrs stand befóre my wounds; * <br> even my close friends hàve stoód fàr off. | |
| 38:13 | Thêy set traps, they who seek my life, † <br> pursuìng *what will hárm me*; * <br> they utter threats and falsehood; thèy múrmur *àll day*. | 35:26 <br> 25:5 |
| 38:14 | Bût I am like one deaf, dèvoid of heáring, * <br> and like one mute, who opèns nót hìs mouth. | |
| 38:15 | Î have become like a pèrson not heáring, * <br> and *in whose mouth* àre nó rèplies. | 5:10 |
| 38:16 | Fôr you indeed, FONT OF BEÌNG, have I waíted; * <br> may you answer, Adonày, my Divìne One. | |
| 38:17 | Fôr I said, *"Nor let them gloat ovèr me* † <br> whenever my foot will stúmble, * <br> nor let them triùmph óvèr me." | 30:2 |
| 38:18 | Fôr I am sèt up for stúmbling, * <br> and my anxiety is *bèfóre me àlways.* | 16:8 |
| 38:19 | Fôr the fault òf mine I dó confess; * <br> of my own sins, Ì stánd ìn dread, | |
| 38:20 | ând my enemies in life have grown númerous, * <br> and many are *they who hate mè fór no reàson,* | 35:19 |
| 38:21 | ând repaying with *èvil in pláce of good,* * <br> they attack me for my pùrsuít of goòdness. | 35:12 |
| 38:22 | *Nôr forsake me,* FONT OF BEÌNG, my Divíne One, * <br> *nor be àloóf fròm me!* | 27:9 <br> 22:12 |
| 38:23 | *Hâsten tò help me,* Ádonay, * <br> with sàlvátion for me! | 22:20 |

# THIRTY-NINE

— Office of Readings on Wednesday II

The author of Psalm 39 is silent (verse 3), speaks (4), becomes silent again (10), and resumes an outcry (13). In the course of his self-dialogue, this psalmist realizes the transitory quality of life (verse 6) and of riches (7). The mid-point of the psalm is self-interrogation: "What do I expect?" (8). By the end the psalmist makes peace with his own mortality (14).

39:1    (For the Director, *for Jeduthun.* A Mizmor of David.)

> **For Jeduthun** (*'al-yeduthun* 39:1, 62:1, 77:1). Jeduthun was chief cantor in the days of Saul. The titles suggest that he contributed musically or textually to the pre-Davidic Hebrew chant tradition.

39:2    **Ônce I statèd, †**
**"I will guard my ways, fròm sinning wíth my tongue, ***
**guard my mouth, with injustìce yét befòre me."**

39:3    **Wrâpped still in silence, I was strùck dumb by goódness, ***
**but my doùbt cóntìnued.**

39:4    **My heart was hot *within my chèst,* in my síghing, ***
**there blazed a flame; I spoke oùt with my tongue:**

> **Within my chest** (*beqirbiy* 39:4, 51:12, 55:5, 94:19, 109:22). Several psalms put the heart within the *qereb* (39:4, 55:5, 109:22), and one places breathing there (51:12). The *qereb*, then, must be the thoracic cavity, the chest. The interior life, underlying speech, is a theme elsewhere as well (51:12, 55:5, 94:19, 109:22).

39:5    **"Lêt me know my end, O FONT OF BEÌNG, †**
**and the tally of my days, whàtever ít may be; ***
**I would like to know *what a lifespàn ís fòr me.***"

> **What a lifespan is for me** (*meh-hadel 'eniy* 39:5; *'eniy meh-hadel* 89:48). A putative answer to the question is given elsewhere: *The span of our years is seventy years, or eighty if strong* (90:10).

39:6     **Bêhold! You have given dimensions to my dàys, †**
        **and my lifespan is like nòthing befóre you. ***
        **Yes, each is a breeze, *everyone lìke Ádam* stànding.**

> *Everyone like Adam* (*kol 'adam* 39:6/12, 64:10, 116:11) reads "every Adam" or "each human being," and is one of several phrases that the psalmist uses twice, like **wrapped still** (*ne'elamtiy* 39:3/10) and **with my tongue** (*bileshoniy* 39:2/4).

39:7     **Yês, in shadow a man goes àbout. †**
        **Yes, like à breeze may weálth grow, ***
        **but who its heir will be rèmaíns ùnknown.**

39:8     **Ând now, what do I èxpect, O Ádonay? ***
        **My hope bèlóngs tò you.**

39:9     **Frôm all my rèbellions sét me free; ***
        **set me not up às spórt fòr fools."**

39:10     **Wrâpped still, Ì open nót my mouth, ***
        ***for yoù háve àcted.***           *22:32*

39:11     **Tûrn your scoùrging awáy from me; ***
        **I would be finished at thè wáve of yoùr Hand.**

39:12     **Whên reproving for sin, you correct à man, †**
        **and like mòth you dissólve his wealth. ***
        **Yes, a breeze is *everyòne líke Àdam!***          *39:6*

39:13a     **Heâr my prayer, O Font of Beìng, †**
        **and lend Ear to mè, crying fór help: ***
        **to my weepìng *bé nòt deaf;***          *28:1*

39:13b     **fôr I have been a sòjourner wíth you, ***
        **a nester like my forebeàrs, áll òf them.**

39:14     **Spâre me, *thàt I may bé at ease,* ***
        ***before I pass away,* and nò lóngèr am.**

> *That I may be at ease, before I pass away* (*we'abliygah beterem 'elek* 39:14, Job 10:20/21) is rather too elaborate to be a common idiom. Rather, the appearance of this material in both Psalm 39 and Job 10 suggests a literary link between those two pieces of writing.

## FORTY

NEW TESTAMENT — Verses 7-9 at Heb 10:5-7
LITURGY OF HOURS — Midday Prayer at Monday II

Psalm 40 seems connected to the call of Samuel (40:8, 99:6), the prophet who anointed David as king. This psalm reflects the prophetic teaching that sacrifice can be no substitute for upright living (verse 7).

40:1 (For the Director. Of David. A Mizmor.)

40:2 **_Ârdently_ I waited for thè FONT OF BÉING, \***
**and he turned to me ànd heárd my cry,**

> *Ardently* (*cognate infinitive absolute*). Infinitive absolute before the cognate verb is a Semitic construction expressing emphasis:
> —**_ardently_ wait** (*qawwoh quwwiythiy* 40:2)
> —**_ardently_ ransom** (*padoh yifdeh* 49:8)
> —**_ardently_ wander** (*noa' yanu'u* 109:10)
> —**_ardently_ push** (*dahoh dehiythaniy* 118:13)
> —**_ardently_ correct** (*yassor yisreniy* 118:18)
> —**_ardently_ go** (*halok yelek* 126:6a)
> —**_ardently_ come** (*bo'-yabo'* 126:6b)

40:3 **ànd lifted me from shaft òf well, from míre of mud, \***
**and set my feet on the bedrock, makìng fírm my steps,**

40:4 **ànd put _into my moùth_ †** *5:10*
**_a song made new_ of praise-craft fòr our Divíne One; \*** *33:3*
**many _saw and had awe_ and trusted thè FÓNT OF BÈING.** *52:8*

40:5 **_Blêssedness belongs to thè man_ †** *34:9*
**who trusts in thè FONT OF BÉING, \***
**and envies none who are proud or bèguíled with ìdols!**

40:6 **Yoû did many things, FONT OF BEING, my Divine Òne; †**
**in your marvels and your plans for ùs, none can équal you! \***
**I speak and declare them bèyónd coùnting!**

40:7 **Ôblation and gift have not pleased yoù; †**
**in the ears you imprìnted it fór me: \***
**you have required no whole òr sín oblàtions.**

40:8 **Sô I said, "Bèhold! I háve come!" \***
**In a scrolled book it wàs wrítten fòr me:**

40:9    **Dôing your will, my Dìvine One, pleáses me, ***
       **and at my heart ìs yoúr Tòrah.**

40:10   **Î heralded justice in *a vast assèmbly*, †**       *22:26*
       **—Behold!—I dìd not restraín my lips, ***
       **as you knew, Ò Fónt of Bèing!**

40:11   **Ât my heart's core I cloaked not your justìce; †**
       **I declared your fidelity ànd your salvátion; ***
       **I hid not *your mercy or your truth* for *à vást assèmbly*.**   *22:26*

40:12   **Âs for you, Font of Bèìng, †**
       **hide not fròm me your ténderness; ***
       ***your mercy and your truth* evèr présèrve me.**   *25:10*

40:13   **Fôr troubles encompass me; *there is no countìng.* †**
       **My offenses engulf mè so I cánnot see; ***
       **they exceed *the hairs of my head*, so my heart ìs óvèrcome.**

*There is no counting* (*'eyn mispar* 40:13, 104:25, 105:34, 147:5) and
*more than the hairs of my head* (*mishha'arot ro'shiy* 40:13, 69:5) are
synonymous idioms for vast numbers—not infinity, but something
beyond the capacity of the Hebrew numerical system.

40:14 = 70:2
       **Bê pleased, O Font of Bèing, to sét me free! ***
       **O Font of Being, *tò hélp me hàsten!***   *22:20*

40:15 = 70:3
       **Bê they shamed and all àbashed †**
       ***who seek my soul*, thàt they might seíze it; ***   *7:2*
       **turned back and confused, whò wísh *what hàrms me*.**   *35:2*

40:16 = 70:4
       **Bê they confoundèd in their vále of shame, ***
       **who say to me, "Oh, *a brother? A brothèr cán hè be?*"**   *35:21*

40:17 = 70:5 see 35:27
       **Lêt them sing and rejoice in you, all who seek yoù; †**
       **let those who love your sàlvation éver say, ***
       **"Great is thè Font of Béing!" ***

40:18 = 70:6
       **Ôf me also, *lowly and ìn need,* †**   *35:10*
       **Adonay thinks of me, my hèlp and my freédom! ***
       **May you, my Divìne Óne, *delày not!***   *70:6*

## FORTY-ONE

NEW TESTAMENT — Verse 10 at Jn 13:18
LITURGY OF HOURS — Vespers on Thursday I

Psalm 41 is framed with blessings. The first verse begins with the word *Ashre'* to bless one empathetic for the poor. The last verse begins with the word *Baruch* to bless God, who shows compassion for all his creatures, who even at their greatest are weak by comparison to their Creator.

41:1    (For the Director.
     A Mizmor of David.)

41:2   **Blêssedness belongs to one caring fòr the poor peóple; \***
     *on a day of evil,* **the FONT OF BEING wìll réscuè him!**     *27:5*

41:3   **FÔNT OF BEING guards him and gives hìm life, †**
     **and he ìs blessed *withín the land*, \***
     **and you do not give him by the neck tò hís rìval.**

> ***Within the land*** (*ba'arets* 41:3, 46:9, 58:3/12, 67:3/5, 72:16, 73:9/15, 74:8, 112:2, 119:19/87, 135:6, 140:12, 141:7) is where the rituals of the Torah can be fulfilled. The poor in the land are more blessed than the rich outside. Rich landless pilgrims come to the land to be blessed by the landed poor to whom they give alms.

41:4   **FÔNT OF BEING sustains hìm on his síckbed; \***
     **you alter all his conditiòns, ín his ìllness.**

41:5   **Saîd I, "O FONT ÒF BEING, pity me; \***
     **heal my soul, though I hàve sínned agaìnst you."**

41:6   **Rîvals of mine speak evil of mè: "How soon wíll he die, \***
     **so that his name mày bécòme nil?"**

41:7   **Ând if one comes to loòk, he speaks nónsense; \***
     **his heart gathers its evil; he goes oùtsíde; he tèlls it.**

41:8   **Âs one against me, all who hate me whìsper agaìnst me; \***
     **they consider *somethìng tó hàrm me*:**     *35:26*

41:9   **"Ôh, let a plague of Bèliäl stríke him, \***
     **and from where he lies, let him not àríse àgain."**

41:10   **Êven one who shared my Shalom, ìn whom I trústed, \***
     **one who ate my bread has raised hìs heél against me.**

41:11   **Bût may you, FONT OF BEING, hàve pity ón me, \***
     **and let me arise, ànd gíve them pàyment.**

41:12   **Ĩn this I know that yoù have been pleásed with me, ***
      **that my enemy may nòt shoút abòve me.**

41:13   **Ând I am one you presèrved *by intégrity*, ***         *7:9*
      **and you set me *before the Face of You ètérnàlly*.**    *17:2, 5:12*

41:14 see 106:48
      **Blêssed be the FONT OF BEING, *Divìne One of Ísraël*, ***
      **from the eternal and to the eternal! *Àmén and àmen!***

*Divine One of Israël* (*'elohey yisra'el* 41:14, 59:6, 68:9, 69:7, 72:18, 106:48) and *Divine One of Jacob* (*'elohey ya'aqob* 20:2, 46:8/12, 75:10, 76:7, 81:2/5, 84:9, 94:7) are interchangeable.

*Amen and amen!* (*'amen we'amen*). Three psalms end with the blessing of God, followed by double *amen* (41:14, 72:19, 89:53). Covenants require mutual consent; the divine covenants are to be affirmed both from the divine side and from the human side. Jesus says *amen amen* twenty-five times in the Gospel of John (Jn 1:50, 3:3/5/11, 5:19/24/25, 6:26/32/47/54, 8:34/51/58, 10:1/7, 12:24, 13:16/20/21/38, 14:12, 16:20/23, 21:18).

# FORTY-TWO

Psalms 42 and 43 share a response (42:6/12 and 43:5) and thus must have originated as a single psalm. Division took place after titles were assigned, because 43 has no title. The psalm divided, perhaps because the first half was on the bottom of one scroll and the second half atop another at a time of recopying. Psalm 42 began with the psalmist drawn to God and Psalm 43 ends with him going in to a holy mountain. The yearning of Psalm 42 finds fulfillment in the liturgical action of Psalm 43.

42:1    (For the Director. A Maskil of *the Sons of Qorah*.)

> **Sons of Qorah** (*beney qorah*), mentioned in twelve psalm titles, are not those who conspired against Moses (Num 16:1-49), but a clan of sacred musicians (1 Chron 6:22).

42:2    **Deêr-like, she is drawn tò *watered górges*; ***    *18:34, 18:16*
       **thus my soul is drawn tò yoú, Divine One.**

> **Deer-like** indicates yearning and desire (*ke'ayyal* 42:2) or fleetness of foot (*ka'ayyalot* 18:34, 2 Sam 22:34). The one is a quality for peace, the other for wartime.

42:3    **Âthirst is my soul for the Divine Òne, for a *Gód of life*; ***
       **when will I come and see thè Fáce Dìvine?**

> **The God of life** (*'el hay* 42:3; *'el hayyay* 42:9) is sovereign over the **land of life** (*'erets hayyim* 27:13, 52:7; *'erets ha-hayyiym* 142:6) or **lands of life** (*'artsot hahayyiym* 116:9). Yet the psalmist says, "Were I shrouded in Sheöl, I would behold you! (139:80)."

42:4    **Fôr me my tears have been bread *day and night*, †**    *22:3*
       **as thèy tell me *áll the day*, ***    *25:5*
       **"Oh, *where ìs yoúr Divìne One?*"**

> The gentiles ask a rhetorical question **Where is your Divine One?** (*'ayyeh 'eloheyka* 42:4/11) or **Where is their Divine One?** (*'ayyeh 'eloheyhem* 79:10, 115:2), expecting the answer "Nowhere." The psalmist turns that into a catechetical question, replying that his Divine One is in the skies, doing whatever he pleases (115:3).

42:5   Lêt me recall these things and refresh my soul ìn me: †
       I crossed the entry, bowed to *the house òf the Divíne One*, *
       *with sound of song and laud*, with a festìve múltìtude.          *26:7*

The *House of the Divine One* (*bet 'elohiym* 42:5, 52:10, 55:15; *bet
'eloheynu* 135:2) means the Jerusalem temple, *House of the FONT OF
BEING* (*bet-yhwh* 23:6, 27:4, 92:14, 116:19, 118:27, 122:1/9, 134:1,
135:2). The two designations stand in parallel once (135:2).

42:6 = 42:12 = 43:5
       Why sink, my soul, and sigh ìn me? †
       Await the Divine Òne; for I laúd him still, *
       the Savior of my fàce, my Divìne One.
42:7   Ôn me my soul weighs dòwn; †
       thus I recall you from the land of Jòrdan and Hérmon, *
       from thè Mítzar Moùntain.
42:8   Deêp calls to deep, at thè sound of yoúr cascade; *
       all your tides and your waves ròll óvèr me.
42:9   *By day*, the FONT OF BEING gives his mèrcy, †
       and *by the night* hìs song is wíth me, *
       a prayer to thè *Gód of* my *life*.          *42:3*

Singular *in the night* (*ballaylah* 42:9, 77:7, 88:2, 119:55, 121:6,
136:9) corresponds to the daytime phrase *at the dawn* (*boqer* 5:4a/b;
*babboqer* 88:14, 90:5/6/14, 92:3). Plural *during the nights* (*leylot*
16:7; *balleylot* 92:3, 134:1) perhaps has distributive phrase *day by day*
(*yom yom* 61:9, 68:20, Prov 8:30/34) as equivalent.

42:10 = 43:2
       Lêt me say to God, my Bedròck: †
       "Why hàve you forgótten me? *
       Why do I go about disguised, oppressed by àn énèmy?"
42:11  Âs I am being slain in my bònes, †
       my rivals taunt me, as thèy tell me *áll the day*, *          *25:5*
       "Oh, *where is yoúr Divìne One?*"          *42:4*
42:12 = 42:6 = 43:5
       Why sink, my soul, and why sigh ìn me? †
       Await the Divine Òne; for I laúd him still, *
       the Savior of my face, ànd my Divìne One.

## FORTY-THREE

LITURGY OF HOURS — Lauds on Tuesday II
See introduction to Psalm 42.

43:1 **Jûdge me, O my Divine Òne, †
and *pursue my suit* with a peoplè undevóted; ***  *35:1*
**from a man of deceit and vice, dèlívèr me.**

43:2 = 42:10

**Fôr you are the Divine One, my Stronghòld, †
Why shoùld you disdaín me? *
Why must I go about in disguise, oppressed by àn énèmy?**

43:3 **Sênd your Light and your Truth to guide mè; †
let them bring me to yoùr *mount of hóliness* ***  *2:6*
**and to yoùr dwéllìng place.**

***Your mount of holiness*** (*har qodsheka* 15:1, 43:3; *har qodshiy* 2:6, 3:5; *har qodsho* 48:2, 99:9; *harrey qodesh* 87:1) is Mount Moriah, where Abraham went to offer up his son Isaac, and where David brought the Ark and Solomon built the temple. Mount Ziön is a different summit, where David built his palace, but the term Ziön was eventually extended to include all of the city, including the temple mount.

43:4 **Sô let me go in to the oblation-table of the Divine Òne, †
to a God òf joy, my révelry, *
and laud you *on a lyre-bow*, Divine, Ò my Divìne One!**  *33:2*

43:5 = 42:6/12

**Why sink, my soul, and why sigh ìn me? †
Await the Divine Òne; for I laúd him still, *
the Savior of my face, ànd my Divìne One.**

# FORTY-FOUR

NEW TESTAMENT — Verse 23 at Rom 8:36
LITURGY OF HOURS — Office of Readings on Thursdays II and IV

Psalm 44 is the first of thirteen psalms that begin with the word *Elohim* (44, 46, 54, 60, 63, 67, 70, 72, 76, 79, 82, 83, and 109), which suggest an Elohist anthology absorbed into the final edition. This psalmist feels keenly a sharp difference between the golden days of the past and the fallen state of affairs at the present. He reasserts the continuing action of God at all times.

44:1   (For the Director.
     Of *the Sons of Qorah*. A Maskil.)          *42:1*

44:2   **Ô Divine One! †**
     **With our ears we heard oùr forebears téll us ***
     **a deed you did in their days,** *in thè dáys òf old*:

> **In the days of old** (*yemey qedem* 44:2, Lam 1:7, 2:17; *yomiym miqqedem* 143:5). The word *qedem* principally means **in the East**, as in divine appellative **Rider in the Heaven of Heavens in the East** (*rokeb bishmey shemey qedem* 68:34). It also means **ancient**, as in divine appellative **Divine One of Old** (*'elohey qedem* Deut 33:27).

44:3   **hôw by your Hànd †**
     **you displaced gentiles ànd had them plánted, ***
     **after crushing nations ànd háving thèm sent.**

44:4   *Nôr surely* **by their blades did they claim lànd, †**    *9:19, 4:7*
     *nor* **did their arm save thèm but your Ríght Hand ***
     **and by your Arm and** *light of your Face*, **yoú fávòred them.**

44:5   **Yoû yourself,** *my Kìng, the Divíne One,* *****       *5:3*
     **ordained victòriés for Jàcob.**

44:6   **Ìn you hàve we repélled our foes, ***
     **in your Name trampled those risìng úp agaìnst us.**

44:7   *Nôr surely* **in my war-bòw do I pláce my trust, ***
     *nor* **in my blade, whìch cánnot sàve me,**      *9:19*

44:8   **bût surely it is you whò saved us fróm our foes, ***
     **and gave shame tò thóse who hàte us.**

44:9   **Wê have gloried in the Dìvine One** *áll the day,* *****    *25:5*
     **and ever do wè laúd yoùr Name.**

44:10 see 60:12 and 108:12
>    **Bût you dìsdained and shámed us, ***
>    **nor have you gone oùt wíth oùr troops.**

44:11   **Yoû push us bàck through distrésses, ***
>    **and those who hate us can foràge fór thèmselves.**

44:12   **Yoû are giving us like a flòck to be eáten, ***          *9:12*
>    **and have scattered us *àmóng the gèntiles*.**

44:13   **Yoû are selling your peoplè at no válue, ***
>    **and have profited nothing ìn séllìng them.**

44:14 = 79:4
>    **Yoû make us *a rebuke tò those who dwéll with us*, ***
>    **scorn and derision tò thóse aboùt us.**

God made his people ***a rebuke to those who dwell with them*** (*herpah lishkeneynu* 44:14, 79:4; *herpah lishkenaw* 89:42; *madon lishekeneynu* 80:7). However, the neighbors rebuke God along with the people, and so ***the rebukes of those who rebuke you*** (*herpot horfeyka* 69:10; *herpatam 'esher herfuka* 79:12) fell on us.

44:15   **Yoû make us a proverb *àmong the géntiles*, ***          *9:12*
>    **a shaking of head *àmóng the nàtions*.**

Three synonyms exist for the non-Hebrew peoples:
—***among the nations*** (*bal'umiym* 44:15, 57:10, 108:4, 149:7)
—***among the gentiles*** (*baggoyim* 9:12, 18:50, 22:29, 44:12, 79:10, 96:3/10, 106:27, 126:2, 149:7)
—***among the peoples*** (*ba'ammiym* 57:10, 77:15, 105:1, 108:4).
The first and second are in remote parallel in this psalm (44:12/15).

44:16   ***Âll the day* my disgràce is befóre me, ***          *25:5*
>    **and my shame òf fáce has cloàked me,**

44:17   **frôm the voice of one mockìng or blasphéming, ***
>    **from the face of *a fiend or a seekèr óf vèngeance*.**          *8:3*

44:18   **Âll this befell us, yet we dìd not forgét you, ***
>    **nor did we deal falsely wíth yoùr bond.**

44:19   **Nôr have wè turned our heárts back, ***
>    **nor have our footsteps wandèred fróm yoùr path,**

44:20   **thoûgh you crushed us in à place of jáckals, ***
>    **and cloaked us ìn *deáthly shàdow*.**          *23:4*

44:21 **Hâd we forgotten the Name òf our Divíne One, ***
      **or stretched out our palms to à fóreìgn god,**

44:22 **woûld the Divine One nòt have discóvered this? ***
      **For he knows the heart, with ìts sécret plàces.**

44:23 **Fôr your sake we have beèn slaughtered *áll the day*, ***       *25:5*
      **seen as sheep fòr óblàtion.**

44:24 **Âwaken! Why are yoù sleeping, Ádonay? ***
      **Be attentive! Be not *for evèr* dísdaìnful.**          *9:7*

44:25 **Why do you turn thè Face of Yoú away? ***
      **Why forget our weakness ànd oúr opprèssion?**

44:26 **Fôr our souls hàve spilled out ónto dust; ***
      **our innards àdhére to thè land.**

44:27 **Rîse up tò be a hélp for us, ***
      **and redeem us for the sake òf yoúr mèrcy!**

# FORTY-FIVE

EARLIEST MANUSCRIPT — Verses 1-3 in pesher 4QpPs45
NEW TESTAMENT — Verses 7-8 in Heb 1:8-9
LITURGY OF HOURS — Vespers on Monday II

The author of Psalm 45 has forged an ode in praise of the king above all other men. Hence the phrase *beney 'adam* (verse 3) is translated "sons of Adam" here rather than "children of Adam" as elsewhere. Dahood conjectures that opening verb *rahash*, which occurs in no other Hebrew text, transposes the consonants of *harash II*, "to engrave, work metal," so that it here means "to compose, to improvise." That conclusion seems to underlie the rendering, "is inditing" (KJV).

45:1     (For the Director, *upon "Lilies."*
      Of *the Sons of Qorah.* A Maskil. A Song of Love.)        *42:1*

> *Upon "Lillies"* (*'al-shoshanniym* 45:1, 69:1, 80:1) probably refers to a long-lost melody.

45:2    **My heart has forged good word-cràft; †
      I tell my opus tò the king wíth my tongue, *
      which is faster than à scríbàl pen.**

45:3    **Yoû are most handsome of the sons of Adàm! †
      Grace hàs poured out thróugh your lips; *
      *Therefore* the Divine One blessed you *ètérnàlly*.**    *25:8, 5:12*

45:4    **Gîrd your blade on your thigh, O stróng màn, †
      in your spendor ànd in your májesty, *
      and conquer in yoùr májèsty!**

45:5    **Rîde on a *word of truth* ànd humble jústice, *
      and teach with marvels àt yoúr rìght hand.**

> *Word of truth* (*debar 'emeth* 45:5, 119:43, Jer 23:28, Qohelet 12:10) may be contrasted with the *word of evil* (*dabar ra'* 64:6, 141:4, Deut 17:1, 23:10, Qohelet 8:3; *dibrey ra'* Jer 5:28).

45:6    **Yoûr sharp arrows, wìth peoples únder you, *
      fall into the heart of the rivàls óf thè king.**

45:7    **Yoûr throne, O Divine One, làsts *ever ánd an age*; ***    *5:12*
      **a staff of equity is the staff òf yoúr dòmain.**

45:8   Yoû loved justice and hated injustìce, †
     *therefore the Divine, your Divìne One,* **anoínted you** *     *25:8*
     **with oil of gladness more than yoùr féllòw men.**

> *The Divine, your Divine One* (*'elohiym 'eloheyka* 45:8, 50:7;
> *'elohiym 'eloheynu* 48:15, 67:7) is a geminated divine appellative,
> which is already a "plural of majesty." As a consequence, there is a
> most heightened emphasis upon the divine nature: "Your Divine One,
> who truly is the Divine One."

45:9   **Myrrh and cinnamon aloes àre all upón your robes,** *
     **from palaces of ivory, from which they rèjoíce ìn you.**

45:10   **Daûghters of kings find à place in yoúr esteem,** *
     **a queen at your right hand, ìn Óphirìte gold.**

45:11   **Lîsten, O daughter, and see, ànd bend your eárlobe,** *
     **and forget your people and yoùr fáthèr's house.**

45:12   **Tâken is the kìng with your beaùty;** *
     **since he is your master, you wìll hónòr him.**

45:13   **Âlso a daughter from the Tyre-Ròck †**
     **is among thè gifts befóre your face,** *
     **for which they seek, the richèst óf the peòple.**

45:14   **Âll glorious is thè daughter óf a king,** *
     **whose garment ìs láced ìn gold.**

45:15   **În her brocade she ìs taken tó the king.** *
     **Maidens follow her; her friends are broùght ín tò you.**

45:16   **Thêy are taken wìth joys and révelry,** *
     **brought into the palàce óf à king.**

45:17   **În place of your fathèrs will your sóns be;** *
     **you will appoint them princelings ìn *áll thè land.***    *8:2*

45:18   **Ï recall your Name *in every àge after án age;*** *    *10:6*
     *therefore* **peoples laud you *evèr ánd àn age.***   *25:8, 5:12*

# FORTY-SIX

Images in the first half of Psalm 46 are planetary in scale—quaking earth, shaking mountains, frothing waves, gladdening channels, groaning nations, falling domains, melting earth. In the second half, the images are military—truces imposed, wars ceased, bows broken, spears shattered, chariots burned. At the transition (verse 8) is the expanded appellative *Elohe-Ya'aqob* (God of Jacob) in parallel with the common Isaian title *Font of Being-Sabaöth* (God of heavenly armies). This juxtaposition is also found in Psalm 84:9.

46:1  (For the Director of *the Sons of Qorah.*　　　　　　　*42:1*
　　　Like "Virgins." A Song.)

46:2  **Fôr us, the Divine One is à refuge ánd a strength, ***
　　　**a help in distresses, oftèn tó bè found.**

46:3  ***Thêrefore* we fear nò quaking óf land, ***　　　　*25:8*
　　　**or tumbling of mountains into thè heárt of thè seas,**

46:4  **thoûgh their wàters may fróth and foam, ***
　　　**though mountains quake àt their swèlling.**

46:5  **Rîver channels gladden *the city òf the Divíne One*, ***
　　　**the holy place, dwellìng óf the Mòst High.**

Some of the appellations for Jerusalem include
—*city of the Divine One* (*'iyr 'elohiym* 46:5, 48:2/9, 87:3)
—*city of the Font of Being* (*'iyr yhwh* 48:9, 101:8)
—*city of the Great King* (*'iyr melek rab* 48:3).
Bishop Augustine of Hippo, in preaching on the psalms, thought deeply about these particular verses and developed them into his magnum opus, the *Civitas Dei.*

46:6  **Wîth the Divine One in her midst, shè cannot stúmble; ***
　　　**the Divine One helps her untìl breák òf dawn.**

46:7  **Gêntiles have groaned; dòmains have túmbled. ***
　　　**He gave his call: "Let thè lánd dìssolve!"**

46:8 = 48:12

　　　**Fônt of Being, Sabàòth is wíth us; ***
　　　**high refuge for us is *the Divine Òne óf Jàcob.***　　　*20:2*

46:9  **Côme, behold the marvels of thè Font of Béing, ***
　　　**who imposed trucès *ín thè land*,**　　　　　　　　*41:3*

46:10   **stôpping battles to *the limit of thè land*: †
breaking wàr-bow and snápping spear, \*
burnìng cháriot wìth flame.**

> *Limit of the land* (singular *qetseh ha'arets* 46:10, 61:3, 135:7; plural *qatsweh-'erets* 48:11, 65:6) can refer to the edges of the land mass, or to the extent of the Holy Land. Jeremiah and Psalm 135 share an interesting image: ***raising up vapors from the limit of the land*** (*ma'aleh nesi'iym miqtseh ha'arets* 135:7, Jer 10:13, 51:16). The fog had to come from somewhere, and it came from the land over the horizon. Note the following related phrases
> —***limit of the land mass*** (*qetseh tebel* 19:5)
> —***limit of the skies*** (*qetseh hasshamayim* 19:7)
> —***ends of land*** (*'afsey 'arets* 2:8, 22:28, 59:14, 67:8, 72:8, 98:3).

46:11   **"Côncede, and acknowledge that I àm the Divíne One. \*
I rise against the gentiles; I rise àgaínst thè land."**

46:12 = 46:8

    **FÔNT OF BEING, Sabàöth is wíth us; \***
    **high refuge for us is *the Divine Òne óf Jàcob.***                  *20:2*

> Israël was the *nom de guerre* of the patriarch Jacob. Therefore, his God is called alternatively ***Divine One of Jacob*** (*'elohey ya'aqob* 20:2, 46:8/12, 75:10, 76:7, 81:2/5, 84:9, 94:7) and ***Divine One of Israël*** (*'elohey yisra'el* 41:14, 59:6, 68:9, 69:7, 72:18, 106:48). So his offspring are called ***children of Israël*** (*beney yisra'el* 103:7, 148:14) or ***children of Jacob*** (*beney ya'aqob* 77:16, 105:6). The terms ***house of Jacob*** (*bet-ya'aqob* 114:1) and ***house of Israël*** (*bet-yisra'el* 98:3, 115:12, 135:19) are not always found to be interchangeable, however, because the latter term came to be used in a narrower sense by later historians.

## FORTY-SEVEN

JEWISH FEASTS — Near Year
LITURGY OF HOURS — Lauds on Wednesday I

Twice (verses 6/9), the author of Psalm 47 uses the word *Elohim*, which usually serves as a divine appellative, as a superlative adjective (as elsewhere at 59:11 and 68:7). Dahood points out that this usage is well documented in Ugaritic literature as well.

47:1   (For the Director of *the Sons of Qorah*. A Mizmor.)                     *42:1*

47:2   **Âll the peoples, give àpplause with á palm! \***
       **Shout to the Divine One *with soúnd òf song*!**                        *26:7*

The phrase **all the peoples** (*kol ha'ammiym* 47:2, 49:2, 96:3, 97:6, 99:2) seems to include Israël, but **all gentiles** (*kol goyiym* 9:18, 59:9, 67:3, 72:11/17, 86:9, 113:4, 117:1) does not. Israël is often called *'am*, but hardly ever *goy*.

47:3   **Fôr the *FONT OF BEING*, Mòst High is áwesome, \***                    *7:18*
       **great King ovèr áll thè land.**                                         *8:2*

**Great King** (*melek gadol* 47:3, 95:3; *melek rab* 48:3) is **the King of Kings** (Aramaic *melek malkaya'* Ezek 7:12; Persian "shah of shahs"). *Rab* and *gadol* are synonyms if singular but not if plural. **Great kings** are *malkiym gedoliym* (136:17) but **many kings** are *malkiym rabbiym* or *'atsumiym* (135:10).

47:4   **Hê subdues peòples beneáth us, \***                                     *18:48*
       **and nations bèneáth oùr feet,**                                         *8:7*

**He subdues peoples beneath us** (*yadber 'ammiym tahteynu* 47:4; *yadber 'ammiym tahtay* 18:48, 2 Sam 22:48; *haroded 'ammiy tahtay* 144:2). God is sovereign, and subjects people to his deputy on earth, the king. The king sat and courtiers stood, but defeated enemies and tributary kings knelt to kiss the royal feet. The prepositional phrase comes in the simpler form first, **beneath us** (*tahteynu* 47:4, *tahtay* 18:40/48, 144:2, 2 Sam 40/48), paralleled in the next line by the ampler form, **beneath our feet** (*tahat ragleynu* 47:4; *tahat raglaw* 8:7, 18:1/39).

47:5   **Hê chooses fòr us our héritage, \***
       **the pride of Jacòb, whóm hè loves.**

47:6  Ône who is Divine has ascended wìth acclamátion, *
the FONT OF BEING, wìth *shófar soùnding.*

*Shofar sounding* (*qol shofar* 47:6, 98:6) follows the pattern shared
by *the sound of laud* (*qol todah* 26:7, 42:5), *the sound of song* (*qol
rinnah* 42:5, 47:2, 118:15), *the sound of my pleading* (*qol tahnunothay*
86:65; *qol tahnunay* 116:1, 130:2, 140:7), *sounding of your thunder*
(*qol ra'amka* 77:19, 104:7).

47:7  Plây chords! Tò the Divíne One, play! *
Play chords! Tò oúr Kìng, play!

47:8  Fôr King of *all the land* ìs the Divíne One; *          *8:2*
play chords as àn áccòlade!

47:9  Hê has ruled divine, àbove the géntiles;
divine he sits upon his seat òf hólìness.

47:10  Ô *princes of peoplès,* †
join the people of the Divìne One of *Ábraham,* *
for earthly shields belong to the Divine Òne, múch exàlted!

*Princes of peoples* (*nediybey 'ammiym* 47:10) are to be joined with
the *princes of his people* (*nediybey 'ammo* 113:8)—*princes of Judah,
princes of Zebulun, princes of Naphtali* (*nediybeh yehudah, nediybeh
zebulun, nediybeh naftaliy* 68:28)—under the divine sovereignty.

# FORTY-EIGHT

**TEMPLE LITURGY** — Monday
**NEW TESTAMENT** — Verse 3 at Mt 5:35
**LITURGY OF HOURS** — Lauds on Thursday I

Psalm 48 (verse 3) contrasts Mount *Ziön* with the northern Mount *Zaphon*, sacred to *Baal*. It climaxes with a tour of the ramparts of Jerusalem (13/14), similar to another passage: "Ascend the walls of Uruk, walk about the top, inspect the base, view the brickwork. Is not the very core made of oven-fired brick? As for its base, was it not laid down by the seven sages?" (*Epic of Gilgamesh*, Tablet I, Column I)

48:1    (A Song. A Mizmor of *the Sons of Qorah.*)         *42:1*
48:2 see 96:4 and 145:3

> **Greât is the FONT OF BEING, and most laudàble,** †
> **in *the city òf our Divíne One*,** *       *46:5*
> **on his *mount òf hóliness*.**       *43:3*

48:3    **Lôvely height, joy to *all the land*, is thè Mount of Zíön;** *   *8:2*
> **like Zaphon is the city òf *thé greàt king*.**       *47:3*

*The Mount of Ziön* (*har tsiyyon* 48:3/12, 74:2, 78:68, 125:1) is only one of the summits on which Jerusalem is built, but later it came to represent the entire city.

48:4    **Ône who is Divine is wìthin her cítadel,** *
> **known to be à hígh rèfuge.**

48:5    **Fôr behold! Thè kings were plédging** *
> **that they would inváde às one.**

48:6    **Thêy were awestrùck! How they wére dismayed!** *
> **They knèw feár! Thèy fled!**

48:7    **Trêmbling seized them àll of a súdden,** *
> **writhing, like a woman givìng bírth to à child.**

48:8    **Wîth the meàns of an *eástward wind*** *
> **you can shatter vessèls fróm Tàrshish.**

*Eastward wind* (*ruah qadiym* 48:8, or simply *qadiym* 78:26) is a strong gale wind that blew in from the Mediterranean, and could cause shipwrecks (as for Paul on more than one occasion).

48:9a   **Jûst as wè have heard, wé beheld \***
      in *the city of the FONT OF BEÌNG*, Sábàöth,

48:9b   *în the city òf our Divíne One,* \*             *46:5*
      which the Divine One founded *for an ètérnìty.*   *18:51*

48:10   **Wê made parables, Divine Òne, for your mércy \***
      in the midst òf yoúr tèmple.

48:11   **Âs your Name, O Divine Òne, †**
      so be your praise-craft to thè *limits óf land*; \*   *46:10*
      your Right Hand ìs fìlled with jùstice.

48:12 see 97:8
      **Lêt the *Mount of Ziön* rejoìce! †**            *48:3*
      Let the daughters òf Judah rével, \*
      because òf yoúr jùdgments.

48:13   **Sûrround Ziön and go àbout her círcuit; \***
      count hèr mány tùrrets.

48:14   *Fîx your focus* **on the walls, exàmine her cítadels, \***
      that you may ìnfórm the nèxt age:

*Fix your focus* (*shiythu libkem* 48:14; *'al-tashiythu leb* 62:11) is a fairly common idiom. The individual words are "set your heart," but for the Hebrews the heart was the seat of the mind, not of the feelings.

48:15   **"Thîs is *the Divìne, our Divíne One!*" \***     *45:8*
      *Ever and an age*, he wìll guíde us pàst death.   *5:12*

# FORTY-NINE

Psalm 49, like Psalm 78, is built around a pre-existing proverb: feeling guilty for being afraid in the face of danger (verse 6). Like a combat soldier, the psalmist must fight through fears to arrive at courage.

| | | |
|---|---|---|
| 49:1 | (For the Director of *the Sons of Qorah.* A Mizmor.) | *42:1* |
| 49:2 | **Lîsten to thìs,** *all the peóples***;** * | *47:2* |
| | **lend ear,** *all whò ín the wòrld dwell,* | *33:8* |
| 49:3 | **yês,** *children of Adam,* **yès,** *children óf rank,* * | *11:4, 4:3* |
| | **together the rich ànd thóse ìn need.** | |
| 49:4 | **Lêt my moùth utter wísdom,** * | |
| | **and my** *heart* **have pèrcéptìve** *thoughts.* | *19:15* |
| 49:5 | **Tô a proverb Ì bend my eárlobe;** * | |
| | **I open my riddlè** *ón a lyre-bow***:** | *33:2* |
| 49:6 | **"Ôh, why do I know fear** *ìn days of évil,* * | *27:5* |
| | **with guilt at my heels, àll aroùnd me?"** | |
| 49:7 | **Âs for those whò trust in thcir wealth,** * | |
| | **and glory in the grandeùr óf their rìches,** | |
| 49:8 | **nô matter how** *ardèntly,* † | |
| | **a brother cànnot be rédeemed;** * | *40:2* |
| | **no man can refund his worth tò thé Divìne One.** | |
| 49:9 | **Toô costly would be thè ransom of one's soul,** * | |
| | **that a lifespan might endure** *ètérnàlly,* | *5:12* |
| 49:10 | **ând that òne might** *for éver* **live,** * | *9:7* |
| | **never tò sée thè grave.** | |
| 49:11 | **Fôr one sees the wise dyìng** † | |
| | **together with** *the sènseless and brútish***;** * | |
| | **they become nil, and leave to othèrs theír rìches.** | |

*Senseless and brutish* (*kesiyl waba'ar* 49:11) appears elsewhere with the terms reversed (*ba'ar ukesiyl* 92:7; *bo'ariym ukesiyliym* 94:8). The psalmist goes on to compare the human race with the brutish cattle (verses 13 and 21) and the senseless sheep (verse 15). These idioms are all of a piece.

49:12  Thêy think their dynasties eternàl, †
　　　 their dwellings *àge after án age*; *                    *10:6*
　　　 they give their names tò plóts òf land.

49:13 = 49:21
　　　 Âdam too has value that òne cannot fáthom, *
　　　 unlike the cattle thàt páss àway,

49:14  whôse way is this, tò fatten thémselves, *
　　　 and whose aim is to bè pleásed *in theìr mouths*;     *5:10*

49:15  *sheêp-like,* they are set for Sheöl, †
　　　 whom death herds and takes dòwn ready *fór dawn*, *    *30:6*
　　　 and whose limbs will rot in Sheöl, fàr fróm their tèmple.

Being *sheep-like* (*katsso'n*) is perfectly fine when shepherded by God
(23:1, 78:52, 80:2, 107:41), by Moses and Aaron (77:21) or by David
with integrity of heart and skill of palm (78:72). When we like sheep
go astray, however (Is 53:6), then we become lost sheep (119:176) and
are led to slaughter (49:15).

49:16  Ônly the Divine One frees my soul *from thè grip of Shéöl*, *
　　　 for he keeps à hóld òn me.

*From the grip of Sheöl* (*miyyad She'ol* 49:15, 89:49), literally "from
the hand of Sheöl." The psalmists pray to be freed from the hand of
sons of a foreign land (*miyyad beney nekar* 144:7/11), of the unjust
(*miyyad resha'iym* 36:12, 82:4, 97:10; *miyyad rasha'*, 140:5), of a
hater (*miyyad sone'* 106:10), and of an enemy (*miyyad 'oyeb* 106:10).

49:17  Hâve no awe for hòw a man gaíns wealth, *
　　　 how the glory of òne's hoúse mày grow,

49:18  whô indeed keèps nothing át one's death, *
　　　 whose glory cannòt fóllow òne down,

49:19  thoûgh one's soul may bè blest in hís life, *
　　　 and they laud you whèn yoú dò well.

49:20  *Tô forever,* to thè forebears sháll you go, *          *9:7*
　　　 who nevèr móre seè light.

49:21 = 49:13
　　　 Âdam has value that òne cannot fáthom, *
　　　 unlike the cattle thàt páss àway.

## FIFTY

NEW TESTAMENT — Verse 12 at 1 Cor 12:26
LITURGY OF HOURS — Office of Readings on Monday II and Saturday IV

God rarely speaks in the psalms, but Psalm 50 issues from the mouth of God in three utterances (verses 5, 7–15, 16b–23) and thus behaves like prophetic literature. The psalm opens with a set of three divine names.

50:1 (A Mizmor of Asaph.)
**Gôd, the Divine One, FONT OF BEÌNG, †**
**has givèn word, has cálled the land \***
*from the rising of sun tò íts sètting.*

*From the rising of sun to its setting* (*mimmizrah-shemesh 'ad-mebo'o* 50:1, 113:3) circumscribes the variable hours of daylight (longer in summer, shorter in winter), but also encompasses the whole physical world of the psalmist, from East to West. The one who makes the sun shine in the sky has his house in Jerusalem (see the next verse).

50:2 **Frôm the Ziön, paràgon of beaúty, \***
**the Divine Òne mákes it shine.**

50:3 **Oûr Divine One comes, and is not silènt, †**
**flame consùming befóre his Face \***
**and about hìm ráging greàtly.**

50:4 **Hê calls from above to thè skies and tó the land, \***
**to decide àgaínst his peòple:**

50:5 **"Gâther to me, Ò my devóted ones, \***
*crafting with me a covenànt thróugh oblàtion."*

*Crafting a covenant* (*korthey briythiy* 50:5, *beriyth yikrothu* 83:6; *korattiy briyth* 89:4) employs the verb for carving (*karath*). In the ancient Middle East, contracts were sometimes carved in stone, like *kudurru* boundary markers of the Kassite period in Babylon (16th to 12th centuries BC). God's finger wrote the decalogue (the covenant with Moses) on two tablets of stone—twice.

50:6 see 97:6a
**Heâvens have tòld of his Jústice, \***
**for the Divine One hìmsélf ìs Judge:**

50:7 see 81:9

"Lîsten, O my peoplè, †
for I accuse Israël and bear wìtness agaínst you! *
*The Divine, your Divíne One* àm I.                         *45:8*

50:8   Nôr do I reprove you fòr your oblátions, *
for your whole oblations are *bèfóre me àlways*;          *16:8*

50:9   nôr do I take from your homesteàd any búllock, *
any rams fròm yoúr stòckade,

50:10  fôr mine are *all the wildlìfe of the fórest*, *
animals on the mountaìns, by the thoùsand.

*Wildlife of the forest* (*haytho-yaday* 50:10) are distinguishable from
*wildlife of the plain* (*haytho-saday* 104:11) by habitat, but both
categories include beasts which have not been domesticated.

50:11  Î have known every bìrd of the moúntains; *
also *insects of thè plaín* are wìth me.

*Insects of the plain* (*ziyz saday* 50:11, 80:14) are among *wildlife
of the plain* (*haytho-saday* 104:11) and they afflict *animals of the
plain* (*behemot sade* 8:8). They infest the *plain of Ya'ar* (*sedeh-ya'ar*
132:6) in Israël as well as the *plain of Tsoän* (*sedeh-tso'an* 78:12/43)
in Egypt. Periodically they appear in vast swarms, as in
—the second plague, of frogs (*tsefarde'iym* Ex 7:28; Ps 105:30)
—the third plague, of gnats (*kinniym* Ex 8:12; Ps 105:33)
—the fourth plague, of flies ('*arob* Ex 8:17)
—the eighth plague, of locusts ('*arbeh* Ex 10:4; Ps 105:34) and of
grasshoppers (*yeleq* Ps 105:34).

50:12  "Îf I were famished, Ì would not téll you, *
for mine is the *world ànd whát fills it.*                *24:1*

50:13  Dô I eat thè flesh of míghty bulls, *
or drink thè bloód òf rams?

50:14  Gîve oblation to the Dìvine One wíth laud, *
and fulfill to the Mòst Hígh yoùr vows,

50:15  ànd call me òn *a day óf distress;* *                    *20:2*
I will free you, and you wìll hónòr me."

50:16  Bût the Divine One says to the unjùst: †
"What does it mean for yoù to recíte my laws, *
or take my bond ùpón yoùr lips,

50:17    whîle you hàve despised díscipline, *
      and cast words òf míne behìnd you?

50:18    Îf you beheld a thief, thèn you were pleásed with him, *
      and with those unfaithfùl ís your pòrtion.

50:19    Wîth your mouth you hàve spread the évil, *
      and yoked your tongue tò thé beguìlement.

50:20    Yoû take the stand; your òwn brother yoú accuse, *
      against the son of your mothèr, yoú bring chàrges.

50:21    Thêse things you did, but I was silènt. †
      Did you think thàt I was *like you?* *          *35:10*
      I will reprove you and set things bèfóre yoùr eyes.

50:22    Kîndly discern this, *those fòrgetting Gódhead,* *
      lest I should prey, while *no rescuèr woúld thère be.*     *7:3*

*Forgetting the Divine One* (*shokekey 'elohiym* 9:18) or *forgetting the Godhead* (*shokhey 'eloah* 50:22) or *forgetting God* (*shokeku 'el* 106:21; *shokhey 'el* Job 8:13) presumes people once knew and put that knowledge out of their minds. This is willful ignorance.

The elative divine appellative **Godhead** appears three times in the singular (*'eloah* 50:22, 114:7, 139:19), including the phrase the **Godhead of Jacob** (*'eloah ya'aqob* 114:7). It also appears in the "plural of majesty" in the common form **Divine One** (*'elohiym*).

50:23    Ône who offers laud honòrs me, †
      and to him I wìll show a fîxed path, *
      with salvation fròm thé Divìne One."

NEW TESTAMENT — Verse 6 at Rom 3:4
LITURGY OF HOURS — Lauds on Friday

Profound contrition makes Psalm 51 the greatest of the seven Penitential Psalms (6, 32, 38, 51, 102, 130 and 143). The psalmist senses that he has been guilty since his conception (verse 7), and he undertakes ritual washings (4/9/12) preparatory to sacrifice (19/21). He waxes poetic with reference to hyssop and snow (9), which falls mainly on Mount *Hermon*; hence the psalmist may be a northerner, like Tobit, who worshiped in Jersusalem (20).

51:1    (For the Director. A Mizmor of David,
51:2    when there came to him Nathan the prophet,
        after he had gone in to Bathsheba.)

51:3    ***Tâke pity on me, O Divine Óne, †***
        ***as befits your mercy, as befits your great ténderness! \****     *25:7*
        **Erase my rèbéllioùs ways.**

*Pity me, O Divine One* (*honneni 'elohiy* 51:3, 56:2, 57:2). The psalmists address the Divine One for pity four times (4:2, 51:3, 56:2, 57:2), the FONT OF BEING ten times (6:3, 9:14, 25:16, 27:7, 31:10/11, 41:5/11, 123:3, 142:2) and Adonay once (30:9).

*As befits your great tenderness* (*kerob rahmeyka* 51:3, 69:17). There are two befittings in this verse (mercy and great tenderness), as again in Psalm 119:149 (mercy and judgment). Mercy usually seems to be the common factor.

51:4    **Mâke me èntirely cleánsed of guilt \***
        **and scour mè óf my sin.**
51:5    **Fôr the rebellion that is mìne I acknówledge \***
        **and my sins are *bèfóre me àlways*.**     *16:8*
51:6    **Âgainst you, only you have Ì sinned, †**
        **and done thè evil ín your Eyes; \***
        **that you be just in your Word, pùre ín your Jùdgment:**
51:7    **thât I wàs brought to bírth in guilt, \***
        **and my mother ìn sín conceìved me;**
51:8    **thât you desire truth in thè inner fórum, \***
        **and make wisdom known tò mé wìthin.**

| | |
|---|---|
| 51:9 | Âbsolve me with hyssop, ànd I will bé clean! *<br>Make me cleansed, and I will be whitèr thán thè snow! | |
| 51:10 | Grânt that I may listen wìth gladness ánd joy; *<br>let them revel, thè bónes that yoù crushed! | |
| 51:11 | *Hîde away the Fàce of You* fróm my sins, *<br>and all my guìlt wípe àway! | *30:8* |
| 51:12 | Creâte a clean heart for mè, O Divíne One, *<br>and renew firm breathing *wìthín my chest.* | *39:4* |
| 51:13 | Nôr cast me out *from bèfore the Fáce of You,* *<br>nor take the gust of your holiness àwáy fròm me. | *17:2* |
| 51:14 | Gîve me back the joy òf your salvátion, *<br>and an eager breath sùstaín ìn me: | |
| 51:15 | tô the rebèls, let me teách your ways, *<br>that sinners may còme báck tò you. | |
| 51:16 | Freê me from deeds òf blood, †<br>O Divine, *my Divine Òne of salvátion;* *<br>my tongue will sing òf yoúr jùst deeds. | *18:47* |
| 51:17 | Ô Adonày, open úp my lips, *<br>and my mouth will pròclaím your praìse-craft. | |
| 51:18 | Fôr you delight not in oblatiòn; †<br>even if I gave à whole oblátion, *<br>it would give nò pleásure tò you. | |
| 51:19 | Ôblations to the Divine One are breath brokèn, †<br>*having a heart that is broken* ánd crushed; *<br>O Divine One, dò nót dìsdain. | |

**Having a heart that is broken** (*leb nishbarah* 51:19) or **broken of heart** (*nishberey leb* 34:19; *nik'eh lebab* 109:16; *sheburey leb* 147:3). Since the Hebrews thought of the heart as the seat of intelligence, the brokenhearted were people who, assaulted by the adversities of life, had run out of solutions to their problems.

| | |
|---|---|
| 51:20 | Dô good, as yoù please, for Zíön; *<br>build up the walls of Jèrúsàlem. |
| 51:21 | Thên will you enjoy due oblatiòns, whole and cómplete; *<br>then will they ascend your oblation tablè, wíth bùllocks. |

# FIFTY-TWO

Psalm 52 holds two contrasting parables. The slanderer has a tongue that resembles a razor (verse 4); the psalmist resembles an olive plant (10). Of course, a razor is used to cut shoots from one vine for attachment to another.

52:1/2  (For the Director.
A Maskil of David, when Doeg the Edomite went and spoke to Saul, and said, "David has gone to the house of Ahimelech.")

52:3  **Whât pride can you take in the faùlts of a stróng man, \***
**while the mercy of God làsts *áll thè day*?**   *25:5*

52:4  **Yoûr tongue invents calamity like à sharpened rázor, \***
**like *one whò cómmits treàson.***

Like ***one who commits treason*** (*'oseh remiyyah* 52:4, 101:7) is the ***tongue of treason*** (*lashon remiyyah* 120:2/3; Mic 6:12). Two verses later it will be called a ***tongue of deception*** (*leshon mirmah* 52:6). The tongue is like a ***sharpened razor*** (*ta'ar meluttash* 52:4) or a ***pointed blade*** (*hereb haddah* 57:5).

52:5  **Yoû loved evìl more than thé good, \***
**falsehood more than speakìng wíth jùstice.**

52:6  **Yoû loved the all-cònsuming phráses \***
**from a tòngue óf decèption.**

52:7  **Sûrely God will *for ever* cast yoù down, †**   *9:7*
**expel you, ànd drive you fróm the tent, \***
**and uproot you from thè *lánd òf life.***   *27:13*

52:8  **Jûst people *wìll see and bé awed*, \***
**and about hìm théy wìll laugh:**

*See . . . and be awed* (*yir'u . . . weyira'u* 40:4, 52:8) is a pleasing phrase that joins two similar verbs, dropping a noun between them:
40:4 *They saw—many!—and were awed*
52:8 *They saw—the just!—and were awed.*

52:9  **"Bêhold the man not making the Divine One his fortrèss, †**
**but trusting in thè greatness óf his wealth. \***
**Can he be strong in his times òf trágèdy?"**

117

52:10  **Bût I am *like an olive tree* bearìng leaf, †**
**in *the house òf the Divíne One*; ***      *42:5*
**I trust in divine mercy *evèr ánd àn age*.**      *5:12*

*Like an olive tree* (*kezayt* 52:10). Elsewhere, too, a just individual is said to be *like a tree* (*ke'ets* 1:3, Jer 17:8). The comparison with an olive tree is expanded later where the just individual is said to have a spouse *like a fruitful branch* (*kegefen poriyyah* 128:3) and children *like olive shoots* (*kishtiley zeytiym* 128:3).

52:11  ***Êternally* will I give laud tò you, †**      *5:12*
***becaùse you have ácted*, ***      *22:32*
**and I await *your Name so good*, with yoùr faíthfùl ones!**

*So good* (*kiy tob*) is the FONT OF BEING (34:9, 100:5, 135:3, 145:9), with the Name "FONT OF BEING" (52:11, 54:8) and Mercy of the FONT OF BEING (106:1, 107:1, 109:21, 118:1/29, 136:1). The little word *kiy* ordinarily functions as the subordinating conjunction *because*, as in the first line of verse 11; however, it can also be a superlative adjective or adverb, as in the second line.

# FIFTY-THREE

NEW TESTAMENT — Verses 2-4 at Rom 3:11-12
LITURGY OF HOURS — Midday Prayer on Tuesday II

Psalm 53 is really the same poem as Psalm 14, except for one very different verse (14:5/6≠53:6). The more complex divine nomenclature in Psalm 14 would make that version seem the original.

53:1 (For the Director, *upon "Mildness."* Maskil of David.)

> *"Mildness"* (*mahalat* 53:1, 88:1) is a musical instrument or chord or melody. It is not mentioned in the title of Psalm 14, which simply reads, "For the Director. Of David."

53:2 *Ín his heart* a fool *says,* "Oh, there ìs no Divíne One." *    10:6
     People are spoiled; they act badly; there is nò dóer òf good.

53:3 Frôm the sky the Divine One espies the *chìldren of Ádam,* *
     to see if any have wisdom, seekìng thé Divìne One.    11:4

53:4 Eâch of them is disloyal, altogèther corrúpted; *
     there is no doer of good, nòt évèn one.

53:5 Dîd they not undèrstand, †
     *doers of evil,* feedìng on my peóple? *    5:6
     They fed on bread; they did not call tò thé Divìne One.

53:6 Thêre! They shook with fright without cause fòr fright, †
     for the Divine One has scattered thè bones of yoúr foes. *
     Are you shamed at how the Divine One rèjéctèd them?

53:7 Whô gives safety from the Ziön to Isràël? †
     As the Divine One *repeals the bondàge* of his peóple, *    14:7
     Jacob will revel, Isràél rèjoice.

# FIFTY-FOUR

Psalm 54 shifts between addressing God in second person (3/4/8) and addressing God in third person (5/6/9). However, perhaps the real shift in the psalm is between two addressees: God in verses 3/4/8 and the reader in 6/7. The word "Behold" in verse 6 is certainly addressed to the reader. Is the psalm a prayer to God interrupted by an aside to the reader?

| | | |
|---|---|---|
| 54:1 | (For the Director, *upon the strings.* A Maskil of David.) | *4:1* |
| 54:2 | (When the Ziphites went and said to Saul, | |
| | "Is not David hidden among us?") | *1 Sam 26:1* |
| 54:3 | **Ô Divine One, by your Nàme give me sáfety, *** | |
| | **and with your Strength intèrcéde fòr me.** | |
| 54:4 | **Ô Divine Òne, listen tó my prayer; *** | |
| | ***lend Ear to thè wórds of my mouth.*** | |

> ***Lend Ear to the words of my mouth*** (*ha'ziynah le'imrey-fiy* 54:4, 78:1) combines the verb derived from the noun ***ear*** (*'ozen*) with the noun for ***mouth*** (*fiy*). The objective is to send the psalm itself from the mouth of the psalmist directly to the Ear of God.

| | |
|---|---|
| 54:5 | **Fôr strangers rose against me, ànd tyrants soúght my soul, *** |
| | **who placed not the Divine Òne béfòre them.** |
| 54:6 | **Bêhold the Divine One, à helper tó me; *** |
| | **Adonay is one of the *sùppórts* for my soul.** |

> ***Support for My Soul*** (*somkey lenafshiy* 54:6) is an appellative of a pattern with ***Support to All Fallen*** (*somek lekol hannofliym* 145:14). Elsewhere God lends support to the psalmist (3:6) and his breathing (51:14), and to those who are just (37:17/24). Consequently, they and their hearts are well supported (111:8, 112:8).

| | | |
|---|---|---|
| 54:7 | **Gîve the evil back tò *those who gláre at me*; *** | *5:9* |
| | **by your truth, reduce thèm tó sìlence.** | |
| 54:8 | **Wîth eagerness I make òblation tó you; *** | |
| | **I laud *your Name, the* "FONT OF BEING;" *hòw goód ìt is!*** | *52:11* |
| 54:9 | **Fôr *from all distrèss* he has freéd me, *** | *34:7* |
| | **and my eye will look down ùpón my foes.** | |

## FIFTY-FIVE

NEW TESTAMENT — Verse 23 at 1 Pet 5:7
LITURGY OF HOURS —
Midday Prayer on Friday II and Office of Readings on Friday IV

Psalm 55 is a prayer of personal appeal. The psalmist uses the first person
pronoun in two-thirds of the verses, but a divine title in fewer than a third. He
wants dove-like wings to fly away from his enemies and fly up to God.

55:1    (For the Director, *upon the strings.* A Maskil of David.)                    *4:1*

55:2    **Lênd an Ear, O Divine Òne, to my práying, ***
        **and do not hide yoùrsélf from my plea.**

55:3    **Bê attuned tò me and ánswer me. ***
        **I have fallen in my ówn èsteem,**

55:4    **ând I shudder at the sound of à fiend, †**
        **in the face of àn unjust búrden, ***
        **for they make the blame fall on me, and in angèr áwaìt me.**

55:5    **My heart is thròbbing *within my chest*, ***                               *39:4*
        **and threats of death have fallèn úpòn me.**

55:6    **Feâr and trembling come upón me, ***
        **and shaking sùbmérgès me.**

55:7    **Thên I stated, "Who càn give me *dóve-like* wings? ***
        **I would fly ànd cóme tò rest.**

> *Dove-like* (*kayyonah* 55:7, Is 60:8, Jer 48:24, Hos 11:11). Direct
> comparison is not odious because doves are not birds of prey, so they
> may be consumed and sacrificed. The name Jonah means "dove." In
> all four gospels, the Spirit descends "like a dove" (Mt 3:16, Mk 1:10,
> Lk 3:22, Jn 1:32). Jesus tells his followers to be "innocent like doves"
> (Matthew 10:16).

55:8    **Hôw far would I gò in escáping? ***
        **I would dwell *in thè wíldèrness*.**

> The phrase *in the wilderness* (*bammidbar*) appears in parallel with
> its exact synonym *in the wasteland* (*biyshiymon*) three times in the
> psalms (78:40, 106:4, 107:4). Psalms mention two wildernesses by
> proper name, the **Wilderness of Qadesh** (29:8) and the **Wilderness of
> Judah** (63:1).

55:9   Lêt me hasten to a plàce that is sáfe for me *
from driving wìnd, fróm the tèmpest.

55:10   Chôke them, Adonay, wìth their own fórked tongue! *
For I have beheld abuse and conflìct ín the cíty.

55:11   *Dây and night* thèy circle hér walls, *      *22:3*
but harm and trouble àre ín hèr midst.

55:12   Dîsastèr is withín her midst, *
and never far from her plazas are fraùd ánd extòrtion.

55:13   *Nôr surely* does a fiend berate me, or I could bear ìt. †
*nor* does one hating mè vaunt abóve me, *      *9:19*
while I àm hídden fròm him.

55:14   Bût you yoùrself are thàt man, *
my fellow, my companiòn ánd my friend;

55:15   wê joined together *in the house òf the Divíne One,* *      *42:5*
as we strolled among à múltìtude.

55:16   Deâth hangs over them; they go down àlive to Shéöl, *
for injustice is in their homes, ìs ín theìr midst.

55:17   Tô the Dìvine One Í call, *
and the FONT OF BEING wìll máke mè safe.

55:18   Ât sunset ànd dawn and noóntime *
I complain and groan, and hè heárs my call,

55:19   rânsoming with Shalom my soùl from my báttle, *
though many wère thére wìth me.

55:20   Gôd heard and answèred them, †
the One seated of old, whò has no chánges, *
yet they revère nó Divìne One!

55:21   Hê put out his hands àgainst his álly; *
he has rènoúnced his òwn bond.

55:22   Hîs mouth was smoother than creàm, †
but near to hìs heart was cónflict; *
gentler his words than oil, thoùgh théy wère blades.

55:23   Câst your burdens on the FONT OF BEÌNG †
and hè will sustaín you; *
he puts no stumbling-block bèfóre the jùst one.

55:24   Bût you lower those into a pit of decay, Divine Òne! †
*Men of bloodshed* and deceìt see not hálf their days, *      *5:7*
but I will hàve trúst ìn you.

LITURGY OF HOURS — Midday Prayer on Thursday II

The fourteen verses of Psalm 56 contain not a single conjunction, in the figure of speech called by the Greeks *asyndeton*, a form of *ellipsis*. (Psalm 78 by contrast has many conjunctions in the figure of *polysyndeton*, a form of *pleonasm*.) The poetical effect is one of breathlessness, as the psalmist stands under attack from a growing number of enemies, happy to join in plundering a victim. When the would-be victim pushes back (10), the pack of predators withdraw, for they are interested only in an easy kill.

56:1    (For the Director, like "The Dove of Far-Off Gods."
        Of David. A Michtam. When the Philistines seized him at Gath.)

56:2    ***Tâke pity on me, O Divine Òne,*** †                 *51:3*
       **because a màn has been húnting me;** *
       **fighting** *all the day*, **hè présses òn me.**          *25:5*

56:3    **Thêy have sought, who glàre at me** *áll the day*; *    *25:5*
       **how many are fighting mè, ín theìr pride.**

56:4    **Ôn a day thàt I can fóresee,** *
       **I will pùt trúst ìn you.** *

56:5 see 56:11/12 and 118:6
       **Ên the Divine One is his word for me tò laud,** †
       **in the Divine Òne have I trústed;** *
       **I fear not what flesh mày dó tò me.**

56:6    *Âll the day* **my words àre turned agaínst me;** *     *25:5*
       **all their intentiòns áre for èvil.**

56:7    **Thêy conspire; thèy hide, those át my heel;** *
       **they** *keep sentinel* **while waitìng** *fór my soul.*

My enemies are like birds of prey that *keep sentinel for my soul* (*yishmoru . . . nafshiy* 56:7) to seize it, but God, too, is *keeping sentinel for my soul* (*yishmor eth-nafsheka* 121:7) to save it.

56:8    **Ênto wickèdness reléase them,** *
       **into the wrath of peoples let thèm fáll, Divìne One.**

56:9    **Tâke account for yourself of my moanìng:** †
       **let my tears be pùt in your párchments.** *
       **Are they not wìthín yoùr scrolls?**

56:10 **Whên my rivals are turned bàck, on a dáy I cry, \***
**I will know this, that the Divine One bèlóngs tò me.**

56:11 see 56:5 and 118:6

**Ín the Divine One is à word for mé to laud; \***
**in the FONT OF BEING is a word fòr mé tò laud.**

56:12 see 56:5 and 118:6

**Ín the Divine Òne have I trústed; \***
**I fear not what Adam's kind mày dó tò me.**

56:13 **Ôn me, O Dìvine One, áre your vows; \***
**I will fulfill thè laúd òf You.**

56:14 **Îndeed, you freed my soul from thè death! †**
**Did you not free my feèt from the stúmbling \***
**to walk before the Divine Face, in thè líght òf life?**

# FIFTY-SEVEN

Psalm 57 has twelve verses. The sixth and twelfth are a refrain that divides the work into two equal halves. That refrain also appears in two other psalms (108:6 and 113:4). An editor has borrowed the second halves of Psalms 57 and 60, and combined them in the composite Psalm 108.

57:1   (For the Director. *Do not destroy!* Of David. A Maskil.
       When he fled from the presence of Saul, into the cave.)    *1 Sam 22:1, 26:1*

> *Do not destroy!* (*'al-tashheth*) stands at the head of four psalms, an editor's instruction to the copyist: after you have made the copy, do not destroy the original. Because of the high cost of materials, old manuscripts were often erased to be reused; such documents, called palimpsests, can sometimes be made to reveal their original text.

57:2  **Pîty me, O Divine One, pity mè,** †                 *51:3*
       **for my soul finds shelter ín you;** *
       **in the shade of your Wings I shelter untìl dángèrs pass.**    *17:8*
57:3  **Î call to** *the Dìvine One, Móst High,* *
       **to the God, Àvénger fòr me.**

> *Divine One Most High* (*'elohiym 'elyon* 57:3, 78:56) is a divine appellative of a pattern with *God Most High* (*'el 'elyon* 78:35) and *FONT OF BEING Most High* (*yhwh 'elyon* 7:18, 47:3, 97:9).

57:4  **Hê sends from the skies and saves mè,** †
       **confoundìng** *those who húnt for me;* *            *7:2*
       **the Divine One sends** *his mercy ánd hìs truth,* *     *25:10*
57:5a

       **whîle among lions my soùl is recúmbent;** *
       **ravenous are** *the childrèn óf Àdam.* †

> *Children of Adam* (*beney 'adam*; note at 11:4). Ancient translators saw this verse as comparing the children of Adam to lions; modern translators have made the children of Adam into the object of hunger for the lions. The ancients were correct, because the word *ravenous* is not in construct state, and so cannot take an object.

57:5b

> Theîr teeth àre spear and árrows, *
> and their tongues à póintèd blade.

57:6/12 = 108:6

> Êxalted *above the skiès*, O Divíne One, *    8:2
> above *all the land* ìs yoúr Glòry.    8:2

57:7   Thêy spread nets for my feet, ìn waiting fór my soul; *
they dug before me a pit, into the midst òf whích thèy fall.

57:8 = 108:2

> *Fîrm is my heàrt*, O Divíne One! *
> *Firm is my heart! I wìll síng ànd play!*    21:14

**Firm is my heart** (*nakon libbiy* 57:8, 108:2; *nakon libbo* 112:7) is the psalmist's declaration of firm intention to remain faithful to the covenant, by the virtue of perseverance. The opposite phenomenon would be the **heart not firm** (*libbam lo'-nakon* 78:37), by the vice of fickleness or inconstancy.

57:9 = 108:3

> Âwaken, *my Glory*! Wake the hàrp and the lyre-bow! *    3:4
> I wìll wáke thè dawn!

57:10 = 108:4

> Lêt me laud you *among thè peoples*, Ádonay, *
> play for you *àmóng the nàtions.*    44·15

**Among the peoples** (*ba'ammiym* 57:10, 77:15, 105:1, 108:4). The singular **people** (*'am*) usually refers to Israël, and the plural **peoples** (*'amiym*) to the rest of the nations. Only the phrase **all you peoples** (*kol ha'ammiym* 47:2, 49:2, 96:3, 97:6, 99:2) seems to associate the gentiles with the Hebrews.

57:11 = 108:5

> Fôr great as the skiès is *your mércy*, *
> and as thè sky-dome *yoùr truth.*    25:10

57:12/6 = 108:6

> Êxalted *above the skiès*, O Divíne One, *    8:2
> above *all the land* ìs yoúr Glòry.    8:2

# FIFTY-EIGHT

LITURGY OF HOURS — Omitted from the cycle.

Interrogative marker *ha-* at the beginning of Psalm 58 keeps its force not just for one verse but well into the body of the psalm. Imperative verbs in verse 7 interrupt the interrogation and shift the mood to that of imprecation (8–11).

| | | |
|---|---|---|
| 58:1 | (For the Director. *Do not destroy!* Of David. A Michtam.) | *57:1* |
| 58:2 | **Dô you, advising silènce, speak with jústice? \*** | |
| | **With fairness do you judge *childrèn óf Àdam?*** | *11:4* |
| 58:3 | **Ôr, in the heart, do yoù fashion *foúl deeds?* \*** | |
| | **Do your hands prepare àbúse *in thè land?*** | *41:3* |

*Foul deeds* (*'olot* 58:3, 64:7) is the plural of *vice* (*'awlah*), as in the expression *those who indulge in vice* (*po'eley 'awlah* 37:1; *po'elu 'awlah* 119:3).

| | | |
|---|---|---|
| 58:4 | **Hâve unjust people stràyed since *the ténder place,* †** | *22:11* |
| | ***speakers of beguilement* erred sìnce thé bòsom?** | *5:7, 22:11* |
| 58:5 | **Îs their venom like the venòm of a sérpent? \*** | |
| | **Are they like a cobrà, deáf with eàrs closed,** | |
| 58:6 | **whìch hears not the voice of those whò handle thé ropes, \*** | |
| | **though the charmers be enchantìng ín their ways?** | |
| 58:7 | **Ô Divine One, *smash their teeth* in theír mouths! \*** | *3:8* |
| | **Defang the lions, Ò FÓNT OF BÈING!** | |
| 58:8 | **Lêt them flow *like water!* Lèt them be trámpled! \*** | *22:15* |
| | **When they aim arrows, let thèm shoót àstray,** | |
| 58:9 | **lîke a worm to dìssolve while móving, \*** | |
| | **like a woman's newborn never tò seé thè sun,** | |
| 58:10 | **bêfore a boxthorn seèn in your caúldrons, \*** | |
| | **whether green, whether glowing, tò blów àway!** | |
| 58:11 | **Lêt a just one know the joy of seèing requítal! \*** | |
| | **Let him wash his feet in the blood òf thé unjùst one!** | |
| 58:12 | **Lêt Adam say, "But there is a fruìt for the júst one! \*** | |
| | **But *there is a Divine One,* judgìng *ín thè land!"*** | *41:3* |

*There is a Divine One* (*yesh-'elohiym* 58:12, 1 Sam 17:4) is the contrary of *There is no Divine One* (*'eyn 'elohiym* 10:4).

LITURGY OF HOURS —
Midday Prayer on Friday II

The author of Psalm 59 finds himself in a city under siege. Much of his language is military: the FONT OF BEING is *Sabaöth* (verse 6); *Elohim* is a fortress (10/17/18); *Adonay* is a shield (12). The besiegers are like howling predators (7/15), but the Divine One is full of mercy (11/18).

| | | |
|---|---|---|
| 59:1 | (For the Director. *Do not destroy!* Of David. A Michtam. | *57:1* |
| | When Saul sent and kept watch on his house, to put him to death.) | |

59:2 **Dêliver me from my rivals, Ò my Divíne One; ***
**from those who rise against mè, líft mè up.**

| | | |
|---|---|---|
| 59:3 | **Dêliver me from *dòers of évil*, *** | *5:6* |
| | **and from *men of bloodshèd* máke mè safe.** | *5:7* |
| 59:4 | ***Tô attention!* They ambush my soùl; †** | *83:3* |
| | **with force thèy turn upón me. *** | |
| | **Nor did I rebel, nor did I sin, Ò FÒNT OF BÈING!** | |

59:5 **Wîth no provocation, they ìnvade and stáke a claim. ***
**Awaken to my àpproách, ànd see!**

59:6 **Ând you, FONT OF BEING! Divine Sabàöth! †**
**Divine One of Israël, awaken to assèmble all géntiles! *** *41:14*
**Take no pity for any who dally wíth èvil.**

*Divine Sabaöth!* (*'elohiym tsaba'ot*) is borrowed military language characteristic of Isaiah. These terms connect two ways:
—*Divine One of the Sabaöth* (*'elohey-tsaba'ot* 89:9), where God is the commander of the heavenly host;
—*Divine Sabaöth* (*'elohiym tsaba'ot* 59:6, 80:5/10, 84:9), where God himself is an army of one.

59:7 = 59:15
**Thêy come bàck toward the súnset; ***
**they whine like the feral dog, and run àroúnd the cìty.**

59:8 **Seê them foam *in their moùths* †** *5:10*
**with dàggers betweén their lips, ***
**for they thìnk, "Whó can lìsten?"**

59:9 **Bût you yourself, FONT OF BÈING, deríde them; ***
**you scoff àt *áll gèntiles.***

59:10 Ô their Mighty One, fòr you will Í watch, *
for the Divine One is hìgh réfuge fòr me.

59:11 My Divine One òf mercy greéts me; *
the Divine One sees me as *thèy gláre àt me.*      *5:9*

59:12 Slây them not, lest you forget which are my peoplè; †
shake them at yoùr walls, and sénd them down. *
Our shield ìs Ádònay.

59:13 Fôr sins of their mouth and words of theìr lips †
let them bè caught in theír pride; *
and for cursing and for deceit, let them bè héld to àccount.

59:14 Êclipsed in wrath—eclipsed and no more will thèy be, †
and they will know a Divine One has còmmand in Jácob, *
to *thè énds òf land.*      *2:8*

59:15 = 59:7
Thêy come bàck toward the súnset; *
they whine like the feral dog, and run àroúnd the cìty.

59:16 Thêy are the ones thàt rummage fór food; *
if they be not filled, thèn théy will bay.

59:17a Bût I àm one who síngs your might, *
and sings for joy until the *mornìng óf your mèrcies*; *      *90:14*

59:17b fôr you have been hìgh refuge fór me *
and refuge *on a day òf neéd fòr me.*

*A day of need* (*beyom tsar* 59:17, 102:3) or *a day of distress* (*beyom
tsarah* 20:2, 50:15; *beyom tsarathiy* 77:3, 86:7) is not yet *a day of evil*
(*beyom ra'ah* 27:5, 41:2; *yomey ra'* 49:6, 94:13).

59:18 Ô my Mighty One, to you I play chòrds, †
for the Divine is hìgh refuge fór me, *
my Divìne Óne óf mèrcy.

# SIXTY

LITURGY OF HOURS — Midday Prayer on Friday II

Psalm 60 begins an Elohist collection of eight psalms (60-67) in which the FONT OF BEING is mentioned only once (64:11). A later redactor connected the second half of this psalm with verses from the Elohist Psalm 57, creating the composite Psalm 108.

60:1 (For the Director, like "The Lily."
An Ordinance.
A Michtam of David. For teaching.)

60:2 (When he fought with Aram-Naharaim and with Aram-Zobah,
and Joab returned and struck Edom in the Valley of Salt — twelve thousand.)

60:3 **Ô Divine One! You raged at us! Yoù burst upón us! \***
**You became angry! Yoù túrned agaìnst us!**

60:4 **Yoû *shook thè land*! You máde her split! \***        *18:8*
**You closed her rìfts! Hów she tùmbles!**

> **You shook the land** (*hir'ashtah 'erets* 60:4; *tir'ash ha'arets* 18:8, 77:19, 2 Sam 22:8; *'erets ra'ashah* 68:9). Earthquakes appear in the psalms, because the region sits on the Great Rift Valley and is prone to earth tremors. Amos dates the start of his ministry two years before a great earthquake (Amos 1:1), to which Zechariah also refers, saying the valley between the two mountains of Jerusalem will be filled up, "as it was filled up by the earthquake in the days of King Uzziah" (Zech 14:5). More than a millennium later there would be a devastating earthquake in the Yemen, and the Qur'an says that on the Last Day people will have vertigo as they do during earthquakes.

60:5 **Yoû showed your peòple a hárd thing; \***
**you made us drink à brácìng wine.**

60:6 **Gîve those who revère you a pénnant, \***
**to be unfurled in the fàce óf the wàr-bow!**

60:7 **Thât your deàr ones be sét free, \***
**may your Right Hand give safety, ànd ánswèr us!**

60:8 = 108:8

    **Ône who is Divine said in his holy plàce: †**
    **"I gladly lày claim to Shéchem, \***
    **and survey thè Vále òf Booths.**

60:9 = 108:9

Mîne is Gileäd, and mine Manasseh, †
and Ephraïm is à helmet fór my head; *
Judàh ís my mace.

60:10 = 108:10

Môab is my washbòwl; †
on Edom Ì toss my sándal; *
above Philistia Ì shoút my joy.

60:11 = 108:11

*Whô* will secure for me à *bulwark cíty*? *                    *31:22*
*Who* will leàd mé to Èdom?"                                   *24:3*

60:12 = 108:12 see 44:10

Nôr are you, Divine Òne, angry wíth us?
Nor do you, Divine One, go oùt wíth oùr troops?

60:13 = 108:13

Êxtend to ùs help from thé siege,
since false security còmes fróm Ádam.

60:14 = 108:14

Ìn the Divine One wè achieve víctory,
for he himself sùbdúes oùr foes.

LITURGY OF HOURS — Midday Prayer on Saturday II

In Psalm 61, an Elohist hymn, Elohim appears three times (verses 2/6/8) and the Name (Shem) appears twice (6/9). The author seems to be a merchant or ambassador a good distance from the homeland (3). The psalm is pre-exilic, because it holds a prayer for the king (7). Despite a tinge of homesickness, the psalmist remains in good spirits and accompanies his own song (9).

| 61:1 | (For the Director, *upon the strings.* Of David.) | *4:1* |
|---|---|---|

**61:2   Lîsten, O Divìne One, to whát I sing; ***
**be attuned tò whát Ì pray.**

**61:3   Frôm *the limit of the land* I call tò you †**     *46:10*
**while my heàrt grows more feéble; ***
**guide me onto a rock tallèr thán Ì am.**

**61:4   Fôr you have been à refuge tó me, ***
***a tower of might* from the face of àn énèmy.**

**Tower of might** (*migdal 'oz* 61:4) describes a castle like the one in the city of Thebez (Judg 9:51), perimeter turrets as in Jerusalem (Ps 48:13) or a temple tower as in the city of Babel (Gen 11:4). It is applied metaphorically to the Name of God (Prov 18:10) and even to God himself, as here (Ps 61:4).

**61:5   Î will sojourn in yoùr tent *for áges*, ***
**take refuge in the covèr óf yoùr wings.**

**For ages** (*'olamiym* 61:5, 77:6; *le'olamiym,* 77:8, *kol-'olamiym,* 145:13) is the plural of the very common expression **for eternity** (*le'olam*). Compare the even more elegant **for an age of ages** (*dor doriym* 72:5, 102:25, Is 51:8).

**61:6   Fôr you, Divìne One, heard my vòw; †**
**you have bèqueathed a héritage ***
**to those who rèvére yoùr Name.**

**61:7   Tô the days of à king, add yét more days; ***
**let his years be lìke *áge aftèr age*.**     *10:6*

**61:8   Lêt him dwell always bèfore the Fáce Divìne; ***
**appoint *mercy and trùth* tó presèrve him.**     *25:10*

**61:9**   **Sô I play chords to honor yoùr Name** *for án age,* *          *9:19*
  **to fulfill my vòws** *dáy by day.*

*Day by day* (*yom yom* 61:9, 68:20, Prov 8:30/34), through doubling,
is a distributive way of expressing *daily* (*yomam* 1:2, 22:3, 32:4, 42:4,
55:11). Other distributive doublings of this kind include:
—*little by little* (*me'at me'at* Ex 23:30), and
—*on all sides* (*sabiyb sabiyb* 2 Chron 4:3, Ezek 37/41/42 passim).

Elsewhere this kind of doubling indicates a superlative:
—*very red* (*ha'adom ha'adom* Gen 15:30)
—*very high* (*ma'alah ma'alah* Deut 28:43)
—*very low* (*mattah mattah* Deut 28:43)
—*very proud* (*gebohah gebohah* 1 Sam 2:3)
—*very deep* (*'amoq 'amoq* Qohelet 7:24)
—*very great* (*me'od me'od* Gen 7:19, 17:2, 30:43, Num 14:7,
1 Kings 7:47, 2 Kings 10:4, Ezek 9:9, 16:13, 37:10).

## SIXTY-TWO

NEW TESTAMENT — Verse 13 at Rev 2:23, 22:12
LITURGY OF HOURS — Vespers on Wednesday II

The first word of Psalm 62 is *ach*, "only" as in the case of Psalm 73. The word starts half the verses of this psalm. Two verses (2/3) are repeated with tiny variants (6/7). This repetition is another kind of reaffirmation, which the psalmist seems to need because of the verbal abuse he has had to endure.

62:1   (For the Director, *for Jeduthun.*           *39:1*
       A Mizmor of David.)

62:2 = 62:6
      **Ônly in the Divine One is thère stillness fór my soul; \***
      **from him còmes my salvàtion.**

62:3 = 62:7
      **Ônly he is my ròck and my sáfety; \***
      **with him as my high refuge, *I cannòt stúmble greàtly.***   *112:6*

62:4   **Hôw long will you assault òne? †**
      **How lòng will you áll attack, \***
      **like a falling wall, à búrsting dam?**

62:5   **Ônly from their safe perch they plan àttack; †**
      **fond of guile, thèy bless *with their mouth,* \***     *5:10*
      **but curse wìthín thèmselves.**

62:6 = 62:2
      **Ônly in the Divìne One, be stíll, my soul; \***
      **from him indeed dèríves my hope.**

62:7 = 62:3
      **Ônly he is my ròck and my sáfety; \***
      **with him as my high refuge, *I cannòt stúmble greàtly.***   *112:6*

62:8   **My salvation and my glory depend upòn the Divíne One; \***
      **my rock of might, my refuge is ìn thé Divìne One.**

62:9   **Trûst him *in every season,* O peoplè; †**     *145:15*
      **pour out yoùr hearts befóre his Face; \***
      **the Divine One is à réfuge fòr us.**

62:10  **Ônly a breeze are *children of Adàm,* †**     *11:4*
      **a beguilement àre *children óf rank.* \***     *4:3*
      **On scales their weight all told ìs léss than à breeze.**

62:11    **Nôr place your trust in extortiòn, †**
         **nor fòr plunder hóld your breath; ***
         **nor *fix your focus* on wealth, evèn whén ìt grows.**

*Fix your focus* (*shiythu libkem* 48:14; *'al-tashiythu leb* 62:11) is a
fairly common idiom, and appears now for the second time in the
Psalms. The phrase means "concentrate your attention."

62:12    ***Ônce* has the Dìvine One spoken; ***
         ***twice* dìd Í lísten: ***

*Once . . . twice* (*'ahat . . . shetayim* 62:12) is an expression shared
with the Book of Job (33:14, 40:5). In this case God spoke once, but
the psalmist heard twice. This suggests that the divine voice echoed in
the psalmist's ear.

62:13    **Thât might belongs to the Divine Òne, †**
         **and yours, O Adònay, is mércy; ***
         **for you repay them, as befits thè deéds òf each.**

# SIXTY-THREE

Psalm 63 starts with drought imagery. The land is dry, and the psalmist's desire for God is compared to the physical sensation of thirst. In the second half of the psalm, the drought imagery is replaced by another issue, which perhaps was the real one all along: that enemies are trying to create disaster for the psalmist and for the king (verse 12).

63:1    (A Mizmor of David,
      when he was in the wilderness of Judah.)

63:2   **Ô Divine One, my God, for you I keep vigìl; †**
      **for you my soul thirsts, fòr you my flésh longs, \***
      **in a *land dry* and exhaustèd, wáterless.**

> ***In a land dry*** (*'erets tsiyyah* 63:2, 107:35) can be shortened to just ***in the dry place*** (*batssiyyah* 78:17) and can also be made plural, both in feminine form ***in the dry places*** (*batssiyyot* 105:41) and in the masculine ***for dry places*** (*letsiyyiym* 74:14).

63:3   **Sô I sought yoù in the hóly place, \***
      **to glimpse *your might* ànd youŕ glòry.**         *132:8*

> The psalmist enters the holy place to glimpse ***the Ark of Might*** (*'aron 'uzzeka* Ps 132:8; 2 Chron 6:41), abbreviated in a couple of places to ***your might*** (*'uzzeka* 63:3; *'uzzo* 78:61). See note 132:8.

63:4   **Sô good is yoùr mercy, móre than life; \***
      **my lips gìve yoú wòrship.**
63:5   **Sô will Ì bless you ín my life; \***
      **in your Name *Ì líft my palms.***

> ***I lift my palms*** (*'essah kappay* 63:5, 119:49) is a ritual gesture, but the palms are the instrument of action, and by lifting up his own agency the psalmist submits it to the guidance of the divine. One similiarly lifts up one's head (83:3), one's eyes (121:1, 123:1), and one's soul (25:1, 86:4, 143:8).

63:6   **Âs with fat or with oìl, let my soúl be filled, \***
      **and my mouth give laud with lips òf jóyfùl song.**

63:7   **Whên I call you to mìnd on my blánket, ***
*as the watches change,* **Ì múse upòn you:**

*As the watches change* (*be-'ashmurot* 63:7, 90:4, 119:148) refers to the night watches, of which the ancient Jews had three, of four hours each. The psalmist is afflicted with insomnia, and hears one watch change after another.

63:8   **Whât a hèlp have you beén to me, ***
**and** *in the shadow of your Wings* **Ì síng fòr joy!**          *17:8*

63:9   **My soul clìngs tightly tó you; ***
**your òwn Ríght Hand hòlds me.**

63:10  **Bût they seek dìsaster fór my soul; ***
**let them go** *into the lower regiòns óf thè land.*

*Into the lower regions of the land* (*betahtiyyoth ha'arets* 63:10; *betahtiyyoth 'arets* 139:15). The noun *lower regions* (*tahtiyyot*) derives from the preposition *beneath* (*tahat*). The psalmist prays that his pursuers be sent into the underworld, or at least into the lowest-lying countryside, which would be seacoast or the plains of the Dead Sea. Another psalmist claims to have been conceived there (139:15), perhaps at the priestly city of Jericho.

63:11  **Lêt people strike them with** *bòth edges óf the blade***; ***          *149:6*
**let them become mannà fór the jàckals.**

63:12  **Bût the king takes joy in the Divine Òne; †**
**they take pride, àll who are swórn to him, ***
**for closed is the mouth of those who speàk wántònly.**

# SIXTY-FOUR

The author of Psalm 64 seems to have been a warrior, a veteran of combat, because of several vivid images he takes from the arena of military conflict: the unjust sharpen tongues like blades and words like darts (verse 4), but *Elohim* shoots one long-distance arrow (8) and the battle is over.

64:1    (For the Director. A Mizmor of David.)

64:2    **"Lîsten, O Divine One!" ìs my cry ín my mind: \***
    **From threat of a foe, prèsérve my life!**

64:3    **Hîde me from thè *league of scoúndrels*, \***      *22:17*
    **from disturbances of *doèrs óf èvil*,**      *5:6*

64:4    **whô sharpèn like a bláde their tongue, \***
    **who aim their dart, a word òf bíttèrness.**

64:4    **Tô target in ambush òne who is ínnocent, \***
    **whom they shoot swiftly while thèy áre nòt seen.**

64:6    **Thêy rally themselves with *à word of wíckedness;* \***
    **they discuss setting traps; they sày, "Oh, whó can seè us?"**

The ***word of wickedness*** (*dabar ra'* 64:6, 141:4, Deut 17:1, 23:10, Qohelet 8:3; *dibrey ra'* Jer 5:28) here parallels the ***word of bitterness*** (*dabar mar* 64:4) and may be contrasted with the ***word of truth*** (*debar 'emeth* 45:5, 119:43, Jer 23:28, Qohelet 12:10).

64:7    **Thêy plan foul deeds: "We have à perfect plán of plans!" \***
    **For the innards of a man and hìs heárt àre deep.**

64:8    **Bût the Divine One shoots thèm with an árrow: \***
    **swiftly àre théy strìcken!**

64:9    **Fôr they are made tò stumble wíth their tongue. \***
    **Moved are all whò loók upòn them.**

64:10    **Ând they see, *everyone like Adàm,* †**      *39:6*
    **and they tell the deeds òf the Divíne One, \***
    **and his works, those which thèy úndèrstand.**

64:11    **Ône who is just rejoices in the FONT OF BEÌNG †**
    **and tàkes refuge ín him, \***
    **and they take pride, all *thè steádfast-heàrted.***      *7:11*

JEWISH FEASTS — Feast of Tabernacles
LITURGY OF HOURS — Lauds on Tuesday II

Psalm 65 is an invitation to join in temple praise (verses 1/5) in the Spring, at the "crowning of the year" (verse 12). At an early period, the Northern kingdom may have adopted the Assyrian New Year in the Spring, but the Jerusalem temple celebrated New Year in the Fall. Dwellers at the ends of the earth are not excluded from the feast, for the rising and setting sun invites them to participate (9). That may also be a rubric indicating this as a psalm of morning and evening.

65:1 (For the Director.
A Mizmor of David. A Song.)

65:2 **Tô you belongs the paùsing in praíse-craft, ***
**O Divine Òne ín Zìön;**

65:2/3 **ând to you bè fulfilled évery vow, ***
**O *Hearèr óf Pleáding.***

> **Hearer of Pleading** (*shomea' tefillah* 65:3) is a participial divine appellative of a pattern with **Hearer of the Needy** (*shome' 'el-'ebyoniym* 69:34).

65:3/4 **Tô you all flesh càn come, conféssing guilt; ***
**our sins overwhelmed us, but yoù cóvèred them.**

65:5 **Blêssedness belongs to the one yoù choose †**
**and bring near to abìde in your pórches! ***
**Full of goodness is your house, the sanctùm óf your tèmple.**

65:6 **Wîth marvels, *with justìce,* †**
**you answer us, *our Divine Òne of salvátion,* ***
**hope of *all limits of land*, and òf fár-òff seas,**

65:7 **raîsing ùp mountains wíth his might, ***
**since he clad hìmsélf ìn strength,**

65:8 **câlming thè roar of óceans, ***
**roar of their waves, and clashìng óf the peòples.**

65:9 **Lêt even border dwellers see sòme of your márvels; ***
**give joy to those sent to the dawn ànd tó the sùnset.**

*9:9*
*18:47*
*46:10*

65:10  Yoû tended the land and gave her embracès; †
       you often enrich hèr, O Divíne One; *
       with a *water-fílled* stream yoù ténd theìr grain. *

*Water-filled* streams (*male' mayim* 65:10; *mey male'* 73:10) are in great contrast with the dry gorges of the southern Negev (126:4), which have no water except when they are flooding.

65:11  Fôr so you tend it: †
       her furrows watered, hèr hedges léveled, *
       you softened her with rains; hèr cróps yoù blessed.
65:12  Yoû crown a yeàr with your goód things, *
       and your pathways àboúnd ìn green.
65:13  Thêy abound in grassès of the wílderness, *
       and the hillsides are girt wìth révèlry.
65:14  Clâd are meadowlands with thè sheep, †
       and the valleys ènfolded wíth grain. *
       They shout for joy! Thèy évèn sing!

LITURGY OF HOURS — Office of Readings on Sunday IV

The author of Psalm 66 was imprisoned but has been released and so can pray again in the temple. This psalmist enthusiastically offers calves, rams, a cow, goats, and incense along with his prayers (66:15); he apparently has no qualms about sacrifice as did another psalmist (51:18).

| | |
|---|---|
| 66:1 | (For the Director. A Song of David.) |
| | **Sîng out tò the Divíne One, *** |
| | *all who àre óf thè land!* |
| 66:2 | **Plây chords to thè glory óf his Name! *** |
| | **Attend to the glory òf hís praìse-craft!** |
| 66:3 | **Sây, "O Divine One, hòw awesome áre your works! *** |
| | **By your great might your foes sùbmít tò you.** |
| 66:4 | **Âll the land worshìps you, and pláys for you. *** |
| | **They** *plày chórds to yoùr Name.***"** |
| 66:5 | **Côme and see deeds òf the Divíne One, *** |
| | **an awesome thing done for** *the childrèn óf Àdam***:** |
| 66:6 | **Hôw he changed a sea into solìd land; †** |
| | **through the rivèr they could cróss by foot: *** |
| | **Therefore, let us rèjoíce ìn him!** |
| 66:7 | **Cômmander by his strength alwàys, †** |
| | **his eyes are fixed ùpon the peóples; *** |
| | **the turncoats shall nòt ríse agaìnst him.** |
| 66:8 | **Blêss, O peoplès, our Divíne One, *** |
| | **and make heard the sound òf hís praìse-craft.** |
| 66:9 | **Hê kept our souls àmong the líving, *** |
| | **and** *gave not our feet to thè stúmblìng-block.* |

8:2

9:3

11:4

*He gave not our feet to the stumbling-block* (lo natan lammot raglenu 66:9; 'al-yitten lammot raglenu 121:3) exculpates God from any imputation of sadistic behavior toward his own creatures.

| | |
|---|---|
| 66:10 | **Fôr you probed ùs, O Divíne One; *** |
| | **you tested us as silvèr ís tèsted.** |
| 66:11 | **Yoû led us ìnto the príson; *** |
| | **you put a burdèn ón oùr backs.** |

66:12   Yoû let someone ride over our heàds; †
      through flame and throùgh water wé passed, *
      but you led ùs ínto plènty.

66:13   Lêt me enter your house wìth whole oblátions; *
      let me fulfill tò yoú my vows,

66:14   thôse which hàve parted my lips, *
      and which my mouth spoke *when dìstréss wàs mine.*     *18:7*

66:15   Lêt me offer you oblations of fatlìngs, †
      with the ìncensing óf rams; *
      let me ready a cow àlóng with hè-goats.

66:16   Côme, hearken, as I tell all who revère the Divíne One *
      what he hàs dóne for my soul.

66:17   Tô him this mouth òf mine has criéd out, *
      with exalting bèneáth my tongue.

66:18   Hâd I, *within my heàrt,* revered évil, *     *10:6*
      Adonay woùld nót have lìstened.

66:19   Bût *the Divìne One has lístened,* *
      attuned to thè soúnd of my plea.

*The Divine One has listened* (*shama' 'elohiym* 66:19, 78:59) hearkens back to participial divine appellative **Hearer of Pleading** (*shomea' tefillah* 65:3) in the previous psalm.

66:20   *Blêssed be the Divine Òne!* †
      He has not turned àway my pleáding *
      or his mercy fròm béing wìth me.

*Blessed be the Divine One!* (*baruch ha'elohiym*) is a concluding formula for two psalms 6:20, 68:36). More common is the version *Blessed be the* FONT OF BEING! (*baruch yhwh* 28:6, 31:21, 41:13, 68:19, 72:18, 89:54, 124:6, 144:1), elaborations of which include *Blessed be the* FONT OF BEING *from the Ziön* (*baruch yhwh mitssiyyon* 135:21) and *Blessed be the* FONT OF BEING, *Divine One of Israël* (*baruch yhwh 'elohey yisra'el* 41:13, 72:18, 106:48).

# SIXTY-SEVEN

Psalm 67 is a big-hearted little psalm that invites all peoples of the earth (verses 4/5) to worship the Divine One of Israel (7). The first and last verses ask *Elohim* to bless, so this psalm is a prayer of benediction like the Yahwist blessing of Aaron (Numbers 6:24/26). At the very middle stands the word "fairness," like the fulcrum of a scale.

67:1 (For the Director, *upon the strings. A Mizmor. A Song.*)  *4:1*

67:2 **Mây the Divine One have pity òn us and bléss us; ***
*may he shine hìs Face* **upòn us,**  *31:17*

67:3 **tô make knòwn** *in the lánd* **your ways, ***  *41:3*
**among** *all gentìles* **yoúr salvàtion.**  *9:18*

67:4 = 67:6
**Lêt peoples laud yoù, O Divíne One! ***
**Let peoples laud yoù, áll òf them!**

67:5 **Lêt nations rejoice and sing fòr joy, †**
**for you judge peòples with faírness, ***
**and nations** *in thè lánd* **yoù guide.**  *41:3*

67:6 = 67:4
**Lêt peoples laud yoù, O Divíne One! ***
**Let peoples laud yoù, áll òf them!**

67:7 see 85:13
**Lêt land gìve forth her boúnty; ***
**may** *the Divine, our Dìvíne One,* **blèss us.**  *45:8*

67:8 **Mây the Dìvine One bléss us, ***
**and let them revere him,** *àll énds òf land.*

*Ends of land* (*'afsey-'arets* 2:8, 22:28, 59:14, 72:8; *kol 'afsey-'arets,* 67:8, 98:3), like synonymous idiom **limits of land** (*qatsweh-'erets* 46:10, 48:11, 61:3, 65:6, 135:7) can mean either the extent of the Holy Land or the edge of the continent. The latter is favored by the usage *from the river to the ends of land* (*minnahar 'ad-'afsey-'arets* 72:8), where the Jordan is the western boundary of tributary territory.

# SIXTY-EIGHT

NEW TESTAMENT — Verse 19 at Eph 4:8
LITURGY OF HOURS — Office of Readings on Tuesday III

Psalm 68 contrasts two processions—one divine (verses 8/9) and one liturgical (25/30). A characteristic of this psalm is high frequency of dual nouns. In Semitic languages, a noun can be singular, dual or plural. Western languages have no dual forms, so the Hebrew duals were all translated as plurals. Thus readers in Greek, Latin, or English can never have known how many duals are found in Psalm 68—"two bare hills" (14), "twice ten thousand" (18), "in double file" (28, after Dahood), "twofold Jerusalem" (30) and "twofold Egypt" (32). Jerusalem was a city built on two mountains (*Ziön* and *Moriah*), and Egypt was a double kingdom (Lower Egypt in the north and Upper Egypt in the south), so both of those proper names have dual endings in Hebrew.

68:1    (For the Director. Of David. A Mizmor. A Song.)

68:2 = Num 10:35

> **Rîsen be the Divine One! Routèd be his énemies, ***
> **and turned from his Face bè thóse who hàte him.**

68:3    **Âs smoke billows, may you billòw; †**
> *like* **melting of** *wàx* **from the fáce of flame, ***          *22:15*
> **let the unjust vanish from thè Fáce Dìvine.**

68:4    **Bût let the just be glad, exulting bèfore the Fáce Divine, ***
> **and rejoicìng wíth glàdness:**

68:5    **"Sîng to the Divine One! Play chords to hìs Name! †**
> **Make way for thè Rider ón the Clouds!" ***
> **They exult in the** *BEING,* **by his Name ànd tó hìs Face.**

*BEING (yah* 68:5/19, 77:12, 89:9, 94:7/12, 102:19, 115:17/18, 118:5/14/17/18/19, 130:3, 135:4, 150:6) is a shortened form of the divine name *FONT OF BEING (yhwh).*

68:6    **Fâther to orphans and defénder of wídows ***
> **is the Divine One in the abode of hìs hóliness.**

68:7    **Ône who is Divine settles lonely people in à home. †**
> **He leads prisoners oùt onto goód ground; ***
> **only rebels dwèll ín the bàdlands.**

68:8    **Ô Divine One, when you went out bèfore your peóple, ***
> **when you marched through à wíldèrness,**

68:9    *lând shook* **and skies fèll †**

from the Face Dìvine of Sínai, *
from the Face Divine, of *the Divine One òf Ísràël.*     *18:8, 41:14*

68:10   Yoû created ample rainfàll, O Divíne One; *
when your heritage was weak, yoù máde hèr strong.

68:11   Yoûr lifeguards wìthin her cán dwell; *
you supply your goods for the lowly, Ò Dívine One.

68:12   Âdonay gìves a repórt with news *
concerning à vást àrmy:

68:13   "Kîngs of àrmies—they fleé! they flee!— *
and domestic beauties dìvíde the boòty,

68:14   thoûgh you lie between twin bare hilltòps, †
with wings of à silver-leáfed dove *
and her feathèrs óf pàle gold."

68:15   Whîle the Shàdday dispérses kings, *
upon her it snows, ùpón Tsàlmon.

68:16   Moûnt Bashan is à mountain óf the gods; *
Mount Bashan is a mountaìn óf rìdges.

68:17   Ô mountains of ridges, why have you been glarìng, †
at the mount the Divine One chòse for his dwélling? *
and where the FONT OF BEING *fòr évèr* dwells!         *9:7*

68:18   Dîvine chariots are twice ten thousànd, †
with thoùsands of bówmen. *
Adonay is with them at Sinai ìn hóliness.

68:19   Yoû went up the heights! You brought back captìves! †
You took tribute along with chìldren of Ádam, *
and again they dwell with *the* BEÌNG, thé Divìne One!    *68:5*

68:20   Blêssed be Adonay; *day by dày* he sustaìns us. *    *61:9*
*Is not Gòd* oúr salvàtion?                                *18:48*

68:21   *Îs not God* for us a Gòd for salvátiòn, *          *18:48*
and FONT OF BEING-*Adonay* gives rèlìef untìl death.      *16:2*

68:22   Ônly the Divine One can crush the heàd of his énemies, *
the scalp of those who keep walking in theìr sínfùlness.

68:23   Âdonay has said, "From Bashàn I will brìng back, *
I will bring back from thè óceàn deeps,

68:24   thât your own foot mày wade in thé blood, *
the tongue of your hounds share in thè énèmy."

68:25   Thêy behold your dìvine procéssions, *
the processions of my God, of my King into thè hóly place.

68:26   Thêy draw near—singèrs, then musícians; *
in the midst àre drúmmer maìdens.

68:27   *În groups* they bless the Divine Òne, FONT OF BÉING, *    *26:12*
from the fountainhead òf Ísràël:

68:28 Thêre little Benjamin leads thèm, †
princes of Jùdah, in doúble file, *
princes of Zebulun, princes òf Náphtàli.

68:29 Âssert yoùr godhead, yoúr might, *
the might divine which you hàve úsed fòr us,

68:30 frôm your temple àbove Jerúsalem, *
where kings offèr yoú tríbute.

68:31 Rêbuke the reed livestock, a herd of mighty bùlls, †
who trample bull-calves of peoples, fòr silver búllion. *
Disperse peoples who dèlíght in fighting!

68:32 Thêy come, cloth merchànts from both Égypts; *
Cush extends his hands tò thé Divìne One.

68:33 Ô domains of the land, sing tò the Divíne One! *
Play chords tò Ádònay,

68:34 tô the Rider in the heaven òf heavens ín the East. *
See, he projects his voice, à voíce òf might!

68:35 Gîve might tò the Divíne One! *
Upon Israël is his majesty and his might ìs ín thè skies!

68:36 Âwesome is the Divine One in your holy placès! †
The God of Israël gives strength and mìght to the peóple! *
*Blessed bè thé Divìne One!*

*Blessed be the Divine One!* (*baruch ha'elohiym*) is a concluding formula (6:20, 68:36). More common is the version ***Blessed be the*** **Font of Being!** (*baruch yhwh* 28:6, 31:21, 41:13, 68:19, 72:18, 89:54, 124:6, 144:1), elaborations of which include ***Blessed be the*** **Font of** **Being** *from the* **Ziön** (*baruch yhwh mitssiyyon* 135:21) and ***Blessed*** *be the* **Font of Being,** *Divine One of Israël* (*baruch yhwh 'elohey yisra'el* 41:13, 72:18, 106:48).

## SIXTY-NINE

NEW TESTAMENT — Verse 5 at Jn 15:25
Verse 10 at Jn 2:17 and Rom 15:3
Verses 23–24 at Rom 11:9–10 / Verse 26 at Acts 1:20
LITURGY OF HOURS — Office of Readings on Friday III

Psalm 69 is a lament by one drowning (verse 2), with symptoms of severe stress (4). The psalmist admits his own guilt (6), but this did not become one of the penitential psalms. Instead, John 15:25 and Matthew 27:34/48 find in this psalm (5/22) antecedents for the suffering of the innocent Christ.

69:1    (For the Director, *upon "Lilies."* Of David.)                                    *45:1*

69:2    **Mâke me sàfe, O Divíne One,** *
        **for waters have come ùp tó thè neck.**

69:3    **Î sank into mire of the deep, and thère is no foóthold.** *
        **I entered the** *watery deeps* **and flood rùshed óvèr me.**

This psalmist likes the phrase **watery deeps** (*ma'amaqqey mayim* 69:3/15, Ezek 27:34) and uses it twice. Isaiah employs the variant **deeps of the sea** (*ma'amaqqey-yam* Is 51:10), but the word **deeps** (*ma'amaqqiym*) appears alone only once (Ps 130:1).

69:4    **Î grew weary in my callìng; rasping wás my throat;** *
        **eclipsed were my eyes from awaitìng my Divìne One.**

69:5    *Môre than hairs of my head, those hating me for nò cause;* †
        **many are they who silenced me, as** *enemiès for no reáson;* *
        **what I took not, mùst Í rèpay?**                          *40:13; 35:19*

69:6    **Ô Divine One, yoù yourself knéw my guilt,** *
        **and my sinfulness was nòt hídden fròm you.**

69:7    **Lêt me bring no disgrace to those who wait fòr you,** †
        *Adonay-FONT ÒF BEING***, Sábaöth,** *                      *16:2*
        **no shame to those who seek you,** *Divine One òf Ísräel.*   *41:14*

69:8    **Hôw much rebuke have Ì borne for yoúr sake!** *
        **My face ìs cloáked wìth shame.**

69:9    **Â stranger I became tò brothers óf mine,** *
        **and unknown to my òwn móthèr's sons.**

69:10   **Bêcause zeal for yoùr house consúmed me,** *
        **and** *the rebukes of those who rebuke yoù* **féll upòn me,**

*The rebukes of those who rebuke you* (*herpot horfeyka* 69:10; *herpatam 'esher herfuka* 79:12) combines a cognate noun and participle, like **bakers of baked goods** (*'agey ma'og* 35:16) and **sufferer of suffering** (*ra'yeroa'* Prov 11:15, 13:20).

69:11 ând I wept at thè fasting óf my soul, *
and at the rebukes thère wére fòr me.

69:12 Î gave myself *tò wearing sáckcloth* *          *35:13*
and became like à próverb tó them;

69:13 thôse sitting at the gàte find a théme ìn me, *
and strumming chords for those ìmbíbing drink.

69:14 Bût my prayer is to you, FONT OF BEÌNG, †
in a time of favòr, O Divíne One, *
*by your great mercy,* answer me truly wìth yoúr salvàtion.   *5:8*

69:15 Dêliver me from the mud lest Ì sink; †
free me fròm *those who háte me,* *          *9:14*
and *from thè wát'ry deeps.*          *69:3*

69:16 Lêt no flood of waters rush ovèr me †
and let nò deeps engúlf me, *
and no pit close ìts moúth upòn me.

69:17 Ânswer me, FONT OF BEING! How goòd is your mércy!*
*As befits your great tendernèss,* túrn tò me,     *51:3*

69:18 nôr *hide the Face of Yòu* from your sérvant; *    *30:8*
for *distress is mine! Swiftly answèr me!*      *18:7*

*Swiftly!* (*maher*) is a verb of urgency that comes before another verb with which it must be in agreement, or before an adjective:
—*Swiftly answer me!* (*maher 'eneniy* 69:18, 102:3, 143:7)
—*Swiftly did they forget!* (*maharu shokhu* 106:13)
—*Very swiftly!* (*maher me'od* Jer 48:16, Zeph 1:14).

69:19 Neâr to my soul ìs her redémption! *
Because of my rivàls, sét mè free.

69:20 Yoû know of my rèbuke †
and of my dìsgrace and óf my shame. *
Present to you àre áll my foes.

69:21 Rêbuke breaks my heart, and sickèns me; †
I wait for compàssion, but thére is none, *
and for comforters, bùt nóne have Ì found.

69:22  Thêy placed a venòm into my food, *
and for my thirst they gave mè gáll tò drink.

69:23  Lêt their table become a snàre tó their faces, *
and a trap fòr theír fèllows.

69:24  Lêt their eyes gròw dim from stáring, *
and their spines ever làck steádìness.

69:25  Poûr out ùpon them yoúr wrath; *
may *the flash of your fury* òvértàke them.

> **Flash of your fury** (*haron 'apka* 69:25; *haron 'appo* 78;49; *haron 'appeka* 85:4). Since the anger of God is *like flame* (*kemo-'esh* 79:5, 89:47; *ke'esh*, 83:15) or *like fire* (*kelehabah* 83:15), there must be a flashpoint when the anger ignites.

69:26  Lêt their càmps be abándoned; *
in their tents lèt nó òne dwell.

69:27  Fôr whenever yoù strike they fóllow, *
and of one who is stabbed thèy coúnt thè wounds.

69:28  Âdd a crìme onto theír crimes, *
and never let them entèr yoúr jùstice.

69:29  Lêt them be remòved from the scróll of life, *
and with the just let them nevèr bé ìnscribed.

69:30  Thoûgh I am òne lowly ánd in pain, *
may your salvation, O Divine Òne, líft mè high.

69:31  Lêt me laud the Name of the Dìvine One ín song, *
and let us magnify hìm wíth thè laud,

69:32  whîch to the FONT ÒF BEING ís good, *
more than an ox, than a bull òf hórns ànd hoofs.

69:33  Lôwly ones saw; they rejoice who seèk the Divíne One, *
and let theír heárts be àlive!

69:34  Fôr *Hearer of the Needy* is thè FONT OF BÉING, *                65:3
and those bound to him he doès nót bèguile.

69:35  Lêt them give laùd to him, skiés and land, *
seas, and all thàt cráwl ìn them.

69:36  Fôr the Divine One gives safety to Zìòn, †
and builds up the cìties of Júdah, *
and there will they dwell, and tò hér lày claim,

69:37  ând her heirs will be the seedlìngs of his sérvants, *
and within her will they dwell whò lóve hìs Name.

# SEVENTY

The whole short Psalm 70 coequals the last five verses of Psalm 40 (verses 14/18). In that part of Psalm 40, the divine appellations are the FONT OF BEING (three times), *'Adonay* (once) and the Divine One (once). In Psalm 70 they are the Divine One (three times) and the FONT OF BEING (twice). Since the three appellations of Psalm 40 become only two in Psalm 70, the latter shows a sign of simplification and thus of being the later edition. The appellation which drops out of the text is *'Adonay*.

70:1    (For the Director. Of David. *For mindfulness*.)          38:1
70:2 = 40:14
    **Ô Divìne One, to sét me free!** *
    **O FONT OF BEING, *tò hélp me hàsten!***      22:20
70:3 = 40:15
    **Bê they shamed and all àbashed, *who seék my soul*;** *   7:2
    **turned back and confused, whò wísh *what hàrms me*.**   35:2
70:4 = 40:16
    **Lêt them go bàck to their vále of shame,** *
    **who say to me, "Oh, *A brother? A brothèr cán he be?*"**  35:21
70:5 = 40:17 see 35:27
    **Let them sing and rejoice in you, all who seek yoù;** †
    **let those who love your sàlvation éver say,** *
    **"Great ìs thé Divìne One!"** *
70:6 = 40:18
    **Tô me also, *lowly and ìn need*,** †       35:10
    **the Divine One hastens to me, my hèlp and my freédom!** *
    **May you, O FONT OF BEÌNG, *délày not!***

   *Delay not!* (*'al-te'ahar* 40:18, 70:6, Dan 9:19) is a verb that derives
   from the preposition *after* (*'ahar*) and is synonymous with
   —*Be swift!* (*maher* 69:18, 102:3, 106:13, 143:7)
   —*Hasten!* (*hushah* 22:20, 38:20, 40:14, 70:2, 71:12).

LITURGY OF HOURS — Midday Prayer on Monday III

Psalm 71 continues the meditation on shame from the last psalm, mentioning shame in the first and last verses, as well as in the middle (verse 13). In these psalms, shame replaces guilt as the main preoccupation. Losing face with other people (shame) may not be as great a theological theme as losing standing with God (guilt), but whole cultures are built around shame-management. The psalmist is not ashamed to admit his own limitations, however. He states clearly that he does not know the full tally of the friendly and saving deeds of God (15).

71:1 = 31:2ab
> **În you, FONT OF BEING, have Ì taken réfuge! \***  $\qquad$ *7:2*
> **Let me not be shamed ètérnàlly.**  $\qquad$ *5:12*

71:2 = 31:2c/3a
> **Wîth your justice free mè and delíver me; \***
> **bend to me your Ear ànd máke mè safe!**

71:3 = 31:3b
> **Bê my rock of abode where I may evèr go; †**
> **give command thàt I be máde safe, \***
> **for *my Bedrock and my Fòrtréss* àre you.**  $\qquad$ *18:3*

71:4
> **Ô my Divine Òne, †**
> **free me from thè hand of óne unjust, \***
> **from the grasp of one wickèd ánd oprèssing.**

71:5
> **Fôr you are my hope, *Adonày-FONT OF BÉING*, \***
> **my confidènce fróm my youth.**

Two appellatives join as ***Adonay-FONT OF BEING*** (*'adonay yhwh* 69:7, 71:5/16, 73:28) or ***FONT OF BEING-Adonay*** (*yhwh 'adonayh* 16:2, 68:21, 109:21, 140:8, 141:8). In the synagogue, FONT OF BEING eventually came to be read as *Adonay*. When the FONT OF BEING and *Adonay* are together, the reading is *Adonay, Adonay.*

71:6
> **Î was helped by you *from the bosòm*; †**  $\qquad$ *22:11*
> **from within my mòther you dréw me; \***
> **ever will my praise-craft bè foúnd ìn you.**

71:7
> **Î became like à sign for mány, \***
> **for you àre my strong rèfuge.**

71:8   *Filled is my moùth* with your praìse-craft, *
    *all the day* wìth yoúr glòry.              *25:5*

*Filled is my mouth* (*yimmale' piy* 71:8) with your praise-craft, our
mouth with laughing (126:2) and the right hand of God with justice
(48:11). The land is filled with mercy (33:5) and glory (72:19) and
creatures (104:24). Nonetheless, my insides are filled with pain (38:8),
for a mouth is filled with deceit and threat (74:20) and his right hand
with bribes (26:10); the darkest places of the land are filled with dens
of abuse (74:20). The near synonym *saba'* means to be filled to the
brim (65:5, 88:4, 104:13/16/28, 123:3/4, 144:13).

71:9   Nôr cast me àside in beárded age; *
    nor, in the eclipse of my mìght, *fórsàke me,*       *27:9*
71:10  fôr my rivals have spòken agaínst me, *
    and those keeping sentinel on my soul consultèd ín coùncil,
71:11  sâying, "The Divine Òne has forsáken him! *
    Follow and seize him, *for no rescuèr wíll thère be!"*   *7:3*
71:12  Ô Divine One, *bè not aloóf from me!* *         *22:12*
    O my Divine One, *tò hélp me hàsten!*         *22:20*
71:13  Shâmed, eclipsed be they who test my soùl, †
    enfoldèd in scorn ánd disgrace *
    be they *seekìng whát hàrms me.*          *35:26*
71:14  Bût as for mè, still do Í hope, *
    as I have enlarged all yoúr praìse-craft.
71:15  Thîs mouth of mine tells your justìce, †
    *all the dày* your salvátion, *         *25:5*
    though the tallies are *ùnknówn tò me.*     *18:44*
71:16  Î come into strength, *O Adonày-*FONT OF BÉING; *   *16:2*
    I keep in mind your justìce, yoúrs àlone.
71:17  Ô Divine One, you hàve taught me fróm my youth, *
    and *to the present* Ì téll your màrvels.
71:18  Ûntil bearded and gray, Divìne One, *forsáke me not,* *   *27:9*
    until I tell of your Arm to an age, tò áll whò come.
71:19  Yoûr Strength and your divìne Justice áre on high! *
    Since you do great, divine thìngs, *whó is lìke you?*   *35:10*
71:20  Thoûgh you showed me many harsh troublès, †
    again revive me ànd again líft me up *
    from deep wìthín thè land.

71:21  Âgain and àgain reléase me, *
       and again bè ténder tò me.
71:22  Sô I laud you on your harp of trùth, my Divíne One; *
       I play *on a lyre-bow* for you, *Holy One òf Ísràël.*          *33:2*

*Holy One of Israël* (*qedosh yisra'el* 71:22, 78:41, 89:19) is a divine
appellative. The Divine One is holy (99:9) along with his Name (*shem*
33:21, 103:1, 105:3, 106:47, 145:21) and his Arm (*zaroa'* 98:1).
Holiness accrues to his place (*maqom* 24:3), his abode (*ma'on* 68:6),
his throne (*kis* 47:9), his temple (*heykal* 79:1, 138:2), his mount (*har*
2:6, 3:5, 15:1, 43:3, 48:2, 99:9), his height (*marom* 102:20) and his
summit (*gebul* 78:54).

71:23  Lêt my lips sing for jòy, yes, play chórds for you, *
       along with my soul, whìch yoú rèdeemed,
71:24  ând let *my tongue all day rèpeat your júst deeds*; *     *25:5, 35:28*
       so shamed, so abashed are they seekìng *hárm fòr me.*       *35:26*

## SEVENTY-TWO

**NEW TESTAMENT** — Verse 10–11 at Mt 2:11
**LITURGY OF HOURS** — Vespers on Thursday II

In Psalm 72 God gives a sense of justice to the royal heir (1), that he may rule with justice for all (2), especially the poor (4/12/13), and extend equity even to the nations (17). The enemy in this psalm seems to be the Canaanite moon god *Yarikh* (verse 7), after whom the city of Jericho got its name.

72:1     (Of Solomon.)
**Ô Divine One! Give yoùr judgment tó a king,** *
**and your justìce tó a kìng's son.**

72:2     **Lêt him decide for your peòple *with jústice*,** *          9:9
**and for your lowly ònes *with jùdgment*.**

*With justice* (betsedek 9:9, 17:15, 65:6, 72:2) and ***with judgment*** (*bemishpot* 72:2, 112:5) stand in strict parallel; elsewhere the two nouns form a unified phrase together (33:5, 89:15, 97:2, 99:4, 119:7/62/106/121/160/164). Justice fills the Right Hand of God (48:11), but judgment is in his Mouth (105:5, 119:13).

72:3     **Lêt mountains arìse in Shalòm for the peóple** *
**and hilltòps ín jùstice.**

72:4     **Lêt him judge for the lowly of the peoplè;** †
**make safe the chìldren of óne in need,** *
**but crush the èxtórtiònist.**

72:5     **Lêt them find yoù awesome wíth the Sun,** *
**and before the faces of the Moon, *àn áge of àges*.**

*An age of ages* (dor doriym 72:5, bedor doriym 102:25, ledor doriym Is 51:8) will be the mathematical square of a single human generation. If the duration of a generation is forty years (95:10), then a generation's worth of generations would be eight centuries.

72:6     **Lêt him descend like rain ùpon a coúntryside,** *
**like showers tò dámpen thè land.**

72:7     **Ín his days let a just one ànd *grand shalóm* sprout up,** *
**until thère bé nò Moon,**          *37:11*

72:8     **ând let him govern fròm the sea tó a sea,** *
**and from the river tò *énds òf land*.**         *2:8*

72:9    **Bêfore his face let desèrt peoples bów down, \***
        **and his rivàls eát thè dust.**

72:10   **Lêt kings of Tarshish and thè isles retúrn with gifts; \***
        **kings of Sheba and Saba àpproách with trìbute,**

72:11   **ând let all thè kings bow dówn to him, \***
        *all thè géntiles* **sèrve him.**           *9:18*

72:12   **Îndeed, let him rescue a needy òne who beseéches, \***
        **and a lowly one for whom** *no helpèr wíll thère be.*

*No helper will there be* ('*eyn-* '*ozer* 22:12, 72:12, 107:12, Is 63:5) is a
defeatist statement, of a pattern with
—*There is no rescuer* ('*eyn-matssiyl* 7:3, 50:22, 71:11)
—*There is no savior* ('*eyn-moshiya*' 18:42, 2 Sam 22:42, Deut
22:27, 28:29/31, Judg 12:3, Is 47:15, Hos 13:4).

72:13   **Lêt him care for òne** *poor and neédy*, **\***
        **and save the souls òf thóse ìn need.**

*Poor and needy* (*dal we'ebyon* 72:13, 82:4) is equivalent to the more
common phrase *lowly and in need* ('*aniy we'ebyon* 35:10, 37:15,
40:18, 70:6, 74:21, 86:1, 109:16/22, 116:16). Though each phrase has
two terms, they describe a single person. Twice the psalmist refers to
himself as *lowly and in need* (86:1, 109:22).

72:14   **Frôm oppression and abuse lèt him redeém their souls, \***
        **and precious let their blood bè, ín hìs eyes.**

72:15   **Lông let him live! And to him be givèn gold of Shéba! \***
        **So pray for him always; bless hìm** *áll thè day.*    *25:5*

72:16   **Lêt stands of grain be** *in thè land*; †          *41:3*
        **waving their fruits atop mountains lìke those of Lébanon; \***
        **let them grow outside the city** *like a plant* **ùpón thè land.**

*Like a plant* (*ke'eseb* 72:16, *kemo 'eseb* 92:8; *ka'eseb* 102:5/12).
Hebrew poetry has many plant similes—*like chaff* (*kammots* 1:4,
35:5), *like grass* (*kehatsiyr* 37:2, 90:5, 103:15, 129:6), *like an olive*
(*kezayt* 52:10, 128:3), *like a tree* (*ke'ets* 1:3, Jer 17:8), *like a vine*
(*keyereq* 37:2), *like a branch* (*kegefen* 128:3).

72:17   **Lêt his name endure** *eternàlly*; †          *5:12*
        **in the face of the Sun, ènduring bé his name, \***
        **and blessed in him be** *all gentìles*; **lét them blèss him.**   *9:18*

72:18    **Blêssed be the FONT OF BEÌNG,** †
        **the Divine,** *the Divìne One of Ísraël,* *             *41:14*
        **who alone is** *Makèr óf màrvels.*

        *Maker of Marvels* (*'oseh nifla'ot* 72:19, 86:10, 136:4; *'oseh pele'*
        77:15) is a divine participial appellative of a pattern with:
        —*Maker of Great Things* (*'oseh gedolot* 106:21)
        —*Maker of the Heavens* (*'oseh hasshamayim* 136:5)
        —*Maker of Heavens and of Land* (*'oseh shamayim wa'arets*
        115:15, 121:2, 124:8, 134:3, 146:6)
        —*Maker of Judgment* (*'oseh mishpot* 146:7)
        —*Maker of Lights* (*'oseh 'oriym* 136:7).

72:19    **Ând blessed** *eternally* **be hìs Name of Glóry,** *      *5:12*
        **and filled with his Glory be** *all the land.*
        *Àmén and àmen!*                     *8:2, 41:14*

LITURGY OF HOURS — Office of Readings on Monday IV

Psalms 62 and 73 both begin with the emphatic word *Ach*. That psalm of twelve verses had six verses starting with this word; this psalm of twenty-eight verses has four, but well distributed throughout (verses 1/13/18/19).

73:1    (A Mizmor of Asaph.)
**Âll-good is the Divìne One to Ísraël, ***
**to** *those whò áre pure-heàrted,*        24:4

73:2    **bût as for me, my feet could slìp** *in a móment*; ***    2:12
**my legs, as if nòt thére, gìve way.**

73:3    **Hôw angry I grew at those whò blandish "Shálom" ***
**when I beheld that they wère únjust peòple.**

73:4    **Îndeed thèy need no shroúds for death, ***
**for sound ìs theír bòdy!**

73:5    **Thêy have nò human troúbles, ***
**nor do they grow sick along wìth Ádàm's kind.**

73:6    **Sô there ìs pride aboút their necks; ***
**they enfold a raiment of àbúse aboùt them.**

73:7    **Theîr eyes secrète milky teárdrops; ***
**they overflow with figmènts óf thè mind.**

73:8    **Thêy mock, ànd speak with málice; ***
**extortion from on high ìs hów thèy speak.**

73:9    **Sêt against thè heavens áre their mouths, ***
**while their tongues are prowlìng** *in thè land.*    41:3

73:10    **Sô his people còme back to thís place, ***
**and siphon** *ample watèrs* **fór thèmselves,**    65:10

73:11    **ând declare, "Woè? How could Gód know? ***
**Is there knowlèdge ín the Mòst High?'**

73:12    **Âttention! These are thè unjust peóple, ***
**and, ever at ease, thèy grów ìn wealth!**

73:13    **"Ônly in vain have I kèpt my heart púrified, ***
**and** *washed my palms intò cleánlìness?*    26:6

73:14    **Î have beèn troubled** *áll the day,* ***    25:5
**and struggled** *t'wàrd thé dàwn times."*    30:6

73:15  Hâd I spoken, had Ì talked like thís, behold: *
    I would have betrayed a generatiòn óf your chìldren.

73:16  Âs I mulled ovèr how to fáthom this, *
    it seemed like troublè ín my eyes,

73:17  ûntil I came into Gòd's holy pláces, *
    that I might fathom theìr héreàfter:

73:18  Ônly onto a slippery slòpe you will sét them; *
    you will make them fall ìntó rùbble.

73:19  Ônly they will grow frightened, àll of a súdden! *
    They will come to an end, takèn by sùrprise!

73:20  *Lîke a dream* on awàkening, Ádonay, *
    on arising you dismiss thèm ás phàntoms.

*Like a dream* (*kahalom* 73:20) is a major literary theme (*La vida es sueño* by Pedro Calderón de la Barca) and Eastern philosophy (world as illusion, or *maya* in Sanskrit). The Hebrew poets consign to a dream only the unjust people (73:12/20), the godless (Job 20:8) and the nations arrayed against Jerusalem (Is 29:8).

73:21  Fôr my heart ìndeed is áching, *
    and I feel as if pierced ìn thé kídneys,

73:22  ând am stunned, ànd cannot fáthom; *
    I have been cow-lìke néxt tò you.

73:23  Bût I àm ever wíth you; *
    grasp me by the hand ùpón my right.

73:24  Wîth your counsèl give me guídance, *
    and later take mè ínto glòry.

73:25  Whô is for mè in the heávens? *
    And with you, I covet nothìng *in thè land.*      *41:3*

73:26  Thoûgh eclipsed bè my heart ánd my flesh, *
    rock of my heart and my eternal portion ìs thé Divìne One.

73:27  Fôr behold how those far fròm you becóme nil; *
    you reduce to silence all whò stráy fròm you.

73:28  Bût I find it good being near the Divine Óne, †
    I put my trust in *Adonày-Font of Béing,* *     *16:2*
    to speak àll yoúr messàges!

# SEVENTY-FOUR

LITURGY OF HOURS — Midday Prayer on Tuesday III

In Psalm 74, Mount Ziön stands in ruins (verse 3). What remains for the remnant of the people, disgrace (1) or return to grace? The psalmist recounts the disaster in detail (3–8), including the Akkadian word for battle axe (6). In the face of great defeat, after the temporal end to the Israëlite state and temple worship, the psalmist writes a poem of hope for the ages.

74:1   (A Maskil of Asaph.)
> **Hôw long, O Divine One, will you dìsdain?** †
> *For ever* **will your angèr be igníted,** *          *9:7*
> **against the** *sheepfold of yoùr pástùre land?*

*Sheepfold of your pasture land* (*tso'n mar'iytheka*) seems a passing metaphor the first couple of times it enters the text (74:1, 79:13), but will grow to become a major central theme (*tso'n mar'iytho* 100:3). The people of the pasture land are indeed like sheep (*'am mar'iytho wetso'n* 95:7), whose holy land has been laid waste.

74:2   **Keêp in mind your band that you bought òf old,** †
        **that you redeemed as the trìbe of your héritage,** *
        *the Mount of Ziön,* **òn whích yoù dwelt.**     *48:3*

74:3   **Lîft your steps** *evèr* **to the rúbble,** *      *9:7*
        **despite all the damage done by a fiend in thè hóly place.**

74:4   **Yoûr besiegers shouted in thè midst of yoúr shrine,** *
        **where they posted their signàl-flágs às signs.**

74:5   **Ît is knòwn how they lífted axe** *
        **as if against à gróve òf trees.**

74:6   **Thên the whole of ìts wooden cárvings** *
        **they chopped with a felling axe ànd báttle àxes.**

74:7   **Thêy cast into thè flame your hóly place;** *
        **to the ground they defiled the dwellìng óf yoùr Name.**

74:8   **Thêy said** *in their hearts,* **"In cònsort we crúsh them!"** * *10:6*
        **They burned all shrines of God** *withín thè land.*  *41:3*

74:9   **Wê have seen none of our signàl-flags.** †
        **No longer is thère any próphet,** *
        **and no one with ùs knóws hòw long.**

74:10 **Hôw long, O Divine One, will à foe show dísrespect? \***
  **Will a fiend *for evèr* scórn yoùr Name?** *9:7*

74:11 **Tô what purpose dò you hold báck your Hand? \***
  **May your Right Hand eclipse thèm fróm your bòsom!**

74:12 **Fôr *the Divìne One, my Kíng* of old, \*** *5:3*
  **doer of saving deeds in the middlè óf thè land:**

74:13 **yoû who divided à sea by yoúr might, \***
  **you who *above the waters* smashed heads òf crócòdiles,** *29:3*

74:14 **yoû who crushed the heàds of Levíathan, \***
  **you who gave it as food for peoplè, *fór dry plàces,*** *63:2*

74:15 **yoû who set spring ànd stream to flówing, \***
  **you who dried up the flowing of à steády stream.**

74:16 **Tô you belongs the dày, and to yoú the night; \***
  **you set in place thè líght and thè sun.**

74:17 **Yoû established àll borders óf land. \***
  **Summer and wintèr: thése yoù made.**

74:18 **Keêp in mind how a fiend taunted yoù, FONT OF BÉING, \***
  **and a foolish peoplè scórned yoùr Name.**

74:19 **Nôr give the soul of your turtle-dòve to the wíldlife, \***
  **nor *ever* forget the lives of yoùr lówly ones.** *9:7*

74:20 **Keêp to the bond, for the *darkèst places* óf the land \*** *88:19*
  **are replete wìth déns of àbuse.**

74:21 **Lêt not their deceit detaìn an oppréssed one;**
  ***those lowly and in need* wìll laúd yoùr Name.** *35:10*

74:22 **Rîse up, O Divine One! *Pùrsue your ówn suit!* \***
  **Keep in mind how a fool taunts yoù, *áll thè day.*** *25:5*

74:23 **Fôrget nòt the call óf your foes! \***
  **Growing still is the din of those who ròse úp agaìnst you!**

## SEVENTY-FIVE

LITURGY OF HOURS — Midday Prayer of Wednesday III

Psalm 75 exhibits a key word *qeren*, "horn," four times (verses 5/6/11a/11b), not as the horn of a living animal (22:22, 69:32, 92:11) or as the horn of the oblation table (118:27) but as the horn of battle. The *Bhagavad Gita* opens with a vivid description of sea shells calling for the start of hostilities on the battlefield. Each battalion had distinct instruments and anthems.

75:1  (For the Director. *Do not destroy!*            *57:1*
       A Mizmor of Asaph. A Song.)

75:2  **Wê give laud to you, Divine Òne! †**
      **We laud you, fòr near is youŕ Name! ***
      **They rècoúnt your màrvels:**

75:3  **"Fôr I wìll seize the móment. ***
      **I myself wíll rùle with faìrness.**

75:4  **Thoûgh land may quake ànd all that dwéll in her, ***
      **I myself set her pillàrs ín position."**

75:5  **Î said to boastful peoplè, "Do no boásting!" ***
      **and to unjust people, "Let nò hórn be lìfted!"**

75:6  **Lîft not yoùr horns agaínst the heights! ***
      **You speak with a posture òf ínsòlence!**

75:7  ***Nôr surely* from the sunrise, nòr *from the súnset ***
      ***nor* from the wildernèss dó they lìft them.**            *9:19*

> ***From the sunset*** (*mimma 'arab* 75:7, 103:12, 107:3) is a territorial idiom "from the West." Temporal idioms are ***at sunset*** (*'ereb* 55:18) or ***towards the sunset*** (*la 'ereb* 59:7/15, 90:6; *'adey- 'areb* 104:23).

75:8  **Fôr the Divìne One gives júdgment; ***
      **this one he casts down, and this one hè raísès up.**

75:9  **Fôr in the Hand of the FONT OF BEING there is à cup †**
      **and mulled wine infused wìth spice he poúrs from it; ***
      **they drained the dregs; they drank, all unjùst óf thè land!**

75:10 **Bût I will còntinue speáking, ***
      **playing chords for *the Divine Òne óf Jàcob,***            *20:2*

75:11 **ând I will clip all the horns òf unjust peóple; ***
      **lifted high will be the hòrns óf the jùst one.**

161

LITURGY OF HOURS — Midday Prayer of Sundays II and IV

Psalm 76 reflects the same sentiments as the famous prophecy of breaking swords into plowshares (Isaiah 2). Other nations also worshipped gods of peace, but gave considerably more cult to their gods of war. In Rome, for example, the Emperor Augustus built a gigantic Temple of Mars but years later a small Altar of Peace. Israël has only one God, who rules in peacetime as well as in wartime, and is more powerful than bow or shield or sword or any instrument of war (verse 4). God has the means at his disposal to impose peace upon the nations (7), whether they want it or not. He is truly awesome (5/8/12/13), and the land is filled with awe for him (9).

76:1    (For the Director, *with strings.*
      A Mizmor of Asaph. A Song.)                       *4:1*

76:2   **Fâmed is the Divìne One in Júdah; ***
      **in Israël, hìs Náme ìs great.**

76:3   **Foûnd is hìs booth in Sálem, ***
      **and his dwellìng pláce in Zìön.**

76:4   **Thêre he has broken thè flamìng wàr-bow, ***
      **shield and blade ànd toóls of còmbat.**

76:5   **Yoû are the òne who is feársome! ***
      **More splendid than thè jágged moùntains!**

76:6   **Stoût-hearted people were cast dòwn; †**
      **into à stupor théy fell, ***
      **and no men of combat coùld fínd theìr hands.**

76:7   **Ûpon your rebuke, *Divìne One of Jácob*, ***      *20:2*
      **both of them halted, both chariòt ánd stàllion.**

*Divine One of Jacob* (*'elohey ya'aqob* 20:2, 46:8/12, 75:10, 76:7, 81:2/5, 84:9, 94:7) is a divine appellative interchangeable with *Divine One of Israël* (*'elohey yisra'el* 41:14, 59:6, 68:9, 69:7, 72:18, 106:48).

76:8   **Yoû are awesòme, †**
      **and *who can stand bèfore the Fáce of You*, ***    *17:2*
      **against yoùr tíme òf wrath?**

*Who can stand?* (*miy ya'amod,* 76:8, 130:3, 147:17, Prov 27:4) is a rhetorical question, the clear answer to which is "no one." Here are other questions of this type:

—*In Sheöl, who can give laud to you?* (6:6)
—*One's own lapses, who can fáthom?* (19:13)
—*Who can deliver him? Who can free him?* (22:9)
—*To whom can he be so pleasing?* (22:9)
—*Who can awe me? . . . Who can frighten me?* (27:1)
—*Who is like you?* (*35:10, 71:19, 89:9*)
—*Who can give me dove-like wings?* (55:7)
—*Who can listen?* (59:8)
—*Who can see us?* (64:6)
—*Who is a god as great as the Divine One?* (77:14)
—*Who in the sky-dome can equal the FONT OF BEING?* (89:7)
—*Who is like the FONT OF BEING among the children of gods?* (89:7)
—*Who can make known the might of your wrath?* (90:11)
—*Who can express the strong deeds of the FONT OF BEING?* (106:2)
—*Who can sound all his praise-craft?* (106:2)
—*Who is like our divine FONT OF BEING?* (113:5)

| | | |
|---|---|---|
| 76:9 | **Frôm the skies yoù sounded júdgment; *** | |
| | **the land wàs áwed and grèw still;** | |
| 76:10 | **rîsing** *for the judgment* **ìs the Divíne One, *** | *25:9* |
| | **to make safe all lowly peoplè óf thè land.** | |
| 76:11 | **Zeâl of Adam's kìnd gives laud tó you; *** | |
| | **with tokens of zeal yoù gírd yoùrself.** | |
| 76:12 | **Sweâr and greet the FONT OF BEÌNG, your Divíne One! *** | |
| | **O you from every side, pay tribute to thè Áwesòme One,** | |
| 76:13 | **snâtching away thè breath of prínces, *** | |
| | **fearsome tò** *eárthly kings!* | *2:2* |

# SEVENTY-SEVEN

Psalm 77 recalls the Divine One with feeling (4). The psalmist asks a set of questions about God's future mercies (8/9/10) and in mid-psalm (11) states the crux of his problem: whether God has changed his modus operandi. The answer is a cascade of concrete examples from the history of salvation. God's past actions are a reliable barometer of present and future activity.

| | | |
|---|---|---|
| 77:1 | (For the Director, *for Jeduthun.* Of Asaph. A Mizmor.) | *39:1* |
| 77:2 | **Câlling am I to the Divìne One, and Í will shout: \*** | |
| | **calling am I to the Divine One, so lend àn Eár tò me!** | |
| 77:3 | ***Ôn a day of distress for me,* I sought Adònay; †** | *20:2* |
| | **my hand, nightly extènded, did nót gròw numb. \*** | |
| | **My soul refuses tò bé consoled.** | |
| 77:4 | **Lêt me call to mind the Dìvine One ánd sigh; \*** | |
| | **let me muse, as *my breáth grows feèble.*** | |

**As my breath grows feeble** (*tith'attef ruhìy* 77:4; *tith'attef 'alay ruhìy* 142:4, 143:4) describes shortness of breath. Other common medical complaints include weakened bones (31:11, 32:3, 33:11), straining bosom (31:10), shuttered eyelids (77:5), dimmed eyes (69:24, 88:10), stumbling ankle (18:37) or foot (116:8), broken heart (34:19, 109:16, 147:3), unsteady spine (69:24), rasping throat (69:4, 102:6), clinging tongue (22:16, 137:6, Lam 4:4).

| | | |
|---|---|---|
| 77:5 | **Yoû have shuttèred up my éyelids; \*** | |
| | **I am troubled and Í cannòt speak.** | |
| 77:6 | **Î have mulled òver the dáys of old, \*** | |
| | **the years *òf ágès past.*** | *61:5* |
| 77:7 | ***În the night* I will recall my sòngs: †** | *42:9* |
| | ***with my heàrt* I will máke reply, \*** | *10:6* |
| | **as my spirìt ís àsking:** | |
| 77:8 | **"Cân it be that Adonay wìll spurn *for áges,* \*** | *61:5* |
| | **and never bè pleásed àgain?** | |
| 77:9 | **Îs his mèrcy *for éver* gone? \*** | *9:7* |
| | **Has his speaking ended fòr *áge aftèr age?*** | *10:6* |
| 77:10 | **Hâs God forgòtten the píties? \*** | |
| | **Has he cut short in anger hìs Téndèrness?"** | |

77:11 Ând I grant thàt my concérn is this: *
a change in the Right Hànd óf the Mòst High!

77:12 Î keep in mind the deèds of *the BÉING*; *  68:5
indeed, I keep in mind your marvèls fróm òf old.

77:13 Î have mùsed over áll your works, *
and reflected on thè thíngs yoù do.

77:14 Ô Divine One, your ways leàd into hóliness. *
Who is a god as great às thé Divìne One?

77:15 Yoû are the God, *Màker of márvels*; *  72:19
you make known *among thè péoples* yoùr might.  57:10

77:16 Yoû redeemed by your Arm your own péople, *
the *children of Jacòb* ánd of Jòseph.

*Children of Jacob* (*beney ya'aqob* 77:16, 105:6) are the **house of Jacob** (*bet-ya'aqob* 114:1) or the **children of Israël** (*beney yisra'el* 103:7, 148:14).

77:17 Wâters behold you, Divine One! Wàters behóld you! *
The deeps are stirring; indeéd, thèy shake.

77:18 Cloûds release water; thè skies give fórth a call. *
How yoùr árròws dance!

77:19 *Soûnding of your thunder* is in the vortèx; †
lightning bolts flash, thè cosmos quívers *
and the *land bègíns tò shake*.  18:8

*Sounding of your thunder* (*qol ra'amka* 77:19, 104:7) follows an idiomatic pattern shared by *the sound of laud* (*qol todah* 26:7, 42:5*)*, *sound of song* (*qol rinnah* 42:5, 47:2, 118:15), *sound of my pleading* (*qol tahnunothay* 86:65; *qol tahnunay* 116:1, 130:2, 140:7) and *shofar sounding* (*qol shofar* 47:6, 98:6).

77:20 Îr the ocean are yoùr lanes †
and your paths *in waters mánifold*, *  18:17
but your deeps rèmaín ùnknown.

77:21 Guîde *like the sheèpfold* your péople, *  49:15
by the hand of a *Mosès* ánd an *Aàron*.

*A Moses and an Aaron* (*mosheh we'ahron* 77:21, 99:6; *mosheh . . . 'ahron* 105:26; *lemoshe le'ahron* 106:16). This psalmist asks for another leader like Moses and another priest like Aaron.

# SEVENTY-EIGHT

NEW TESTAMENT — Verse 2 at Mt 13:35
Verse 24 at Jn 6:31 / Verse 37 at Acts 8:21
LITURGY OF HOURS — Office of Readings on Friday and Saturday IV
only in the seasons of Advent and Christmas, Lent and Easter

Psalm 78 is based on a proverb about Ephraïmite archers failing to join battle (verse 9). The tribe of Ephraïm is mentioned five times in the psalms, twice in this psalm (2/67). Joshua was a member of that tribe, which exercised leadership in times of both war and peace. The psalmist situates the Ephraïmite withdrawal among the historic failures of the nation.

78:1   (A Maskil of Asaph.)
*Lênd an ear,* **my peoplè, to my teáching;** *
    **bend your ears** *to thè wórds of my mouth.*     *54:4*

78:2   **Wîth a proverb I wìll open my mouth,** *
    **pour forth riddlès fróm òf old,**

78:3   **whîch we hàve heard and únderstood,** *
    **and which oùr fórebears tòld us,**

78:4   **whîch we did not hide from their offsprìng,** †
    **but told a later age the praise-craft of thè** FONT OF BÉING, *
    **and his might, and his marvèls whích hè did.**

78:5   **Hê set statutes in Jacob, and in Israël hè put a Tórah,** *
    **which he told our forebears tò shów their òffspring,**

78:6   **thât they would show the next age, childrèn yet to bé born,** *
    **to grow up ànd téll their òffspring,**

78:7   **ând they would place in the Dìvine One theír trust,** *
    **and not forget the deeds of God, bùt keép his còmmands,**

78:8   **nôt to be** *like their forebears,* **à hard and bítter brood,** *
    **a brood unwise of heart, whose breath assentèd nót tò God.**

*Their forebears* (*'abotham* 78:8/57) is from the noun *father* (*'ab*), which is purely masculine in the singular. In the plural it takes a feminine ending (*-ot*) and can have masculine or common gender.

78:9   **"Sôns of Ephraïm, armed proùdly with wár-bows,** *
    **retreated on à dáy of còmbat."**

78:10  **Thêy did not keep the bond òf the Divíne One,** *
    **and they refused to** *follòw hís Tòrah.*

*Follow his Torah* (*ubetoratho laleketh* 78:10; *holekiym betorath yhwh* 119:1). The combination of the verb *to walk* (*halak*) with the preposition *by* (*be-*) is a characteristic Hebrew idiom for *to follow*. Within the psalms, things followed in this way are advice (1:1), the Torah (78:10, 119:1), and pathways (128:1).

78:11 **Thêy did not keep in mind thè things he hád done, ***
**and his marvels whìch hé had shòwn them.**

78:12 **Bêfore their forebears hè made a márvel ***
**in the *land of Egypt, on thè plaín of Tsòän.***

The *land of Egypt* (*'erets mitsrayim* 78:12, 81:6/11) is the *land of Ham* (*'erets ham* 105:23/27, 106:22), *both lands* (*'artsayim* for *'artsam* 105:30/32/35/36), *both topsoils* (*periy 'admathayim* for *'admatham* 105:35, Deut 28:4/18), and *Rahab* (*rahab* 87:4, 89:11).

*The plain of Tsoän* (*sedeh-tso'an* 78:12/43). The capital of Egypt's 24th to 26th Dynasties (724 to 526 BC) was the Delta city of Zau, called in Hebrew *tso'an*. That name (Is 19:11/13, 30:4; Ezek 30:14) dates this psalm to the period between the fall of North and South.

78:13 **Hê divided à sea and lét them cross, ***
**and made waters stand ùp líke à wall.**

78:14 **Hê led thèm with a cloúd by day, ***
**and all the night with à líght òf flame.**

78:15 **Hê divided ròcks *in the wíldèrness*, *** 55:8
**and gave drink as if from thè *greát àbyss*.** 36:7

78:16 **Hê brought forth *running watèrs* from the bédrock, ***
**and like the rivers, he sent thè wátèrs down.**

*Running waters* (*nozliym* 78:16/44) is another term that appears in no other psalm, but connects this psalm with other books of the Hebrew Bible (Ex 15:8, Is 44:3, Prov 5:15).

78:17 **Thêy added still to thè sin agaínst him, ***
**for begrudging the Most High, *in thé dry place*.** 63:2

78:18 **Ín their hearts thèy put God tó the test, ***
**to demand sustenànce fór their lives.**

78:19 **Thêy spoke out agaìnst the Divíne One; ***
**they said, "Could God spread a table *in thè wíldèrness*?** 55:8

78:20 **Îf he strikes rock so watèrs gush and cúrrents flow, ***
**can he also give bread, or hang up meat fòr hís peòple?"**

78:21 **Thên the FONT OF BEING heard and respondèd, †**
**and flame was enkìndled at Jácob, ***
**and wrath too rose up agaìnst Ísràël.**

78:22 ***Nôr surely* did they believe ìn the Divíne One, ***
***nor* did they trust ìn hís salvàtion.** 9:19

78:23 Hê commandèd the skies fróm above, *
and opened the floodgàtes óf thè skies.

78:24 Hê rained on thèm manna tó eat, *
and gave them graìn fróm thè sky,

78:25 breâd of mighty bèings that mén could eat; *
he sent enough fòr thém to bè filled.

78:26 Hê stirred *eàstward winds* ìn the skies, *                48:8
and by his might he drove à désèrt wind.

78:27 Hê rained meat ùpon them *líke dust*, *                18:43
and bird of wing lìke sánd of thè seas.

78:28 Hê caused them to drop into thè midst of theír camps, *
all àroúnd their dwèllings.

78:29 Thêy ate; they wère greatly sátisfied, *
and he brought thèm whát thèy craved.

78:30 Frôm their cràvings they swérved not; *
still their food wàs *in theìr mouths,*                5:10

78:31 âs the anger of the Divine One rose up against thèm, †
and he slaughtèred some of theír troops, *
and made the young men of Israël tò bénd thè knee.

78:32 Ín all of thìs, still did théy sin, *
and did not assent tò hís màrvels.

78:33 Hê eclipsed their days in á breeze *
and theìr yeárs in thè dread.

78:34 Îf he struck them, thèn would they seék him, *
and return tò thoúghts òf God.

78:35 Thêy called to mind that the Dìvine One wás their rock, *
and that God Most High was a Rèdeémer tò them.

78:36 Bût they dèceived him *ín their mouths*, *                5:10
and beguiled hìm wíth theìr tongues,

78:37 ând their *heart wàs not made firm* for him, *                57:8
nor did they gìve àssént to hìs bond.

78:38 Bût he tenderly covered their guìlt and did nót destroy. *
Again he abated his anger and fanned nòt áll hìs wrath.

78:39 Hê kept ìn mind how théy were flesh, *
a breeze that goes ànd wíll not còme back.

78:40 Hôw many times they begrudged hìm *in the wílderness!* *
They grieved hìm *in the wàsteland!*                55:8

*In the wilderness* (*bammidbar* 55:8, 78:15/19/40a, 95:8, 106:14/26, 107:4) is more common than the exactly synonymous phrase **in the wasteland** (*biyshiymon* 78:40, 106:4, 107:4). The latter occurs only in parallel with the former in the psalms.

78:41 Âgain and àgain they témpted God, *
and provoked *the Holy One òf Ísràël.*                    71:22

78:42 Thêy kept not in mind hòw helpful hé had been *
on the day he ransomed thèm fróm dìstress,

78:43 whên he posted ìn Egypt hís signs, *
and his portents *on thè plaín of Tsòän:*                    78:12

78:44 trânsforming theìr channels ínto blood
(their *running waters* thèy coúld nòt drink);                    78:16

78:45 sênding against them à swarm to feéd on them, *
and froglèts tó pollùte them;

78:46 gîving to the grasshòpper their hárvest,
and their hard work tò thé lòcust;

78:47 strîking down wìth the hailstórm their vines, *
and their mulberry bushès wíth thè frost;

78:48 cônsigning tò the hailstórm their flocks,
and their herds to thè flásh-lìghtning;

78:49 sênding against them *the flash of his fury* †                    69:25
(invasion ànd rancor ánd siege, *
a phalanx of àvénging àngels);

78:50 cleâring a pathway for hìs wrath; †
sparìng not from deáth their lives; *
giving even their livestòck tó thè plague;

78:51 see 105:36
strîking every firstborn in Égypt *
(first fruits of their potency in thè ténts òf Ham);

78:52 brînging out *like the sheèpfold* his peóple, *                    49:15
and guiding them like a herd through thè wíldèrness;

78:53 leâding them *to a plàce of secúrity*, *                    4:9
lest they should fear as the sea engulfed theìr énèmies;

78:54 brînging them to his sùmmit of hóliness, *
to the mountain his Rìght Hánd hàd made;

78:55 drîving out gentiles before their facès; †
making a heritage fall tò them by súrvey line; *
settling in their tents the tribes òf Ísràël,

*Driving out gentiles* (*yegaresh goyim* 78:55; *tegaresh goyim* 80:9) uses
the same verb as to divorce a wife (Lev 21:7). The gentiles who defiled
the land by human sacrifice are being divorced from it.

78:56 whô tested and begrudged *the Dìvine One Móst High*, *
and kept nòt hís dècrees.

*Divine One Most High* (*'elohiym 'elyon* 57:3, 78:56) is a divine

appellative of a pattern with:
—*God Most High* (*'el 'elyon* 78:35)
—*FONT OF BEING Most High* (*yhwh 'elyon* 7:18, 47:3, 97:9).

78:57   *Lîke their forebears* again thèy acted wíthout faith, *     *78:8*
        undone like a hunting-bòw oút of bàlance.

78:58   Thêy provoked him òn their high pláces, *
        and with their carvings aroused hìs jeáloùsy.

78:59   *Ône who is Divine heàrd,* and grew ángry, *     *66:19*
        reacting strongly agaìnst Ísràël;

78:60   fôrsaking the dwellìng place of Shíloh, *
        a tent of dwelling wìth Ádàm's kind;

78:61   gîving up *his might* ìnto captívity, *     *132:8*
        and his splendor into thè hánd of à foe;

The psalmist refers to the Ark under the title *the Ark of Might* (*'aron 'uzzeka* Ps 132:8; 2 Chron 6:41). This title is abbreviated here to *his might* (*'uzzo* 78:61; *'uzzeka* 63:3). See 132:8.

78:62   dêlivering hìs people tó a blade; *
        becoming enraged against hìs hérìtage,

78:63   âgainst their young mèn with consúming flame, *
        so their maidens would have nò sérènade.

78:64   Wîth the blade their priests were broúght down, *
        but their widòws coúld nòt weep.

78:65   Âwakenìng like a sleéping man, *
        Adonay was like a strong man, who knèw jóy fròm wine;

78:66   pûshing bàckwards his énemies; *
        giving them ètérnàl shame;

78:67   tûrned against thè tent of Jóseph, *
        and against the tribe of Ephraìm, which hè díd nòt choose;

78:68   choôsing thè tribe of Júdah, *
        the *Mount of Zìon,* whích hè loved;     *48:3*

78:69   buîlding up like thè heights his hóly place, *
        which *like the land* he supports ètérnàlly;     *5:12*

*Like the land* (*ka'arets* 78:69). God supports the temple as he does the land; elsewhere my soul thirsts like the land (143:6).

78:70   choôsing Dàvid his sérvant; *
        taking him from pens òf thé sheèpfold;

78:71   frôm the care of sucklìng lambs †
        he gave him to shepherd Jàcob his peóple, *
        and Israël hìs hérìtage,

78:72 **ând as befits his _integrity òf heart_ he pástured them, ***
**and with the skill of hìs pálms he lèd them.**

*His integrity of heart* (*kethom lebabo* 78:72; *bethom lebab* 1 Kings 9:4; *bethom lebabiy* 101:2, Gen 20:5; *bethom lebabka* Gen 20:6) describes David's inner qualities, but *skill of his palms* (*bithbunoth kappaw* 78:72) describes his outer abilities. Hence these two phrases are not synonymous, though they stand in parallel.

# SEVENTY-NINE

LITURGY OF HOURS — Midday Prayer on Thursday III

Mention of the temple in the first verse indicates that Psalm 79 is post-Davidic. Clearly from the first verse onwards, Jerusalem lies in ruins, so the psalm comes from the time of exile. The psalmist himself is a prisoner (verse 11) and seeks vindication from the Divine One. Nonetheless, the last verse declares an intention to praise *Adonay* regardless of the outcome of this prayer. Our praise is not conditional on the Lord obeying our will.

79:1    (A Mizmor of Asaph.)
**Ô Divine One! Gentiles invàded your héritage, ***
**defiled *your temple of holiness*, made a ruin of Jèrúsàlem.**

*Your temple of holiness* (*heykal qodsheka* 79:1, 138:2) is literally ***"the temple of your holiness."*** Semitic grammar precludes that the first noun in a genitive phrase may take a prefix or suffix; these must be attached to the last noun in the phrase. This is an ironclad rule in Arabic even today; on the other hand, Chancery Aramaic apparently lost the genitive phrase altogether during Persian times.

79:2    **Thêy gave the bodies of your servànts †**
**as food to *thè birds of heáven*, ***
**flesh of your devoted ones to *wildlífe óf thè land*.**

*The birds of heaven* (*'of hasshamayim* 79:2, 104:12) are the larger birds that fly and nest in the trees. Those that ate carrion were not kosher for the Mosaic kitchen. The Assyrians and Persians had the custom of exposing the dead to be eaten by the birds; the psalmist shares the horror of Tobit at this practice.

*Wildlife of the land* (*haytho-'arets* 79:2; *hayyath ha'arets* Gen 1:30, 9:2/10 etc.) comprise undomesticated, non-flying creatures of the land, who happily compete with the birds for the carcasses of dead animals or of warriors fallen in battle.

79:3    **Thêy poured their blood *like water*, àbout Jerúsalem, ***
**and there was no one tò búry them.**     *22:15*
79:4 = 44:14
      **Wê became a *rebuke tò those who dwéll with* us, ***     *44:14*
      **scorn and derision tò thóse aboùt us.**

172

79:5 = 89:47

**Hôw long, O FONT OF BÈING, will yoú reject?**
*For ever* **will your angèr bláze** *like flame*?                    *9:7*

*Like flame* (*kemo-'esh* 79:5, 89:47; *ke'esh* 83:15) stands parallel to *like fire* (*kelehabah*) in Psalm 83. The psalmist did not like the exposure of corpses to birds in verse 2; now he seems to exclude cremation. Flame is a sign of anger to the psalmist, and for him not the kind of funerary rite that would bespeak the mercy of God.

79:6    **Poûr your wrath on the gentiles whò do not knów you, ***
        **and on domains that fail to call ùpón yoùr Name.**
79:7    **Fôr one of them hàs fed on Jácob, ***
        **and they have emptied hìs pástùre lands.**
79:8    **Keêp not in mind against us the guilt of orìginal peóples; ***
        **let your tenderness quickly come to us, for we àre véry low.**
79:9    **Hêlp us, our** *Divine Salvation*, **for the glory of yoùr Name, †**
        **and deliver us and còver our sínfulness ***          *18:47*
        *for thè sáke of yoùr Name.*                          *25:11*
79:10   **Why do gentiles say,** *"Where is their Divine Òne?"* **†**     *42:4*
        **Be it known** *among the gèntiles*, **befóre our eyes: ***      *9:12*
        **for the spilled blood of your servants thère ís rèdress.**

79:11 see 102:21 see 79:11

        **Let there come** *before the Face òf You* **†**               *17:2*
        **the groanìng of a cáptive;**
        **by your great Arm reprieve** *thòse doómed tò death,*

*Those doomed to death* (*beney themuthah* 79:11, 102:21) are the *"children of the death penalty."* The psalmist asks for the granting of executive clemency, to lift the penalty from himself and others.

79:12   **ând repay our neighbors** *seven-fòld*, **in their bósoms, ***   *12:7*
        **for** *their rebukes by which they rebuked yoù*, **Ádònay.**      *69:10*
79:13   **Bût we, your people and** *sheep of your pastùre land,* **†**    *74:1*
        **we wìll laud you álways, ***
        *for age after age* **rècíte your praìse-craft.**                 *10:6*

Lauds on Thursday II / Midday Prayer of Thursday III

Psalm 80 presents the little tribe of Benjamin nestled between the two Joseph tribes, Ephraïm and Manasseh (verse 3). So this psalmist's point of view is Benjaminite rather than Judahïte. Use of the appropriated military term *Sabaöth* (5/15) suggests a dating in the time of Isaiah.

80:1 (For the Director, *upon "Lilies."* An ordinance. Of Asaph. A Mizmor.)      *45:1*

80:2 **Shêpherding Isràël, †**
   **lend an Ear, guiding Josèph** *like the sheépfold,* *      *49:15*
   *seated upon thè Chérùbim.*

*Seated upon the Cherubim* (*yosheb hakkerubiym* 80:2, 99:1) is one of the participial divine appellatives, along with *Seated in the Skies* (*yosheb basshamayim* 2:4, 123:1) as well as *Seated in Ziön* (*yosheb tsiyyon* 9:12). Also related are *Rider on the Clouds* (*rokeb ba'arabot* 68:5) and *Rider in the Heaven of Heavens in the East* (*rokeb bishmey shemey qedem* 68:34).

80:3 **Shîne on the face of Ephraïm and Benjamìn and Manásseh!***
   **Bestir your strength ànd cóme to sàve us!**
80:4 = 80:8/15/20
   **"Ô Divine Òne, come back tó us,** *
   **and shine your Face, ànd wé will bè saved!"**
80:5 *Ô FONT OF BEING! Ò Divine Sábaöth!* *      *59:6*
   **Why have you fumed at the prayer òf yoúr peòple?**
80:6 **Yoû made thèm eat bread teárfully,** *
   **and drink teardròps by the threè-fold.**
80:7 **Yoû made us contention** *for those who dwéll with us,* *      *44:14*
   **and our enemies hàve scórn fòr us.**
80:8 = 80:4/15/20
   **"Ô Divine One! O Sabaòth! Come back tó us,** *      *59:6*
   **and shine your Face, ànd wé will bè saved!"**
80:9 **Yoû uprooted à branch from Égypt;** *
   **you** *drove out gentiles* **and caused hèr tó be plànted.**      *78:55*
80:10 **Yoû dug fùrrows befóre her face;** *
   **she spread her roots; shè fílled thè land.**

80:11 Êclipsed were mountaìns in her shádow, *
and the cedars of Gòd by her brànches.

80:12 Shê sent forth hèr tendrils *tóward sea,* *
*and toward rivèr* hér òffshoots.

*Toward sea and toward river* (*'ad-yam we'el nahar* 80:12; *bayyam ubanneharot* 89:26). Israël appears as a branch (*gefen*) in verse 9. The next three verses elaborate the metaphor. As a branch sends out roots toward sources of water, the vine of Israël spread west to the Mediterranean and east to the Jordan. Compare *from the sea to a sea* (*miyyam 'ad-yam,* 72:8a) and *from the river to ends of land* (*minnahar 'ad-'afsey-'arets,* 72:8b).

80:13 Why did *yoù split her báttlements?* *
That they might poach her, *all whò páss thè way?*

This verse contains two idioms, *you split her battlements* (*paratsta gedereyha*) and *all who pass the way* (*kol-'obrey-darek*), which are both reprised in Psalm 89:41/42. The second idiom, which means passing along the way and not crossing the highway, also appears in the first two chapters of Lamentations (1:12 and 2:15).

80:14 Trâmpling her is a boàr from the fórest, *
and upon her an *insect of thè plaín* mày feed.                    *50:11*

80:15 = 80:4/8/20
"Ô Divine One! Sabaòth! Kindly cóme back!" *                    *59:6*
Bend down from the skies and see, ànd ténd thìs vine,

80:16 ând the root which your Rìght Hand has plánted, *
and the son you strengthèned ás yoùr own.

80:17 Hâving beèn scorched in prúning flame, *
they become nil at the rèbúke of yoùr Face.

80:18 Mây your Hand be on someòne, †
your own Right Hand on à *son of Ádam* *                    *8:5*
whom you strengthèned ás yoùr own.

80:19 Sô let us nòt turn awáy from you; *
give us life, as in yoùr Náme wè call:

80:20 = 80:4/8/15
"Ô FONT OF BEING! Ò Divine Sábaöth! *                    *59:6*
Come back to us! Shine your Face, and wè wíll bè saved!"

# EIGHTY-ONE

EARLIEST MANUSCRIPT — Verses 3–17 in Masada Psalm Scroll
TEMPLE LITURGY — Thursday
JEWISH FEASTS — New Year
LITURGY OF HOURS — Lauds on Thursday II

Psalm 81 provides liturgy for one of the holy days of Israël, with song (verse 1) and playing instruments (3), including the ram's horn (4). New Year took place at New Moon (4), but Passover at Full Moon. The *Torah* mandates temple worship for adult males on those high holy days (5), which remained harvest festivals with ritual meals (17).

| 81:1 | For the Director, *upon the Gittith.* Of Asaph. | *8:1* |
|---|---|---|
| 81:2 | **Sîng with joy to our mìghty Divíne One; ***<br>**shout to *the Divine Òne óf Jàcob.*** | *20:2* |
| 81:3 | **Plûck a string ànd tap a tímbrel, ***<br>**a lovely lyre with thé hàrp-bow.** | |
| 81:4 | **Plây the shofàr on a Néw Moon, ***<br>**on the Full Moon, fòr oúr feàstday.** | |
| 81:5 | **Îndeed, that is à law for Israël, ***<br>**a judgment of *the Divine Òne óf Jàcob,*** | *20:2* |
| 81:6 | **împosed on Joseph as he left thè *land of Égypt.* ***<br>**I hear lips *ùnknówn tò me:*** | *78:12*<br>*18:44* |
| 81:7 | **"Frôm the shoulder I have tàken their búrden; ***<br>**from their palms has thè báskèt passed.** | |
| 81:8 | ***Dûring the siege* you called, and I set yoù free; †**<br>**I answered you, disguìsed in a thúnder-bolt: ***<br>**I probed you *by the watèrs óf Merìbah.*** | |

*The waters of Meribah* (*mey meriybah* 81:8, 106:32), also called Massah (95:8, Ex 17:7) in the wilderness of Kadesh, were the turning point in the life of Moses, the moment of doubt that kept him from entering the promised land. It becomes a paradigm for the moment of truth in our moral lives, when we show who we really are in the face of adversity.

81:9 see 50:7

**Lîsten, O my people, as I bear wìtness agaínst you! ***
**O Israël, if only you woùld lísten tò me!**

81:10 Âmong you there shàll be no stránge god, *
nor shall you worship à fóreìgn god.

81:11 *Î am the* FONT OF BEING, *your Divine Òne,* †
who brought you up from thè *land of Égypt.* *     *78:12*
Open your mouth ànd Í will fill it!

> *I am the* FONT OF BEING, *your Divine One* (*'anokiy yhwh 'eloheyka*
> 81:11) is God's introduction to the Decalogue (Ex 20:1, Deut 5:6);
> compare ***The Divine, your Divine One am I*** (*'elohiym 'eloheyka*
> *'anokiy* 50:7). The psalmist's own affirmation is ***My Divine One are***
> ***you!*** (*'elohay 'attah* 31:15; *'eliy 'attah* 140:7).

81:12 Nôr did my peòplè hearken tó my voice, *
nor did Isràél obèy me.

81:13 În their hardness of heàrt I gave reín to them: *
'Let them proceed *by theìr ówn devìces.*'     *5:11*

81:14 Îf only my peòple would heár me! *
If Israël woùld wálk in my ways,

81:15 Î would suppress their rivàls *in a móment,* *     *2:12*
and turn my Hand àgaínst theìr foes."

81:16 Thôse hating the FONT OF BEING feign sùbmission tó him, *
so that will be their móment àlways,

81:17 bût he would feèd one *with creám of wheat*: *
"and from the rock, with honèy woúld I fill you!"

> ***Cream of wheat*** (*heleb hittiym* 81:17, 147:14). Fatty cream rises to the
> surface in the separation of milk. By extension, the word cream comes
> to mean the best of anything, as in ***the cream of land*** (*heleb ha'arets*
> Gen 45:18). This is an idiom in modern languages as well (*la crème*
> *de la crême*).

## EIGHTY-TWO

**EARLIEST MANUSCRIPT** — Masada Psalm Scroll
**TEMPLE LITURGY** — Tuesday
**NEW TESTAMENT** — Verse 6 at Jn 10:34
**LITURGY OF HOURS** — Midday Prayer on Monday IV

Psalm 82 uses the divine appellative *Elohim* four times, referring twice to the Hebrew God (verses 1/8) and twice to pagan gods (1/6). The relationship between them seems one of greater and lesser, not of true versus false. By the end of the psalm, the gods seem reduced to the level of mortal beings (7), but they are in progressive decline to the state of nullity (96:5, 97:7).

82:1 (A Mizmor of Asaph.)
**Ône who is Divine has presided in à council óf God; ***
**in midst of 'divine ones' hè óffers jùdgment:**

82:2 **"Hôw long will yoù judge unfaírly, ***
**lifting up the faces òf únjust peòple?**

82:3 **Jûdge on behalf of òne poor and órphaned; ***
**to one lowly and dèpríved, give jùstice.**

82:4 **Dêliver one who is *poor and neédy*; ***          *72:13*
**from the *hand of unjust peoplè* sét hìm free."**      *36:12*

82:5 **Nôr did they know, nor did they undèrstand;**
**in thè gloom they gó about, ***
**as the *bases of the world* tottèr, áll òf them.**      *18:16*

82:6 **Î asked, "Àre you 'divíne ones?' ***
**Are you children of the Most Hìgh, áll òf you?**

82:7 **Râther, you shàll die like Ádam, ***
**and like one of the princès, yoú shàll fall."**

82:8 **Ârise, O Dìvine One! *Júdge the land!* ***
**Indeed, you make heirs amòng áll the gèntiles!**

*Judging the land* (*shoftah ha'arets* 82:8; *lishpot ha'arets* 96:13, 98:9) was a sovereign task, which God delegated to the uncrowned *judges of the land* (*shoftey ha'arets* 2:10, 148:11).

# EIGHTY-THREE

EARLIEST MANUSCRIPT — Masada Psalm Scroll
LITURGY OF HOURS — Excluded from the cycle

Psalm 83 is a litany of Israël's enemies of Israël present (verses 7/8/9) and past (10/11/12). The great enemy Assyria appears almost as an after-thought (9). The neighbors allied with Assyria seem to have done much of the heavy work in bringing down the Israëlite state.

83:1 (A Song.
A Mizmor of Asaph.)

83:2 **Ô Divine Òne!** *Nor take yoúr rest!* *
*Nor be deaf,* **and nor bè stíll, Ò God!**  *28:1*

83:3 *Tô attention!* **Your rìvals are híssing,** *
and *those hating you lifted òne úp às head.*  *9:14, 24:7*

> **To attention!** (*kiy hinneh* 11:2, 59:4, 83:3). Being a conjunction of emphatic *kiy* with equally emphatic *hinneh*, this issues a strong call for the attention of the addressee. This may be a standard military order, like "On your guard!" or "Look sharp!"

83:4 **Âgainst your peòple they fórm a league,** *
**and counsel each other àgaínst your deàr ones.**

83:5 **Thêy said, "Come, let us strìp them of nátionhood,** *
**and call no more to mind the name òf Ísràël."**

83:6 **Fôr they are conspiring, in heart unìted agaínst you;** *
*they are crafting à cóvènant:*  *50:5*

83:7 **tênts of Edom and òf Ishmaélites,** *
**of Moab and òf Hágàrites,**

83:8 **ôf Gebal and Àmmon and Ámaleq,** *
**Philistia with dwellèrs ón the Tyre-Rock.**

83:9 **Âshur as wèll is alliéd with them,** *
**become a right arm for thè chíldren òf Lot.**

83:10 **Deâl with them as with Midiàn, as with Sísera,** *
**as with Yabin at thè Ríver Qìshon.**

83:11 **Thêy were destròyed at the Sprìng of Dor;** *
**they becàme dúng for thè fields.**

83:12 **Mâke them, their princes, like Orèb and like Zéëb** *
**and like Zebah and like Zalmunna, àll their èlite,**

83:13  whô declared, "Let ùs claim for oúrselves *
　　　　the grazing lands òf thé Divìne One."

83:14  Ô my Divine One, make thèm like the stúbble, *
　　　　like thistle *toward thè fáce òf wind,*　　　　　　　*35:5*

83:15  *lîke flame* thàt burns a fórest, *　　　　　　　　　*79:5*
　　　　or like fire that enkíndlès thé moùntains.

> *Like flame* (*kemo-'esh* 79:5, 89:47; *ke'esh*, 83:15) stands parallel to
> *like fire* (*kelehabah* 83:15) in the central imagery of this psalm. In verse
> 14 desiccated desert foliage creates a danger; in verse 15 the mountain
> forests ignite in a conflagration, and in verse 16 updrafts push the winds
> to gale force. The poet has seen this happen before.

83:16  Thûs pursue thèm with your témpests, *
　　　　and with your gale wìnds búffèt them.

83:17  Fîll up theìr faces wìth shame, *
　　　　that they may seek your *Name, thè "FÓNT OF BÈING."*　　*7:18*

83:18  Lêt them be shamed ànd shaken *fór an age,* *
　　　　and be disgraced, ànd bécòme nil,

> *For an age* (*'adey-'ad* 83:18, 132:12/14) is equivalent to the more
> common phrase *for an age* (*la'ad* 9:19, 19:10, 21:7, 22:27, 37:29, 61:9,
> 111:3/8/10, 112:3/9, 148:6). The preposition *for* (*'ad*) takes a fuller
> form (*'adey-*) when preceding a word that begins with the consonant
> Ayin, as in the phrase *towards the sunset* (*'adey-'areb* 104:23). The
> preposition *'ad* and the noun *'ad* seem to come from the same root, and
> add up to something like "beyond the beyond."

83:19  ôr let them knòw †
　　　　that you are the one whose Name ìs "FONT OF BÉING," *
　　　　that you alone are Most High ovèr *áll thè land.*　　*8:2*

# EIGHTY-FOUR

EARLIEST MANUSCRIPT — Masada Psalm Scroll
LITURGY OF HOURS — Lauds on Monday III

Psalm 84 (verse 7) describes the pilgrim path through the Valley of *Baca* ("weeping," mentioned only here) and the Plain of *Moreh* ("rain," also at Gen 12:6 and Deut 11:30). The language is metaphorical, for pilgrims must pass through *Baca* and *Moreh*, Weeping and Rain. On arrival the pilgrims go before the oblation tables of the Lord (verse 4), of which there were two—one for incense (141:2) and one for animals (51:21). In the rafters above both of the altars, birds nested with their young. The irony must have been striking. The birds on the altar symbolized the ram and the free birds, Isaac.

| | | |
|---|---|---|
| 84:1 | (For the Director, *upon the Gittith.* | *8:1* |
| | Of *the Sons of Qorah.* A Mizmor.) | *42:1* |
| 84:2 | **Hôw lovely are thè places whére you dwell, *** | |
| | **O Font of Beìng, Sábàöth!** | |
| 84:3 | **Pîning and even fainting is my soùl †** | |
| | **for the porches of thè Font of Béing; *** | |
| | **my heart and my flesh sing for joy to thè lívìng God.** | |
| 84:4a | **Êven a bird finds her home, and thè swallow hér nest, *** | |
| | **in which she càn pút hèr young,** | |
| 84:4b | **ât your oblation-tables, O Font òf Being, Sábaöth, *** | |
| | ***my King ànd my Divìne One!*** | *5:3* |
| 84:5 | **Blêssedness belongs to thòse dwelling ín your house! *** | |
| | **For evèr wíll they laùd you.** | |
| 84:6 | ***Blêssedness belongs to Adàm's kind, †*** | *84:13* |
| | **to those whò find their stréngth in you! *** | |
| | ***Within their heàrts áre the pàthways:*** | *10:6* |
| 84:7 | **crôssing the Baca Vallèy, †** | |
| | **to thè Spring they sét their route; *** | |
| | **while Moreh enfolds thèm ín blèssing.** | |
| 84:8 | **Thêy go from a statiòn to a státion; *** | |
| | **God, the Divine One, comes intò víew in Zìön!** | |
| 84:9 | ***Ô Font of Being! Ò Divine Sabaöth! *** | *59:6* |
| | **Listen to my prayer! Lend an Ear, *Divine Òne óf Jàcob!*** | |

181

*Divine One of Jacob* (*'elohey ya'aqob* 20:2, 46:8/12, 75:10, 76:7, 81:2/5, 84:9, 94:7) is a divine appellative interchangeable with *Divine One of Israël* (*'elohey yisra'el* 41:14, 59:6, 68:9, 69:7, 72:18, 106:48).

84:10     **Loôk to our shièld, O Divíne One, ***
            **and gaze on the face òf yoúr anoìnted.**

84:11a    **Fôr better is à day in yoúr courts ***
            **than a thousand elsewhere òf my own choòsing;**

84:11b    **bêtter is the threshold of the house òf my Divíne One ***
            **than a pavilion among the tents òf ínjùstice!**

84:12a    **Fôr a Sun and a Shield is thè FONT OF BÉING, ***
            **the Divine One who gìves gráce and glòry;**

84:12b    **FÒNT OF BEING deniès nothing thát is good ***
            **to those who pursue ìntégrìty.**

84:13      **Ô FONT OF BÈING! O Sábaöth! ***
            ***Blessedness belongs to Adam's kind* whò trúst ìn you!**

*Blessedness belongs to Adam's kind* (*'ashrey 'adam* 32:2, 84:6, 84:13) extends the blessings of happiness to all people of every race who place their trust in the Divine One of Jacob. This is theocentrism, but not ethnocentrism.

# EIGHTY-FIVE

EARLIEST MANUSCRIPT — Verses 1–10 in Masada Psalm Scroll
LITURGY OF HOURS — Lauds on Tuesday III

The masterly author of Psalm 85 uses nearly every form of the Hebrew verb—precative perfect (verses 2/3/4), imperative (4/8), interrogative (6/7), hortative (9), imperfect (10/11/12), future (13/14).

| | | |
|---|---|---|
| 85:1 | (For the Director. Of *the Sons of Qorah*. A Mizmor.) | *42:1* |
| 85:2 | **Bê pleased, O FONT òF BEING, wíth your land! \*** | |
| | ***Repeal the bondàge óf Jàcob!*** | *14:7* |
| 85:3 | ***Lïft up the guìlt of your peóple! \*** | *32:5* |
| | **Cloak ovèr áll theìr sins!** | |
| 85:4 | **Hôld back àll of your ráging! \*** | |
| | **Turn back from *the flash òf yoúr fúry!*** | *69:25* |
| 85:5 | **Cóme back to us, our *Divine Òne of salvátion*, \*** | *18:47* |
| | **and set aside yoùr wráth wìth us.** | |
| 85:6 | **Wîll you for ever bè angry wíth us? \*** | |
| | **Will you prolong your anger? *For àge áftèr age?*** | *10:6* |
| 85:7 | **Wîll you nòt give us lífe again, \*** | |
| | **and let your people rèjoíce ìn you?** | |
| 85:8 | **Shôw us, O FONT OF BÈING, your mércy, \*** | |
| | **and grant ùs yoúr salvàtion.** | |
| 85:9 | **Lêt me hear what the God, the FONT OF BEÌNG, says, †** | |
| | **how he says "Shalom!" to his people ànd his devoút ones; \*** | |
| | **and "Let them not rètúrn to fòlly."** | |
| 85:10 | **Trûly near is his salvation to thòse who revére him, \*** | |
| | **for the dwelling of glory wìthín oùr land.** | |
| 85:11 | ***Mèrcy ànd truth* have émbraced; \*** | *25:10* |
| | **justice and shàlóm hàve kissed.** | |
| 85:12 | **Trûth will sproùt upward fróm the land, \*** | |
| | **and Justice has loòked down fróm thè sky.** | |
| 85:13 see 67:7a | | |
| | **Trûly the FONT OF BEING wìll give the goódness, \*** | |
| | **and our land wìll yíeld her boùnty.** | |
| 85:14 | **Jûstice will pròceed befóre his Face \*** | |
| | **and blaze for hìs stéps a pàthway.** | |

The divine appellative *Adonay* occurs seven times in Psalm 86 (verses 3/4/5/8/9/12/15) out of sixty appearances in the psalms. The psalmist builds up to a grand request: "Make me into a sign of goodness." Like the prophets who acted out their message, the psalmist volunteers to act out his poetry.

86:1 (A Prayer of David.)
**Bênd your Ear, Ò Font of Béing! ***
**Answer me!** *So lowly and ìn neéd àm I!*

> The phrase **lowly and in need** (*'aniy we 'ebyon*) occurs eight times in the psalms (35:10, 37:15, 40:18, 70:6, 74:21, 86:1, 109:16/22) but only twice refers to the psalmist (86:1, 109:22). Here in the first verse, it sets the tone for the whole psalm.

86:2 **Keêp sentinel over my soul! So dèvoted ám I! ***      *16:1*
**Save your servant, my Divine One, whò trústs ìn you.**

86:3 **Hâve pity upòn me, O Ádonay, ***
**for to you I cry oùt** *áll thè day.*      *25:5*

86:4 **Mâke joyful the soùl of your sérvant, ***
**for to you, Adonay,** *Ì lift my soul.*      *25:1*

86:5 **Fôr you, Adonay, are goòd and forgíving, ***
**and manifold in mercy to all whò cáll upòn you.**

86:6 **Lênd Ear to my prayer, Ò Font of Béing, ***
**and be attuned** *to the sound òf my pleàding.*

> **The sound of my pleading** (*qol tahnunothay* 86:6; *qol tahnunay* 116:1, 130:2, 140:7) follows an idiomatic pattern shared by **the sound of laud** (*qol todah* 26:7), **the sound of song** (*qol rinnah* 47:2, 118:15), **the sound of song and laud** (*qol rinnah wetodah* 42:5), **sounding of your thunder** (*qol ra'amka* 77:19, 104:7), the **shofar sounding** (*qol shofar* 47:6, 98:6).

86:7 *Ôn a day of distress for mè,* **I call oút to you, ***      *20:2*
**for you wìll ánswèr me.**

86:8 **Nône of the "divine ones" àre** *like you,* **Ádonay, ***      *35:10*
**and nothing ìs líke yoùr deeds.**

| 86:9 | Lêt *all gentiles*, whom you made, còme † | 9:18 |
| | and bow *before the Fàce of You*, Ádonay, * | 17:2 |
| | and give honòr tó yoùr Name. | |
| 86:10 | Hôw great you are, and *Màker of márvels*, * | 72:19 |
| | you are thè sóle Dívine One! | |
| 86:11 | Teâch me, FONT OF BEING, your wàys; † | |
| | I àm walking ín your truths, * | |
| | single-hearted to rèvére yoùr Name. | |
| 86:12 | Î laud you *wholeheartedly*, Adonày, my Divíne One, * | 9:1 |
| | and honor fòr éver yoùr Name. | |
| 86:13 | Fôr your mercy upon me is greàt, † | |
| | and you pluck my soùl from the Shéöl, * | |
| | from thè deépest plàces. | |
| 86:14 | Ô Divine One, insolent people rose against mè, † | |
| | and a pack of ruthlèss people soúght my life, * | |
| | and they kept yoù nót besìde them. | |
| 86:15 | Bût you are Adonay-God, tènder and grácious, * | |
| | *slow to wrath* but manifold *in mercy ánd trúthfùlness.* | 25:10 |

*Slow to Wrath* (*'erek 'appayiym* 86:15, 103:8, 145:8, Nah 1:34) is a
divine appellative that literally means "Long of Nose." The Nose is an
anthropomorphic symbol of anger.

The phrase *lowly and in need* (*'aniy we 'ebyon*) occurs eight times
in the psalms (35:10, 37:15, 40:18, 70:6, 74:21, 86:1, 109:16/22) but
only twice refers to the psalmist (86:1, 109:22). Here in the first verse,
it sets the tone for the entire psalm.

| 86:16 | *Bênd to me and pity mè*; † | 25:16 |
| | give your Mìght to your sérvant * | |
| | and make safe *the son òf yoúr hàndmaid.* | |

The crown prince of Judah, speaking to his father the king, would
have called himself as *the son of your handmaid* (*ben 'ematheka*
86:16, 116:16). The queen consort had little role to play in the state
structure; the woman of power was the king's mother.

| 86:17 | Mâke me a sign of goodnèss, † | |
| | *those who hate me* will bèhold and bé shamed: * | 9:14 |
| | how you, FONT OF BEING, help me ànd cómfòrt me! | |

## EIGHTY-SEVEN

— Lauds of Thursday III

Psalm 87 defends Jerusalem against northern shrines such as Bethel, but the psalmist extends Jerusalemite citizenship west to Rahab (Egypt), east to Babel, north to Tyre, and south to Cush (Somalia). The Roman Empire, by contrast, did not have universal citizenship until a thousand years later.

87:1 (Of *the Sons of Qorah.* A Mizmor. A Song.)  *42:1*
    **Âssemblèd as they háve been** *
    **on *mountains òf hóliness,*** *43:3*
87:2 **FÔNT OF BEING loves *thè gates of Ziön*** *  *9:14*
    **more than all the dwellìngs óf Jàcob.**

Nehemiah systematically enumerates eight *gates of Ziön* (*sha'arey tsiyyon* Ps 87:2; *sha'rey bat-tsiyyon* Ps 9:15), some of which may go by different names in other books:
—*Gate of the Valley* (*sha'ar haggay'* Neh 2:13, 3:13)
—*Gate of the Dung* (*sha'ar ha'ashpot* Neh 2:13, 3:13/14)
—*Gate of the Spring* (*sha'ar ha'ayin* Neh 2:14, 3:15, 12:37)
—*Gate of the Sheep* (*sha'ar hatsso'n* Neh 3:1, 3:32)
—*Gate of the Fish* (*sha'ar haddagiym* Neh 3:3, 12:39, 2 Chron 33:14)
—*Gate of the Water* (*sha'ar hammayim* Neh 3:26, 8:1/3/16)
—*Gate of the Horses* (*sha'ar hassusiym* Neh 3:28, Jer 31:40)
—*Gate of Ephraïm* (*sha'ar 'efrayim* Neh 12:39, 2 Kings 14:13)
—*Gate of the Prison* (*sha'ar hammattarah* Neh 12:39)

87:3 **Glôrious things are spòken aboút you,** *
    **O *city òf thé Divìne One.*** *46:5*
87:4 **"Î call to mind Rahab and Babel with those who know mè;** †
    **behold Philistia and thè Tyre-Rock ánd Cush:** *
    **there wàs bórn eàch one."**
87:5 **Ând of Ziön is saìd:** †
    **"In her was born thìs one and thát one,** *
    **and her foundèr ís the Mòst High."**
87:6 **FÔNT OF BEING counts thè peoples ín a scroll:** *
    **"There wàs bórn thìs one."**
87:7 **Ând they will sìng as a chórus:** *
    **"All my fountainheàds áre withìn you!"**

# EIGHTY-EIGHT

LITURGY OF HOURS — Friday Compline

The author of Psalm 88 cries by day (verse 1) and by night (1/19), as a "man with no support" (5). The noun *'eyal* occurs only here but comes from the same root as *'eyaluth*, found only at Psalm 22:20b. Zerr seems to note the paradox in his rendering, "a warrior who has no strength."

| | | |
|---|---|---|
| 88:1 | (A Song. A Mizmor of *the Sons of Qorah.* | *42:1* |
| | *Upon "Mildness."* For a Responsory. | *53:1* |
| | A Maskil of *Heman the Ezrahite.*) | *1 Kings 5:11* |
| 88:2 | **Ô FONT OF BEING! Our *Divine Òne of salvátion!* *** | *18:47* |
| | **In the day I wail, *in thè night* befòre you.** | *42:9* |
| 88:3 | **Lêt my prayer come *bèfore the Fáce of You!* *** | *17:2* |
| | **Turn yoùr Eár to my cry!** | |
| 88:4 | **Hôw replete wìth troubles ís my soul *** | |
| | **and they have tossed my lìfe dówn to Shèöl!** | |
| 88:5 | **Î was counted *with those goìng down intó a pit*; *** | *28:2* |
| | **I was like à hélplèss man.** | |
| 88:6 | **Î was thought to lie entombed among thè dead, †** | |
| | **like those slain whom you nò longer cáll to mind; *** | |
| | **and those cùt óff from yoùr Hand.** | |
| 88:7 | **Yoû put me into a Pit, intò deepest pláces, *** | |
| | **into *darkest placès*, ínto dùngeons.** | *88:19* |
| 88:8 | **Prêssing was your fùry upón me, *** | |
| | **and with all your waves yoù gáve rèply.** | |
| 88:9 | **Yoû drove my friends from me, caused mè to repél them. *** | |
| | **I am finished and Ì cánnòt flee.** | |
| 88:10 | **Dîmmed is my eye from my illnèss; †** | |
| | **I call to you, Ò FONT OF BÉING; *** | |
| | **each day I reach out tò yoú my palms.** | |
| 88:11 | **Dô you màke marvels fór the dead? *** | |
| | **Can phantoms rise up? Can thèy gíve yoù laud?** | |
| 88:12 | **Îs your mercy bèspoken ín the grave? *** | |
| | **Or your fidelity ìn Ábàddon?** | |
| 88:13 | **Âre your marvels knòwn in the dárkness? *** | |
| | **Or your justice in a land of fòrgétfùlness?** | |

187

88:14 **Bût I have sought you, Ò Font of Béing, \***
**and *at the dawn* my prayer wìll dráw neàr you.**    *5:4*

88:15 **Why, O Font of Beìng, do you spúrn my soul? \***
**Why *hide the Face òf Yoú fròm me*?**    *13:2*

88:16 **Lôwly am I, ànd mortal fróm my youth; \***
**I bore your terròrs; Í grèw numb.**

88:17 **Ûpon me hàve passed your rágings;**
**your horrors hàve sílènced me.**

88:18 **Thêy surrounded me lìke waters *áll the day;***    *25:5*
**they circled altogethèr aboùt me.**

88:19 **Fâr from me have you drivèn lover ánd friend. \***
**Known to mè ís *a dàrk place*.**

*Dark place* (*mahshak* 88:19) is related to the noun for *darkness* (*hoshek*), and appears as the very last word of this gloomy psalm. This should be a psalm for Winter, when the hours of daylight are shortest. Elsewhere the word is favored in the plural as *darkest places* (*mahshakkiym* 88:7, 143:3) or in a fuller phrase as *darkest places of the land* (*mahshakkey-'erets* 74:20).

## EIGHTY-NINE

NEW TESTAMENT —
Verse 4 at Acts 2:30 / Verse 21 at Acts 13:22
Verses 28 and 38 at Rev 1:5 / Verse 38 at Rev 3:14
LITURGY OF HOURS —
Office of Readings on Wednesday and Thursday III

David appears four times in Psalm 89, out of only twelve times in the Psalms (18:51, 78:70, 89:4/21/36/50, 122:5, 132:1/10/11/17, and 144:10). Three times the psalmist says God swore an oath to David (verses 4/36/50). The four David references all take place near mercy and fidelity.

| | | |
|---|---|---|
| 89:1 | (A Maskil of Ethan the Ezrahite.) | |
| 89:2 | **Mêrcies of the FONT OF BEÌNG †** | |
| | **ever will Ì sing, *age áfter age*; \*** | *10:6* |
| | **I make known *with my mouth* your fidélìty.** | *5:10* |
| 89:3 | **Fôr I declared, mercy is evèr built up tó the skies, \*** | |
| | **in which you confirm your fidélìty.** | |
| 89:4 | **Î *crafted a bónd* for my chósen one; \*** | *50:5* |
| | **I swore to Davìd my servant:** | |
| 89:5 | **"Fôr ever will I cònfirm your seédling, \*** | |
| | **and *age after age* buìld úp yoùr seat."** | *10:6* |
| 89:6 | **Lêt the skies laud your marvels, Ò FONT OF BÉING, \*** | |
| | **and your fidelity in the assembly òf hóly ones.** | |
| 89:7 | **Fôr who in the sky-dome can equal the FONT OF BEÌNG? †** | |
| | ***Who is like thè FONT OF BÉING* \*** | *35:10* |
| | **among thè *chíldren òf gods*?** | *29:1* |
| 89:8 | **Gôd is dreaded ìn league with hóly ones, \*** | |
| | **grand and awesome ovèr áll aboùt him.** | |
| 89:9 | **Ô FONT OF BEÌNG! †** | |
| | **Divine One of Sabaòth! *Who is líke you?* \*** | *35:10* |
| | **Might of *the BEING* and your fidelìty surroùnd you.** | *68:5* |
| 89:10 | **Yoû are in charge even in thè swelling óf the sea; \*** | |
| | **when his waves àríse, you càlm them.** | |
| 89:11 | **Yoû struck Rahab lìke one who ís stabbed; \*** | |
| | **with your mighty Right Hand you dispelled yoùr énèmies.** | |

89:12 Tô you belong the skies and tò you belóngs the land; *
 you established the *world ànd whát fills it.          *24:1*

89:13 Zâphon and Yamin, you yoùrself creáted; *
 Tabor and Hermon sing in yoùr Náme fòr joy.

89:14 Tô you belongs à Right Arm wíth strength; *
 you clench your Hand; yoù raíse your Rìght Hand.

89:15 *Jûstice and judgment are thè basis óf your throne*; *    *33:5*
 *mercy and truth* are directed to thè Fáce òf You.       *25:10*

89:16 *Blêssedness belongs to the peoplè* †
 those whò know the jóyful shout! *
 O FONT OF BEING, in the light of yoùr Fáce thèy walk.

*Blessedness belongs to the people* (*'ashrey ha'am* 89:16, 144:15)
but also *to the man* (*'ashrey ha'iysh* 86:16; *'ashrey 'iysh* 112:1). The
psalmists see no clash between common and individual good.

89:17 În your Name let thèm revel *áll the day*, *          *25:5*
 and be lifted high ìn yoúr Jùstice.

89:18 Fôr you are thè marvel óf their might, *
 and by your favor our horn ìs líftèd high:

89:19 "Fôr to the FONT OF BÈING belóngs our shield! *
 And to the *Holy One of Israël* bèlóngs oùr king!"       *71:22*

89:20 Ônce you spoke in a dream to your dèvoted ónes and said *
 "I helped a strong man, lifted one chosèn fróm the peòple.

89:21 Î found David tò be my sérvant, *
 anointed him with my oil òf hóliness,

89:22 thât my Hand mày stand besíde him, *
 and my Right Arm bè stróng fòr him,

89:23 thât there be nò foe to griéve him, *
 or an offspring of vice tò weákèn him,

89:24 bût I will beat hìs foe from hís face, *
 and battèr thóse who hàte him,

89:25 fôr *my fidelity and my mèrcy* are wíth him, *
 and *lifted high is hìs hórn* in my Name,

*My fidelity and my mercy* (*we'emunathiy wehasdiy* 89:25) flips the
terms in *his mercy and his fidelity* (*hasdo we'emunatho* 98:3, 100:5).
*Lifted high is his horn* (*tarum qarno* 86:25) reverses *let his horn be
lifted high* (*qarno tarum* 112:9).

| 89:26 | ând I will put hìs hand *intó the sea*, * | |
| | and *into the rìvèrwáys* his rìght hand. | 80:12 |
| 89:27 | Hê will call to me, 'O my fàther, you áre my God, * | |
| | and my rock òf sálvàtion.' | |
| 89:28 | Î am the one whò made my fírstborn son * | |
| | most high ovèr *eárthly kings*. | 2:2 |
| 89:29 | *Êternally* I keep sentinel over hìm with my mércy, * | 5:12 |
| | and my bond is màde súre fòr him. | |
| 89:30 | Î will establish for èver his seédling, * | |
| | and his seat like thè dáys of heàven. | |
| 89:31 | Îf his children fòrsake my Tórah, * | |
| | and follòw nót my jùdgments, | |
| 89:32 | îf they prèscind my láw codes, * | |
| | and do nòt keép my prècepts, | |
| 89:33 | thên I will punish theìr revolt wíth the rod, * | |
| | and theìr guílt with làshing. | |
| 89:34 | Bût from him I wìll nòt take my mércy, * | |
| | nor annul my fidélìty. | |
| 89:35 | Nôr will Ì break my ówn bond, * | |
| | nor alter what has issuèd fróm my lips. | |
| 89:36 | Ônce I swòre by my hóliness * | |
| | never to bèguíle Dàvid | |
| 89:37 | hîs seedling to rèmain *etérnally*, * | 5:12 |
| | and his seat like thè Sún befòre me, | |
| 89:38 | lîke the Moon, to bè standing álways; * | |
| | assenting as a witnèss ín the sky-dome." | |
| 89:39 | Bût you were angèred, and offénded, * | |
| | trespassed against by your ànoíntèd one. | |
| 89:40 | Yoû suspended the bònd with your sérvant; * | |
| | you doomed his diadem ùpón thè land. | |
| 89:41 | *Yoû split asundèr* all *his báttlements*; * | 80:13 |
| | you turned his defensès ínto rùbble. | |
| 89:42 | Thêy plunder hìm, *all who páss the way*; * | 80:13 |
| | he has become a rebuke *to those whò dwéll wìth* him. | 44:14 |
| 89:43 | Yoû *lifted up thè right hand* óf his foes; * | |
| | you gave joy to all hìs énèmies. | |

*You lifted up the right hand* (*heriymotha yamiyn* 89:43; *yemiyn yhwh romema* 118:16). Raising up the hand of a victor is still a common gesture; here the idiom is used metaphorically.

| 89:44 | Yoû even turned back thè flintstone óf his blade, * | |
| | and did not leave him standìng ín the bàttle. | |

89:45   Ôf his splèndor you máde an end, *
and cast his throne ùpón thè ground.

89:46   *Yoû cut short thè days* of hís youth; *
you have mantlèd hím ìn shame.

> *Cutting short the days of his youth* (*hiqtsarta yemey 'alumaw* 89:46)
> means that he grew prematurely gray, but ***cutting short my days***
> (*qitssar yomay* 102:24) means shortening my lifespan.

89:47 = 79:5

  Hôw long, O Font òf Being, wíll you hide? *
*For ever* will your indignatiòn bláze *lìke flame?*     *9:7, 79:5*

89:48   Keêp in mind *what à lifespan ís to me!* *     *39:5*
For what vain end did you make all *childrèn óf Àdam?*    *11:4*

89:49   Whô is the man that can live ànd not behóld death? *
Can one deliver one's own soul *from thè gríp of Shèöl?*   *49:16*

89:50   Whêre are your primàl Mercies, Ádonay? *
Those you swore to David by your Fìdélìty?

89:51   Keêp in mind, O Adonay, the rebukìng of your sérvants! *
I harbor in myself how all thè mány gèntiles,

89:52   hôw your rivals rebuked, Ò Font of Béing, *
how they rebuked the footsteps of your ànoíntèd one.

89:53   Blêssed be thè Font of Béing *
*eternally*! *Àmén and àmen!*     *5:12, 41:14*

## NINETY

NEW TESTAMENT — Verse 4 at 2 Pet 3:8
LITURGY OF HOURS — Lauds on Thursday III and Monday IV

Psalm 90 is the only psalm that begins with *Adonay*, which is also at the end by way of "inclusion." The psalmist contrasts the eternal *Adonay* (verses 1/2) with mortal humans (3/5/6). In verse 4 he gives two yardsticks to compare divine and human time; these are cited in Second Peter.

90:1     (A prayer of Moses, the man of the Divine One.)
**Ô Adonày, you have beén for us \***
**a homestead in *àge àfter àn age*.**     *10:6*

90:2     **Bêfore the mountains were begottèn, †**
**or the wòrld was born, ór the land, \***
**even *from eternity* to eternity yoù áre thè God.**     *25:6*

90:3     **Yoû change humàn beings báck to dust, \***
**and say, "Go back, O *childrèn óf Àdam*!"**     *11:4*

90:4     **Fôr a thousand years in yoùr Eyes †**
**are like yesterdày—how it pásses!— \***
**or like a *watch changìng* ín thè night.**     *63:7*

90:5     **Yoû release them from sleèp *in the mòrning*; \***     *5:4*
**they are *like thè* chángìng *grass*.**     *37:2*

90:6     ***Ât the dawn* it blooms but chànges toward súnset, \***     *5:4*
**it wilts and ìt driés àway.**

90:7     **Hôw eclipsed have wè been in yoúr wrath, \***
**and by your anger becòme térrìfied!**

90:8     **Yoû have placed our offènces befóre you, \***
**our secrets before *the light of thè Fáce òf You*.**     *4:7*

90:9     **För all our dàys pass in yoúr wrath; \***
**we are eclipsed; our years àre líke à sigh.**

90:10     **Spânning our days are seventy years, or eighty ìf strong, †**
**and many of them àre toil and troúble, \***
**but need compels, and àwáy wè fly.**

90:11     **Whô can màke known your míghty wrath? \***
**Or your foresight? Or yoùr índignàtion?**

90:12     **Mâke known thè number óf our days, \***
**that we may attain à heárt of wìsdom.**

90:13 *Côme back, O FONT òF BEING, hów long ... ? *       *6:4*
and pity thèm, ás your sèrvants.
90:14 Fîll us *at the dàwn with your mércies*, *
and let us sing and rejoice throùgh áll oùr days.

*At the dawn with your mercies* (*babboqer hasdeka* 90:14, 92:3, 143:8; *labboqer hasdeka* 59:17). Morning is a fresh time, when the thirsting ground is moistened by the fallen dew, like the dewfall on Mount Hermon (133:3). To be awakened, alive and intact, after surviving the terrors of the night, is in itself a mercy.

90:15 Lêt us rejoice as befits thè days you weákened us, *
the years whèn wé saw èvil.
90:16 Mâke known your deèds to your sérvants, *
and your splendòr tó their chìldren.
90:17 Ând may the favor of Adonay, our Divine One, be on ùs, †
and let the works of oùr hands be fìrm for us, *
and let the works of our hands bè fìrm fòr him.

## NINETY-ONE

EARLIEST MANUSCRIPT — 4QPs[b]
NEW TESTAMENT — Verses 11–12 at Mt 4:6 and Lk 4:10–11
LITURGY OF HOURS — Sunday Compline

The first two verses of Psalm 91 juxtapose four divine names: *Elyon, Shadday, Yhwh,* and *Elohim.* The least common is *Shadday,* which appears most often in Job (thirty-one of forty-eight times in the Bible). That word parses as a plural of majesty with a first-person singular suffix, like *Adonay* or *Elohay.* The Septuagint and Vulgate, in line with their policy of reducing divine vocabulary, replaced *Shadday* with the phrase "God of heaven" (136:26). No etymology seems to support that, or Bea's *Omnipotentis* (followed by RSV, Grail, NAB, Zerr, EUB, Alonso-Schökel). Dahood, BdJ, JB, and NJB simply leave *Shadday* as such in the text. In recent years, the name *Shadday* has appeared in a popular song and become more familiar to English speakers.

91:1 **Dwêlling in the refùge of the Móst High, ***
**staying in thè sháde of Shàdday,**

91:2 **sây, "O FONT OF BEING, my Refùge and my Fórtress! ***
**My Divine One, ìn whóm Ì trust!"**

91:3 **Fôr he frees yoù from the fówler's trap, ***
**from the ìmpéndìng plague.**

91:4 **Wîth his feathers he covèrs you, †**
**and you can shèlter beneáth his Wings; ***
**a buckler and a cordon is his Arm òf faíthfùlness.**

91:5 **Nêver be àwed with the dreád of night, ***
**with the arrow flyìng ín the dàytime,**

91:6 **wîth the plague spreadìng in the dárkness, ***
**with the stinger strikìng át noòntimes.**

91:7 **Thoûgh at your side a thousand may fàll, †**
**and ten thousànd at your ríght hand, ***
**you yourself ìt cánnòt touch.**

91:8 **Wîth your òwn eyes you wíll look ***
**and see the recompense òf únjust peòple.**

91:9 **"Fôr you, FONT OF BEING, are to me à refuge ón high, ***
**where you hàve pláced your dwèlling."**

91:10 **Lêt nothing hàrmful approách you, ***
**nor any ailment come ìnsíde yoùr tent.**

91:11 **Fôr he sends hìs angel tó you, ***
**to guard you ìn áll yoùr ways.**

91:12 **Ûpon pàlms they will líft you up, ***
**lest you stub your foot àgaínst à stone.**

91:13 **Ôn asp or òn viper yoú can tread, ***
**can trample on liòn ór on dràgon.**

91:14 **"Fôr he trusts in me, ànd I delíver him; ***
**I will lift him high, if hè knóws my Name.**

91:15 **Hê calls on me, and I answèr him; †**
*during the siège* **I am wíth him; ***
**I rescue him, and bestow honòr úpòn him.**

91:16 **Wîth *length of dàys* I fulfíll him, ***
**and am made known to him throùgh my salvàtion."**

*4:2*

**Length of days** (*'orek yomiym* 21:5, 91;15; *le 'orek yomiym* 23:6, 93:5) indicates a duration that remains unspecified, but is of great length. The word *yom* has a secondary meaning of lifetime, so this phrase could signify "lengthy life" or even "a length of lifetimes." Compare **Slow to Wrath** (*'erek 'appayiym* 86:15, 103:8, 145:8, Nah 1:34), a divine appellative literally meaning "Long of Nose." The Nose is an anthropomorphic symbol of anger.

## NINETY-TWO

EARLIEST MANUSCRIPT — 4QPs[b]
TEMPLE LITURGY — Sabbath
LITURGY OF HOURS — Lauds on Saturdays II and IV

Psalm 92 contrasts two images—the psalmist himself is like a cedar of Lebanon in the house of God (92:13, elsewhere a literal tree at 29:5, 80:11, 104:16, and 148:9), but unjust people are sprouting like grass (37:2, 92:8, 102:5/12, 103:15, and 129:6). Of course, the forest cedar is an evergreen, while the desert grass thrives only briefly.

| | | |
|---|---|---|
| 92:1 | (A Mizmor. | |
| | A Song for the Sabbath Day.) | |
| 92:2 | Goôd it is to laud thè FONT OF BÉING, * | |
| | and *play chords to yoùr Náme*, Mòst High, | *9:3* |
| 92:3 | têlling *in the mòrning your mércy*, * | *90:14* |
| | and your faithfulnèss *ín thè nights*, | *16:7* |
| 92:4 | *ôn ten strings* ànd on a hárp-bow, * | *33:2* |
| | on the chòrds, *ón a lyre-bow.* | *33:2* |
| 92:5 | Fôr you gave me joy, FONT ÒF BEING, wíth your deeds; * | |
| | at *the works of your Hands* Ì síng fòr joy! | *8:7* |
| 92:6 | Hôw great are your works, Ò FONT OF BÉING, * | |
| | how very deèp áre yoùr plans. | |
| 92:7 | Nôr can a *brutìsh* person knów this, * | |
| | nor one who ìs *sénseless* fàthom. | *49:11* |
| 92:8 | Âs the unjùst people sproút *like plants*, * | *72:16* |
| | and all *doers of evil* flourish, to theìr lástìng doom. | *5:6* |
| 92:9 | Bût you yoùrself are ón the heights, * | |
| | *eternally*, Ò FÓNT OF BÈING. | *5:12* |
| 92:10 | Bêhold your rivals, FONT OF BEÌNG, † | |
| | behold your rìvals becóme nil; * | |
| | scattered are all *doèrs óf èvil.* | *5:6* |
| 92:11 | Yoû *lifted my horn*, às do the óxen; * | |
| | with leafy oils I hàve beén anoìnted, | |
| 92:12 | ând you let my eye see *those glaring at mè*, † | *5:9* |
| | those who rìse up agaínst me; * | |
| | let my ears hear òf súch scoùndrels. | |

92:13 **Sproûting like the palm treè is the júst one, \***
**growing like *a cedar in thè Lébànon*.**

*29:5*

> *Like the palm tree* (*kattamar* 92:13) and *like a cedar* (*ke'erez*) are not images chosen at random. Palm trees are a noted feature of the southern city of Jericho, called the **city of palms** (*'iyr hattamariym* Deut 34:3; Judg 1:16, 3:13, 2 Chron 28:15), while in the north are the **cedars of Lebanon** (*'arzey lebanon* 104:16; *'erez ballebanon* 92:13, Ezek 31:3; *'erez 'esher ballebanon* 1 Kings 5:13; *'arzey hallebanon* Ps 29:5, Judg 9:15, Is 2:13). So the just one can flourish in the south, close by the temple, but also in the far north.

92:14 **Plânted in *the house of thè* FONT OF BÉING, \***
**they will sprout up in porticos òf thé Divìne One.**

*42:5*

92:15 **Stîll will they be growìng, into óld age; \***
**green and leafy wíll thèy be,**

92:16 **têlling how steadfast is *the* FONT ÒF BEING, my Rock, \***
**and how there is nothing vicioùs áboùt him.**

> FONT OF BEING, my Rock (*tsuriy* 19:15, 92:16, 144:1) is a divine appellative, under which God trains a psalmist for combat (144:1). This is not synonymous with **God, my Bedrock** (*'el sal'iy* 42:10). Bedrock is the foundation for house or city; good for a fortress are rocky outcroppings like **Tyre-Rock** (*tsur* 45:13, 83:8, 87:4), once an island, now a peninsula on the coast of Lebanon.

# NINETY-THREE

EARLIEST MANUSCRIPTS — 4QPs[b] / Verses 1–3 in 11QPs[a]
TEMPLE LITURGY — Friday
LITURGY OF HOURS — Lauds on Sunday III

A crescendo of water images lies at the heart of Psalm 93 (verses 3/4), from whispering streams to the roaring sea—a relentlessly rising tide, a metaphor for the din of rebellious upstarts. Noun *dakya* "beating" (3) belongs more properly to a battle drum than to a water fall. Louder than war or nature is the FONT OF BEING in his great Amen.

93:1 see 96:10

> *FÔNT OF BEING has ruled*, robed in Majèsty, †
> robed is FONT OF BEÌNG, tightly gírded! *
> Surely is the world foundèd, nót to tùmble!

*The FONT OF BEING has ruled* (*yhwh malak* 93:1, 96:10a, 97:1, 99:1) opens three psalms and appears in a fourth, to mark them as royal. The verb *to rule* (*malak*) is related to the noun *king* (*melek*). Apart from the opening line, the cosmic hymn Psalm 93 has little in common with Psalms 95-100, which are hymns to divine kingship.

93:2 **Foûnded is yoùr seat from lóng ago; ***
**you yourself are *from ètérnìty.***      *25:6*

93:3 **Rîvers have lifted, Ò FONT OF BÉING, ***
**rivers lifted their voice; rivèrs líft their beàting.**

93:4 **Môre than the sound of *waters manìfold,* †**      *18:17*
**more splendid thàn breakers óf the sea, ***
**splendid in the heights is thè FÓNT OF BÈING.**

93:5 **Yoûr decrees are amply ratìfied: †**
**your house has pleasing holiness, Ò FONT OF BÉING, ***
**for à *léngth òf days.***      *21:5*

## NINETY-FOUR

EARLIEST MANUSCRIPT — 4QPs[b]
TEMPLE LITURGY — Wednesday
NEW TESTAMENT —
Verse 11 at 1 Cor 3:20
Verse 14 at Rom 11:2
LITURGY OF HOURS — Midday Prayer on Wednesday IV

The author of Psalm 94 has had to endure the babbling of the insolent. It is not enough for them to slay the widow and the alien, and even the orphans. They have to brag about it, also. They rationalize that the God named *Yah* does not care to see what they do (verse 7). Finally, however, the Font of Being reduces them to silence. So the psalm ends with a blessed stillness.

94:1 **Gôd of redress is thè Font of Béing! ***
**O God of redress, rèveál yoùrself!**
94:2 **Bê raised ùp, judging thé land, ***
**giving what is due tò proúd peòple!**
94:3 **Hôw long will the unjust, Ò Font of Béing, ***
**how long will unjust peoplè keép exùlting?**
94:4 **Thêy babble on, thèy speak with ínsolence, ***
**they boast among themselves, all *doèrs óf èvil.*** *5:6*
94:5 **Thêy crush your people, Ò Font of Béing, ***
**and they sicken yoùr héritage.**
94:6 **Thêy slay the widow ànd foreign résident; ***
**they slaughter evèn thé òrphans.**
94:7 **Ând they declare, "Oh, nòr does the *Béing* see, *** *68:5*
**nor does *the Divine One òf Jácob* fàthom."** *20:2*
94:8 **Fâthom for yoùrselves! †**
***Brutes* among the peòple and sénseless ones, *** *49:11*
**when wìll yoú becòme wise?**
94:9 **Cân the planter of an ear, càn he not lísten? ***
**Can the molder of an eye, càn hé nòt see?**
94:10 **Cân the corrector of natiòns, can he nót chastise? ***
**The one who tutored Adàm ín knòwledge?**
94:11 **Fônt of Being knew thè plans of Ádam, ***
**how thèy wére à breeze.**

| | | |
|---|---|---|
| 94:12 | *Blêssedness belongs to thè man* † | *34:9* |
| | whom you còrrect, *O Béing,* * | *68:5* |
| | and whom you teach fròm yoúr Tòrah, | |
| 94:13 | tô spare hìm *dáys of évil* * | *27:5* |
| | until a pit be dug fòr thé unjùst one. | |
| 94:14 | *Nôr surely* will the FONT OF BEING càst off his peóple, * | |
| | *nor* abandon hìs hérìtage. | *9:19* |
| 94:15 | Îndeed, for justice he wìll bring back júdgment, * | |
| | and behind him are all *thè steádfast-heàrted.* | *7:11* |
| 94:16 | *Whô* will rise fòr me by scoúndrels? * | *23:4* |
| | *Who* will stand for me by *doèrs óf èvil?* | *5:6* |
| 94:17 | *Hâd not the FONT OF BEÌNG been* a hélp for me, * | |
| | *in a moment* my soul would hàve dwélt in sìlence. | *2:12* |

*Had not the FONT OF BEING* . . . (*luley yhwh* 94:17, 124:1/2) is a synonymous with *If the FONT OF BEING had not* . . . (*'im yhwh lo'* . . .). Both formulas allow the psalmist to speculate on what would have happened without the blessing of God—the psalmist would dwell in silence (94:17), the people would have been swallowed up (124:1/2), the house would not have been built (127:1), nor would the city have been guarded (127:2).

| | | |
|---|---|---|
| 94:18 | Thoûgh I declared, "Hòw my foot stúmbles!" * | |
| | your mercy, FONT OF BEÌNG, sústaìns me. | |
| 94:19 | Whên my disarray ìs great *withín my chest,* * | *39:4* |
| | your consolations dèlíght my soul. | |
| 94:20 | Coûld you relate to tribùnals that threáten, * | |
| | enforcing crime ìnsteád òf law? | |
| 94:21 | Thêy indict à soul that ís just, * | |
| | and on blood that is guiltless thèy láy thè blame. | |
| 94:22 | FÒNT OF BEING has beèn my high réfuge, * | |
| | and my Divine One a rock òf shélter fòr me, | |
| 94:23 | ând he turns against them their wickèdness, † | |
| | and by their injustìce he will sílence them; * | |
| | silence them, O FONT OF BEÌNG, oúr Divìne One. | |

NEW TESTAMENT — Verses 7b–14 at Heb 3:7–11
LITURGY OF HOURS — Daily Invitatory Psalm

Psalm 95 begins with the plural imperative *lechu* "Come!" which reappears in verse 6. Other psalms of this invitatory type are 34 and 100. A third imperative is found in verse 8, not to harden our hearts. In addition to these imperatives, the psalm has a string of exhortations. The first half of the psalm hearkens back to the creation story in Genesis, but the second half recalls the sojourn in the desert from Exodus through Deuteronomy.

95:1 **Côme! Let us sing with joy to thè FONT OF BÉING, ***
**shout to the Rock òf oúr Salvàtion!**

95:2 **Lêt us còme near his Fáce with laud, ***
**cry out to him wìth mélòdy!**

95:3 **Fôr a great God is thè FONT OF BÉING, ***
**and the *great King*, ovèr áll àngels,**            *47:3*

95:4 **în whose Hànd are the clèfts of land, ***
**and whose are thè moúntain rìdges,**

95:5 **whôse is the seà, since he máde it, ***
**and the solid land to which hìs Hánds gàve shape.**

95:6 **Côme! Let us adore and bow dòwn! ***
**Let us bless the Face of thè FONT OF BÉING, ***
***the Òne Whó Màde Us,***

*The One Who Made Us* (*'osenu* 95:6) is a divine imperative in participial form like the following:
—*The One Who Made Them* (*'osaw* 149:2)
—*Maker of Marvels* (*'oseh nifla'ot* 72:19, 86:10, 136:4)
—*Maker of A Marvel* (*'oseh pele'* 77:15)
—*Maker of Great Things* (*'oseh gedolot* 106:21)
—*Maker of the Heavens* (*'oseh hasshamayim* 136:5)
—*Maker of Heavens and of Land* (*'oseh shamayim wa'arets* 115:15, 121:2, 124:8, 134:3, 146:6)
—*Maker of Judgment* (*'oseh mishpot* 146:7)
—*Maker of Lights* (*'oseh 'oriym* 136:7).

95:7 **fôr he is our Divine Òne, †**
**and we are *people of his pasture ànd sheep* of hís Hand, ***
**if today yoù heéd hìs call.**            *74:1*

95:8     **Hârden not your hearts às at Meríbah, ***
        **as on the day of Massah *in thè wìldèrness,***       *55:8*

95:9     **whên your forebeàrs put me tó the test; ***
        **they probed me, though thèy sáw my deeds.**

95:10    **Fôrty years I take offense, against àn age! †**
        **I stated: "A people òf wayward heárt are they, ***
        **and thèy knów not my ways!"**

95:11    **Sô I swore whèn I was ángry: ***
        **"They shall not come *into my pláce òf rest.*"**

*The place of rest* (*menuhah*) is the watering place for the sheep (23:1), the Holy Land where the wandering Hebrews can take their ease (*'el-menuhathiy* 95:11), the resting place of the Ark of the Covenant (*limnuhatheyka* 132:8), and the place where the soul itself can be at peace (*limnuhaykiy* 116:7). To be given no rest is like the curse of Sisyphus.

## NINETY-SIX

EARLIEST MANUSCRIPT — 4QPs[b]
LITURGY OF HOURS — Lauds on Monday III

Psalm 96 begins and ends with the same phrases as Psalm 98. This psalm is longer, and the extra length is liturgical (verses 7/8/9). Otherwise the two psalms are strikingly parallel. The author of both psalms is probably a priest. The opening verses invite the priestly clan to join in service. If they are young ones who have just reached the age to participate, then even old songs are new to them. Then the invitation is extended to the family of nations (7) and to the entire cosmos (11/12), to whom the song of praise is entirely new.

96:1    **Sîng to the Font of Bèing a sóng made new: ***      *33:3*
       **sing to the Font of Bèing, áll thè land!**     *8:2*

96:2    **Sîng to the Font òf Being, bléss his Name! ***
       **Tell from day to day hìs sálvàtion!**

> **Bless his Name** (*borku shemo* 96:2, 100:4) is a euphemism for **bless the Font of Being** (*borku yhwh* 103:20/21/22 and *borku et-yhwh* 134:1/2, 135:19/20). The euphemisms eventually would be mandatory usage for all public reading. Beyond euphemism is blessing the Name with other divine characteristics—**his Name of glory** (*shem kebodo* 72:19) and **his Name of holiness** (*shem qodsho* 33:21, 103:1, 105:3, 106:47, 145:21).

96:3    **Dêclare *among the gèntiles* his glóry, ***      *9:12*
       **among *all the peoplès* hís màrvels!**     *47:2*

96:4 see 48:2 and 145:3
       **Hôw great is the Font of Bèing and most laúdable! ***
       **Awesome is he, abòve *áll "divìne ones!"***

> **All "divine ones"** (*kol 'elohiym* 96:4, 97:7/9, 135:5) are *"divine ones" of the peoples* (*'elohey ha'ammiym* 96:5). Because Psalm 97 says they should adore the Font of Being (97:7), who is higher than they (97:9), "divine ones" are often translated as angels there. However, both psalms declare clearly that "divine ones" are *empty things* (*'eliyliym* 96:5 and 97:7), and that is not true of angels.

96:5    **Fôr *all "divìne ones"* of the peòples are émpty things, ***      *96:4*
       **but the Font of Bèing máde thè skies.**

96:6     *Mâjesty and grandeùr* are befóre his Face! *        *21:6*
       Might and splendor are in hìs hóly place!

96:7 see 29:1/2
       Brîng to the FONT OF BEING, you fàmilies of géntiles, *
       bring to the FONT OF BEÌNG glóry ànd might!

96:8     Brîng the FONT OF BEING thè glory óf his Name! *
       Carry a gift and come, into hìs pórtìco!

96:9     Âdore the FONT OF BEING ìn robes of hóliness! *
       Reel from hìs Fáce, *all thè land!*        *8:2*

96:10 see 93:1
       Sây *among gentiles, "The FONT OF BEING has rùled!* †   *9:12, 93:1*
       Surely is the world foundèd, not to túmble; *
       he decides among peoplès *wíth faìrness."*        *9:9*

96:11    Heâvens rejoice ànd *the land révels;* *
       *the sea resounds ànd whát fills it.*

*The land revels* (*tagel ha'arets*) both here and at the beginning of
Psalm 97. *The sea resounds and that which fills it* (*yir'am hayyam
umlo'o*) here and at verse 7 of Psalm 98. This verse binds the three
psalms tightly, along with everything else they share.

96:12    Plaîns exult, and èverything ín them; *
       they sing for joy, all thè fórèst trees,

96:13 see 98:9
       bêfore the Face of the FONT OF BEÌNG! †
       For he comes! For hè comes *to júdge the land,* *      *82:8*
       to judge a world justly, and peoples with his Fìdélìty!

EARLIEST MANUSCRIPT — 4QPs[b]
NEW TESTAMENT — Verse 7 at Heb 1:6
LITURGY OF HOURS — Lauds on Wednesday II

Psalm 97 is one of three (93/97/99) that begin with the sentence: "The FONT OF BEING has ruled." Though the verb comes from the milieu of kingly rule, nothing else about these psalms that is monarchical. They could come from the post-exilic periods when sovereignty had returned to God alone.

97:1　*FÒNT OF BEING has rùled! The land révels! ￼ \**　　93:1, 96:11
　　　*Islands manìfóld rèjoice!*

97:2　*Cloûd and fùnnel surroúnd him;*
　　　*Justice and Judgment are the basìs óf* hìs *throne.*　　33:5

　　　*Cloud and funnel* ('anan wa'arafel) were among those signs that attended Moses on Sinai (Deut 4:11) and will reappear on the day of wrath (Joel 2:2 and Zeph 1:15); the sheep of Israël were scattered on such a day (Ezek 34:12). 'Arafel is usually translated "gloom," but it derives from the word 'aref (**nape of the neck**, 18:41) and so it most likely describes a neck-shaped, funnel cloud.

97:3　**Flâme will gò forth befóre his Face, \***
　　　**and shine àboút hìs Brow.**

97:4　**Tô the world his bolts òf lightning gáve light; \***
　　　**the land bèhólds and dànces.**

97:5　**Moûntains** *like wax* **have meltèd, †**　　　　22:15
　　　**before the Face of thè** FONT OF BÉING, **\***
　　　**before the Face of the Master òf** *áll thè land.*　　8:2

97:6 see 50:6a
　　　**Heâvens have reláted his Jústice, \***
　　　**and** *all the peoples* **bèhéld his Glóry.**　　47:2

97:7　**Shâmed are all slaves of idols, takìng pride in émptiness; \***
　　　**let** *all "divine ònes"* **ádòre him!**　　96:4

97:8 see 48:12
　　　**Lêt Ziön listen and rejoìce, †**
　　　**and let the daughters òf Judah rével \***
　　　**on account of your judgmènts,** FÓNT OF BÈING.

97:9    Fôr you are *FONT OF BEÌNG,* †             *7:18*
         the *Most Hìgh* over *áll the land,* *         *8:2*
         far higher thàn *áll "divìne ones."*       *96:4*

         *FONT OF BEING Most High* (*yhwh 'elyon* 7:18, 47:3, 97:9) is a divine
         appellative of a pattern with:
         —*Divine One Most High* (*'elohiym 'elyon* 57:3, 78:56)
         —*God Most High* (*'el 'elyon* 78:35).

97:10   Thôse who love the FONT OF BEING hate injustìce; † 
         he guards the souls òf his devóted ones; * 
         from the *hand of the unjust people* hè séts thèm free.    *36:12*
97:11   Lîght has been plantèd for the júst one, * 
         and joy for *thè steádfast-heàrted.*          *7:11*
97:12   Rêjoice, you just, in thè FONT OF BÉING, * 
         and give laud, to stay mindful of hìs hóliness.

# NINETY-EIGHT

EARLIEST MANUSCRIPT — 4QPs[b]
LITURGY OF HOURS — Midday Prayer on Wednesday III

Psalm 98 begins and ends with the same phrases as Psalm 96, but is shorter and more tightly structured. Again, the psalmist wishes to reinvent his art.

98:1    (A Mizmor.)

*Sîng the* FONT OF BEING *a song màde new;* †      *33:3*
such are thè marvels hé made! *
He saves him by his right Hand and his Arm òf hólìness.

98:2    FÔNT OF BEING makes knòwn his Salvátion, *
in eyes of the gentiles, the triùmph óf his Jùstice.

98:3    Hê calls to mind *his mercy* †      *89:25*
*and his fidelity* for thè *house of Ísraël.* *
*All ends of land* see the Salvation òf oúr Divìne One.   *2:8*

*House of Israël* (*bet-yisra'el* 98:3, 115:12, 135:19) usually means all twelve tribes. So Isaiah once refers to the divided kingdom as *two houses of Israël* (*sheney battey yisra'el* Is 8:14). Jeremiah distinguishes between *the house of Israël and the house of Judah* (*bet-yisra'el ubet-yehudah* Jer 11:17). When he wrote, however, only one kingdom was left, so his language is anachronistic. Both dynasties claimed the right to rule over all twelve tribes.

98:4    Shoût to the FONT OF BEING, *àll who are óf the land!* *   *8:2*
Find pitch and sing fòr jóy ànd play.

98:5    Plây for the *FONT OF BEÌNG on a lyre-bow,* *
*on a lyre-bow* and with the sound òf mélòdy.   *33:2*

98:6    Wîth trumpets and *à shofar soúnding,* *   *47:6*
sing out before the Face of the King, thè FÓNT OF BÈING.

98:7    *Seâ resoùnds and what fills it,*   *96:11*
*a world and they whò dwéll within it:*   *24:1*

98:8    Rîvers applaud with à palm! †
Togethèr mountains síng for joy, *
before the Face of thè FÓNT OF BÈING!

98:9 see 96:13

Fôr he is còming *to júdge a land,* *   *82:8*
to judge a world with justice, and peoplès *wíth faìrness!*   *9:9*

## NINETY-NINE

EARLIEST MANUSCRIPT — 4QPs[b]
LITURGY OF HOURS — Lauds on Thursday III

Psalm 99 elevates the prophet Samuel to a status equal to that of Moses and Aaron (verse 6). No other prophets are named in the text of a psalm, and the very word "prophet" occurs only twice (74:9, 105:15). The singers of Ziön were not very much concerned with the phenomenon of prophecy.

| | | |
|---|---|---|
| 99:1 | *Fônt of Being has rùled,* peoples ráging! * | *93:1* |
| | He is *seated on Cherubim;* tremblìng ís thè land! | *80:2* |
| 99:2 | Fônt of Being ìn Ziön ìs great, * | |
| | and he is high ovèr *áll the peòples.* | *47:2* |
| 99:3 | Thêy have givèn laud to yoúr Name: * | |
| | "Great and awesòme, hóly ìs he!" | |
| 99:4 | Mîght of a king is love for justìce; † | |
| | you hàve made fair vérdicts; * | |
| | you enacted *judgment and justìce* ín Jàcob. | *33:5* |
| 99:5 | Thêy exalt the Font of Beìng, our Divíne One, * | |
| | and *worship before his footstoòl*: "Hóly ìs he!" | |

*Worship before his footstool* (*hishtahwu lahadom raglaw* 99:5; *histahweh lahadom raglaw* 132:7). *Footstool* (*hadom*) is a term for the Ark, as is made clear by the two terms being in parallel in Psalm 132. See other terms for the Ark listed in the note at 132:8.

| | | |
|---|---|---|
| 99:6 | *Môses and Aaron* are among hìs priests, † | *77:21* |
| | and Samuel among thòse calling hís Name, * | |
| | calling the Font of Being, and hè ánswèrs them. | |
| 99:7 | În a pillar òf cloud he spóke to them; * | |
| | they kept his decrees, and thè láw he gàve them. | |
| 99:8 | Ô Font of Being, our Divine One, you answèred them; † | |
| | O God, you were ùplifting fór them, * | |
| | but rèdréssing theìr crimes. | |
| 99:9 | Êxalt the Font of Being, our Divine Òne; † | |
| | and adore him before hìs *mount of hóliness*: * | *43:3* |
| | "How holy is the Font of Beìng, oúr Divìne One!" | |

# ONE HUNDRED

EARLIEST MANUSCRIPT — 4QPs<sup>b</sup>
LITURGY OF HOURS — Lauds on Fridays I and III

Psalm 100 begins with a rubric specifying the psalm is to be sung loudly. Every sentence in this psalm is exclamatory! The psalmist speaks only to the readers, not to God directly. This is not a prayer as such, then, but a call to prayer, an invitatory like Psalms 34 and 95.

100:1 (A Mizmor of Thanksgiving.)
**Sîng out to thè Font of Béing, ***
*all who àre óf thè land!*                                    8:2
100:2 **Sêrve the Font of Beìng with rejoícing! ***
**Come before his Face wìth jóyfùl song!**
100:3 **Knôw the Font of Being as the Divine Òne. †**
**He màde us and hís are we, ***
*his people and the sheepfold of hìs pástùre land!*          74:1

His people and the sheepfold of his pasture land (*'ammo wetso'n mar 'iytho* 74:1, 79:13, 100:3) gives meaning first, metaphor second, which is like reading the last chapter of a book first. Even more scrambled is **the people of your pasture and sheepfold** (*'am mar 'iytho wetso'n* 95:7), putting people in the pasture instead of the sheep! This kind of mixing would be possible only with a metaphor that had become so familiar that the terms were virtually equivalent.

100:4 **Ênter his gates wìth thanks, †**
**his pòrches with praíse-craft! ***
**Give laud to hìm!** *Bléss hìs Name!*                      96:2
100:5 *Sô good is thè Font of Béing, ***
**everlasting** *his mercy,* **and** *age after age his fidélity.*

                                                    89:25, 10:6

*So good is the Font of Being* (*kiy tob yhwh* 34:9, 100:5, 135:3, 145:9), with the Name (52:11, 54:8) and the Mercy of the Font of Being (106:1, 107:1, 109:21, 118:1/29, 136:1). Usually the word *kiy* functions as a subordinating conjunction with the meaning *for* or *because*, but it can also be a superlative adjective or adverb.

# ONE HUNDRED ONE

EARLIEST MANUSCRIPTS — 4QPs[b] / Verses 1–8 in 11QPs[a]
LITURGY OF HOURS — Lauds on Tuesday IV

Psalm 101 begins with the same figure as the opening words of Virgil's *Aeneid*, *Arma virumque cano* ("Of arms and of a man I sing"), which is *hendiadys*, "one through two." Mercy and judgment are paired only here in the psalms. Also unique is "path of integrity" (*derek tamiym*, verses 2 and 6).

101:1 (Of David. A Mizmor.)
**Ôf mercy and òf judgment lét me sing; ***
**to you, the FONT OF BEÌNG, lét mè play.**

101:2 **Lêt me gain wisdòm †**
**on a path of integrity, ùntil you cóme to me; ***
**let me go about *with integrity of heart*, withín my home.**     *78:72*

101:3 **Lêt me set before my eyes nòthing of Béliäl. ***
**Weaving of webs I shun; they do nòt clíng tò me.**

101:4 **Lêt a devious heart bè turned awáy from me, ***
**with an evil that Ì dó nòt know.**

101:5 **Lêt me silence one who slanders his neìghbor in sécret; ***
**one proud of eyes and gross of heart I cànnót àbide.**

101:6 **My eyes are on faithful ones in thè land, to dwéll wìth me; ***
**one who goes by a path of integrity can be òf sérvice tò me.**

101:7 **Nôr does *one who commits treasòn* †**     *52:4*
**dwell in thè apses óf my home, ***
**nor do speakers of idle things stand bèfóre my eyes.**

101:8 ***Tôward the mornìngs* †**     *30:6*
**I will silence all unjùst people ín the land ***
**to cut from the *city of the FONT OF BEING* all *doèrs óf èvil*.**     *5:6*

Some of the appellations for Jerusalem include:
—*city of the Divine One* (*'iyr 'elohiym* 46:5, 48:2/9, 87:3)
—*city of the FONT OF BEING* (*'iyr yhwh* 48:9, 101:8)
—*city of the Great King* (*'iyr melek rab* 48:3).
Bishop Augustine of Hippo, in preaching on the psalms, thought deeply about these particular verses, and developed them into his magnum opus, the *Civitas Dei*.

# ONE HUNDRED TWO

EARLIEST MANUSCRIPTS — 4QPs[b] / Verses 18–29a in 11QPs[a]
NEW TESTAMENT — Verses 26-28 at Heb 1:10–12
LITURGY OF HOURS — Office of Readings on Tuesday IV

Psalm 102 is the fifth Penitential Psalm (6, 32, 38, 51, 102, 130, and 143). This psalmist searches similes for the way to convey his distress—he is like an oven (verse 4), like grass (5/12), like an owl (7), like a sparrow (8), like bread (10), like a shadow (12), like a garment (27). These are not metaphors, because the word "like" is always expressed. (If the psalmist had said "I am an owl" that would be a metaphor, but he says "I have been like an owl," and that is a simile.) The long form of a simile is the parable. Here in this psalm is the seed material for seven parables. In mid-psalm there is a small detour (12/24) when the ill person is distracted from his own pain to meditate on the compassion of God; during this section the psalmist steers clear of metaphor.

102:1 (Prayer of one lowly—hòw he grows feeble!—
but to the Face of the FONT OF BEING he poùrs out his need.)

102:2 **Ô FONT OF BEING, hearkèn to my práying, ***
**and let my beseechìng cóme tò you.**

102:3 *Hîde not your Face fròm me* †
*On my day of neèd,* **bend your Eár to me!**     *13:2*
**On the day I call,** *swiftly ánswèr me!*     *59:17*
    *69:18*

102:4 **Fôr my days hàve been eclípsed in smoke ***
**and my bones billòwed líke a fùrnace.**

102:5 **Bruîsed** *like the plant,* **my heart ìtself was wílting, ***     *72:16*
**so I have forgotten tò eát my bread.**

102:6 **Frôm the soùnd of my coúghing, ***
**my bones are clingìng tó my flesh.**

102:7 **Î became like an òwl of the wílderness; ***
**I was like a screech-òwl ín rùbble.**

102:8 **Î awoke and wàs like a spárrow, ***
**alone òn á roòftop.**

102:9 **Âll the day my rìvals were taúnting me; ***
**cursing me, thèy swóre àt me.**

102:10 **Îndeed, the bread that I consùme is like áshes, ***
**and my tears are in my drink thàt Í hàve mixed.**

102:11 Frôm the Face of yoùr anger ánd your rage, *
how you lift me up, bùt cást mè down.

102:12 Dâys for me, *like à shadow*, fáde away, *
and I, *like thè plánt*, am wìlting.          *72:16*

> *Like a shadow* (*ketsel*) describes the days of this psalmist (102:12)
> and elsewhere the days of Adam (144:4). A growing shadow is no
> longer light and not yet darkness, but light becoming darkness. The
> shadow also insinuates itself into the composite word *tsal-maweth*
> ("shadow of death" 23:4, 44:20, 107:10/14, Jer 13:16).

102:13 Bût you, FONT OF BEING, are *seàted etérnally*, *          *9:8*
and your memorial is *for àge áftèr age*.          *10:6*

102:14 Mây you arise! Feel tendèrly for Zíön, *
for the time to pity her, for thè móment hàs come.

102:15 Hôw pleasing to yoùr servants áre her stones; *
even for her dust thèy feél the pìty.

102:16 Lêt gentiles revere *the Nàme "FONT OF BÉING,"* *          *7:18*
and all the kings of thè lánd your Glòry.

102:17 Fôr the FONT OF BEÌNG builds up Zíön *
that she may be seen ìn hís Glòry.

102:18 Hê faces toward thè prayer of thóse in need, *
and their prayer he doès nót dèspise.

102:19 Lêt this be writtèn for a láter age, *
that a later people may give laud tò *thé* BEÌNG.          *68:5*

102:20 Fôr he looks down from hìs height of hóliness; *
from the skies, the FONT OF BEING tàkes nóte òf land,

102:21 see 79:11
tô hear the groanìng of a cáptive, *
to set free *thòse doómed tò death*,          *79:11*

102:22 thât in Ziön be retold *the Nàme "FONT OF BÉING,"* *          *7:18*
and his praise-craft in Jèrúsàlem,

102:23 ât the gathering òf gentiles ás one *
and of domains, to serve thè FÓNT OF BEÌNG.

102:24 Âlong thè way, he sápped my strength; *
*he has cùt shórt my days.*          *89:46*

102:25 Tô my God I say: "In midst of my dàys do not táke me; *
*an age of ages* are bùt yeárs fòr you.          *72:5*

102:26 *Ât their first appearance*, yoù founded thé land, *
and the *works of your Hands* àre the heávens.                    *8:7*

> *At their first appearance* (*lefaniym*) is an idiom found at only two
> places in the Hebrew Bible (102:26, 1 Sam 9:9). It is like the Latin
> *prima facie*, which means "on first viewing." Here, the land and the
> skies are obvious works of a divine Hand.

102:27 Thêy become nil, but you wìll stand; †
they are all wòrn *like a gárment*; *
*like clothing* you change them, and thèy fáde àway,

> *Like a garment* (*kabbeged* 102:27, 109:19; *kebeged* Job 13:28) and
> *like clothing* (*kallebush* 102:27, 104:6) are true synonyms, standing
> in parallel only here. Cloth disintegrates, torn in the wearing, moth-
> eaten in the storage. The very act of living ages a human being, but the
> divine FONT OF BEING suffers no such effect.

102:28 bût you will còntinue ás yourself, *
and your years àre wíthoùt end.
102:29 Lêt the children of your sèrvants be séttled, *
and their seedlings stand *before thè Fáce òf You*."           *17:2*

EARLIEST MANUSCRIPTS — 4QPs[b] / Verse 1 in 11QPs[a]
NEW TESTAMENT — Verse 8 at Jas 5:11 / Verse 17 at Lk 1:50
LITURGY OF HOURS — Office of Readings on Wednesday IV

Psalm 103 begins and ends "Bless, O my soul." The reader is privileged to hear the interior dialogue of this articulate self-interlocutor, who addresses his "inner self" (verse 1) and talks with angels (20/21).

| | | |
|---|---|---|
| 103:1 | (Of David.) | |
| | *Blêss, O my soul, thè FONT OF BÉING,* * | *104:35* |
| | **and, all my inner self, his *Name òf hóliness.*** | *33:21* |
| 103:2 | *Blêss, O my soul, thè FONT OF BÉING,* * | *104:35* |
| | **and forget not all thàt ís duè him—** | |
| 103:3 | **whô pardòns all your státe of guilt,** * | |
| | **who heals all òf yoúr ìllness,** | |
| 103:4 | **whô ransòms from the pít your life,** * | |
| | **who crowns you with mercy ànd téndèrness,** | |
| 103:5 | **whô fills your assèmbly with whát is good,** * | |
| | **that your youth be made nèw, *líke the eàgle.*** | |

*Like the eagle* (*kannesher* 103:5, Is 40:31). The psalmist wishes the youth of his soul to be renewed, like an eagle. There must be some backstory to this, like the resurrection of the phoenix bird from the ashes. The eagle was not a kosher animal, because of its diet, and so the reader is not compared directly to the bird.

| | | |
|---|---|---|
| 103:6 | **Crâfting *just deeds* is thè FONT OF BÉING,** * | *143:1* |
| | **and of judgmènts fór all vìctims,** | |
| 103:7 | **whô made known hìs ways to Móses,** * | |
| | **things he had done for *the children òf Ísràël.*** | |

*Children of Israël* (*beney yisra'el* 103:7, 148:14) means not just the babies of the land, but offspring of every generation. This phrase is same as *children of Jacob* (*beney ya'aqob* 77:16, 105:6).

| | | |
|---|---|---|
| 103:8 | **Tênder and gracious is thè FONT OF BÉING,** * | |
| | ***slow to wrath*, but manìfóld in mèrcy,** | *86:15* |
| 103:9 | **nòr will he *for ever* màke accusátion,** * | *9:7* |
| | **nor *eternally* pùt tó thè test,** | *5:12* |

103:10 nôr has he treated ùs as befíts our sin, *
nor dealt with us as bèfíts oùr guilt.

103:11 Fôr as the heavens àre high abóve the land, *
*mighty is his mercy upon* those whò révère him.

> **Mighty is his mercy** (*gabar hasdo* 103:11, 117:2) is the felicitous rendering of a powerful Hebrew idiom. Divine mercy has its own massive force, drawing humanity away from sin and death.

103:12 Âs sunrise is fàr *from the súnset,* *        75:7
so far he has put our rèbéllions fròm us.

103:13 Âs a father is tendèr to his chíldren, *
so tender is the FONT OF BEING to those whò révère him.

103:14 Fôr he is aware òf how he máde us; *
it is kept in mind hòw wé àre dust.

103:15 Dâys of a human bèing are *líke the grass,* *        37:2
like a blossom of the meadòw, thús hè blooms,

103:16 fôr a wind goes past hìm, †
*and thère is no móre of him,* *        37:10
and he is found no longèr át hìs place.

103:17 Bût the mercy of the FONT OF BEÌNG †
is *from eternity* to eternity on thòse who revére him, *        25:6
and his Justice belongs to the childrèn óf their children,

103:18 tô those who keep his bond †
and keep ìn mind his précepts, *
to àct úpòn them.

103:19 FÒNT OF BEING in thè skies has sét his seat, *
and his dominion has commànd óvèr all.

103:20 Blêss the FONT OF BEING, O his heràlds, †
O strong ones of might, àcting on hís command *
that the sound of hìs wórd be heèded.

103:21 Blêss the FONT OF BEÌNG, all his sábaöth, *
his acolytes whò dó hìs will.

103:22 Blêss the FONT OF BEING, all hìs works †
in all pòrtions of hís domain. *
*Bless, O my soul, thè FÓNT OF BÈING.*        104:35

# ONE HUNDRED FOUR

EARLIEST MANUSCRIPT — 11QPsᵃ
NEW TESTAMENT — Verse 4 at Heb 1:7
Verse 12 at Mt 13:32, Mk 4:32, Lk 13:19
CHRISTIAN FEASTDAY — Pentecost
LITURGY OF HOURS — Office of Readings on Sunday II

Psalm 104 borrowed its opening and closing lines from the previous, but the rest of this psalm is highly original, and displays high majesty of expression.

| | | |
|---|---|---|
| 104:1 | *Blêss, O my soul, the FONT OF BEÌNG*; † | *104:35* |
| | FONT OF BEING, my Divine Òne, you are greát indeed! * | |
| | With *Majesty and Grandeur* yoù áre bèdecked, | *21:6* |
| 104:2 | drêssed in light às with a mántle, * | |
| | arching across the skiès líke à tent, | |
| 104:3 | âssembling on the wàters his úpper decks, * | |
| | making clouds his chariot, wending *òn wíngs òf wind*, | *18:11* |
| 104:4 | mâking hìs heralds óf winds, * | |
| | his acolytes òf glówìng flame, | |
| 104:5 | fîxing thè land upón her poles, * | |
| | unlikely to tumble, *evèr ánd àn age!* | *5:12* |
| 104:6 | Dêpths cloaked hìm *like a gárment*; * | *102:27* |
| | above the mountaìns, wátèrs stood. | |
| 104:7 | Ât your roàring they túrned about! * | |
| | At *the sounding of yoùr thúnder* thèy fled! | *77:19* |
| 104:8 | Thêy went up the mountains, they went down the válleys, * | |
| | to the place that you hàd fíxed fòr them. | |
| 104:9 | Yoû placed a bordèr for them nót to cross, * | |
| | for them never again to sùbmérge thè land, | |
| 104:10 | yoù who send fountaìnheads intó the streams, * | |
| | winding bètweén the moùntains. | |
| 104:11 | Ôf them, all wildlìfe of the plaín can drink; * | |
| | donkeys quench thè thírst thèy have. | |
| 104:12 | Ôver them perch *bìrds of the heávens*; * | *79:2* |
| | from among the branches thèy gíve theìr call. | |
| 104:13 | Gîving drink to the mountaìns from your úpper decks, * | |
| | with the fruit of your works yoù fíll thè land, | |

104:14 grôwing grass for the cattlè, †
and plants for thè care of Ádam, *
to bring bread fòrth fróm thè land:

104:15 ând wine to make one's heart rèjoice, †
oil tò make the fáces shine, *
and bread to make òne's heárt mìghty.

104:16 Fûll-branched are the trees of thè FONT OF BÉING: *
*the cedars of Lebanòn* whích he plànted,                29:5

104:17 în which thè birds can séttle, *
the stork, which in junipèrs hás hèr home.

104:18 Moûntains, the steep ones, bèlong to thé goats; *
bedrocks to the badgèrs ás a rèfuge.

104:19 Hê made a Moòn for the móments, *
a Sun thàt knóws its sètting.

104:20 Yoû send dàrkness and thére is night, *
in which roam *all wildlìfe óf the fòrest*:                50:10

104:21 cûbs of the liòns, bawling fór prey, *
begging fròm Gód their food.

104:22 Sûn rises, and then thèy reassémble, *
and gathèr ín their dens.

104:23 Âdam goès out to hís work, *
and to his servìce úntil sùnset.

104:24 *Hôw many are* your works, FONT OF BEÌNG, †      3:2
all of which yoù made in wísdom; *
the land is filled wìth yoúr creàtions:

104:25 Hêre is the sea, grand and wide òf reach: †
there are species, and *thère is no coúnting*, *          40:13
*small* wildlìfe *with the greàt ones*.

Like many Hebrew phrases, **small ones with the great ones** (*qetannot
'im-gedolot* 104:25, *haqqetanniym 'im-gedoliym* 115:13) conjoins
two opposing polarities, comprising everything between.

104:26 Thêre are the vèssels that návigate; *
there is Leviathan, to laugh àt whích you made.

104:27 Âll of them àre looking tó you, *
to give their foód *in seàson*.                          145:15

104:28 **Whên you give tò them, they hárvest; ***
*when you open your Hand,* **they are filled wìth whát ìs good.**

> *You open your Hand* (*tiftah yadka*) appears twice in the psalms (104:28, 145:16) and both times the next verb is to fill to the brim (*saba'a*). The open Hand is an anthropomorphic metaphor for the generosity of God. Hand is singular rather than dual here, because God needs only one Hand. Thus the imagery here is not slavishly anthropomorphic, as with the idols of the false gods.

104:29 **Whên you turn your Fàce, they grow fríghtened; ***
**you halt their breath: they die and go bàck tó theìr dust.**

104:30 **Yoû send your Breath: thèy are creáted, ***
**and you make new thè fáce of thè field.**

104:31 **Fôr ever be the Glory of thè FONT OF BÉING: ***
**may the FONT OF BEING in hìs wórks find joy.**

104:32 **Hê stares at the lànd, and it trémbles; ***
**he taps on the mountaìns, ánd thèy smoke!**

104:33 see 146:2

**Lêt me sing to the FONT ÒF BEING ín my life! ***
**Let me play for my Divine One in my rèmaínìng time!**

104:34 **Sweêt be my contèmplation óf him! ***
**I am one who rejoices in thè FÓNT OF BÈING!**

104:35 **Lêt sinners desist from thè land, †**
**and unjust peóple bé no more! ***
*Bless, my soul, the FONT OF BEÌNG! Hállelù-YAH!*

> *Bless, my soul, the FONT OF BEING* (*borkiy nafshiy  eth-yhwh* 103:1/2/22, 104:1/35) appears at the beginning and the end of adjacent psalms 103 and 104, and nowhere else. It is an indication, along with others, that the two psalms have a common provenance. Either the same psalmist wrote them both, or another psalmist used 103 as a skeletal form for 104. In Hebrew anthropology, blessing emerges from one's soul ("neck"), while thought derives from one's heart.

> *Hallelu-Yah* (104:35, 105:45, 106:1/48, 111:1, 112:1, 113:1/9, 116:19, 117:2, 135:1/21, 146:1/10, 147:1/20, 148:1/48, 149:1/9, 150:1/6) appears twenty-one times, always at the beginning or the end of a psalm. The plural imperative verb *Hallelu* takes as object the short divine name *Yah*.

NEW TESTAMENT —
Verses 8-9 at Lk 1:72-73
LITURGY OF HOURS —
Office of Readings on Saturday I
only in the seasons of Advent and Christmas, Lent and Easter

Psalm 105 appeals to the historical memory. The Greeks invented history as secular chronicle, leaving out their gods, but the Hebrews were no people without their God (verse 5), without whose help they could never have left Egypt. The psalmist uses several different expressions for that dual kingdom —"Egypt" (*mitsrayim,* verses 23 and 38, with dual ending), "both lands" (30/32/35/36), "both topsoils" (35), and "land of Ham" (23/27).

| | | |
|---|---|---|
| 105:1 | **Gîve laud to the FONT OF BEING; càll out in hís Name! *** | |
| | **Make known his deeds** *àmóng the peòples!* | *57:10* |
| 105:2 | **Sîng to hìm! Play your stríngs for him! *** | |
| | **Contemplàte áll his màrvels!** | |
| 105:3 | **Tâke pride in hìs** *Name of hóliness! *** | *33:21* |
| | **Rejoice at heart, you who seek thè FÓNT OF BÈING!** | |
| 105:4 | **Pûrsue the FONT ÒF BEING ánd his might; *** | |
| | *seek the Face òf Hím* **àlways.** | *24:6* |
| 105:5 | **Keêp in mind his màrvels that hé has done, *** | |
| | **his portents and** *the judgmènts óf hìs Mouth.* | |

*Judgments of his Mouth* (*mishpetey-piw* 105:6, 119:13) seems to indicate that the word *mishpot* is verbal judgment, and not merely judgment in the mind. Of course, judgment requires forethought, but this term emphasizes completion of the act in verbal utterance.

| | | |
|---|---|---|
| 105:6 | **Ô seedlings of Abràham, his sérvant! *** | |
| | **O** *children of Jacob,* **hìs chósèn one!** | *77:16* |
| 105:7 | **Hê is the FONT OF BEÌNG, our Divíne One; *** | |
| | **through** *all the land* **àre hís jùdgments.** | *8:2* |
| 105:8 | **Hîs bond is a memòrial** *etérnally,* ***** | *5:12* |
| | **a promise he made for à thoúsand àges,** | |
| 105:9 | **whìch he has cràfted with Abráham, *** | |
| | **and by hìs oáth to Ìsaac,** | |

105:10 ând which he set up fòr Jacob ás a law, *
      for Israël as an ètérnàl bond,

105:11 sâying, "To you I give thè land of Cánaan *
      as the measure of yoùr hérìtage,"

105:12 wîthin which they residèd *for a móment,* *
      still in numbèr pérsòns few.

105:13 Thêy roamed from nàtion to nátion, *
      from one domain to yet ànóther peòple.

105:14 Hê let none of Adàm's kind extórt from them, *
      and rebuked kings òn theír bèhalf:

105:15 "Toûch none òf my anoínted ones, *
      and to my prophets caùse nó dìstress."

105:16 Hê called a fàmine upón the land; *
      he broke all thè stálks òf grain.

105:17 Hê sent someone bèfore their fáces, *
      Joseph, who wàs sóld as à slave.

105:18 În the shacklè his feet wére held; *
      into an *iron collàr* wént hìs neck,

*2:12*

An *iron collar* (*barzel* 105:18, *bekabley barzel* 149:8) constrains the legs (mobility) or the neck (soul), but not the hands, because a manacled man needs too much assistance from the guards. The narrative (Gen 37:27) does not indicate that Joseph was shackled.

105:19 ûntil the tìme when his wórd came; *
      a statement from the FONT OF BEÌNG próved hìm true.

105:20 Â king sent and released him as commànder of peóples, *
      and hè sét hìm free.

105:21 Hê made hìm master óf his house, *
      and warden ìn áll his hòldings,

105:22 tô teach his prìnces aboút their souls, *
      and to make hìs éldèrs wise.

105:23 Thên Israël càme into Égypt, *
      and Jacob stayed *in thè lánd òf Ham.*

*The land of Ham* (*'erets ham* 105:23/27, 106:22) means the land of Egypt (*mitzrayim*). Ham, son of Noah, was forefather of Cush, Egypt, Put and Canaan (Gen 10:6). The Coptic language of Egypt was unintelligible to the Hebrews (114:1) but the Canaanites spoke a Northwest Semitic language like Hebrew or Aramaic.

105:24 Hê increased hìs people greátly, *
and made them oùtnúmber theìr foes,
105:25 whôse hearts he turned to hatrèd of his péople, *
and to abuse òf hís sèrvants.
105:26 Hê sent forth *Mòses*, his sérvant, *
*Aaron*, whom he had chosèn fór hìmself.  77:21
105:27 Thêy took to themselves hìs promise óf signs *
and marvels *in thè lánd òf Ham*.  105:23
105:28 Hê sent forth dàrkness and dárkening, *
for were they not bitter tò hís dècrees?
105:29 Hê changed theìr waterwáys to blood, *
and caused theìr físh tò die.
105:30 *Bôth the lands* were teèming with fróglets, *  105:35
even within the chambers of theìr róyàlty.
105:31 Hê spoke and a swarm òf gnats inváded, *
into all theìr bórdèrlands.
105:32 Hê gave hail at theìr rainy seásons, *
forks of flàme ínto *bòth the lands*.  105:35
105:33 Hê struck down theìr vines and theír figs, *
and split the trees of theìr bórdèrlands.
105:34 Hê spoke and the lòcusts inváded, *
and grasshoppers, and *thère wás no coùnting*.  40:13
105:35 Thêy consumed eàch plant in *bóth the lands*; *
they consumed thè fruít of theìr fields.

Reading **both the lands** results from repointing *'artsam* with a dual
ending. The name *mitsrayim*, "Egypt," is dual in Hebrew, because
the Hebrews knew that Egypt actually comprised two kingdoms,
combined into a dual monarchy like the Austro-Hungarian Empire.

105:36 see 78:51

Hê struck each firstborn in *bóth the lands*, *  105:35
first fruits of all theìr pótèncy.
105:37 Hê brought them out wìth silver ánd gold, *
and among his tribes nò óne stùmbled.
105:38 Êgypt rejoiced àt their depárting, *
for fear of them had fallèn úpòn them.
105:39 Hê spread out cloùds as a cánopy, *
and flame tò bríghten thè night.

105:40 Thêy were insistènt, and he broúght them quail, *
and with bread from thè skiés he filled them.

105:41 Hê opened a rock, ànd waters gúshed out; *
they wended like a wadi *in thè dry plàces.* 63:2

105:42 Fôr he kept in mind his pròmise of hóliness *
to Abràhám, his sèrvant.

105:43 Hê brought forth hìs people wíth joy, *
with joyful song hìs chósèn ones.

105:44 Hê gave to them thè lands of géntiles, *
and wealth of nations fòr thém tò claim.

105:45 For this, let them keep sentinèl over hís laws, *
and preserve his teachìngs! *Hállelù-YAH!* 104:35

# ONE HUNDRED SIX

LITURGY OF HOURS — Office of Readings on Saturday II
only in the seasons of Advent, Christmas, Lent, and Easter

Psalm 106 continues the appeal to memory from the previous psalm. Though our forebears did not grasp the wonders as they happened (verse 7), we grow in appreciation by calling them back to mind again and again. The really important things are those that reveal new dimensions of meaning every time they are recalled. Memory exists in the service of meaning.

106:1 = 107:1, 118:1/29, 136:1

*Hâllelu-YAH!* "Give laud to thè FONT OF BÉING! *       *104:35*
How good, how eternàl ís his mèrcy!"

106:2  Whô can tell the strengths of thè FONT OF BÉING? *
Who can sound àll hís praìse-craft?

106:3  Blêssedness belongs to thòse who have júdgment, *
acting with justice *in évery seàson!*      *145:15*

106:4  Keêp me in mind, FONT OF BEÌNG, †
with favòr for your peóple; *
draw near me with yoùr sáving help:

106:5  tô behold goodnèss for your chósen ones, *
to rejoice in joy of your nation, to glory in yoùr hérìtage.

106:6  Âlong with oùr forebears, wé have sinned; *
we have done wrong, have actèd únjùstly.

106:7  Nôr did our forebears in Egypt understand your marvèls, †
nor did they keep in mind the grandeùr of your mércy; *
they were bitter beside a seà, ín the Reèd Sea.

106:8  Hê saved them *for thè sake of hís Name,* *      *25:11*
to màke knówn hìs Strength.

106:9  Hê rebuked the Reed Seà, and it draíned away; *
he led them through the deeps as through thè wíldèrness.

106:10  Hê saved them from the hand òf one who háted, *
and he redeemed them from the *hand of àn énèmy.*      *31:9*

106:11  Îd the watèrs were submérged their foes, *
not one òf whóm sùrvived.

106:12  Tô his words thèy gave assùrance; *
they sàng praíse-craft tò him.

106:13 *Swîftly* did they fòrget the thíngs he did; *     *69:18*
they did not cling tò hís coùnsel.

106:14 Thêy *wanted what they wantèd in the wílderness* *     *78:40*
and tested God *ìn thé wàsteland.*     *55:8*

> *They wanted what they wanted* (*wayyith'awwu ta'awah* 106:14, Prov
> 21:26) is an instance of the internal accusative, when the verb takes a
> direct object that derives from the same root. See also:
> —*sing a song* (*shiyru shiyr* 33:3, 96:1, 98:1, 149:1)
> —*offer oblation* (*zibhu zebah* 4:6, 27:6, 107:22, 116:17)
> —*contest a contest* (*riybah ribiy* 43:1, 119:154; . . . *ribeka* 74:22)
> —*do a deed* (*po'al pa'alta* 44:2).

106:15 Hê gave them whàt they requésted, *
but sent a wasting disease àgaínst theìr life.

106:16 Thêy were jealous òf *Moses* ín the camp,
of *Aaron*, sacred to thè FÓNT OF BÈING.     *77:21*

106:17 Groûnd opened ànd swallowed Dáthan *
and covered the clan òf Ábìram.

106:18 Ând there blazed à fire agaínst their clan, *
a flame that consumed thè únjust peòple,

106:19 thôse who had fashioned a bùll-calf at Hóreb, *
and adored a thing càst óf mètal,

106:20 thôse who had èxchanged their Glóry *
for the image of an herb-eàtíng bùll-calf,

106:21 thôse who *forgot God*, à Savior tó them, *     *9:18*
maker of great thìngs ín Ègypt,

106:22 ôf the marvèls *in the lánd of Ham*,     *105:23*
of wonders bèsíde the Reèd Sea.

106:23 Hê would have decreed their extinctiòn †
had not his chosen Moses stood in thè gap befóre his Face *
to turn his fury fròm déstrùction.

106:24 Thêy objected against à land of beaúty; *
to his word they àsséntèd not.

106:25 Thêy complained withìn their encámpments; *
they heeded not the call of thè FÓNT OF BÈING.

106:26 Hê lifted up hìs Hand agaínst them *
to toss them *into thè wíldèrness,*     *55:8*

| | |
|---|---|
| 106:27 | ând to cast their seedlings *àmong the géntiles*, *<br>and to scatter them àmóng thè lands. |

9:12

106:28 Tô the Baäl of Peòr they had yóked themselves; *
they ate things offèred tó thè dead.

106:29 Thêy incurred wràth by their deálings; *
among them there bròke oút à plague.

106:30 Phînehas rose up ànd issued júdgment; *
liftèd wás thè plague.

106:31 Thîs was held for him as àn act of jústice
*for age after age*, to ètérnìty.

10:6

106:32 Thêy caused anger *by the watèrs of Meríbah*; *
things went badly for Moses bècaúse òf them,

81:8

106:33 fôr they embìttered his spírit; *
they put nonsense ùpón hìs lips.

106:34 Thêy did not ùproot the peóples, *
as the Font of Beìng hád tòld them.

106:35 Thêy comminglèd with the géntiles; *
they learned òf theír deàlings.

106:36 Thêy gave servìce to their ídols, *
which became à snáre fòr them.

106:37 Thêy offèred up their ówn sons *
and their daughtèrs tó the dèmons.

106:38 Thêy shed innocent blood, blood of their sòns, †
and of their daughters, offered to the ìdols of Cánaan. *
They polluted the land wìth bloódy deeds.

106:39 Thêy defiled themsèlves in their deálings; *
they committed adultery ìn theír àctions.

106:40 Îre of the Font of Beìng ignited àgainst his peóple, *
offended by his òwn hérìtage.

106:41 Hê gave them into thè hand of géntiles; *
they who commandèd thém despìsed them.

106:42 Thêy oppressed thèm as their rívals; *
they were humbled bèneáth theìr hands.

106:43 Ôften he delivèred them, †
yet they were bittèr in their coúnsels; *
they sank into theìr státe òf guilt.

106:44 Hê perceìved when *they hád distress*, *
when hè heárd their cries.

18:7

106:45 Hê kept ìn mind his bónd with them; *
he felt pity as befits hìs greát mèrcy.

106:46 Hê bestowed tò them the ténderness *
in the face of all whò détaìned them.

106:47 Sâve us, FONT OF BEING, our Divine Òne! †
Gather us from àmong the géntiles *
to laud your *Name of holiness*, to glory ìn yoúr praìse-craft.

106:48 see 41:14                                                    *33:21*

Blêssed be the FONT OF BEING, *Divine One of Isràël,* †     *41:14*
from the eternal and tò the etérnal!
Let all the people say, "Amèn! *Hállelù-YAH!"*              *104:35*

# ONE HUNDRED SEVEN

LITURGY OF HOURS — Office of Readings on Saturday III

Psalm 107 holds recurring verses to affirm God's response (7/13/19/28) and invite thanks (8/15/21/31). A key phrase occurs three times in this psalm (4/7/36) and nowhere else—"a city in which to dwell." The Israëlites were not interested in urbanization as such. Their goal was the "city of our Divine One" (Psalm 48:2/9), a city worth living in, a city of life.

107:1 = 106:1, 118:1/29, 136:1
> **"Gîve laud to thè FONT OF BÉING! \***
> **How good, how eternàl ís his mèrcy!"**

107:2    **Lêt them speak, redeemed by thè FONT OF BÉING, \***
         **whom he redeemed from thè hánd òf need,**

107:3    **ând whom he gathered from thè lands, †**
         **from sunrìse and *from súnset*, \***               *75:7*
         **from the Zaphon ànd fróm thè Sea.**

107:4    **Thêy roamed *in the wildernèss, in the wásteland*; \***    *55:8, 78:40*
         **they could find no routc to *a city ìn whích tò dwell.***

The goal of Exodus was ***a city in which to dwell*** (*'iyr moshab* 107:4/7/36), in a land flowing with milk and honey. A habitable city required nearby farm land, internal water sources, and a defensible position.

107:5    **Fâmished people—yès, thirsting peóple—**
         **their life within thèm ébbed àway.**

107:6 see 107:13/19/28
> **Tô the FONT OF BEING they crièd *when they hád distress*; \***
> ***from their anguish he dèlivered them.***        *18:7, 25:17*

107:7    **Hê directed them onto à level páthway \***
         **so they could journey to *a city ìn whích tò dwell.***     *107:4*

107:8 = 107:15/21/31
> **Lêt them laud the FONT OF BEÌNG for his mércy, \***
> **and his marvels to *the childrèn óf Àdam:***         *11:4*

107:9    **hôw he can satisfy a soùl that is thírsting, \***
         **and fill a famished soul wìth whát ìs good.**

107:10 Thêy dwelt in darkness ànd *deathly shádow,* *                     *23:4*
       bound with sicknèss ánd with shàckles,
107:11 fôr they resènted the wórds of God, *
       and rejected the advice òf thé Mòst High,
107:12 bût their heart was brought down thròùgh tribulátion; *
       they stumbled, and *no helpèr woúld thère be.*          *22:12*
107:13 = 107:6/19/28
       Tô the Font of Being they crièd *when they hád distress*; *
       *from their anguish hè sét thèm free.*          *18:7, 25:17*
107:14 Hê led them out of darkness ànd *deathly shádow,* *          *23:4*
       and hè bróke theìr bonds.
107:15 = 107:8/21/31
       Lêt them laud the Font of Beìng for his mércy, *
       and his marvels for *the childrèn óf Àdam:*          *11:4*
107:16 hôw he hàs shattered doórs of bronze *
       and bars of iròn hé has bròken.
107:17 Thêy were made foolish on their pàth of rebéllion, *
       and enfeeblèd wíth theìr sin;
107:18 theîr soul repèlled every kínd of food, *
       as they neared *thè gátes òf death.*          *9:14*
107:19 = 107:6/13/28
       Tô the Font of Being they crièd *when they hád distress*; *
       *from their anguish hè sét thèm free.*          *18:7, 25:17*
107:20 Hê sent out hìs word and heáled them, *
       and released thèm fróm their pìtfalls.
107:21 = 107:8/15/31
       Lêt them laud the Font of Beìng for his mércy, *
       and his marvels for *the childrèn óf Àdam:*          *11:4*
107:22 ând *offer òblations óf laud,* *
       and recount his deeds wìth jóyfùl song,

*Offer oblations of laud* (*zibhu zibhey todah* 107:22, 116:17) is an
"internal accusative," verb and noun coming from the same root.
Another example is to **sing a song renewed** (*shiyru shiyr hadash*
33:3, 96:1, 98:1, 144:9, 149:1). In both cases the internal nature of the
construction is mitigated by the addition of a third word.

107:23 fôr those going down to thè sea in véssels, *
       those making embassy *in watèrs mánìfold:*          *18:17*
107:24 Thêy beheld the works of thè Font of Béing, *
       and his marvèls ín a deèp place:

107:25 Hê spoke up ànd stirred *a gústing wind*, *
whose waves liftèd thém òn high;

*Gusting wind* (*ruah se'arah* 107:25, 148:8) pushes the water and produces high waves. This is more dangerous to ships at sea than *driving wind* (*ruah so'ah* 55:9).

107:26 thêy went up skyward, went downwàrd into thé deeps; *
in the danger, theìr soúls were shàken.

107:27 Thêy reeled and swàyed like a drúnken one, *
and all theìr skíll was ùseless.

107:28 see 107:6/13/19
Tô the FONT OF BEÌNG they crièd *when they hád distress*; *
*from their anguish hè réscued them.*                    18:7, 25:17

107:29 Hê caused thè storm to stánd still, *
and the waves wère sílenced fòr them.

107:30 Thêy rejoiced thàt they becáme still; *
he towed them to the port òf their choòsing.

107:31 = 107:8/15/21
Lêt them laud the FONT OF BEÌNG for his mércy, *
and his marvels for *the childrèn óf Àdam:*              11:4

107:32 Lêt them exalt him in an assèmbly of peóple *
and in a session of elders gìve laúd tò him,

107:33 whô changed rivèrs into wílderness *
and outlets of water intò thírstìng ground,

107:34 lând of fruit ìnto a *sálty plain*, *
from the injustice of those dwellìng ín thàt place.

*Salty plain* (*melohah* 107:34, Job 39:6) stands in parallel to *wilderness* and *thirsty ground* in the previous verse and *wilderness* and *dry land* in the following verse. In every respect a salty plain is the antithesis of a *city in which to dwell* ('*iyr moshab* 107:4/7/36)—as a plain, it offers no defensible position in case of attack; its salty soil allows for no agriculture; and there are no water sources.

107:35 Hê changed a wildernèss into wétlands *
and *a land that was dry* intò wátered oùtlets,       63:2

107:36 ând he settled there à famished peóple, *
that they might found *a city ìn whích tò dwell.*     107:4

107:37 Thêy planted the meàdows; they gráfted vines; *
they harvested thè fruíts of pròduce.

107:38 Hê blessed them; thèy greatly múltiplied, *
yet their cattle dìd nót dimìnish.

107:39 Whênever they were rèduced and sánk low *
from accidents of disastèr ánd of troùble,

107:40 hê poured contèmpt onto prínces, *
and made them roam ìn tráckless lòwlands

107:41 whîle one in need was liftèd up from weákness; *
he gathered their familiès *like the sheèpfold.*     49:15

107:42 Steâdfast people bèheld and knéw joy, *
but every vice kèpt íts moùth closed.

107:43 Whô has wisdom both to see sùch things *
and to reflèct on the Mércies *
of thè Fónt of Bèing?

LITURGY OF HOURS — Lauds on Wednesday IV

Psalm 108 has only one unique verse (7). The first six are borrowed from Psalm 57, and the last seven from Psalm 60. Both source psalms are Elohist and never use the name FONT OF BEING. The editor of Psalm 108 left Elohist language intact, but changed *'Adonay* (57:10) to FONT OF BEING (108:4).

108:1   (A Song.
      A Mizmor of David.)

108:2 = 57:8

**Fîrm is my heàrt, O Divíne One! \***             *57:8*
**I will sing and play chòrds! Yés, my Glòry!**     *21:14*

108:3 = 57:9

**Wâke the hàrp and the lyre-bow! \***
**I woùld wáke thè dawn!**

108:4 = 57:10

**Lêt me laud you *among the peoplès*, FONT OF BÉING, \***   *57:10*
**and play for you *àmóng the nàtions*.**            *44:15*

The editor of Psalm 108 changed *among the peoples, O Adonay* (*baggoyim 'adonay* 57:10) to *among the peoples, FONT OF BEING* (*baggoyim yhwh* 108:4). This is the only sign that the editor was a Yahwist, since he left untouched *the Divine One* (*'elohiym*).

108:5 = 57:11

**Fôr greater than the skiès is *your mércy*, \***
**and as thè sky-dome *yoùr truth*.**              *25:10*

108:6 = 57:6/12

**Êxalted *above heavèns*, O Divíne One, \***       *8:2*
**and above *all the land* ìs yoúr Glòry.**          *8:2*

108:7  **Thât your loved ones be set freè, †**
**may your Rìght Hand grant sáfety, \***
**and may yoù ánswèr me:**

108:8 = 60:8

**Ône who is Divine said in his holy plàce: †**
**"I gladly lày claim to Shechem, \***
**and survey thè Vále òf Booths.**

108:9 = 60:9

> Mîne is Gilead, mine Manassèh, †
> and Ephraïm is à stronghold fór my head; *
> Judàh ís my mace.

108:10 = 60:10

> Môab is my washbòwl; †
> on Edom Ì toss my sándal; *
> above Philistia Ì shoút fòr joy!

108:11 = 60:11

> *Whô* will secure for me à *bulwark cíty*? *                    *31:22*
> *Who* will lead mè tó Èdom?"                                    *24:3*

The editor of Psalm 108 changed *a bulwark city* (*'iyr matsor* 31:22,
60:11) to the synonymous *'iyr mibtsar* (108:11, 2 Kings 3:19, Jer
1:18). That accorded the idiom with the usage of Jeremiah's time, and
indicates that the editing was done around 600 BC.

108:12 = 60:12 see 44:10

> Nôr are you, Divine Òne, angry wíth us?
> Nor will you, Divine One, go oùt wíth oùr troops?

108:13 = 60:13

> Êxtend to ùs help from thé siege, *
> since false security còmes fróm Àdam.

108:14 = 60:14

> În the Divine One wè achieve víctory, *
> for he himself sùbdúes oùr foes.

# ONE HUNDRED NINE

EARLIEST MANUSCRIPT — Verses 21–31 in 11QPs[a]
NEW TESTAMENT — Verse 8 at Acts 1:20
LITURGY OF HOURS — Excluded from the cycle

The author of Psalm 109 has an enemy unjust and deceitful, who has perjured him "gratuitously." The adverb is *hinnam* (35:7/19, 69:5, 109:3, 119:161), synonymous with adverb *reqam* "without cause" (7:5, 25:3). Peter ascribes this psalm to David (Acts 1:15) and quotes verse 8 (Acts 1:20).

109:1   (For the Director. Of David. A Mizmor.)
**Ô Divine Òne of my praíse-craft! ***
**May yoù *nót bè deaf!***           *28:1*

109:2   **Fôr a mouth of injustìce †**
**and a mouth of deceit òpened agaínst me; ***
**they accuse me wìth *idlè tongue,***

> The idle tongue (*leshon shaqer*) appears four times in Proverbs (Prov 6:17, 12:19, 21:6, 26:28) and once in the Book of Psalms (109:2). Other psalms castigate the **idle lip** (*sefath sheqer*, 31:19, 120:2) and the **speakers of idle things** (*dobrey sheqariym*, 101:7).

109:3   **ând speaking hatrèd they encírcled me; ***
**they attacked mè fór nò cause.**

109:4   **În response to my affèction they slánder me, ***
**evèn whíle Ì pray.**

109:5   **Thêy imposed on me *èvil in pláce of good,* ***     *35:12*
**and loathing in answèr tó my love:**

109:6   **"Âppoint an unjùst man agaínst him, ***
**and a *satan to stand àt hís rìght hand.***

> A satan to stand at his right hand (*satan ya'amod 'al-yemiyno* 106:9, Zech 3:1; *ya'amod satan* 1 Chron 21:1). *Satan* is a generic Hebrew noun for a tempter or tormenter. God sent the heavenly satan to tempt the righteous man, Job. In this psalm, the satan is a court official appointed to cross-examine the accused and the defense witnesses.

109:7   **Ât *his indictment* let hìm be held guílty; ***     *37:33*
**let his plea itself be countèd ás à crime.**

109:8   Lêt the days that belong tò him *becóme few,* *
       by another let hìs póst be tàken.

> **Become few** (*yihyu meʿattiym* 109:8, Qohelet 5:1) is the antonym
> of **become many** (*rabbu* 3:2, 4:8, 104:24). Peter quotes this verse to
> characterize the death of Judas (Acts 1:20).

109:9   Lêt his childrèn become órphans, *
       and hìs wífe a wìdow.

109:10  *Ârdently* let his childrèn wander ánd beg, *           40:2
        and be driven fròm theír shànties.

109:11  Lêt a lender seize ìn forfeit áll he has; *
        let strangèrs raíd his sàvings.

109:12  Tô him let no òne offer mércy, *
        nor anyone be tendèr tó his òrphans.

109:13  Lêt his hereàfter be cút off; *
        in the next age let theìr náme be èrased.

109:14  Lêt his father's guilt be recalled by thè FONT OF BÉING, *
        and let his mother's sins nevèr bé èrased."

109:15  Lêt them stand before the FONT ÒF BEING álways, *
        but may he *cut off memory of thèm fróm thè land.*     34:17

109:16  Fôr they did not keep in mind the works of mèrcy, †
        yet drove to death òne *lowly ánd in need* *          35:10
        *and bròkénheàrted.*                           34:19

109:17  Lêt cursing, which hè loved, come báck to him, *
        let blessing, which he scorned, bè fár fròm him.

109:18  Âs his garment, let cursing bedeck hìm, †
        come *like thè waters* ínto him *            22:15
        and like the oil ìntó hìs bones,

109:19  bêing his, *like a gàrment* enfólding,*          102:27
        like a sash evèr tó gìrd him.

109:20  Bê this done to my accusers by thè FONT OF BÉING, *
        and to those speaking ill àgaínst my soul.

109:21  Bût you, *FONT OF BEING-Adònay!* †          16:2
        Deal with me *for thè sake of yoúr Name.* *      25:11
        How good is your mercy! Dèlívèr me!

109:22  Fôr that one *lowly ànd in need* ám I, *         35:10
        and my heart is pierced *wìthín my chest.*       39:4

109:23   *Líke a shadow*, like ìts trail, I tápered off; *         *102:12*
       like a locùst brúshed àside.

109:24   My knees stumblèd from the fásting *
       and my flesh grew lean fròm thé anoìnting.

109:25   Sô I have beèn a rebúke to them; *
       when they behold me, thèy túrn theìr heads.

109:26   Hêlp me, O FONT OF BEÌNG, my Divíne One; *
       *save me as bèfíts your mèrcy.*            *25:7*

The phrase *as befits your mercy* (*kehasdeka* 25:7) expands one way
into *save me as befits your mercy* (*hoshiy'eniy kehasdeka* 109:26;
*hoshiy'eniy behasdeka* 31:17) and another way into *as befits your
mercy give me life* (*kehasdeka hayyeni* 119:88/159).

109:27   Lêt them know thàt this is yoúr Hand, *
       that you, the FONT OF BEÌNG, háve dòne it.

109:28   Thêy curse, thèy do, but yoú bless; *
       they rise and are shamed, but your servànt wíll bè glad.

109:29   Lêt those who tempt me bè clad with dísgrace, *
       enfolded like a mantlè ín theìr shame.

109:30   *Wíth my mouth* loudly, †          *5:10*
       I give laud to thè FONT OF BÉING, *
       and in the midst of many tàke príde ìn him.

109:31   Fôr he stands at the rìght hand of óne in need *
       to save from those whò júdge òne's soul.

NEW TESTAMENT —
Verse 1 at Mt 22:44, Mk 12:36, Lk 20:42–3
Verse 1 at Acts 2:34, 1 Cor 15:25, Heb 1:13
Verse 4 at Heb 5:6 and 7:20
LITURGY OF HOURS — Second Vespers of Sunday

Psalm 110 begins at the feet and concludes at the head. The word *rosh* "head" can mean a head of state (as *ra'is* in modern Arabic). Melchisedek (verse 4) was priest-king of Salem (Gen 14:18), and David, in taking the city, assumed that monarch's titles, including the priestly order.

110:1   (Of David. A Mizmor.)
**Ôracle of the FONT OF BEÌNG: †**
**"O my master, sìt at my Ríght Hand, \***
**that I may set your rivals as à stoól for yoùr feet."**

110:2   **Yoûr scepter of might will he sènd, †**
***the FONT OF BEÌNG from the Zíön: \****
**march into the midst of yoùr énèmies!**

*FONT OF BEING from the Ziön* (*yhwh mitssiyyon* 110:2, 128:5, 134:3, 135:21) connects the Hebrews' God with their capital city. The "gods of Rome" is a similar expression.

110:3   **Wîth your people was princedom on your day òf birth, †**
**with holy honòrs from *the ténder place*; \***
**from your dawn, at dewfàll Í begòt you.**

110:4   **FÔNT OF BEING has swòrn and will nót relent: \***
**you are priest eternally in the line of Mèlchísèdek.**

110:5   **Âdonay ìs at your ríght hand; \***
**he shattered kings on hìs dáy òf wrath.**

110:6   **Hê decides against the gentìles, †**
**laden with corpsès is the wíde land, \***
**upon which he hàs crúshed theìr head;**

110:7   **Frôm the stream by the road, sòmeone is drínking; \***
**thus he will be *liftèd úp às head.***                   *24:7*

# ONE HUNDRED ELEVEN

LITURGY OF HOURS — Second Vespers of Sunday III

Psalms 111 and 112 each have 22 lines, one for each letter of the alphabet, and share the Waw line: "and his Justice is standing for an age." The first psalm is about divine justice, however, and the second about human justice.

| | | |
|---|---|---|
| 111:1 | *Hâllelu-Yàh!* † | *104:35* |
| | *Aleph:* **I laud** *wholeheartedly* **thè Font of Béing.** * | *9:1* |
| | *Beth:* **in league with steadfast peoplè, ánd in coùncil.** | |
| 111:2 | *Ghimel:* **Greât are the works of thè Font of Béing,** * | |
| | *Daleth:* **to be sought for àll theír dèlights.** | |
| 111:3 | *He: Mâjesty and Grandeùr* **are in hís deeds,** * | *21:6* |
| | *Waw:* **and his justice is** *standìng fór àn age.* | *19:10* |
| 111:4 | *Zain:* **Mêmorial he has màde of his márvels;** * | |
| | *Heth:* **gracious and tender is thè Fónt of Bèing.** | |
| 111:5 | *Teth:* **Foôd he gives to thòse who revére him;** * | |
| | *Yod:* **he keeps in mind eternàlly hìs bond.** | |
| 111:6 | *Coph:* **Mîght of his deeds speàks to his péople,** * | |
| | *Lamedh:* **to bequeath them a herìtáge of gèntiles.** | |
| 111:7 | *Mem: Wôrks of his Hands* **àre Truth and Júdgment;** * | *19:2* |
| | *Nun:* **ratified are all òf hís dècrees,** | |
| 111:8 | *Samech:* **ûpheld** *for an age, fòr an etérnity,* * | |
| | *Ain:* **to be performed ìn Trúth and Faìrness.** | |

*For an age* (*la'ad* 9:19 *et al.*) appears twelve times in the psalms and *for an eternity* (*le'olam* 5:12 *et al.*) thirty-two, but they appear side-by-side only twice (111:8, 148:6).

| | | |
|---|---|---|
| 111:9 | *Pe:* **Rêdemption he sent to his peoplè;** † | |
| | *Tsade:* **he decreed etèrnally hís bond.** * | |
| | *Qoph:* **Holy and awesòme ís hìs Name!** | |
| 111:10 | *Res:* **Prîme wisdom is** *awe for the Font of Bèing,* † | *19:10* |
| | *Shin:* **with insights good for àll who perfórm them.** * | |
| | *Tau:* **His praise is** *standíng fór àn age.* | *19:10* |

# ONE HUNDRED TWELVE

EARLIEST MANUSCRIPT — 4QPs[b]
NEW TESTAMENT — Verse 9 at 2 Cor 9:9
LITURGY OF HOURS — Second Vespers of Sunday IV
**See introduction to Psalm 111**

112:1    *Hâllelu-Y*ÀH! †                                        *104:35*
       *Aleph:* **Blessedness belongs to** revering thè FONT OF BÉING, *
       *Beth:* delighting above all ìn hís còmmands!           *1:1*

112:2    *Ghimel:* **Strông** *in the lànd* let his seédlings be; *       *41:3*
       *Daleth:* a generation of steadfast peoplè wíll be blèssed.

112:3    *He:* **Lêt** riches ànd wealth be ín his house, *
       *Waw:* and his justice be *standìng fór àn age.*         *19:10*

112:4    *Zain:* **Hê** shines in darkness as lìght for the steádfast, *
       *Heth:* as grace and tendèrnéss and jùstice.

112:5    *Teth:* **Goôd** is a man *feeling pìty and lénding,* *     *37:26*
       *Yod:* selecting hìs wórds *with jùdgment.*            *72:2*

112:6    *Coph:* **Fôr** *he wìll never stúmble;* *
       *Lamedh:* in eternal memorial will thè júst òne be.

The just one *will never stumble* (*bal yimmot* 21:8; *lo' yimmot* 15:5,
112:6, 125:1); *I do not stumble* (*bal-'emmot* 10:6, 16:8, 30:7; *lo'*
*'emmot* 62:3/7). When one stumbles by foot (38:17, 37:31) or by
tongue (64:9), one's enemies rejoice (38:17). The unjust stumble in
their winding paths (125:5) and into bogs (140:11).

112:7    *Mem:* **Hê** fears nò news of évil; *
       *Nun:* firm is his heart, trusting in thè FÓNT OF BÈING.

112:8    *Samech:* **Sûpported** is hìs heart, which feárs not, *
       *Ain:* until he looks ùpón hìs foes.

112:9    *Pe:* **Hê** gives, he distributes to the needy; †
       *Tsade: let his justice bè standing fór an age,* *       *19:10*
       *Qoph: let his horn be liftèd hígh* in glòry.         *89:25*

112:10 *Res:* **Ône** who is unjust sees and is troublèd; †
       *Shin:* he *gnashes hìs teeth* and fádes away. *        *35:16*
       *Tau:* The desire of the ùnjúst becòmes nil!

# ONE HUNDRED THIRTEEN

EARLIEST MANUSCRIPT — 4QPs[b]
JEWISH FEASTS — Tabernacles, Weeks, before Passover meal
LITURGY OF HOURS — First Vespers of Sunday III

Psalm 113 begins the section of psalms called the "Egyptian Hallel," from the word *hallel*, which means "laud!" This section is not coextensive with the usage of the word *Hallelu-Yah*. That word first appears at the end of Psalm 104 and appears twenty-one times, finally at the end of the last psalm. This Hallel section stretches from Psalm 113 to Psalm 118, during the course of which the word *Hallelu-Yah* occurs only three times (113:1/9, 117:2).

113:1  *Hâllelu-YÀH!* †  104:35
**Give laud, O** *servants of thè FONT OF BÉING!* *
**Give laud to** *the Nàme "FÓNT OF BÈING"!*  7:18

*Servants of the FONT OF BEING* (*'abdey yhwh* 113:1) may or may not belong to the levitical priesthood. They stand and worship in the porticos of the temple (135:1/2); they stand as temple guards during the night hours (134:1)

113:2  **Lêt** *the Name, the "FONT ÒF BEING"* **bé blessed** *  7:18
*from now, and to ètérnìty!*  131:3
113:3  *Frôm rising of the sùn to its sétting,* *  50:1
**may laud be given to** *the Nàme "FÓNT OF BÈING"!*  7:18
113:4  **Hîgh above** *all gentiles* **is thè** FONT OF BÉING, *  9:18
*above thè skiés* **his Glòry!**  8:2
113:5  *Whô is like our divìne FONT OF BÉING?* *  35:10
**—One exalted tò bé ènthroned,**
113:6  **Ône descènding to óversee** *
**both the heavèns ánd thè land,**
113:7  **lîfting from thè dust a poór one,** *
**from an ash heap raisìng óne ìn need,**
113:8  **gîving them à seat with prínces,** *
**with** *princès óf his peòple,*  47:10
113:9  **mâking the barren womàn settled ín a home,** *
**a joyful mother of childrèn:** *Hállelù-YAH!*  104:35

240

EARLIEST MANUSCRIPT — 4QPs[b]
JEWISH FEASTS — Tabernacles, Weeks, before Passover meal
LITURGY OF HOURS — Second Vespers of Sunday I

Psalm 114 is a short historical psalm, which seeks to go beyond the external events to their inner meaning. The psalmist asks the question "What was it with you?" (verse 5), or in other words, "Why did you act as you did?" The answer is that the Red Sea and the Jordan River rolled back because of divine intervention in history (verse 7). This psalm is sung on the *Tonus Peregrinus* in both the Gregorian and Yemenite repertories, as described in the introduction to this volume. All the psalms, including this one, have been pointed for chanting to that ancient tone.

114:1 **Whên Israël èmerged from Égypt, ***
**the *house of Jacob* from a people òf cloúdèd speech,**

> *House of Jacob* (*bet-ya'aqob* 114:1; Gen 46:27; Ex 19:3; Is 8:17, 10:20, 14:1, 41:8, 46:3, 58:1; Jer 2:4, 5:20; Amos 3:15, 9:8; Obad 1:17/18; Mic 2:7, 3:9, 4:2) is a version of the increasingly frequent *house of Israël* (*bet-yisra'el* 98:3, 115:12, 135:19; four times in Isaiah, twelve in Jeremiah and a whopping fifty-nine in Ezekiel). Likewise, the *children of Jacob* (*beney ya'aqob* 77:16, 105:6) are coextensive with *children of Israël* (*beney yisra'el* 103:7, 148:14).

114:2 **Jûdah would bècome his hóly place, ***
**Israèl hís dòmain.**

114:3 **Dîd not the sea bèhold and róll back, ***
**the Jordan flòw báck àgain?**

114:4 **Dîd not thè mountains júmp like rams, ***
**hilltops like lambs fròm thé sheèpfold?**

114:5 **Whât was with you, the seà, that you rólled back, ***
**Jordan, that you flòwed báck àgain?**

114:6 **Whât was with you, the mountaìns, jumping líke rams, ***
**hilltops, like lambs fròm thé sheèpfold?**

114:7 **Bêfore the Face of thè Master, dánce, O land, ***
**before the Face of the Godheàd óf Jàcob,**

114:8 **dîd he not turn the rock into à wateríng pool, ***
**the stone intò wáterìng springs?**

EARLIEST MANUSCRIPT — 4QPs[b]
JEWISH FEASTS — Tabernacles, Weeks, after Passover meal
NEW TESTAMENT — Verse 13 at Rev 11:18 and 19:5
LITURGY OF HOURS — Second Vespers of Sunday II

The Septuagint combines Psalms 114 and 115 into a single psalm, but their styles are very different. With its three-fold responsory "Their help and their shield is He" (9b/10b/11b), this psalm is more expansive.

115:1 **Nôt to us, O Font of Being, not tò us, †
but rather to your Nàme give the glóry, \*
*along with your mercy, àlóng wíth yòur truth.***

*Along with your mercy, along with your truth* (*'al-hasdeka 'al-'emitteka* 115:1, 138:2). The psalmist wishes us to give glory (115:1) and praise (138:2) to the Name, in company with mercy and truth, given to us as guardian angels (40:12, 61:8).

115:2 **Why should the gòntiles be sàying: \*
*"Where, oh kindly, ìs theír Divìne One?"*** 42:4

115:3 = 135:6
**Meânwhile our Divìne One is ín the skies; \*
whatever pleasès hím, hè does.**

115:4 = 135:15
**Theîr idols àre silver ánd gold, \*
works of the hands òf Ádàm's kind.**

115:5 = 135:16
**Thêy have à mouth, but speák not; \*
they have twò éyes, but seè not;**

115:6 = 135:17
**thêy have twò ears, but heár not; \*
they have à nóse, but smèll not,**

115:7 **twô hands but feel not, twò feet but wálk not; \*
they utter nòt wíth theìr throat.**

115:8 = 135:18
**Lîke them will bè those who máke them, \*
all who put theìr trúst ìn them.**

115:9 = 135:19a
    **Îsraël? Trust in thè FONT OF BÉING! ***
    *Their help and theìr shiéld is He!*           *33:20*
115:10 = 135:19b
    **Hoûse of Aaron? Trust in thè FONT OF BÉING! ***
    *Their help and theìr shiéld is He!*           *33:20*
115:11 = 135:20
    **Hâving awe for the FONT OF BEÌNG? †**
    **Trust in thè FONT OF BÉING! ***
    *Their help and theìr shiéld is He!*           *33:20*
115:12  **FÔNT OF BEING has kept us ìn mind; †**
    **he blesses, blessing *thè house of Ísraël*, ***     *98:3*
    **blessing thè hoúse of Aàron,**
115:13  **blêssing those who revere thè FONT OF BÉING, ***
    *the small ònes wíth the greàt ones.*         *104:25*
115:14  **Mây the FONT OF BEÌNG give you íncrease, ***
    **for yourselves ànd fór your chìldren.**
115:15  **Blêssed may you be to thè FONT OF BÉING, ***
    *maker of heavèns ánd òf land.*

> *The Maker of Heavens and of Land* (*'oseh shamayim wa'arets* 115:15, 121:2, 124:8, 134:3, 146:6) has a shortened form *Maker of the Skies* (*'oseh hasshamayim* 136:5). Both follow the pattern of:
> —*Maker of Marvels* (*'oseh nifla'ot,* 72:19, 86:10, 136:4)
> —*Maker of A Marvel* (*'oseh pele'* 77:15)
> —*Maker of Great Things* (*'oseh gedolot* 106:21)
> —*Maker of Judgment* (*'oseh mishpot* 146:7)
> —*Maker of Lights* (*'oseh 'oriym* 136:7)
> —*The One Who Made Us/Them* (*'osenu* 95:6; *'osaw* 149:2).

115:16  **Heâvens are heavens of thè FONT OF BÉING, ***
    **but the land he gave to *the childrèn óf Àdam.***     *11:4*
115:17  **Nôr do those who are dead give laùd to *the BÉING*, ***     *68:5*
    **nor those going down ìntó sìlence.**
115:18  **Bût we can! We càn bless *the BÉING*, ***     *68:5*
    *from now, and to eternity: "Hàllélù-YAH!"*     *104:35*

> *From now and to eternity* (*me'attah we'ad-'olam* 113:2, 115:18, 121:8, 125:2, 131:3) is a phrase that brings three psalms (115, 121, 133) to cosmic conclusions.

# ONE HUNDRED SIXTEEN

EARLIEST MANUSCRIPT — 4QPs[b]
JEWISH FEASTS — Tabernacles, Weeks, after Passover meal
LITURGY OF HOURS —
first half — Vespers of Friday II
second half — First Vespers of Sunday III

The Septuagint splits Psalm 116 into two psalms, but there is a refrain on both sides of their split: "I call in the Name FONT OF BEING" (verses 4/13/17).

116:1 **Î have loved how thè FONT OF BÉING *
hears** *the sound òf my pleàding*;                86:6
116:2 **hôw he hàs turned his Eár to me, *
and on thè dáy that Ì call.**
116:3 *Snâres of death entanglè me,* †                18:5
**and anguish of Shèöl discóvers me; *
distress and torment àre whát Ì find.**
116:4 **Bût I call** *in the Nàme "FONT OF BÉING"*: *        7:18
**"Kindly, O FONT OF BEÌNG, spúrc my soul!"**

*Kindly, O FONT OF BEING* ('*annah yhwh* 116:4/16, 118:25a/b). '*Annah* is an adverb meaning "please" or "kindly," and it can be used absolutely (116:16). Otherwise it precedes the verb. Often the simplified form – *na* is suffixed to the verb (7:10, 50:22, 118:2/3/4, 124:1, 129:1, 145:6).

116:5 **Grâcious and just is thè FONT OF BÉING, *
and our Divine One acts wìth téndèrness.**
116:6 **FÔNT OF BEING is a sentinel fòr simple peóple; *
I was no one, but hè máde mè safe.**
116:7 **Gô back** *to yoùr place of rést*, **my soul; ***        95:11
**for the FONT OF BEING hàs deált wìth you:**
116:8 **"Fôr you have rèscued my soúl from death, *
my eye from tears, my foòt fróm stùmbling!"**
116:9 **Bêfore the Face of thè FONT OF BÉING *
I will go into thè** *lánds òf life.*                27:13

116:10 Wîth assurànce, nonetheléss I said, *
    "Weary have Ì grówn ìndeed!"

116:11 Ìn my hàste, I mysélf said, *
    *"Everyone like Adam* ìs déceìtful!"             *39:6*

116:12 Whât could I repay thè FONT OF BÉING *
    for all his benèfíts tò me?

116:13 Â cup of salvatiòn, that will Í raise, *
    and call *in the Name, thè "FÓNT OF BÈING."*       *7:18*

116:14 = 116:18
    Vôws of mine to the FONT OF BEÌNG, these will Í fulfill; *
    be it so before all òf hís peòple.

116:15 Prêcious in the eyes of thè FONT OF BÉING *
    is the death of his dèvótèd one.

116:16 *Kîndly, FONT OF BEING,* for I am your servànt; †     *116:4*
    I am your servant, the *sòn of your hándmaid,* *     *86:16*
    whom you rèleásed from bòndage.

116:17 Tô you I *offer òblation óf laud,* *            *107:22*
    and call *in the Name, thè "FÓNT OF BÈING."*       *7:18*

116:18 = 116:14
    Vôws of mine to the FONT OF BEÌNG, these will Í fulfill; *
    be it so before all òf hís peòple.

116:19 în the porches of *the house of thè FONT OF BÉING,* *     *42:5*
    in your midst, O Jerusalèm! *Hállelù-YAH!*         *104:35*

# ONE HUNDRED SEVENTEEN

**EARLIEST MANUSCRIPT** — 4QPs[b]
**JEWISH FEASTS** — Tabernacles, Weeks, after Passover meal
**NEW TESTAMENT** — Verse 1 at Rom 15:11
**LITURGY OF HOURS** — Midday Prayer of Saturdays I and III

Psalm 117, like Psalms 113, 148 and 150, begins and ends with imperative *Hallelu,* "give laud." These psalms are extended tropes or midrashes of that beloved word, *Hallelu-YAH.* All the words between are exegetical, answering the questions Who, Whom, Why, and How Long? Who should praise? All nations, all peoples. Whom? The FONT OF BEING. Why? Because his mercy is mighty on us. How long? Eternally, for that is how long the why shall endure. The universalism in verse 1 appealed to Paul, who includes it in a chain of four quotations (Rom 15:11).

117:1 **Gîve laud to the FONT OF BÈING, *all géntiles!* ***
**Adore hìm, *áll the peòples*:**

The phrase **all gentiles** (*kol goyiym* 9:18, 59:9, 67:3, 72:11/17, 86:9, 113:4, 117:1) seems to exclude Israël, but the phrase **all the peoples** (*kol ha'ammiym* 47:2, 49:2, 96:3, 97:6, 99:2, 117:1) seems to be all-inclusive. Israël is hardly ever called *goy*, but often called *'am*.

117:2 **"Hôw *mighty upon* us *is his mèrcy* †**
**and truth of thè FONT OF BÉING ***
***eternally* endùres: *Hállelù-YAH!*"**                    *15:12, 104:35*

*Mighty is his mercy* (*gabar hasdo* 103:11, 117:2) is the felicitous rendering of a powerful Hebrew idiom. Divine mercy has its own massive force, drawing humanity away from sin and death. Power created the world, but mercy re-creates it. Here mercy parallels truth in the next line. They may seem odd bedfellows, but in the psalms they embrace one another (85:11). They are greater than the skies (57:11, 108:5) and point to the Divine Face (89:15), but they give the path to follow (25:10) and have been appointed our protectors (40:12) and travel companions (61:8).

# ONE HUNDRED EIGHTEEN

EARLIEST MANUSCRIPTS — 4QPs[b]
Verses 1/15/16/8/9/29 in 11QPs[a]
JEWISH FEASTS — Tabernacles, Weeks, after Passover meal
NEW TESTAMENT — Verse 6 at Heb 13:6
Verse 22 at Acts 4:12 and 1 Pet 2:7 / Verses 22–23 at Mt 21:42
Verses 25-26 at Mt 21:9 and 23:39, Mk 11:10 and Lk 19:38
CHRISTIAN FEASTS — Octave of Easter
LITURGY OF HOURS — Lauds of Sundays I and III
Midday Prayer of Sundays II and IV

Psalm 118 begins with a short form of the litany in Psalm 136. There follows an encomium on the God named *YAH*, "BEING." This abbreviated version of the divine Name appears in prefixes, in suffixes such as *Hallelu-YAH*, alone (Ex 15:2; Ps 68:5/19, 77:12, 89:9, 94:7/12, 102:19, 115:17/18, 118:5 twice, 118:14/17/18/19, 130:3, 135:4, 150:6) and even as a human name, notably that of King Jehu of Northern Israël.

118:1 = 106:1, 107:1, 118:29, 136:1
> **"Gîve laud to thè FONT OF BÉING! ***
> **How good, how eternàl ís his mèrcy!"**

118:2    *Lêt Israël kìndly be sáying: ***
> **"How eternàl ís his mèrcy!"**

> *Let Israël kindly say* (*yomar-na yisra'el* 118:2/3/4, 124:2, 129:1). This psalm is like a drama, with choral responsories (verses 2/3/4) and victory songs (verse 15). *Please* or *kindly*, *'annah*, is often reduced to *–na* and attached to the end of a verb (7:10, 50:22, 118:2/3/4, 124:1, 129:1, 145:6), to make it subjunctive.

118:3    **Lêt the house of Aaron kìndly be sáying: ***
> **"How eternàl ís his mèrcy!"**

118:4    **Lêt those who revere FONT OF BEING kìndly be sáying: ***
> **"How eternàl ís his mèrcy!"**

118:5    **Frôm the state of siege I càlled to *the BÉING*; ***      *68:5*
> **the BEING gave me answer *in thè ópen spàces*.**      *18:20*

118:6 see 56:5/12
> **FÔNT OF BÈING is fór me; ***
> **I fear not what Adam's kind mày dó tò me.**

118:7 Fônt of Being is fòr me, in hélping me; *
and I will look upòn *thóse who hàte me.*  *9:14*

118:8 Goôd it is taking refuge with thè Font of Béing, *
more than trusting ìn Ádàm's kind!

118:9 Goôd it is taking refuge with thè Font of Béing, *
more than trusting ín prìnces!

118:10 Thoûgh all the nàtions surroúnded me, *
*in the Name, the "Font of Being,"* how Ì cút thèm off!  *7:18*

118:11 Thêy encircled mè and surroúnded me, *
*in the Name, the "Font of Being,"* how Ì cút thèm off!  *7:18*

118:12 Thêy encircled me like beès; †
they blazed lìke flame amóng thorns; *
*in the Name, the "Font of Being,"* how Ì cút thèm off!  *7:18*

118:13 *Ârdently* they pushed me to thè point of fálling, *  *40:2*
but the Font of Bèìng wás my help.

118:14 see 118:21b
Mîght of mine and melody—these belòng to the Béing, *
who for me has been thè Óne whò Saves.

118:15 *Soûnding of song* and vict'ry ìn the tents óf the just: *  *26:7*
"Right Hand of the Font of Bèìng gíves vìct'ry!

118:16 *Rîght Hand* of the Font of Bèìng *is exálted!* *  *89:43*
Right Hand of the Font of Bèìng gíves vìct'ry!"

118:17 Lêt me not die, bùt rather lét me live *
and declare the deeds òf thé Bèìng.

118:18 *Ârdently* did the Bèìng corréct me, *  *40:2*
but did not bestow mè tó thè death.

118:19 Ôpen to me the gàteways of jústice; *
let me enter them; let me give laud tò thé Bèìng.

118:20 Thîs is the gate that belongs to thè Font of Béing; *
they who are just mày éntèr it.

118:21 see 118:14b
Î laud you, fòr you have ánswered me, *
and have been for me thè Óne whò Saves.

118:22 Stône which the buìlders rejécted *
has become the keystòne óf the àrchway.

118:23 By the Font of Bèìng has this cóme to be, *
which is a marvèl ín oùr eyes.

118:24 **Thîs is the day thè FONT OF BÉING made; ***
    **let us revel and rèjoíce ìn it.**

118:25 *Kîndly, FONT OF BEING,* **kìndly give sáfety! ***         *116:4*
    *Kindly, FONT OF BEING,* **kindly bèstów rèlief!**      *116:4*

118:26 **Blêssed be the òne †**
    **who comes** *in the Nàme "FONT OF BÉING"; ***     *7:18*
    **we bless you all from** *the house of thè FÓNT OF BÈING.*

118:27 **Gôd is the FONT OF BEING and shines òn us; †**
    **proceed festìvely with bránches ***
    **to the horns of the òblátion-tàble.**

118:28 *Yoû are my Gòd,* **and I laúd you; ***          *31:15*
    **O my Divine Òne, Í exàlt you!**

118:29 = 106:1, 107:1, 118:1, 136:1
    **"Gîve laud to thè FONT OF BÉING! ***
    **How good, how eternàl ís his mèrcy!"**

# ONE HUNDRED NINETEEN

EARLIEST MANUSCRIPT — 11QPs<sup>a</sup> (Verses 17–24, 37–49, 59–72, 82–96, 105–120, 128–142, 150–164, 171–176)
LITURGY OF HOURS — Midday Prayer on weekdays

119:1 *Aleph.*

**Blêssedness belongs to finding pèrfection ín the way,** *
*following the Torah of thè FÓNT OF BÈING!*          *78:10*

> **Torah of the FONT OF BEING** (*torath yhwh* 1:2, 19:8, 119:1) is not yet
> the Five Books of Moses, nor the laws contained within them. The root
> Hebrew word means "teaching." *Torah* or one of seven synonyms appears
> in each of the 176 verses of this, the longest Hebrew poem.

119:2 *Aleph.*

**Blêssedness belongs tò keeping hís Decrees,** *
*wholeheartedly* **seárching fòr him,**          *9:1*

119:3 *Aleph.*

**îf truly they dìd not** *indúlge in vice,* *          *5:6*
**if they hàve wálked in hìs Ways.**

119:4 *Aleph.*

**Yoû yourself òrdained your Précepts,** *
**to keep sentinèl tó the ùtmost.**

119:5 *Aleph.*

**Lêt my footsteps bè firm upón my path** *
**to keep sentinèl fór yoùr Laws.**

119:6 *Aleph.*

**Thûs I will not be shàmed in discérning** *
**all òf yoúr Còmmands.**

119:7 *Aleph.*

**Î laud you wìth** *steadfast-heártedness* *          *7:11*
**as I learn** *the Judgmènts óf your jùstice.*          *33:5*

119:8 *Aleph.*

**Fôr your Làws I keep séntinel;** *
*do not forsake mè tó the ùtmost.*          *27:9, 38:7*

119:9 *Beth.*
**Hôw can a youth keèp to his páthway, ***
*as befits your Word,* **to keèp séntìnel?**

Since **Word** (*dabar*) is a synonym for **Torah** in this psalm, the phrase *as befits your Word* (*kidebareyka* 119:9/25/28/65/107/169) is more or less the same as saying *as befits your Torah* (*ketorateka*, 119:85).

119:10 *Beth.*
*Whôleheartedly* **hàve I sought áfter you; ***                    *9:1*
**I will not stray fròm youír Còmmands.**

119:11 *Beth.*
*Wîthin my heart* **I esteèm your Pronoúncements; ***              *10:6*
**that I may nòt sín agaìnst you.**

119:12 *Beth.*
**Blêssed are you, Ò** FONT OF BÉING; *****
*instruct mè ín yoùr Laws.*

**Instruct me in your laws** (*lammedeniy huqqeyka* 119:12/26/68; *lammedeniy 'et-huqqeyka* 119:135; *telammedeniy huqqeyka* 119:171; *huqqeyka lammedeniy* 119:64/124). **Law** is *hoq*; **teaching** is *torah*.

119:13 *Beth.*
**Wîth my lips Ì have reláted ***
**all** *the Judgmènts óf yoùr Mouth.*                             *105:6*

119:14 *Beth.*
**Ìn the way of your Tèstaments Í rejoiced ***
**as àbóve all rìches.**

119:15 *Beth.*
**Ôn your Prècepts I cóntemplate, ***
**and I cònsíder yoùr ways.**

119:16 *Beth.*
**Ìn your Làws I will táke delight; ***
**your Word I wìll nót fòrget.**

119:17 *Ghimel.*
**Deâl with your sèrvant that Í may live, ***
**and over your Word I keèp séntìnel.**

119:18 *Ghimel.*
**Ûnveil my èyes and make cleár to me ***
**the marvèls óf your Tòrah.**

119:19 *Ghimel.*
**Thoûgh I be an alien rèsident** *ín the land*; *****              *41:3*
**hide not from mè youír Còmmands.**

119:20 *Ghimel.*
Cômpelled is my soul to yeàrn for your Júdgments *
*in èvery seàson.*                                                     *145:15*

119:21 *Ghimel.*
Yoû have rèbuked the prídeful, *
the doomed who stray fròm yoúr Còmmands.

119:22 *Ghimel.*
Rôll away fròm me disgráce and shame, *
for I have kept yoùr Téstàments.

119:23 *Ghimel.*
Thoûgh princès sat and chállenged me, *
your servant contèmplátes yoùr Laws.

119:24 *Ghimel.*
Êven more, your Testamènts are delíghts to me, *
like men of goòd coúnsel fòr me.

119:25 *Daleth.*
Clînging tò the dust ís my soul; *
*as befits yoùr Wórds,* revìve me.                                     *119:9*

119:26 *Daleth.*
Wâys of mine I recounted, ànd you repliéd to me; *
*instruct mè ín yoùr Laws.*

119:27 *Daleth.*
Shôw me the wày of your Précepts, *
and I will muse aboút your màrvels.

119:28 *Daleth.*
Teârful is my soùl from the griéving; *
*as befits your Words,* lèt mé àrise.                                  *119:9*

119:29 *Daleth.*
Tûrn from mè any wánton path, *
and have pity on mè wíth your Tòrah.

119:30 *Daleth.*
Faîthfulness is the wày have I chósen; *
I have bèstówed your Jùdgments.

119:31 *Daleth.*
Clînging was I to your Testamènts, FONT OF BÉING; *
put mè nót tò shame.

119:32 *Daleth.*
>    În the way of your Còmmands I hásten, *
>    for you hàve sét my heàrt free.

119:33 *He.*
>    Teâch me, O FONT OF BEING, thè way of yoúr Laws, *
>    and I will preserve thèm deép wìthin.

119:34 *He.*
>    Rêveal to me and I will prèserve your Tórah, *
>    and keep sentinel over her *whòleheártèdly.*                    *9:1*

119:35 *He.*
>    Poînt me in thè path of yoúr Commands, *
>    for I am wèll pleásed ìn that.

119:36 *He.*
>    Tûrn my heàrt to your Téstaments *
>    and not tò sélfish gain.

119:37 *He.*
>    Tûrn away my eyes fròm seeing whát is vain; *
>    let mè líve in yoùr Way.

119:38 *He.*
>    Fûlfill for your sèrvant your Prómises, *
>    which are for thòse whó revère you.

119:39 *He.*
>    Tûrn away my rebukes whìch I have dreáded, *
>    for your Còmmánds are goòd things.

119:40 *He.*
>    Bêhold, I have yeàrned for your Précepts; *
>    let me live ìn yoúr jùstice.

119:41 *Waw.*
>    Brîng me your merciès, FONT OF BÉING, *
>    your salvation *as bèfíts your Pròmise,*

Since *Promise* (*'imrah*) is a synonym for *Torah* in this psalm, *as befits your Promise* (*ke'imrateyka* 119:41/58/76/116/170) is like *as befits your Torah* (*ketorateka* 119:85). The Torah of Moses contains many promises made to Adam, Noah, Abraham, Jacob, and Moses.

119:42 *Waw.*
>    ând let me reply with a word to òne who rebúkes me, *
>    for in your Words Ì pút my trust.

119:43 *Waw.*

Sô take no *wòrd of truth* fróm my mouth, *
I await your Commands *tò thé ùtmost,*

*45:5*
*38:7*

119:44 *Waw.*

ând keep sentinel over yoùr Torah álways, *
*for evèr ánd àn age,*

*5:12*

119:45 *Waw.*

ând let me walk about *in thè open spáces,* *
for I hàve soúght your Prècepts,

*18:20*

119:46 *Waw.*

ând of your Testaments let mè speak befóre kings *
and I wìll nót bè shamed,

119:47 *Waw.*

ând I take dèlight in yoúr Commands *
which are thè thíngs that Ì love,

119:48 *Waw.*

ând let me *lift my palms,* to your Còmmands, †
which are thè thíngs that Ì love, *
and let me contèmpláte yoùr laws.

*63:5*

119:49 *Zain.*

Keêp in mind a Wòrd for your sérvant, *
by which you càn gíve mè hope.

119:50 *Zain.*

Wîth this have I beèn consoled ín my pain, *
that your Pròmíse revìves me.

119:51 *Zain.*

Proûd people may scorn mè *to the útmost*; *
I will not turn fròm yoúr Tòrah.

*38:7*

119:52 *Zain.*

Yoûr Commands from of old, FONT ÒF BEING, Í recalled, *
and I hàve beén cònsoled.

119:53 *Zain.*

*Seâring wind* hàs taken hóld of me *
because of the unjust people who fòrsáke your Tòrah.

*11:6*

119:54 *Zain.*

Yoûr laws are mèlodies fór me *
whenever I rèláx àt home.

119:55 *Zain.*
   **În the nightìme, †**          *42:9*
   **I have called to mind your *Nàme,* "FONT OF BÉING," ***       *7:18*
   **and I keep sentinel ovèr yoúr Tòrah.**
119:56 *Zain.*
   **Thîs thing is whàt has befállen me ***
   **because Ì képt your Prècepts.**
119:57 *Heth.*
   **Pôrtion for me is thè FONT OF BÉING; ***
   **over your Words I promised to keèp séntìnel.**
119:58 *Heth.*
   **Î have sought the Face òf You *wholeheártedly*: ***      *9:1*
   **pity me *as bèfîts your Pròmise.***      *119:41*
119:59 *Heth.*
   **Î have been mùlling upón my ways, ***
   **and turn my feet toward yoùr Téstàments.**
119:60 *Heth.*
   **Î have hastèned and have nót delayed ***
   **in keeping sentinel ovèr yoúr Còmmands.**
119:61 *Heth.*
   **Thoûgh snares of unjust peòple entwíne me, ***
   *your Torah I hàve nót forgòtten.*

   *Your Torah I have not forgotten* (*torathka lo shakahtiy* 119:61/109/153).
   *Zakar* (keep in mind) occurs in three verses (49/52/55), in the *zain* stanza,
   recalling Word, Command, and Name. *Shakah* (forget) is in nine verses (1
   6/61/83/93/109/139/141/153/176), including the last; the psalmist seeks
   not to forget Torah (61/109/153), Words (16/139), Commands (141/176),
   Laws (83), or Precepts (93).

119:62 *Heth.*
   **Mîdway through the night I àrise to laúd you ***
   **for *the Judgmènts óf your jùstice.***      *33:5*
119:63 *Heth.*
   **Î am befriending àll who revére you, ***
   **and who keep sentinel ovèr yoúr Prècepts.**
119:64 *Heth.*
   **Yoûr mercy, FONT ÒF BEING, fílls the land; ***
   *by yoùr Láws instrùct me.*      *119:12*

119:65 *Teth.*
> Wêll have you providèd for your sérvant, *
> *as befits your Words,* Ò FÓNT OF BÈING.

*119:9*

119:66 *Teth.*
> Teâch me the value of discèrnment and knówledge, *
> for I assent tò yoúr Còmmands.

119:67 *Teth.*
> Bêfore I wàs weakened, Í strayed, *
> but now I keep sentinel ovèr yoúr Pròmise.

119:68 *Teth.*
> Yoû are good, and thè cause of goódness; *
> *instruct mè ín yoùr Laws.*

*119:12*

119:69 *Teth.*
> Proûd people commit slànder agaínst me; *
> I am one who keeps your Precepts *whòleheártèdly.*

*9:1*

119:70 *Teth.*
> Bloâted àre their hearts líke the fat; *
> for me, *my delight ìs yoúr Tòrah.*

**My delight is your Torah** (*torathka shiʻshaʻthiy* 119:70; *torathka shaʻashuʻay* 119:77/92/174). Other objects of this psalmist's delight include Laws (16), Testaments (24), and Commands (47/143), but those are synonyms for Torah, and so they amount to the same thing. Only one other psalm uses this root verb, and finds delight in God's consolations to the soul (94:19).

119:71 *Teth.*
> Goôd it was for mè to be weákened, *
> that I mìght leárn yoùr Laws.

119:72 *Teth.*
> Tôrah from your lips ìs better fór me, *
> than thousands of gold òr sílver pièces.

119:73 *Yod.*
> Yoûr Hands create`d me and sét me straight; *
> show me and I wìll leárn your Còmmands.

119:74 *Yod.*
> Thêy who revère you behóld me *
> and rejoice that for yoùr Wórd I waìted.

119:75 *Yod.*
 Âware have I been, O FONT OF BEÌNG, †
 that justice is foùnd in your Júdgments; *
 and that you weakened me for the sake of Fìdélìty.

119:76 *Yod.*
 Kîndly may your mercy be òf comfort tó me, *
 *as befits your Promìse* tó your sèrvant.                    *119:41*

119:77 *Yod.*
 Yoûr tenderness bring tò me, and Í will live, *
 for *my delìght ís your Tòrah.*                              *119:70*

119:78 *Yod.*
 Shâmed are the proud for they òppress me wántonly; *
 I myself meditàte ón your Prècepts.

119:79 *Yod.*
 Lêt those who revère you retúrn to me, *
 and know yoùr Téstàments.

119:80 *Yod.*
 Lêt my heart becòme whole in yoúr Laws, *
 that I may not bè pút tò shame.

119:81 *Coph.*
 Pîning has my soul been fòr your salvátion; *
 for yoùr Wórd Ì hope.

119:82 *Coph.*
 Pîning have my eyes been fòr what you prómise, *
 saying, "When will yoù cómfòrt me?"

119:83 *Coph.*
 Thoûgh I became lìke parchment ín smoke, *
 I did not fòrgét yoùr Laws.

119:84 *Coph.*
 Hôw long are the days of your servànt? †
 When wìll you give Júdgment *
 against *those whò húnt fòr me*?                             *7:2*

119:85 *Coph.*
 Proûd peoplè have dug píts for me, *
 which does not bèfít your Tòrah.

119:86 *Coph.*
 Âll of your Còmmands are faíthful! *
 Wantonly, people pùrsué me! Hèlp me!

119:87 *Coph.*

**În a moment, they could èclipse me *in the land*,** *       2:12, 41:3
**but I did not fòrsáke your Prècepts.**

119:88 *Coph.*

**Âs befits yòur mercy, gíve me life,** *       25:7
**as I keep sentinel over the Testamènts óf yoùr Mouth.**

*Mercy* (*hesed*) is not one of the synonyms for *Torah* in this psalm, but the giving of the *Torah* was an act of mercy, and the teachings of the *Torah* reveal the merciful intentions of God. Thus the phrase **as befits your mercy** (*kehasdeka* 119:88/124/149/159) is roughly equivalent to saying **as befits your Torah** (*ketorateka* 119:85).

119:89 *Lamed.*

**Êternally, Ò FONT OF BÉING,** *       5:12
**your Word is kept ìn thé heàvens.**

119:90 *Lamed.*

**Fôr age after age ìs your Fidélity;** *       10:6
**you founded the land, ànd ít wìll stand.**

119:91 *Lamed.*

**Thêy have stood to this dày for your Júdgments,** *
**for they are all àt yoúr sèrvice.**

119:92 *Lamed.*

**Wêre *my delìght* not *your Tórah*,** *       119:70
**I would have become nil then, whèn Í wàs sick.**

119:93 *Lamed.*

**Nêver let me fòrget your Précepts,** *
**for by them yoù gáve mè life.**

119:94 *Lamed.*

**Tô you do I belòng; give me sáfety,** *
**for I hàve soúght your Prècepts.**

119:95 *Lamed.*

**Fôr me the unjust are waìting, to máke me nil;** *
**I am attentive to yoùr Téstàments.**

119:96 *Lamed.*

**Tô every goal I hàve beheld límits;** *
**utterly vast ìs yoúr Còmmand.**

119:97 *Mem.*

Hôw I hàve loved your Tórah, *
which concerns mè *áll thè day!*                                        *25:5*

119:98 *Mem.*

Yoûr Command makes me wisèr than my rívals, *
because it is mine *ètérnàlly.*                                          *5:12*

119:99 *Mem.*

Bêyond all my teachers Ì have gained ínsight, *
for your Testaments àre whát concèrn me.

119:100 *Mem.*

Bêyond the elders Ì am atténtive, *
for I hàve képt your Prècepts.

119:101 *Mem.*

Frôm every wrong pàth I restraíned my feet; *
thus over your Word I keèp séntìnel.

119:102 *Mem.*

Frôm your Judgmènts I turned nót away, *
for you are thè óne who taùght me.

119:103 *Mem.*

Hôw sweet were your Wòrds to my pálate, *
*more than honèy* tó my mouth.                                           *19:11*

119:104 *Mem.*

Frôm your Precepts I bècome atténtive; *
*therefore* I detestèd *eách fàlse path.*                                *25:8*

*Each false path* (*kol 'orah shaqer* 119:61/153). The psalmist avoids
connecting the noun *way* (*derek*) with the adjective *false* (*shaqer*). The
word *derek* is inherently positive, because the root word means straight
or true (in a directional sense). There is one path, but two directions to
go—the *way of the just* (*derek tsaddiqiym* 1:6) is to go toward goodness,
and the *way of sinners* (*derek hatta'iym* 1:1) is to go away from it. The
road is not false, but only the direction traveled.

119:105 *Nun.*

Yoûr Word is à lantern tó my feet, *
and enlightenmènt tó my pàthway.

119:106 *Nun.*

Î have sworn ànd have arísen *
to keep sentinel over *the Judgmènts óf your jùstice.*                   *33:5*

119:107 *Nun.*

Îll have I been *to the utmòst*, FONT OF BÉING; *　　　　*38:7*
as befits yoùr Wórd,* give mè life.　　　　　　　　　　*119:9*

119:108 *Nun.*

Bê pleased by oblations of my moùth, FONT OF BÉING, *
and by yoùr Júdgments, teàch me.

119:109 *Nun.*

În my pàlms ever ís my soul, *　　　　　　　　　　　　
but *your Torah I hàve nót forgòtten.*　　　　　　　　　*119:61*

119:110 *Nun.*

Ûnjust people hàve set a snáre for me, *
but I strayed nòt fróm your Prècepts.

119:111 *Nun.*

Î inherited your Testamènts *for etérnity*; *　　　　　　*5:12*
to my heart, they àre súch à joy.

119:112 *Nun.*

Î directed my heàrt to perfórm your Law *
for evèr, deép wìthin.

119:113 *Samech.*

Dûplicitous people hàve I detésted, *
but I hàve lóved your Tòrah.

119:114 *Samech.*

Rêfuge to me ànd shield to mé are you; *
for your Wòrd háve I waìted.

119:115 *Samech.*

Tûrn away fròm me, O scoúndrels, *
and I will keep the Commands òf my Divìne One.

119:116 *Samech.*

Sûpport me *as befits your Pròmise* and Í will live, *　　*119:41*
and not bè shámed for hòping.

119:117 *Samech.*

Mâke me strong ànd I will bé safe, *
and gaze always ùpón yoùr Laws.

119:118 *Samech.*

Yoû have rejected all whò stray from yoúr Laws, *
for fruitless ìs theír decèption.

260

119:119 *Samech.*
   Frôm the land you remove all unjùst people líke dross; *
   thus I have loved yoùr Téstàments.
119:120 *Samech.*
   Shûddering was my flèsh from the dreád of you, *
   and I am in àwe óf your Jùdgments.
119:121 *Ain.*
   Î have acted with *Jùdgment and jústice*; *
   to my extortionists dò nót consìgn me.                    33:5
119:122 *Ain.*
   Guârantee yoùr servant whát is Good; *
   let not the proud èxtórt fròm me.
119:123 *Ain.*
   Pîning were my eyes fòr your salvátion, *
   and for the Promìse óf your jùstice.
119:124 *Ain.*
   Deâl with your servant *as bèfits your mércy,* *       25:7
   and *by yoùr Láws instrùct me.*                         119:12
119:125 *Ain.*
   Tô me, yoùr servant, shów me, *
   and I will learn yoùr Téstàments.
119:126 *Ain.*
   Tîme for action belongs to thè Font of Béing; *
   they have brokèn yoúr Tòrah.
119:127 *Ain.*
   *Thêrefore* I lòved your Commándments *                25:8
   *more than the gold òr thé gìlding.*                    19:11
119:128 *Ain.*
   *Thêrefore* I upheld yoùr Precepts, áll of them; *      25:8
   I detestèd *eách fàlse path.*                           119:104
119:129 *Pe.*
   Mârvelous thìngs are your Téstaments; *
   *therefore* my soùl hás kèpt them.                       25:8
119:130 *Pe.*
   Mây unscrolling òf your Words shéd light, *
   giving discernmènt tó the sìmple.

119:131 *Pe.*
> Î have òpened my moúth and gaped, *
> for I longed fòr yoúr Còmmands.

119:132 *Pe.*
> Tûrn toward me, and give me lìfe as a Júdgment *
> for those whò lóve yoùr Name.

119:133 *Pe.*
> Wîth your Promise sècure my foótpath, *
> and let no evìl thíng contròl me.

119:134 *Pe.*
> Spâre me presumption lìke that of Ádam, *
> as I keep sentinel ovèr yoúr Prècepts.

119:135 *Pe.*
> *Shîne the Face of You ùpon your sérvant* *
> *and instruct mè ín yoùr Laws.*

31:17
119:12

119:136 *Pe.*
> *Wâter-filled streams* wère running dówn my eyes, *
> for those not keeping sentinel ovèr yoúr Tòrah.

1:3

119:137 *Tsade.*
> Jûst are you, Ò FONT OF BÉING, *
> and steadfàst áre your Jùdgments.

119:138 *Tsade.*
> Yoû decreed the justice of your Téstaments, *
> and hòw véry faìthful.

119:139 *Tsade.*
> Zeâl of mine redùced me to sílence, *
> for my foes have yoùr Wórds forgòtten.

119:140 *Tsade.*
> Prôven indeèd is your Prómise, *
> which yoùr sérvànt loves.

119:141 *Tsade.*
> Ûnimportant though I be, ànd disregárded, *
> your Precepts I dìd nót fòrget.

119:142 *Tsade.*
> Yoûr justice is jùstice *etérnally*, *
> and your Toràh ís thè truth.

5:12

119:143 *Tsade.*
> Neêd and ànguish have foúnd me, *
> but my delight ìs ín your Còmmands.

119:144 *Tsade.*
> Jûst are your Testàments *etérnally*; *
> show them to me ànd Í wìll live.

*5:12*

119:145 *Qoph.*
> Câlling was I *wholeheàrtedly*: Ánswer me!
> O FONT OF BEING, I will prèsérve yoùr Laws.

*9:1*

119:146 *Qoph.*
> Câlling was Ì to you: Máke me safe, *
> and I will keep sentinel over yoùr Téstàments.

119:147 *Qoph.*
> Fâcing dawn in the dim light, ìndeed I bégged for help; *
> for your Word wàs Í hòping.

119:148 *Qoph.*
> Fâcing dawn were my èyes, *as the wátches changed*, *
> to muse ùpón your Pròmise.

*63:7*

119:149 *Qoph.*
> Heâr my call *as befits your mercy*, Ò FONT OF BÉING; *
> *as befits your Jùdgmént revìve me.*

*25:7*

There are two befittings in this verse (mercy and judgment), as in Psalm 51:3 (mercy and tenderness). Mercy is not, but Judgment is one of the seven synonyms for *Torah* in this psalm. Here, both *as befits your mercy* (kehasdeka 119:88/124/149/159) and *as befits your Judgment* (kemishpoteka 119:149/156) are equivalent to saying *as befits your Torah* (ketorateka 119:85).

119:150 *Qoph.*
> Neâr drew they *who huntèd me* with cúnning; *
> far were thèy fróm your Tòrah.

*7:2*

119:151 *Qoph.*
> Neâr are you, Ò FONT OF BÉING, *
> and all your Còmmánds àre truth.

119:152 *Qoph.*
> Lông have I knòwn from your Téstaments *
> that you *eternàlly* suppòrt them.

*5:12*

119:153 *Resh.*
**Bêhold my weaknèss and delíver me, ***
**for** *your Torah I hàve nót forgòtten.*                    *119:61*

119:154 *Resh.*
***Pûrsue my suìt* and redeém me; ***                        *35:1*
**for your Pròmíse, revìve me.**

119:155 *Resh.*
**Fâr from unjust peoplè is salvátion, ***
**for they have nòt soúght yoùr Laws.**

119:156 *Resh.*
**Yoûr tender deeds are many, Ò** FONT OF BÉING; *****
*as befits your Jùdgmént revìve me.*                         *119:149*

119:157 *Resh.*
**Hûnting me and besiegìng me are mány; ***
**from your Testaments I have nòt túrned àway.**

119:158 *Resh.*
**Î beheld those who compromise, ànd was offénded ***
**by those who kept no sentinel ovèr yoúr Pròmise.**

119:159 *Resh.*
**Bêhold how I loved your Precèpts,** FONT OF BÉING; *****
*as befits your mèrcy, revìve me.*                           *25:7*

119:160 *Resh.*
**Ât the head of yoùr Word is trúthfulness ***
**and eternal are all** *the Judgmènts óf your jùstice.*     *33:5*

119:161 *Shin.*
**Prîncelings have pùrsued me fór no cause, ***
**but your Word is what made my heárt àfraid.**

119:162 *Shin.*
**Jôyful am I òver your Prómise, ***
**like one who discovers à treásùre great.**

119:163 *Shin.*
**Fâlsehood I detested ànd found offénsive; ***
**your Toràh háve Ì loved.**

119:164 *Shin.*
***Sêven times* in thè day, I gáve you laud, ***             *12:7*
**for** *the Judgmènts óf your jùstice.*                     *33:5*

119:165 *Shin.*
> ***Grând Shalom*** belongs to those whò love your Tórah, *       37:11
> and for whom it is nò stúmblìng-block.

119:166 *Shin.*
> Î awaited your salvatiòn, FONT OF BÉING, *
> as I enactèd yoúr Còmmands.

119:167 *Shin.*
> My soul keeps sentinel òver your Téstaments, *
> and I love thèm tó the ùtmost.

119:168 *Shin.*
> I kept sentinel over your Testamènts and your Précepts; *
> indeed, all my wàys áre befòre you.

119:169 *Tau.*
> Neâring the Face of You is my sòng, FONT OF BÉING; *
> *as befits yoùr Wórd,* instrùct me.                        119:9

119:170 *Tau.*
> Côming *before the Face of Yoù* is my pleáding; *           17:2
> *as befits your Promìse,* gíve me rèlief.                   119:41

119:171 *Tau.*
> Ôverflowing are my lìps with the praíse-craft; *
> indeed, you will *instruct mè ín yoùr Laws.*               119:12

119:172 *Tau.*
> Rêplying is my tòngue to your prómise; *
> how just are all òf yoúr Còmmands!

119:173 *Tau.*
> Lêt my help bè within yoúr Hand, *
> for I have chosèn yoúr Prècepts.

119:174 *Tau.*
> Lônging have I been for your salvatiòn, FONT OF BÉING, *
> and *my delight ìs yoúr Tòrah.*                            119:70

119:175 *Tau.*
> Lêt my soul lìve and give laúd to you, *
> and yoùr Júdgments hèlp me.

119:176 *Tau.*
> Roâming was I like a lost sheèp; †
> seek àfter your sérvant, *
> for I have not forgottèn your Còmmands.

# ONE HUNDRED TWENTY

LITURGY OF HOURS — Midday Prayer on Monday IV
Complementary Psalm for Midday Hours

Psalm 120 is the first of the fifteen psalms of the Great Hallel, also known as the Gradual Psalms or Psalms of Ascent.

120:1 (A Song of Ascents.)
    **Tô the FONT OF BEING** *whèn I was ùnder siege,* *      *4:2*
    **I called, that he mìght ánswèr me:**
120:2 **"Ô FONT OF BEÌNG!** †
    **Free my soul from thè** *lip of fálsehood,* *      *31:19*
    **from thè** *tóngue of treàson."*

The ***tongue of treason*** (*lashon remiyyah* 120:2/3; Mic 6:12) is also called the ***one who commits treason*** (*'oseh remiyyah* 52:4, 101:7). Hardly different is the ***tongue of deception*** (*leshon mirmah* 52:6).

120:3 **Whât can be given you, òr whàt will prófit you,** *
    **O yoù** *tòngue of treàson?*      *120:2*
120:4 *Ârrows of à strong man,* **shárpened** *
    **with thè coáls of brùshwood!**

The ***arrows of a strong man*** (*hittssey gibbor* 120:4; *hitssiym beyad gibbor* 127:4) are part of his standard military equipment. The technical term for a bowman, however, is ***master of arrows*** (*ba'al hitssiym* Gen 49:23).

120:5 **Woê to me! Would that I hàd stayed in Méshek,** *
    **or** *among the tents òf Qédàr* **camped.**

***Among the tents of Qedar*** (*'ohley qedar* 120:5, Cant 1:5). Qedar is in the north and Meshek in the south. So this verse expresses a span like that between southerly Ziön and northerly Zaphon in Psalm 48. In both expressions, the point-of-view comes from the south.

120:6 **Ôften has my soùl found hersélf encamped** *
    **with those whò háte Shàlom.**
120:7 **Î am for the Shàlom, but Í must say:** *
    **"They àre fór the bàttle!"**

EARLIEST MANUSCRIPT — Entire in 11QPs[a]
LITURGY OF HOURS — Vespers on Friday II
Complementary Psalm for Midday Hours

Psalm 121 looks up to the helpful mountains, including Ziön and Moriah, on which Jerusalem is built. Most ancient and medieval towns straddled summits, like Rome's seven hills, for defense from raiders and from disease.

121:1 (A Song of Ascents.)
**Î lift my èyes to the moúntains,** *
**from which aid wìll cóme fòr me.**

*I lift my eyes* (*'essa 'eynay* 121:1, *nasa'thiy eth-'eynay* 123:1) and my head (83:3) in attention, my gates (24:7/9) in welcome, my soul (25:1, 86:4, 143:8), and my palms (63:5, 119:48) in prayer.

121:2 **Hêlp is mine from thè FONT OF BÉING** *
*maker of heavèns ánd òf land.*                    115:15

121:3 **Nôr does he** *give your foòt to the stúmbling-block,* *    66:9
**nor does he slumber, yoùr Séntìnel.**

121:4 **Âttention! Nor does he slumbèr nor does hé sleep,** *
**the Sentinel òf Ísràël.**

121:5 **FÔNT OF BEING is Sèntinel fór you,** *
**FÔNT OF BEING is your Shade àt hánd, your rìght hand.**

121:6 **Nôr by day wìll the Sun stríke you,** *
**nor à Moón** *in thè night.*                    42:9

121:7 **FÔNT OF BEING guards yoù from all évil,** *
*he keeps sentinèl fór yoùr soul.*                 56:7

121:8 **FÔNT OF BEING keeps sentìnel †**
**over your going oùt and your cóming in,** *
*from now, and to ètérnìty!*

*From now and to eternity* (*me'attah we'ad-'olam* 113:2, 115:18, 121:8, 125:2, 131:3) contrasts this single point of time with the vast expanse of eternity that lies beyond. This idiom brings three psalms to cosmic conclusion. Even more vast in scope are:
—*from eternity to eternity* (*me'olam 'ad-'olam* 90:2)
—*from eternity and to eternity* (*me'olam we'ad-'olam* 103:17).

EARLIEST MANUSCRIPT — 11QPsª
LITURGY OF HOURS — First Vespers on Sunday IV
Complementary Psalm for Midday Hours

The author of Psalm 122 recalls sharing the joy of his fellow pilgrims, as they set foot within the holy city. The law of worship required, however, that they enter the temple itself. So they traversed the city, built on two summits, but bound up into a single city (verse 3).

122:1   (A Song of Ascents. Of David.)
        **Jôyful was I wìth those who tóld me, \***
        **"To the *house of the Font of Bèing*, lét ùs go!"**     *122:9*
122:2   **Oûr feet were standìng in your gáteways, \***
        **O Jèrúsàlem!**
122:3   **Ô Jerusalem, which they buìlt as a cíty \***
        **all tògéthèr bound!**
122:4   **Tô her go up tribes, the tribes of the Bèing; †**
        **to Israël bèlòngs the dúty \***
        **to laud the *Nàme*, "*Fónt of Bèing*."**     *7:18*
122:5   **Fôr there sit thè thrones for júdgment, \***
        **thrones for thè hoúse of Dàvid.**
122:6   **Seêk the Shalòm of Jerúsalem: \***
        **let those whò lóve yoù thrive.**

*Seek the Shalom of Jerusalem* (*sha'alu shalom yerushalayim* 122:6) is a pun. The name Jerusalem contains the word *shalom*; each word appears three times, and they are together in verse 6.

122:7   **Lêt Shalom bè found withín your walls, \***
        **surplùs ín your stòrerooms.**
122:8   **Fôr my brothers ànd friends let mé say, \***
        **"Shalom bè wíthìn you!"**
122:9   **Fôr the *house of the Font of Bèing*, our Divíne One, \***
        **let me beseech what ìs goód fòr you.**

*House of the Font of Being* (*bet-yhwh* 23:6, 27:4, 92:14, 116:19, 118:27, 122:1/9, 134:1, 135:2; *bet 'elohiym* 42:5, 52:10, 55:15; *bet 'elohenu* 135:2) bookends the psalm (verses 1/9).

# ONE HUNDRED TWENTY-THREE

EARLIEST MANUSCRIPT — Verses 1–2 in 11QPs[a]
LITURGY OF HOURS — Vespers on Monday III
Complementary Psalm for Midday Hours

In Psalm 123 the psalmist lifts his eyes, but even higher than before. Two psalms ago, he lifted his eyes to the mountains, but now his eyes rise higher, to the skies. Whether traveling by sea or by land, the pilgrim had to keep a constant lookout for the weather, for the danger of downpours or sandstorms. The words "sovereign lady" in verse two render the Hebrew word *gebirah*, the title of the queen mother in Judah and Israel, as also in Egypt (1 Kings 11:19). That position was so important in the constitution of the Jerusalem state, that a nearly complete queen mother list survives, covering the whole history of the House of David. On the domestic level the title refers to the presiding female, called *domina* in Latin.

123:1   (A Song of Ascents.)
      **Tô you I hàve lifted my eyes, ***          *121:1*
      **to the One *Seatèd ín thè Skies*.**          *2:4*

123:2a  **Seê, *like eyes* of slaves on the hànd of their sóvereigns, ***
      ***like eyes* of a slave girl on the hand of hèr sóvereign lády,**

> *Like eyes* (ke'eyniym 123:2) is the central image, repeated twice for emphasis and to advance the step-by-step progress of the poem. The psalmist lifts his eyes to God as a liberator, as a slave looks to be manumitted by his slave-owner. The master's hand can remove the shackles, and God can set the psalmist free from the taunting of the complacent and the contempt of the proud.

123:2b  **sô our eyes are on the FONT OF BEÌNG, our Divíne One, ***
      **that he may tàke píty òn us.**

123:3    **Tâke pity on us, O FONT ÒF BEING! Píty us! ***
      **How often have we been satèd wíth còntempt!**

123:4    **Ôften our souls have been sated with tauntìng, †**
      **with the còmplacent peóple, ***
      **with the contempt òf thé proud peòple.**

# ONE HUNDRED TWENTY-FOUR

EARLIEST MANUSCRIPT — Verse 8 in 11QPsᵃ
LITURGY OF HOURS — Vespers on Monday III
Complementary Psalm for Midday Hours

This author of Psalm 124 seems reluctant to commit himself to a single image; thus it seems his party has narrowly escaped being metaphorically swallowed alive (verse 3), drowned (4), or chewed as prey (6) until he settles on the beautiful simile of being like a bird sprung from the hunter's trap (7). Apparently more than one bird was trapped in that snare, because of the plural language "our soul was like a bird."

124:1  (A Song of Ascents. Of David.)
       *Hâd not the FONT OF BÈING been fór us, ∗*          *94:17*
       *let Israël kìndly be sàying,*                       *118:2*
124:2  *Hâd not the FONT OF BÈING been fór us, ∗*          *94:17*
       **when Adam's kind ròse úp agaìnst us,**
124:3  **thên would they hàve swallowed ús alive, ∗**
       **when their anger was ignitèd ágaìnst us.**
124:4  **Thên the watèrs would have drówned us, ∗**
       **the flood sùbmérged oùr souls;**
124:5  **Thên it woùld have submérged our souls, ∗**
       **with thè wáters ràging.**
124:6  **Blêssed be thè FONT OF BÉING, ∗**
       **who did not give us às préy to their teeth.**
124:7  **Lîke a bird was our soul releàsed from the húnters' trap. ∗**
       **The trap was sprung, ànd wé wère freed.**

Here the soul is ***like a bird*** (*ketsippor* 124:7), which can fly away to escape the trap set by enemies. Given similarly metaphorical wings are the wind (18:11, 104:3, 2 Sam 22:11) and the cherubim (18:11), as well as God (17:8, 36:8, 57:2, 63:8).

124:8  **Aîd for us is in *the Nàme, "FONT OF BÉING," ∗***     *7:18*
       ***maker of heavèns ánd òf land.***                     *115:15*

# ONE HUNDRED TWENTY-FIVE

EARLIEST MANUSCRIPT — 11QPsᵃ
LITURGY OF HOURS — Vespers on Tuesday III
Complementary Psalm for Midday Hours

In Psalm 125, the pilgrims are on their way to Ziön (verse 1), to Jerusalem (2). Their prayer is not for the city alone, but for the nation. One might think this is a southern psalm until the last verse, which prays for the peace of Israël. So this psalmist could be a northerner. Literal mountains do encircle Jerusalem (2) but perhaps they here represent the neighboring tribes.

125:1 (A Song of Ascents.)
**Thôse trusting in the FONT OF BEÌNG** †
**are like the *Mount of Ziòn, not to stúmble,*** *       48:3, 112:6
***seated ètérnàlly.***       9:8

125:2 **Ô Jerusalem, ringed with mountaìns!** †
**The FONT OF BEING, too, sùrrounds his peóple,** *
***from now and to ètérnìty!***       131:3

125:3 **Fôr the rod of the unjust òne** †
**will not touch the portiòn of just peóple,** *
**lest the just should try theìr hánds àt crime.**

125:4 **Gîve what is good, Ò FONT OF BÉING,** *
**to those who are good, and *in theìr heárts* are steàdfast.**       10:6

125:5 **Bût tend those who stumble in their windìng paths,** †
**with the *doers of evil,* Ò FONT OF BÉING.** *       5:6
***Shalom be wìth Ísràël!***

***Shalom be with Israël!*** (*shalom leyisra'el* 125:5, 128:6). The standard greeting formula is ***Shalom*** (peace or prosperity) followed by the preposition ***with*** (*'el-*) as in the colloquial *Shalom 'eleykem,* "Peace be with you." Also attested are the alternative greetings:
—***Peace be within you*** (*shalom bak* 122:8)
—***Peace be to you*** (*shalom lak* Judg 19:20).

EARLIEST MANUSCRIPT — 11QPs<sup>a</sup>
LITURGY OF HOURS — Vespers on Wednesday III
Complementary Psalm for Midday Hours

Psalm 126 begins with the phrase *shub . . . shibah*, "repealing the bondage," a juridical term for paroling prisoners (Deut 30:3; Ps 53:7, 85:2, 126:1/4). The psalmist says it is like "gorges in the Negev" (verse 4). When prison doors open, prisoners burst forth like floods after a rain. The psalmist knows the rhythm of rural life—the planting (5) and the harvest (6).

126:1  (A Song of Ascents.)
**Whên the Font of Being *repealed the bòndage* of Zíön, ***
**we were lìke dreáming peòple.**                                    *14:7*

*Like dreaming people* (*keholmiym* 126:1) establishes the point of view, an atmosphere of wonder on the part of the psalmist. He does not say that life is *like a dream* (*kahalom* 73:20), but only that he reacts to the wondrous deeds of God as if he were sleep-walking. He had experienced a living nightmare or two and is now is seeing wonderful things.

126:2a **Thên *our mouth wàs filled* with laúghing, ***            *71:8*
**and our tongue wìth jóyfùl song.**

126:2b **Thên they will say *àmong the géntiles*, ***               *9:12*
**"Font of Being hàs dóne much fòr them!"**

126:3  **Fônt of Being hàs done much fór us; ***
**we have been à jóyful peòple.**

126:4  ***Rêpeal*, O Font of Bèing, *our bóndage*, ***             *14:7*
**like gorgès ín the Nègev.**

126:5  **Thôse who are plànting with teárs now ***
**will reap a harvest wìth jóyfùl song.**

126:6  ***Ârdently* one goes and weeping, beàring the bág of seed; ***
***ardently* one comes with joyful sòng, beáring hìs bales.**      *40:2*

# ONE HUNDRED TWENTY-SEVEN

EARLIEST MANUSCRIPT — Verse 1a in 11QPs[a]
LITURGY OF HOURS — Vespers on Wednesday III
Complementary Psalm for Midday Hours

Psalm 127 debunks our works, as does Qohelet: "Vanity of vanities, all is vanity."
The dignity of leisure is part of the great heritage of Israël. Other ancients had an
elite leisure class and an enslaved labor class. By the Third Commandment all
are entitled to rest on every seventh day—rich or poor, slave or free, human or
animal. On that one day each week, the punishment of Adam is lifted, and there
is a return to Paradise.

127:1a  (A Song of Ascents. Of Solomon.)
> ***Woûld the FONT OF BÈING* not buíld a house,** *        *94:17*
> **vainly have its buildèrs wórked withìn it;**

127:1b  ***Woûld the FONT OF BEING* not keep sentinel òver a cíty,** *
> **vainly has à séntry kèpt watch.**        *94:17*

127:2    **Vaîn for you is early rising, delay òf rest,** †
> **eating of thè bread of hárdship;** *
> **so he gives to hìs deár one, ìn sleep.**

127:3    **Bêhold, children are a gift from thè FONT OF BÉING;** *
> **a reward is *the fruit òf thé bòsom.***        *22:11*

127:4    **Lîke *arrows* in the hànd of a *stróng man,*** *    *120:4*
> **so are the childrèn óf òne's youth.**

*Like arrows in the hand of a strong man* (*kehitssiym beyad gibbor*
127:4; *hitssey gibbor* 120:4) continues the military imagery from the
sentinel in verse 1. Bows and arrows were part of the standard military
equipment for sentries. The technical term for a bowman, however, is
***master of arrows*** (*ba'al hitssiym* Gen 49:23).

127:5    ***Blêssedness belongs to the màn* †**        *34:9*
> **who has filled hìs quiver wíth them;** *
> **unshamed, how they contend with rivàls át the gàteway!**

# ONE HUNDRED TWENTY-EIGHT

EARLIEST MANUSCRIPT — Verses 3–6 in 11QPsª
LITURGY OF HOURS — Midday Prayer on Thursday IV
Complementary Psalm for Midday Hours

Psalm 128 begins with a singular verb, so *kol* must mean "each." Many translators erred by rendering "all" here and making the verb plural, though a few have done the verse correctly (Nova Vulgata, Dahood, Zerr, RSV, EUB, Alonso Schökel). The subject is also masculine, but this only becomes clear two verses later, when he has a wife and children!

128:1  (A Song of Ascents.)
    **Blêssedness belongs to each òne †**         *2:12*
    **who reveres thè FONT OF BÉING, ***
    **who *walks àlóng* his pàthways!**         *78:10*
128:2  **Lêt you indeed eat of *thè work of yoúr palms!* ***    *9:17*
    **Blêssedness be yours, ànd yoúrs be goòdness!**

*Blessedness belongs to each one ('ashrey kol* 128:1) is the same genitival construction as **blessedness be yours** *('ashreyka* 128:2, Deut 33:29). The first is governed by a noun, the second by a pronoun. The person shifts from third to second for the remainder.

128:3  **Lêt your wife be like à branch, †**
    **fruitful in thè apses óf your home, ***
    **your children *like shoots of olives* aboút your tàble.**    *52:10*
128:4  **Bêhold, how thùs blessed ís the man ***
    **who reveres thè FÓNT OF BÈING.**
128:5  **Mây *the FONT OF BEING from the Zïön* bless yoù, †**    *110:2*
    **and may you look on the goòd of Jerúsalem ***
    ***all yoùr dàys òf life,***    *23:6*
128:6  **ând may you see the childrèn of your chíldren. ***
    ***Shalom be wìth Ísràël!***    *125:5*

LITURGY OF HOURS — Midday Prayer on Thursday IV

In Psalm 129, grass sprouts in a place which has no soil for roots, as in the parable of the Sower (Mt 13, Mk 4, Lk 8). Several other psalms also use the imagery of grass (37/92/102/103).

129:1 (A Song of Ascents.)
    **"Ôften they bèsieged me, from my youth," ***
    *let Israël kìndly be sàying.*        *118:2*

129:2 **"Ôften they bèsieged me, fróm my youth, ***
    **but they coùld nót seìze me.**

129:3 **Ôn my back thèy plowed, like thóse who plow; ***
    **they reached as far às theír hèdgerows."**

129:4 **FÒNT OF BÈING, the Júst One, ***
    **breaks any bonds wìth únjust peòple.**

129:5 **Thêy will bè shamed and túrned back, ***
    **all of them dèspísing Zìön.**

129:6 **Thêy are *like thè grass* on roóftops, ***    *37:2*
    **that, early sproutèd, wílts àway,**

*Like the grass* (kehatsiyr 37:2, 90:5, 103:15, 129:6) is the central simile of this psalm, filled with images of rural life. None of this language indicates, however, that the psalmist had a vineyard or an orchard. He tends the soil as a small farmer or a share-cropper.

129:7 **thât will never fill the palm òf one who harvests, ***
    **nor the bosom of one whò bínds thè bale.**

129:8 **Nôr will the passers-by sày: †**
    **"The blessing of the FONT ÒF BEING tó you!" ***
    **"We bless you *in the Nàme 'FÓNT OF BÈING!'"***    *7:18*

The final verse of Psalm 129 contains a versicle and responsory. One passerby says the first line, and the others answer as a group:
—*Blessing of the FONT OF BEING to you* (birkat yhwh 'eleykem)
—*We bless you in the Name FONT OF BEING* (beraknu beshem yhwh).
Similarly in the Book of Ruth, one field hand says the first line, and the others reply:
—*The LORD OF BEING be with you* (yhwh 'immakem Ruth 2:4)
—*The LORD OF BEING bless you* (yebarekeka yhwh Ruth 2:4).

LITURGY OF HOURS —
First Vespers on Sunday IV
Wednesday Compline

Psalm 130 is the sixth of the seven Penitential Psalms (6, 32, 38, 51, 102, 130, and 143). The point seems to be redemption in the last verse, coupled with mercy in second last, the only time in the Book of Psalms that they are together.

130:1 (A Song of Ascents.)
 *Frôm the deepèst places háve I called* *    69:3
 to you, Ò FÓNT OF BÈING!
130:2 Ô Adonày, listen tó my call; *
 be your Ears attuned *to the sound òf my pleàding.*  86:6
130:3 Îf you kept an Eye òn guilt, *O BÉING,* *
 O Adonay, *who woùld bé left stànding?*   76:8

BEING (*yah* 68:5/19, 77:12, 89:9, 94:7/12, 102:19, 115:17/18, 118;5/14/17/18/19, 130:3, 135:4, 150:6) is a shortened form of the divine name FONT OF BEING (*yhwh*).

130:4 Râther, with yoù is the párdon, *
 that òne máy revère you.
130:5 Wîth ardent soul I have awaited thè FONT OF BÉING, *
 and to his word hàve beén attèntive.
130:6 Tô Adonày does my soúl belong *
 more than sentinels to the dawn, sentinèls tó thè dawn.
130:7 *Âttentive be Israël to the FONT OF BEÌNG,* †
 for with the FONT OF BEÌNG is the mércy, *
 and breadth of Redemptiòn ís wìth him,

Attentive be Israël to the FONT OF BEING (*yahel yisra'el 'el-yhwh*) appears twice, near the end of adjacent Psalms 130 and 131, which helps to indicate that they are a connected pair.

130:8 ând he himsèlf redeems Ísraël *
 from àll óf theìr guilt.

# ONE HUNDRED THIRTY-ONE

**LITURGY OF HOURS —**
Office of Readings on Saturday I
Vespers on Tuesday III

The central simile of Psalm 131 likens the psalmist's soul to a weaned child. A suckling child has variable moods, contented one minute, crying out the next. After the child is weaned, the relationship of the child to the mother becomes more steady and peaceable. The psalmist is still a spiritual child but one who is taking first steps toward maturity.

131:1 (A Song of Ascents. Of David.)

**Ô FONT OF BEÌNG! †**
**My heart was not vain, nòr my eyes haúghty, ***
**nor was I directed by things too great òr wóndrous fòr me.**
131:2 **Râther, I stilled and calmed my soùl †**
*like a weaned chìld* **at his móther's side; ***
*like the weaned child* **is my soúl withìn me.**

*Like a weaned child* (*kegamul* 131:2) and *like the weaned child* (*kaggamul* 131:2) is the central, single image, describing the calm state of the psalmist's soul. The image is repeated for emphasis and to advance the step-like character of the psalm. Isaiah provides the clear definition of the term as *children weaned from milk* (*gemuley mehalab* Is 28:9). At the climax of the great Isaian vision of peace, *the weaned child shall place his hand* (*gemul yado hadah* Is 11:8) upon the den of the adder, and parents will be weaned from worry about what will happen next.

131:3 *Âttentive be Israël to thè FONT OF BÉING ***                    *130:7*
*from now and to ètérnìty!*

*From now and to eternity* (*me'attah we'ad-'olam* 113:2, 115:18, 121:8, 125:2, 131:3) contrasts this single point of time with the vast expanse of eternity that lies beyond. This idiom brings three psalms to a cosmic conclusion. Even more vast in scope are
—*from eternity to eternity* (*me'olam 'ad-'olam* 90:2)
—*from eternity and to eternity* (*me'olam we'ad-'olam* 103:17).

EARLIEST MANUSCRIPT — Verses 8–18 in 11QPs[a]
NEW TESTAMENT — Verse 11 at Acts 2:30
CHRISTIAN FEASTDAY — Assumption of the Virgin
LITURGY OF HOURS —
Office of Readings on Saturday I
Vespers on Thursday III

The name of King David appears four times in Psalm 132, out of only twelve times in the entire Book of Psalms (18:51, 78:70, 89:4/21/36/50, 122:5, 132:1/10/11/17, and 144:10). Here David is to be found in the very first verse, and also in the second-last, in the poetical figure called "inclusion" or "framing." The psalm speaks only of his plan to build a temple, and does not speak of the temple as already existing. Instead, the Ark is the central image of the Psalm, and the action of David in moving the Ark to Jerusalem was a major first step toward building the temple.

132:1 (A Song of Ascents.)
**Ôf David be mindful, Ò FONT OF BÉING, ***
**of all his húmblèness,**

132:2 **whên he swore to thè FONT OF BÉING, ***
**an oath to the Mighty Òne óf Jàcob:**

132:3 **"Lêst I ènter my hoúse-tent, ***
**lest I climb onto my cúshiòn-bed;**

132:4 **lêst I gìve sleep to my eyes, ***
**repose tò my èyelids,**

132:5 **bêfore I find a place for thè FONT OF BÉING, ***
**dwelling chambers for the Mighty Òne óf Jàcob?"**

132:6 **Bêhold, that which we heàrd of in Éphrathah, ***
**on the plain of Yà'ar we foúnd it:**

132:7 **how we could ènter his dwélling place, ***
*worship bèfóre his foòtstool.*     99:5

132:8 **Gô up *to your place of rest*, Ò FONT OF BÉING, ***     95:11
**you and yoùr *árk òf might*.**

Exodus introduces the ***ark of the commandments*** (*'aron ha'edut*, Ex 25:22, 26:33/34, 30:6/26, 39:35, 40:3/5/21; Num 4:5, 7:89). Many variants show the centrality of the ark in Hebrew religion:

—*ark of the covenant of the* FONT OF BEING (Deut 10:8, 31:25/26)
—*ark of the covenant of the Lord of All the Land* (Josh 3:11)
—*ark of the covenant of the Divine One* (Judg 20:27)
—*ark of the covenant* (Josh 3:6; Is 3:8)
—*ark of the Divine One* (1 Sam 4:13/19/21)
—*ark of the Divine One of Israël* (1 Sam 5:7/8)
—*ark of the* FONT OF BEING (1 Sam 6:1/11/15/18/21, Is 3:13)
—*ark of Adonay-*FONT OF BEING (1 Kings 2:26)
—*ark of the covenant of Adonay* (1 Kings 3:15)
—*ark of our Divine One* (1 Chron 13:3)
—*ark of holiness* (*'aron haqqodesh* 2 Chron 35:3)
—*your ark of might* (*'aron 'uzzeka* Ps 132:8; 2 Chron 6:41)
—*your might* (*'uzzeka* 63:3; *'uzzo* 78:61)
—*his footstool* (*hedom raglaw* 99:5, 132:7).

132:9 see 132:16

> Yoûr priests will be vèsted with jústice, *
> and your devoted ones wìll síng fòr joy.

132:10 Fôr the sake of Dàvid your sérvant, *
turn not away the face of your ànoíntèd one.

132:11 FÔNT OF BEING swore David a truth not to revòke: †
"From *the fruìt of your bósom* *　　　　　　　　　　22:11
I will put one ùpón yoùr throne.

132:12 Îf your sons keep my bond and the stàtutes I teách them, *
their sons, too, *for an age* will sit ùpón yoùr throne."　83:18

132:13 Fôr the FONT OF BEING hàs chosen Zíön; *
he desires her as a dwellìng fór hìmself:

132:14 "Thîs is my rèsting place *fór an age*; *　　　　　　83:18
here will I dwell, fòr Í desìre it.

132:15 Hêr meat will I blèss with a bléssing, *
her needful ones will Ì fíll wìth bread,

132:16 see 132:9

> ând bedeck her prièsts with salvátion, *
> and her devoted ones to sing wìth jóyfùl song.

132:17 Hêre I make sprout à horn for Dávid, *
set a lamp fòr my Messíah.

132:18 Hîs rivals wìll I bedéck with shame, *
but his diadem wìll shíne upòn him."

# ONE HUNDRED THIRTY-THREE

EARLIEST MANUSCRIPT — 11QPs[a]
LITURGY OF HOURS — Midday Prayer on Friday IV

Psalm 133 holds out an ideal of fraternal unity. When ancient kings had more than one wife, there would be competition within the palace to see which mother's son would accede to the throne. A new king would often slay his half-brothers to prevent them from attempting any palace coup. This psalm suggests a better way.

133:1  (A Song of Ascents. Of David)
**Bêhold how goòd and how lóvely ***
**is the leisure of brothèrs trúly one,**
133:2 **lîke the best of oil, on thè head, †**
**flowing down the beard, thè beard of Aáron, ***
**flowing onto the hèm óf his vèstment;**
133:3 ***lîke the dèwfall** **of Hérmon, ***
**flowing down by the mountaìns óf Zïön,**

> ***Like the dewfall*** (*ketal hermon* 133:3; *kattal* Hos 6:4, 13:3, 14:6) is a positive image for the psalmist, who likens brotherly love to the waters of the Jordan that bless the holy land (133:3). Hosea uses the same simile negatively and positively. The piety of Israël evaporates quickly like the dewfall (6:4) and prefigures their doom (13:3), but God will be like a dewfall for Israël (14:6).

133:4 **fôr there the FONT OF BEING dècreed the bléssing ***
**of life** *for* **ètérnìty.**

> ***For eternity*** brings three psalms to poetically apt endings (*'ad-ha'olam* 28:9, 133:4; *'ad-'olam* 18:51, 48:9, 113:2, 2 Sam 22:51). See synonymous phrases listed at 5:12.

# ONE HUNDRED THIRTY-FOUR

EARLIEST MANUSCRIPT — 11QPs[a]
LITURGY OF HOURS — Saturday Compline

The very short Psalm 134 addresses those keeping vigil in the outer court of the temple, both guarding and praying. Jewish night guards kept a four-hour tour, and so the night was broken down into three watches. The Romans, who had a much larger standing military force, kept a three-hour tour of duty, with the night segmented into four watches. The Roman usage appears in the description of Jesus as abroad "on the fourth watch of the night" (Mt 14:25), the last hours before sunrise.

134:1 (A Song of Ascents.)
    **Âttention! Bless the FONT OF BEÌNG, †**
    **all *servants of thè FONT OF BÉING,* \***        *113:1*
    **stationed in *the house of FONT OF BEÌNG, in thè nights.***     *42:5*

> ***In the nights*** (*leylot* 16:7; *balleylot* 92:3, 134:1) corresponds to the distributive phrase ***day by day*** (*yom yom* 61:9, 68:20, Prov 8:30/34). Singular ***in the night*** (*ballaylah* 42:9, 77:7, 88:2, 119:55, 121:6, 136:9) is equivalent to the daytime phrase ***at the dawn*** (*boqer* 5:4a/b; *babboqer* 88:14, 90:5/6/14, 92:3).

134:2 **Lîft up your hànds to the hóly place \***
    **and bless thè FÓNT OF BÈING.**
134:3 **Mây he bless you, *the FONT OF BEÌNG from the Zíön,* \***
    **maker of heavèns ánd òf land.**     *115:15*

> **FONT OF BEING *from the Zïön*** (*yhwh mitssiyyon* 110:2, 128:5, 134:3, 135:21) is a divine appellative connecting the Hebrews' God with his dwelling place on earth. Zion here is not the mountain as such, for the temple was built on Mount Moriah nearby. Rather, the term has come to mean the city as a whole as well as both summits within. This accords with the usage in the previous psalm, ***the mountains of Zïön*** (*harrey-tsiyyon* 133:3).

NEW TESTAMENT — Verse 14 at Heb 10:30
LITURGY OF HOURS — Vespers on Friday III 961

Psalm 135 reprises a panegyric against idolatry from 115:3/11: idols mimic humans, but their makers forfeit their own humanity.

| | |
|---|---|
| 135:1 **Hâllelu-YÀH!** † | *104:35* |
| **Laud** *the Nàme "FONT OF BÉING"!* * | *7:18* |
| **Laud, O** *servants of thè FÓNT OF BÈING,* | *113:1* |
| 135:2 **stâtioned in** *the house of thè FONT OF BÉING,* * | *42:5* |
| **in the porches of** *the house òf oúr Divìne One!* | *42:5* |
| 135:3 **Laûd the FONT OF BEÌNG!** † | |
| *How good is thè FONT OF BÉING!* * | *34:9* |
| **Play chords to his Name! Hòw lóvely ìt is!** | |
| 135:4 **Fôr** *the BEING* **has chosèn Jacob for hímself,** * | |
| **Israèl fór his pòrtion.** | |

BEING (*yah* 68:5/19, 77:12, 89:9, 94:7/12, 102:19, 115:17/18, 118:5/14/17/18/19, 130:3, 135:4, 150:6) is a shortened form of the divine name FONT OF BEING (*yhwh*).

| | |
|---|---|
| 135:5 **Fôr I have known that the FONT ÒF BEING ís great,** * | |
| **and our Adonay more thàn** *áll "divìne ones."* | *96:4* |
| 135:6 **Whàtever pleases the FONT ÒF BEING, hé does,** * | |
| **in the skies and** *on the land,* **in thè seás and àll deeps.** | *41:3* |
| 135:7 *Raîsing up vapors from the limit of thè land,* † | *46:10* |
| **he creates lightning bòlts for the raínfall,** * | |
| **sending wind oùt fróm hìs vaults;** | |

Jeremiah and Psalm 135 share the image *raising up vapors from the limit of the land* (*ma'aleh nesi'iym miqtseh ha'arets* 135:7, Jer 10:13, 51:16). The fog had to come from somewhere, and it came from the land over the horizon. Note the following related phrases:
—*limit of the land* (*qetseh ha'arets* 46:10, 61:3, 135:7)
—*limits of land* (*qatsweh-'erets* 48:11, 65:6)
—*limit of the land mass* (*qetseh tebel* 19:5)
—*limit of the skies* (*qetseh hasshamayim* 19:7)
—*ends of land* (*'afsey 'arets* 2:8, 22:28, 59:14, 67:8, 72:8, 98:3).

135:8  whô struck the firstborn of Égypt, *
    *from Adam's kìnd tó the càttle*;               *36:7*

135:9  whô sent signs and marvels into yoùr midst, O Égypt, *
    against Pharaoh and àgaínst all hìs slaves;

135:10  whô struck dòwn many géntiles, *
    and slew à númber òf kings:

135:11  *Sîhon, king of Amorites, and Òg, king of Báshan,* *
    and all the dòmaíns of Cànaan,

Before crossing the Jordan, the Hebrews defeated kings Sihon of
Heshbon (Num 21:21–35) and Og of Bashan (Deut 3:1–11), mentioned
together in adjacent psalms (135:11 and 136:19/20).

135:12  ând gave their lànd as a héritage, *
    a heritage for Isràél, his peòple.

135:13  "FÔNT OF BEING" is yoùr Name *etérnally*; *         *5:12*
    "FONT OF BEING" is your memorial *for àge áftèr age.*    *10:6*

135:14  Fôr the FONT OF BEING decìdes for his peóple, *
    and feels tenderly t'wàrd thóse who sèrve him.

135:15 = 115:4
    Îdols of the gentiles àre silver ánd gold, *
    works of the hands òf Ádàm's kind.

135:16 = 115:5
    Thêy have à mouth, but speák not; *
    they have twò éyes, but seè not.

135:17 = 115:6
    Thêy have twò ears, but heàr not; *
    but *in their mouth* thère ís nò breath.        *5:10*

135:18 = 115:8
    Lîke them will bè those who máke them, *
    all who put theìr trúst ìn them.

135:19 = 115:9/10
    *Hoûse of Israël?* Blèss FONT OF BÉING! *        *98:3*
    House of Aaron? Blèss FÓNT OF BÈING!

135:20 = 115:11
    Hoûse of Levi? Blèss FONT OF BÉING! *
    You revere FONT OF BEING? Blèss FÓNT OF BÈING!

135:21  Blêssed be *FONT OF BEÌNG from the Zìön,* *    *110:2*
    dwelling in Jerusalèm! *Hállelù-YAH!*    *104:35*

# ONE HUNDRED THIRTY-SIX

EARLIEST MANUSCRIPT — Verse 1–16 and 26 in 11QPs[a]
JEWISH FEASTS — Passover
LITURGY OF HOURS — Office of Readings on Saturday II
Vespers on Monday IV

Psalm 136 constitutes a major litany, expanding on the brief litany that starts Psalm 118. The same verse opens this along with three other psalms (106 and 107, as well as 118). The divine title *Adonim* (Lordly One, verse 3) occurs as such only in this psalm, in parallel with *Elohim* (Divine One, 4). Nearly every verse of this psalm names God under a specific title.

136:1 = 106:1, 107:1, 118:1/29
  "Gîve laud to thè FONT OF BÉING! *
  How good, how eternàl ís his mèrcy!"

136:2 Gîve laud to the Divìne of divíne ones! *
  How eternàl ís his mèrcy!

136:3 Gîve laud to thè Lord of lórdly ones! *
  How eternàl ís his mèrcy!

136:4 Tô the sole *maker of màrvels*, of greát ones! *   *72:19*
  How eternàl ís his mèrcy!

136:5 Tô the *makèr of the skiés* with skill! *   *115:15*
  How eternàl ís his mèrcy!

136:6 Tô the implanter of the land *àbove the wáterways*! *  *29:3*
  How eternàl ís his mèrcy!

136:7 Tô the maker òf lights, the greát ones! *
  How eternàl ís his mèrcy!

136:8 Sûn for rulìng in the dáytime! *
  How eternàl ís his mèrcy!

136:9 Moôn and Stars for rulìng *in the níghttime*! *   *42:9*
  How eternàl ís his mèrcy!

136:10 Tô the striker of Egypt in their fírstborn! *
  How eternàl ís his mèrcy!

136:11 Ând usher of Israèl from the mídst of them! *
  How eternàl ís his mèrcy!

136:12 Wîth Hand clenched ànd Arm exténded! *
  How eternàl ís his mèrcy!

136:13 **Whô cut intò halves the Reéd Sea! ***
How eternàl ís his mèrcy!

136:14 **Ând who escorted Isràël betweén them! ***
How eternàl ís his mèrcy!

136:15 **Ând who cast Pharaoh and his army ìnto the Reéd Sea! ***
How eternàl ís his mèrcy!

136:16 **Tô the prompter of his peoplè through a wílderness! ***
How eternàl ís his mèrcy!

136:17 **Tô the striker òf kings, of greát ones! ***
How eternàl ís his mèrcy!

136:18 *Hê slaughtèred kings,* the spléndid ones! *      *135:10*
How eternàl ís his mèrcy!

136:19 *Sîhon, thè king of Ámorites!* *      *135:11*
How eternàl ís his mèrcy!

136:20 *Ând Og, thè king of Báshan!* *      *135:11*
How eternàl ís his mèrcy!

136:21 **Ând gave their lànd** *as a héritage!* *      *33:12*
How eternàl ís his mèrcy!

136:22 **Âs a heritage for Isràël, his sérvant! ***
How eternàl ís his mèrcy!

136:23 **Whô, when we had fallèn, called us tó mind! ***
How eternàl ís his mèrcy!

136:24 **Ând snatched us from thòse who besiéged us! ***
How eternàl ís his mèrcy!

136:25 **Tô the** *Giver òf Bread* **to áll flesh! ***
How eternàl ís his mèrcy!

**Giver of Bread** (*nothen lehem* 136:25, 146:7, *nothen libehemah lahmah* 147:9) is a participial appellative describing how God sustains his creatures—all flesh (136:25) who are hungry (146:7), even the beasts (147:7).

136:26 **Gîve laud to thè God of thé skies! ***
How eternàl ís his mèrcy!

# ONE HUNDRED THIRTY-SEVEN

LITURGY OF HOURS — Vespers on Tuesday IV

Psalm 137 refers to the period of exile in Babylon in the past tense, and so the psalmist seems to be writing after the return. Even in exile the vanquished nation of Israël remained justly famous for her music. The author, however, took no pleasure in being reduced to the status of a homeless minstrel. He wanted to sing at home, or not at all. Now he has in fact returned, and now he can sing of that songless time.

137:1 **Âlong the rivers òf Babel, thére we sat, ***
**and wept as we remémbered Zìön;**
137:2 **âlong the pòplar trees ín her midst, ***
**where wè húng our lyre-bows.**
137:3 **Thoûgh there our captors asked us for words òf song, †**
**and our wàrdens for jóyful song: ***
**"Oh, sing to us à sóng of Zìön!"**
137:4 **Hôw could we sing a song of thè** FONT OF BÉING ***
**on the fields of à fóreign land?**
137:5 **Îf I forget yoù, O Jerúsalem, ***
**let this be forgotten, my ówn rìght hand!**
137:6 **Lêt** *my tongue cling to my palàte* †
**should I rèmember yoú not, ***
**should I not lift Jerusalem as thè heád of my joy.**
137:7 **Rêmember, O** FONT OF BEING**, against the sons of Edòm,**
**those saying on the dày of Jerúsalem: ***
**"Destroy! Destroy! Down tò hér foundàtion!"**
137:8 **Ô daughter of Babel, the assailànt! †**
**Blessedness belongs tò one repáying you ***
**for the dealings that yoù deált tò us!**
137:9 **Blêssedness belongs to one seìzing and smáshing ***
**your nurselings àgaínst thè rock.**

22:16

# ONE HUNDRED THIRTY-EIGHT

LITURGY OF HOURS — Vespers on Tuesday IV

The second verse of Psalm 138 contains the phrase "your full Name"—a reference to the complete nomenclature revealed to Moses: "FONT OF BEING, Divine One of your fathers, Divine One of Abraham, Divine One of Isaac, Divine One of Jacob" (Ex 3:15), later reduced to *YHWH-El* (Ps 10:12, 31:6), then to *YHWH*, and at last to *YAH*.

138:1 (Of David.)
   **Tô you I give the laud *wholeheártedly*; ***      *9:1*
   **before angels I plày chórds tò you.**
138:2 **Î adore at *your temple of holiness* and laud yoùr Name †**    *79:1*
   ***along with your mercy and àlong with yoúr truth*, ***    *115:1*
   **for you made great your promises fòr yoúr fùll Name.**
138:3 **Ôn a day I càlled, and you ánswered me; ***
   **you set me free, wìth stréngth in my soul.**
138:4 **Lêt them laud you, FONT OF BÈING, all *eárthly kings*, ***    *2:2*
   **for they have heard thè wórds of yoùr Mouth,**
138:5 **ând they sang on the paths of thè FONT OF BÉING: ***
   **"How great is the Glory of thè FÓNT OF BÈING!"**
138:6 **Hôw exalted is the FONT OF BEING! Yet thè fallen hé sees, ***
   **while the proud he espies *fròm fár àway*.**

*From far away* (*merahoq* 139:2; *mimmerhaq* 138:6, Prov 31:14) appears in adjacent psalms, a sign they come from the hand of the same psalmist, who seems to find himself in a far-off land (139:2). God's long-distance vision is a consolation to him (138:6).

138:7 **Thoûgh I enter the middle of a siege, you revive mè; †**
   **against my rivals' anger, yoù stretch out yoúr Hand, ***
   **and your own Right Hand wìll keép mè safe.**
138:8 **FÓNT OF BEING *gives requital for mè*. †**      *57:3*
   **FONT OF BEING, your mercy èndures *etérnally*; ***    *5:12*
   **dismiss not thè wórks of yoùr Hands.**

# ONE HUNDRED THIRTY-NINE

EARLIEST MANUSCRIPT — Verses 8–24 in 11QPsª
LITURGY OF HOURS — Vespers on Wednesday IV

The text of Psalm 139 contains several foreign words. There are two Aramaisms—"edict" in verse 4 and "taken up" in verse 8. If the phrase "to dwell beyond the sea" (verse 9) is autobiographical, then this psalm might come from *Tarshish* (Spain) or an isle of the Mediterranean. Verses 8 to 24 are found intact atop Column XX of the Qumran Psalm Scroll.

139:1 (For the Director. Of David. A Mizmor.)
  Ô Font of Being, yoù have asséssed me *
  and yoù háve the knòwledge:

139:2 Yoû knew my sittìng and my stánding; *
  you discerned my thought *fròm fár àway.*   *138:6*

139:3 Yoû distinguished my stridìng and my paúsing, *
  and were aware òf áll my ways.

139:4 Fôr there is nò edict ón my tongue, *
  without the Font of Being knowìng áll òf it.

139:5 Frôm behind and befòre, you besiéged me, *
  and you placed yoùr Pálms upòn me.

139:6 Mârveloùs is the knówledge; *
  above me so high, that Ì cánnot reàch it.

139:7 Whêre could Ì go from yoúr breath? *
  And where could I flee from thè Fáce òf You?

139:8 Wêre I taken into the skiès, there would yoú be! *
  Were I shrouded in Sheöl, Ì woúld behòld you!

139:9 Wêre I liftèd up on wíngs of dawn, *
  were I to dwell bèyónd thè sea,

139:10 êven there yoùr Hand would guíde me, *
  and your own Rìght Hánd would gràsp me.

139:11 Lêt me say, "Even darknèss may reveàl me, *
  by night also, there ìs líght aboùt me!"

*May disclose me* (*yeshuffeni* 139:11) is a hapax legomenon, which Dahood connected to the Arabic verb "to see" (*shafa*). The Qumran Psalm Scroll has a less difficult reading for this verse: "I say, even darkness may hide me, and night may gird me about."

139:12 Êven darkness cannot becloud what is fròm you; †
night, too, can shìne like the dáytime; *
alike is the darkening, àlíke the brìght'ning.

139:13 Fôr it was you who fàshioned my ínner self; *
you wove me within *my mòthér's bòsom.*          *22:11*

139:14 Ǐ give you laud, for I am defíned by your márvels; *
defíned are your works, ànd wéll my soùl knows.

139:15 Nôr was my form hidden fròm you, when Í was made; *
in secret was I woven, *in the lower regìòns óf thè land.*    *63:10*

In the lower regions of the land (*betahtiyyoth ha'arets* 63:10;
*betahtiyyoth 'arets* 139:15). The noun **lower regions** (*tahtiyyot*)
derives from preposition **beneath** (tahat). This is the underworld, or at
least the lowest-lying countryside, seacoast or the plains of the Dead
Sea. This psalmist claims to have been conceived there, perhaps at the
priestly city of Jericho.

139:16 Yoûr Eyes have beheld my progrèss, †
and all the days are wrìttèn, shaped in yoúr book, *
and each one òf thém ìs his.

139:17 Sô, to me, how precioùs are your thoúghts, O God! *
How num'roùs áre theìr themes.

139:18 Îf I could count them—thèy are more thán the sand—*
I awaken, ànd stìll am wìth you.

139:19 Îf only you would slay the unjùst one, O Gódhead, *
and *men of bloodshed* would turn àwáy fròm me,    *5:7*

139:20 thêy who would ìnvoke you fór a plot, *
while they dèspíse yoùr thoughts.

139:21 Dô I not hate *those who hate you*, Ò FONT OF BÉING, *    *9:14*
and take offense at those who rìse úp agaìnst you?

139:22 Wîth utter loàthing I loáthe them; *
fiends have thèy beén tò me.

139:23 Sûrvey me, O God, ànd know this heárt of mine, *
*probe me,* and know my dísàrray.          *26:2*

139:24 Seê if there be any trace of idòlatry ín me, *
and lead me on the way to ètérnìty.

EARLIEST MANUSCRIPT — Verses 1–5 in 11QPs[a]
NEW TESTAMENT — Verse 4 at Rom 3:13
LITURGY OF HOURS — Midday Prayer on Thursday IV

The "man of abusive deeds" rears his head three times in Psalm 140 (verses 2/5/12) and once at Psalm 18:49. This is not the unjust mob, as in Psalm 1, but perhaps the leader of the mob (3/5). The psalmist feels powerless against such evil, unless *Adonay* should protect him (8).

140:1   (For the Director. A Mizmor of David.)

140:2   **Dêliver me, O Fᴏɴᴛ ᴏꜰ Bᴇɪ̀ɴɢ, †**
      **from a wickèd one of Ádam's kind, ***
      **preserve me *from a man of àbúsìve deeds,***      *18:49*

140:3   **whô at heart has còncocted évils, ***
      **who each day rèpeát the bàttles,**

140:4   **whôse tongue is shàrp as a sérpent's, ***
      **with venom of a viper bèneáth theìr lips.**

140:5   **Fᴏ̂ɴᴛ ᴏꜰ Bᴇɪɴɢ, keep me from a *hand of one ùnjust*; †**   *36:12*
      ***keep sentinel over me, from a màn of abúsive deeds,***   *16:1*
      **from those who plan tò tríp my feet.**

The psalmist prays for deliverance ***from a man of abusive deeds*** (*me'iysh hemasiym* 140:2/5; *me'iysh hamas* 18:49, 140:12, 2 Sam 22:49) three times in this psalm. The abuse changes from plural the first two times to singular the third time. The unjust one may have committed many abusive deeds, but he needs only to be convicted of one in order to be banished from the land.

140:6   **Proûd people have laid a trap fòr me, †**
      **and rope handlèrs let out nétting; ***
      **they set snares for mè neár the pàthway.**

140:7   **Î said to the Fᴏɴᴛ ᴏꜰ Bᴇɪ̀ɴɢ: *"My Gód are you!"*** *    *31:15*
      **Lend Ear, Fᴏɴᴛ ᴏꜰ Bᴇɪɴɢ, to the *sound òf my pleàding!***  *86:6*

140:8   **Ô *Fᴏɴᴛ ᴏꜰ Bᴇɪɴɢ-Adònay,* †**                *16:2*
      **Strength òf my salvátion, ***
      **you shielded for my head on a day òf weapònry.**

140:9   **Grânt, O Fᴏɴᴛ ᴏꜰ Bᴇɪɴɢ, no wishes òf the unjúst one, ***
      **to his plotting gìve nó cònsent.**

140:10  **Proûd headed àre those aboút me; \***
**let the evil from theìr líps submèrge them.**
140:11  **Lêt them fall on each òther like spárks in flame; \***
**let them stumble *into bogs*; nevèr lét thèm rise.**

*Into bogs* (*bemahmoroth* 140:11) is a hapax legomenon (single reading) found just here in the Hebrew Bible, though it probably appeared also in the original Hebrew text of Sirach (12:16).

140:12  **Â man of tongue cannot bè settled *ín the land*; \***          *41:3*
***a man of abuse* is driven by evil intò bánìshment.**          *18:49*
140:13  **Î have known how the FONT OF BEÌNG acts, †**
**with decisiòn for the lówly, \***
**with judgment fòr thóse ìn need.**
140:14  **Ônly the just gìve laud to yoúr Name; \***
**let the steadfast dwell before thè Fáce òf You.**

# ONE HUNDRED FORTY-ONE

EARLIEST MANUSCRIPT — Verses 5–10 in 11QPs[a]
LITURGY OF HOURS — First Vespers on Sunday I

Psalm 141 is a prayer for evening, which begins the Jewish day (Gen 1:5). Romans computed the day from sunrise.

141:1   (A Mizmor of David.)
**Ô Font of Being, I call to yoù: "Hasten tó me!" ***
**Lend an Ear to my voice as Ì cáll tò you!**

141:2   **Lêt my prayer rise up as ìncense *befóre your Face*, ***     *17:2*
**lifting my palms as àn évenìng gift.**

141:3   **Ô Font of Being, put sòmething to guárd my mouth, ***
**to keep the doorwày óf my lips.**

141:4   **Tûrn not my heart to *a word of evìl*, †**     *64:6*
**to involvement with injustice, with mèn *doing évil*, ***     *5:6*
**or breaking bread àt their bànquet.**

141:5   **Âs mercy, the just one may strike me and rebuke mè, †**
**as virgin oil for my heàd not to sháke off, ***
**but still I pray àgaínst their troùbles.**

141:6   **Whên they are brought dòwn from the clíff of rock, ***
**their judges then will heed my wòrds, só lòvely.**

141:7   **Âs when one furrows ànd plows *intó the land*, ***     *41:3*
**their bones must be scattered into thè moúth of Shèöl.**

141:8   **Fôr my eyes are on you, *Font òf Being-Ádonay*; ***
**I have taken refuge in you, lest my soúl bè lost.**

*Font of Being-Adonay* (yhwh 'adonayh 16:2, 68:21, 109:21, 140:8, 141:8) appears in adjacent psalms 140 and 141, indicating they may have common provenance. This title is the mirror-image of *Adonay-Font of Being* ('adonay yhwh 69:7, 71:5/16, 73:28). When the Font of Being and *Adonay* are together, the synagogue reading is *Adonay, Adonay.*

141:9   ***Keêp sentinel ovèr me*** †     *16:1*
**from the hands òf those ensnáring me, ***
**and from the snares of *doèrs óf èvil*.**     *5:6*

141:10  **Lêt the unjust fall altògether ín their nets; ***
**let me, however, be one whò pássès by.**

# ONE HUNDRED FORTY-TWO

EARLIEST MANUSCRIPT — Verses 4–8 in 11QPs[a]
LITURGY OF HOURS — First Vespers on Sunday I

The author of Psalm 142 finds himself in a place of imprisonment, where a trap was hidden (4) and his soul is secluded (8), but he no longer has a place of refuge (5). As a prisoner himself, Paul in two letters (Rom 3:20, Gal 2:16) quotes the first verse, to imply the whole psalm. Elsewhere Paul employs a term from verse 3, to speak of seeing God "face-to-face" (1 Cor 13:12).

142:1 (A Maskil of David, when he was in the cave.      *1 Sam 22:1, 26:1*
       A prayer.)

142:2 ***With my voice* I cry to thè Font of Béing! ***      *3:4*
       ***With my voice* I beg for pity to thè Fónt of Bèing!**

142:3 **Tô his Face will I pour fòrth what concérns me, ***
       **tell my needs bèfóre hìs Face.**

142:4 ***Âs my breath grows more faint within mè,* †**      *77:4*
       **and you are thè one to knów my thoughts, ***
       **they set a trap for me on thè páth Ì tread.**

142:5 **Loôk to the right and see how thère is no friénd for me. ***
       **Gone for me is a refuge where none càn *seék my soul*.**      *7:2*

142:6 **Î cried out to you, Ò Font of Béing! ***
       **I said: "You are my refuge, my portion in *thè lánd òf life*."**

The **land of life** (*'erets hayyim* 27:13, 52:7; *'erets ha-hayyiym* 142:6), also called the **lands of life** (*'artsot hahayyiym* 116:9, Is 38:11, Job 28:13), will be ruled by the **God of life** (*'el hay* 42:3; *'el hayyay*, 42:9). The opposite is the land of death.

142:7 **Bê attuned to my pleading, for I am much rèduced; †**
       **deliver me fròm those who seék me, ***
       **for they are strongèr thán Ì am.**

142:8 **Rêlease my soul from hidìng, †**
       **that I may gìve laud to yoúr Name. ***
       **Gather the just about me, for you hàve deált wìth me!**

# ONE HUNDRED FORTY-THREE

EARLIEST MANUSCRIPT — Verses 1–8 in 11QPs<sup>a</sup>

EARLIEST MANUSCRIPT — Verses 1–8 in 11QPsᵃ
NEW TESTAMENT — Verse 2 at Rom 3:20, Gal 2:16
LITURGY OF HOURS — Compline on Tuesday

Psalm 143 is the last of the seven Penitential Psalms (6, 32, 38, 51, 102, 130, and 143), and it joins other psalms that mention mercy in connection with morning (59:17, 90:14, 92:3, and 143:8, with Lam 3:22/23). Psalm 59 bids us rejoice in mercy until morning; other psalms suggest that surviving the dangers of night is a mercy that calls for thanksgiving. Hence the morning temple service seems to have incorporated a mercy theme.

143:1    (A Mizmor of David.)

Ô Font of Being, to my prayer hearkèn! †
Lend Eàr to my pleáding! *
With your Fidelity answer me, wìth yoúr *jùst deeds.*     *5:9*

Justice is an abstract noun that has both grammatically masculine (*tsedeq*) and grammatically feminine forms (*tsedaqah*) in Hebrew. The masculine appears only in the singular, but the feminine appears in both singular and plural. In the plural it must mean something like ***just deeds*** (*tsidqatheka* 5:9, 143:1; *tsidqot* 103:6).

143:2    Ând enter not into judgmènt with your sérvant; *
indeed no living thing acts justly *bèfóre yoùr Face.*     *17:2*

143:3 see 7:6

Fôr a fiend *hunts my soul*, grindìng to the groúnd my life. *
He settles me in *dark places* lìke thóse lòng dead.    *7:2, 88:19*

143:4    *Breâthing of mine gròws faint withín me,* *     *77:4*
my heart numbs within thè mídst òf me.

143:5    Î have called to mind *days from òf old*; †     *44:2*
I hàve mused on áll your deeds; *
I contemplate *thè wórks of yoùr Hands.*     *8:7*

143:6    Î have extèndèd my hánds to you, *
my soul being *like land* thàt thírsts fòr you.     *78:69*

143:7    *Swîftly answer me,* O Font of Beìng! †     *69:18*
Spent is my breath; *hìde not your Fáce from me,* *     *13:2*
lest I be compared *with those going down ìntó à pit.*     *28:2*

143:8a  *Ín the morning* I will heàr *of your Mércies,* *　　90:14
for in you I hàve pút my trust.

143:8b  Shôw me *the way thàt I should fóllow,* *　　32:8
for to you *have I liftèd úp my soul.*　　25:1

143:9  Freê me from my rivals, Ò Font of Béing; *
within you, I hàve cloáked myself.

143:10  Teâch me to do your will, for you àre my Divíne One; *
your good wind will lead me *ontò lévèl land.*

Onto level land (*be'erets miyshor*) describes the topography of the
sanctuary city of Bezer, standing on the table-land in the portion of
Reuben in the Transjordan (Deut 4:43). The psalmist prays that the
divine wind will lead him onto such land, where going is easy because
there are no deep valleys or high mountains (143:10).

143:11  *Fôr the sake of your Nàme,* †　　25:11
O Font òf Being, gíve me life; *
in your Justice, bring my soul oùt fróm thè siege,

143:12  ând in your mercy silence my rivàls †
and make nil àll the foes óf my soul, *
for Ì ám your sèrvant.

EARLIEST MANUSCRIPT — Verses 1–7 and 15 in 11QPsᵃ
LITURGY OF HOURS — Lauds on Tuesday IV; Vespers on Thursday IV

The author of Psalm 144 received his military training directly from the Font of Being (verse 1), upon whom he showers military appellations (2). He prays for deliverance from a foreign army (7) and asks for victory so that the arts of peace may return (9/12/13/14).

144:1  (Of David.)
**Blêssed be** *the Font òf Being,* **my Rock,** \*          *92:15*
**who trains my hands for combat, my fingèrs fór bàttle.**

144:2  **My mercy and my fortress, my high refuge and my rèlief,** †
**my shield and ìn whom I trústed,** \*
*who subdues* **my** *peoplè úndèr me.*          *18:48*

144:3  **Ô Font of Beìng!** †
**What was Adam, yèt you took nóte of him?** \*
**The son of man, yet yoù thoúght òf him?**

144:4  **Âdam wàs equal tó a breeze,** \*
**his days** *like à shádow* **pàssing.**          *102:12*

144:5  **Ô Font of Beìng!** †
**Leave yoùr skies and cóme down;** \*
**tap on mountains that they bè wrápped ìn smoke.**

144:6  **Flâsh a lightnìng bolt and scátter them;** \*
**toss your arròws ánd confoùnd them.**

144:7  **Strêtch forth your Hands from thè heights!** †
**Deliver me and free me** *from thè waters mánifold,* \*          *18:17*
**from the hand of sons of à fóreìgn land,**

144:8 = 144:11bc
**whôse mouth hàs spoken whát is vain,** \*
**and whose right hand is à hánd of fàlsehood.**

144:9  **Ô Divine Òne,** †
**let me sing tò you** *a sóng made nèw,* \*          *33:3*
**play to you** *on à hárp of tèn strings.*          *33:2*

144:10  **Ô giver of safety to kìngs,** †
**deliverer of Dàvid his sérvant,** \*
**from a wicked blade dèlívèr me,**

144:11 = 144:7b/8
>ând free me from the hand of sons of a foreìgn land, †
>whose mouth hàs spoken whát is vain *
>and whose right hand is à hánd of fàlsehood.

144:12 Bê our sons like saplìngs towering ín their youth, *
our daughters *like pillars* holdìng úp a pàlace.

> Maidens appear *like pillars* (*kezawiyyot* 144:12, Zech 9:15) in the
> Caryotid temple on the Acropolis in Athens, and elsewhere in ancient
> architecture. The Psalmist hopes to have real daughters as magnificent
> as those idealized in art.

144:13 Lêt our lofts be filled, stocked with this ànd that, †
our sheepfolds *yieldìng by the thoúsands* *
and by tens of thousands in oùr coúntryside.

> *Yielding by the thousands* (*ma'aliypot* 144:13, Job 15:5) is a verb
> related to the ordinal number *one thousand* (*'elef*). Literally here it
> means "thousanding and ten-thousanding."

144:14 Lêt our oxen bear theìr loads; †
be there nò breach and nó flight, *
and no alarm ìn oúr plàzas.

144:15 *Blêssedness belongs to the people,* for whom this ìs so! †    89:16
*Blessedness belòngs to the peóple* *
*whose Divine One is thè FÓNT OF BÈING.*    33:12

# ONE HUNDRED FORTY-FIVE

EARLIEST MANUSCRIPT — Verse 5 in 11QPs[a]
**LITURGY OF HOURS —**
Office of Readings on Sunday III
Vespers on Friday IV

Psalm 145 praises God as King (verse 1) and the glory of his majesty (5) and of his domain (11). These statements apply language from human monarchy to divine rule. This nearly complete alphabetical psalm has a verse for each letter. The *Nun* verse, lacking in the received Hebrew text, is found in the Septuagint (in Greek) and the Qumran Psalm Scroll (in Hebrew).

(A Praise-Craft of David.)

145:1 *Aleph.*
**Î exalt you, my Dìvine One, thé King, \***         *30:2*
**and bless your Name** *for evèr ánd àn age.*         *5:12*

145:2 *Beth.*
**Êvery dày will I bléss you, \***         *7:12*
**and laud your Name** *for evèr ánd àn age.*         *5:12*

145:3 *Ghimel.*
**Greât is the FONT OF BEÌNG and most laúdable; \***
**to his greatness thère ís no èqual.**

145:4 *Daleth.*
**Ône age honors your works ùntil the néxt age, \***
**and relates yoùr deéds òf strength,**

145:5 *He.*
**splêndor of the glory of the màjesty óf you; \***
**and as they speak of your marvels, let mè cóntèmplate.**

145:6 *Waw.*
**Thêy relate the mìght of your áwesome deeds \***
**and of your greatness kindly let mè táke àccount.**

145:7 *Zain.*
**Thêy extend memory of the greatnèss of your goódness, \***
**and joyfully sìng óf your jùstice.**

145:8 *Heth.*
**Grâcious and tender is thè FONT OF BÉING, \***
*slow to wrath,* **bùt greát in mèrcy.**         *86:15*

145:9 *Teth.*
**Goôd is the FONT ÒF BEING tó all,** *            *34:9*
**with his tenderness òn áll hìs works.**

145:10 *Yod.*
**Âll of your works laud yoù, FONT OF BÉING,** *
**and your dèvoút ones blèss you.**

145:11 *Coph.*
**Thêy relate the glòry of yoúr domain,** *
**and of yoùr stréngth thèy speak,**

145:12 *Lamedh.*
**tô show the children of Àdam his deéds of strength** *
**and the glory of hìs spléndid dòmain.**

145:13 *Mem.*
**Yoûr domain is a domaìn** *for* **all** *áges,* *            *61:5*
**and your command** *in every àge áfter àn age.*            *10:6*

*Nun. LXX and 11QPs*[a]
**Fîrm is the FONT OF BÈING in áll his words,** *
**and reliable ìn áll hìs deeds.**

145:14 *Samech.*
**FÔNT OF BEING is a** *support* **tò all the fállen,** *            *54:6*
**and** *a staff tò áll those bòwed down.*

*A staff to all those bowed down* (*zoqef lekol haqefufiym* 145:14; *zoqef qefufiym* 146:8) is a participial appellative that describes how God lends support to those stooped under the heavy weights that they have to carry through life.

145:15 *Ain.*
**Êyes of all àre fixed upón you,** *
**and you give them theìr foód** *in seàson,*

*In season* (*be'itto*) occurs three times in the Book of Psalms (1:3, 104:27, 145:15) and is like the phrase *in every season* (*bekol 'eth* 34:2, 62:9, 106:3, 119:20). Neither is clock time of the twenty-four-hour day; both are calendar time of the four seasons of the year.

145:16 *Pe.*
**hôlding oùt** *open yoúr Hand,* *            *104:28*
**and fulfilling the desire òf eàch thing lìving.**

145:17 *Tsade.*
**Jûst is the FONT OF BÈING in áll his ways,** *
**and merciful ìn áll hìs deeds.**

145:18 *Qoph.*
> Neâr is the Font of Being tò those who cáll him, *
> to all who call òn hím ìn truth.

145:19 *Res.*
> Whât they desire, he does for thòse who revére him, *
> and he hears their cry ànd mákes thèm safe.

145:20 *Shin.*
> Sêntinel is the Font of Being fòr all who lóve him, *
> but he destroys all thè únjust peòple.

145:21 *Tau.*
> Lêt my mouth speak praise-craft of the Font of Beìng †
> and all flesh bless hìs *Name of hóliness,* *   33:21
> *for evèr ánd àn age.*   5:12

EARLIEST MANUSCRIPT — Verses 9–10 in 11QPs[a]
NEW TESTAMENT — Verse 6 at Acts 4:24
LITURGY OF HOURS — Lauds on Wednesday IV

Psalm 146 acknowledges people as incapable (verse 3) but the God of Jacob (5) as able. The Septuagint adds the names of Haggai and Zechariah to the titles of Psalms 146 to 148, indicating that they are post-exilic.

146:1   *Hâllelu-Yàh!* **O my soúl, give laud, ***      *104:35*
       **to thè FÓNT OF BÈING!**

146:2   **Lêt me laud the FONT ÒF BEING ín my life! ***
       **Let me play for the Divine One in my rèmaínìng time!**

146:3   **Trûst not in princelings, in à son of Ádam, ***      *8:5*
       *for whom there ìs nó salvàtion,*      *3:3*

146:4   **whôse breath goes oùt, back to hís fields; ***
       **on the same day hìs goáls becòme nil.**

146:5   **Blêssedness belongs tò one †**
       **in whose help is thè God of Jácob, ***
       **whose hope is upon the FONT OF BÈING, hís divìne one.**

146:6   *Mâker of heavens and land,* **sea and àll that is ín them, ***
       **sentinel of ètérnàl truth,**      *115:15*

146:7   **âgent of judgment for victìms, †**
       *giver of breàd* **to the húngry, ***      *136:25*
       **FONT OF BEING releasès thóse in bòndage!**

146:8   **FÒNT OF BEING is an opening for thè blind! †**
       **FONT OF BEING** *is à staff for thóse bowed down!* ***     *145:14*
       **FONT OF BEING loves thè júst peòple!**

146:9   **FÒNT OF BEING is a sentinel for alièns; †**
       **for an orphan or a widòw he gives wítness, ***
       **but makes rough** *the path òf únjust peòple.*      *1:6*

**The path of unjust people** (*derek resha'iym* 1:6, 146:9; Prov 4:19, 12:26). Injustice belongs not to the path but to those treading it.

146:10 **FÒNT OF BEING rules** *eternàlly,* **†**      *5:12*
        **your Divìne One, O Zïön, ***
        *age after àge! Hállelù-YAH!*      *10:6, 104:35*

LITURGY OF HOURS —
Part One (Septuagint 146) — Lauds on Thursday IV
Part Two (Septuagint 147) — Lauds on Fridays II and IV

Psalm 147 teaches that God freely gives rain to earth (verse 8) and snow to mountains (16), and food to beasts (9) and to people (14). The laws, too, are inestimable gifts (19), to which we should respond by playing musical instruments and singing glory and praise (1/7/12)!

147:1   *Hâllelu-Yàh!* †                       *104:35*
       **How good to play chords fòr our Divíne One!** *
       **How lovely ìs fítting praìse-craft!**

147:2   **Âs Buildèr of Jerúsalem,** *
       **Font of Being assembles outcasts òf Ísràël:**

147:3   **âs healer for *thè brokenheárted*,** *             *34:19*
       **who will bínd up theìr wounds,**

147:4   **âs the One who keèps tally óf the stars,** *
       **calling out the names fòr eách òf them.**

147:5   **Greât is our Master ànd manifóld his might;** *
       **of his insights *thère ís no coùnting*.**        *40:13*

147:6   **Wîtness for the weak is thè Font of Béing,** *
       **casting unjust peoplè tó thè ground.**

147:7   **Ânswer the Font òf Being wíth laud;** *
       **play to our Divine Òne *ón a lyre-bow*.**     *33:2*

147:8   **Hê is the One who cloaks the skies with cloùds,** †
       **who supplies thè land with raínfall,** *
       **who makes the mountaìns sproút wìth grass,**

147:9   ***gîver of their feèd* to the cáttle,** *           *136:25*
       **to the *raven chicks* that fòr whích thèy cry.**

> **Raven chicks** (*beney 'oreb* 147:9, Job 38:41) describes nestlings with the same word as for human offspring. Whereas the children of Israel are people of all ages, raven chicks are tiny, young birds.

147:10  **Hê delights not in the strèngth of a stállion,** *
        **nor takes pleasure in the physique òf ány man.**

147:11 **FÔNT OF BEING is pleased with thòse who revére him, \***
**with those attentìve tó his mèrcy.**

Here the Greek Septuagint divided Psalm 147, and in this way arrived at a total of 150 psalms along with the received Hebrew. Verse 12 does seem to introduce a new poetic thrust. To both halves the Septuagint affixed the surtitle "Alleluia: of Haggai and of Zechariah" (as they did also atop Psalms 146 and 148).

147:12 **Âdore, O Jerusalem, thè FONT OF BÉING! \***
**Laud your Divine Òne, Ó Zìön!**
147:13 **Fôr he strengthens thè bars of yoúr gates, \***
**blessing your childrèn wíthìn you.**
147:14 **Ône placing Shalòm in your bórderland \***
**will fill you *wìth creám òf wheat*!** *81:17*

*Cream of wheat* (*heleb hittiym* 81:17, 147:14). Fatty cream rises to the surface in the separation of milk. By extension, the word cream comes to mean the best of anything, as in *the cream of land* (*heleb ha'arets* Gen 45:18). This is an idiom in modern languages as well (*la crème de la crème*).

147:15 **Ône sending hìs promise tó the land \***
**has a word that rùns swíftly on!**
147:16 **Gîver òf snow like thé wool, \***
**frost he distrìbutes líke thè ash,**
147:17 **sêndìng lìke pellets hís sleet! \***
**In the face of hìs chíll, *who càn stand*?** *76:8*
147:18 **Hê sends hìs word and mélts them: \***
**he releases his breath; thè wátèrs flow.**
147:19 **Rêlating hìs words to Jácob, \***
**his laws and his judgments tò Ísràël,**
147:20 **hê has not done so fòr any géntiles; \***
**he never shows them his judgmènts. *Hállelù-YAH!*** *104:35*

# ONE HUNDRED FORTY-EIGHT

EARLIEST MANUSCRIPT — Verses 1–12 in 11QPs<sup>a</sup>
LITURGY OF HOURS — Lauds on Sunday III

Psalm 148 begins and ends with *Hallelu-Yᴀʜ*, as is also true of three other psalms (113, 117, 150). They are tropes or midrashes. The Septuagint adds the names of Haggai and Zechariah to the titles of Psalms 146 to 148.

148:1    *Hâllelu-Yᴀʜ*! †                                          *104:35*
         **Laud the Fᴏɴᴛ ᴏꜰ Bᴇɪ̀ɴɢ from the heávens! ***
         **Laud him *ùpón thè heights!***

> ***On the heights*** (*bameromiym* 148:1, Job 16:19, Qohelet 10:6) are the high places where pagan worship was conducted, but summits were also important in the worship of the Samaritans and Jews, on Mount Gerizim and Mount Moriah.

148:2    **Gîve laud to him, àll you his héralds! ***
         **Laud him, all hìs sábàöth!**

148:3    **Gîve laud to hım, yoù Sun and yoú Moon! ***
         **Laud him, all thè stárs òf light!**

148:4    **Gîve laud to him, you heavèns of the heávens, ***
         **and the waters *àbóve the heàvens!***         *8:2*

148:5    **Thêy laud the *Name*, thè *"Fᴏɴᴛ ᴏꜰ Bᴇ́ɪɴɢ,"* ***    *7:18*
         **for he commanded and thèy wére creàted,**

148:6    **ând set them *for an age, fòr an etérnity;* ***    *111:8*
         **as a law which he gave, not tò bé rèvoked.**

148:7    **Gîve laud to the Fᴏɴᴛ ᴏꜰ Bᴇɪɴɢ, Ò you from thé land, ***
         **O whales ànd áll thè deeps,**

148:8    **Ô flame and hail, O snòw and fog, O *gústing wind*, ***    *107:25*
         **doing whatever hìs wórd màicy be,**

148:9    **Ô mountaìns and all híllsides, ***
         ***O fruit trees*** **and àll cédàr woods,**

> ***Fruit trees*** (*'ets periy* 148:9) are defined as "trees bearing fruit in which is their seed, each according to its kind" (Gen 1:11). They include the vine (*gefen* 105:33), the fig (*te'enah* 105:33), the olive (*zayt* 52:10), and also the date-bearing palm (*tamar* 92:13).

148:10 **Ô livestock ànd all the cáttle, \***
**O creeping thing ànd *bírd òf wing*,**

*Bird of wing* (*tsippor kanaf* 148:10, Deut 4:17) refers to the small winged birds like the dove (*yonah*, 55:7). Large winged birds, such as the eagle (*nesher* 103:5), are called *'of kanaf* (78:27).

148:11 ***Ô earthly kings* ànd nations, évery one, \***
**O princelings and *earthly judgès*, évèry one,**

*Earthly kings* (*malkey 'arets* 2:2, 76:13, 89:28, 138:4, 148:11) and *earthly judges* (*shoftey 'arets* 2:10, 148:11) are in parallel here, and they bookend Psalm 2. Whether anointed as king or acclaimed as judge, earthly rulers hold authority by sufferance of the divine monarch and contradict their mandate by opposing the rule of heaven.

148:12 **Ô young men ànd also maídens, \***
**O eldèrs with thè young—**

148:13 **lêt them laud the *Nàme, "Font of Béing," \***       *7:18*
**so exalted is only his Name, his majesty ovèr lánd ànd sky!**

148:14 **Hê has lifted the horn of his peoplè, †**
**praise-craft of all his devout *chìldren of Ísraël*, \***       *103:7*
**a people near to hìm! *Hállelù-YAH!***       *104:35*

EARLIEST MANUSCRIPT — Verse 5 in 11QPsᵃ
LITURGY OF HOURS — Lauds on Sunday I

Psalm 149 makes an odd turn from victory celebration in the first half to military posturing in the second half. Normally the celebration takes place after the conflict. Is this a pre-celebration? The psalm does not say that a battle actually took place but only that the celebrants were well armed and ready for action if necessary.

| | | |
|---|---|---|
| 149:1 | *Hâllelu-YÀH!* † | *104:35* |
| | **Sing to the FONT OF BÈING** *a sóng made new,* * | *33:3* |
| | his *praise-craft in an assembly* of dèvótèd ones. | *22:26* |
| 149:2 | **Lêt Israël rejoice in** *thè one who máde them*; * | *95:6* |
| | let the children of Ziön revèl ín theìr King. | |
| 149:3 | **Lêt them laud hìs name** *with dáncing,* * | |
| | *with timbrel,* **and with lyre-bòw pláy tò him.** | *150:4* |
| 149:4 | **Fôr the FONT OF BEING delights in his peóple,** ᴀ | |
| | dìgnìfìes the lowly ònes wíth salvàtion. | |
| 149:5 | **Lêt devoted ones èxult in glóry,** * | |
| | sing for joy *on thè pláce where thèy lie.* | *4:5* |
| 149:6 | **Lêt exalting òf God be ín their throats,** * | |
| | and *two-edged blades* bè ín theìr hands, | |

**Two-edged blades** (*hereb piypiyyot* 149:6, Is 41:15) designates blades with two "mouths" (*piy-piy*), or two-edged. The same idea may be expressed by *both edges of the blade* (*yedey-hareb* 63:11), dual in number. Of course, all blades have two edges, but some are sharpened on both. These are such blades.

| | | |
|---|---|---|
| 149:7 | **tô exact redress** *àmong the géntiles,* * | *9:12* |
| | strikings *amóng the nàtions,* | *44:15* |
| 149:8 | **tô bind their kings with mánacles,** * | |
| | and their notables *wìth íron shàckles,* | *105:18* |
| 149:9 | **tô execute against them à writ of júdgment;** * | |
| | he is splendor to all his devout ònes. *Hállelù-YAH!* | *104:35* |

**EARLIEST MANUSCRIPT** — Entire in 11QPs[a]
**LITURGY OF HOURS** — Lauds on Sundays II and IV

The first ten lines of Psalm 150 each begin with the word *Hallelu* "give laud" and the eleventh (verse 6) ends with the full expression *Hallelu-YAH*! Each line invokes a different musical instrument or singer. Here is a musical ensemble. In 1976 Suzanne Haïk-Vantoura accompanied a small group of players and singers in her musical setting of the Hebrew text of Psalm 150, based on her interpretation of the Masoretic accents. In 1991 Esther Lamandier recorded that setting again, accompanying herself on the harp. Such efforts remain in the realm of the hypothetical. Not so with the *Tonus Peregrinus*, attested in the Gregorian chant repertory, in synagogue chants of Yemenite Jews, and in the folk melodies of the Ashkenazy.

| | | |
|---|---|---|
| 150:1 | *Hallelu-YÀH*! † | *104:35* |
| | **Give laud to Gòd, in his hóliness!** * | |
| | **Give laud to him within hìs témplate òf strength!** | |
| 150:2 | **Gîve laud to hìm in his míghty deeds!** * | |
| | **Give laud to him as befits his greatnèss mánìfold!** | |
| 150:3 | **Gîve laud to him with thè shófar blàring!** * | |
| | **Give laud to him on a harp ànd *ón a lyre-bow!*** | *33:2* |
| 150:4 | **Gîve laud to him *with timbrèl and with dáncing!*** * | |
| | **Give laud to him with the flutes ànd wíth thè strings!** | |

*With timbrel and with dancing* (*betof umahol* 150:4, *bemahol . . . betof* 149:3) refers to using small drums to accompany dancers. Maiden drummers (*'alamot tofefot* 68:26) could appear alongside dancers in the procession.

| | |
|---|---|
| 150:5 | **Gîve laud to him wìth cymbals rínging!** * |
| | **Give laud to him wìth cymbals cràshing!** |
| 150:6 | **Lêt everythìng that is breáthing** * |
| | **give laud to the BEÌNG:** *Hállelù-YAH!* |

*104:35*

The last divine appellative that appears in the book of the psalms is *THE BEING* (*yah* 68:5/19, 77:12, 89:9, 94:7/12, 102:19, 115:17/18, 118:5/14/17/18/19, 130:3, 135:4, 150:6), the shortened form of the divine name *FONT OF BEING* (*yhwh*).

## Divine Names and Appellatives in the Psalms

**Adon Family** — Master or Lord (*'adon* 97:5, 110:1, 114:7, 136:3), Lord of All the Land (*'adon kol-ha'arets* 97:5), Lord of the Lordly Ones (*'adon ha'adoniym*), Adonay ("plural of majesty" of *'adon* with first-person singular suffix, 57 times in the psalms), Adonay-FONT OF BEING Sabaöth (*'adonay yhwh saba'ot* 69:7), Adonay-FONT OF BEING (*'adonay yhwh* 69:7, 71:5/16, 73:28), Adonay my Divine One (*'adonay 'elohay* 38:16), Adonay our Divine One (*'adonay 'eloheynu* 90:17)

**El Family** — God (*'el* 29:1, 89:7), God-Savior to Them (*'el-moshiy'am* 106:21), God-Avenger for Me (*'el gomer 'alay* 57:3), God of Life (*'el hay* 42:3), God of My Life (*'el hayyay* 42:9), God Divine One (*'el 'elohiym* 50:1, 84:8), God Divine FONT OF BEING (*'el 'elohiym yhwh* 50:1), God Most High (*'el 'elyon* 78:35), God My Bedrock (*'el sal'iy* 42:10), God of Israël (*'el yisra'el* 68:36), God of Jacob (*'el ya'aqob* 146:5), God of Glory (*'el hakkabod* 29:3), God of Joy My Revelry (*'el simhat giyliy* 43:4), God-Our Salvation (*ha'el yeshu'athenu* 68:20), God of the Skies (*'el hasshamayim* 136:26), God of Truth (*'el-'emeth* 31:6), God for Salvation (*'el lemosha'ot* 68:21), God of Redress (*'el neqamoth* 94:1/1), God the FONT OF BEING (*'el yhwh* 85:9), God-Maker of Marvels (*'el 'oseh pele'* 77:15), Great God (*'el gadol* 95:3), God Who Is Uplifting (*'el-nose'* 99:8), God Who Is Zealous (*'el zo'em* 7:12).

**Eloah Family** — Godhead (*'eloah* 50:22, 114:7, 139:19), Godhead of Jacob (*'eloah ya'aqob* 114:7), Divine One (*'elohiym* the "plural of majesty" of *'eloah* with first-person singular ending), My Divine One (*'elohay* 31:15), Your Divine One (*'eloheynu* 68:29), His Divine One (*'elohaw* 33:12, 144:15 etc.), Divine One in Ziön (*'elohiym betsiyyon* 62:2), Divine One of Abraham (*'elohey 'abraham* 47:10), Divine One of Divine Ones (*'elohey ha-'elohiym* 136:3), Divine One Most High (*'elohiym 'elyon* 57:3, 78:56), Divine One of Israël (*'elohey yisra'el* 41:14, 59:6, 68:9, 69:7, 72:18, 106:48), Divine One of Jacob (*'elohey ya'aqob* 20:2, 46:8/12, 75:10, 76:7, 81:2/5, 84:9, 94:7), Divine One of Justice (*'elohey tsidqiy* 4:2), Divine One of Mercy (*'elohey hasdiy* 59:11/18), Divine One of My Stronghold (*'elohiym ma'ozziy* 43:2), Divine One of Sabaöth (*'elohey tsaba'ot* 89:9), Divine One of Salvation (*'elohey teshu'ah* 18:47, 24:5, 25:5, 278:9, 51:16, 65:5, 79:9, 85:5, 88:2), Divine One My God (*'elohiym 'eliy* 63:2), Divine One! Sabaöth (*'elohiym tsaba'ot* 80:8/15), Divine One Who Is Just (*'elohiym tsaddiyq* 7:10), Divine Your Divine One (*'elohiym 'eloheyka* 45:8, 48:15, 50:7, 67:7).

**Yah Family** — The BEING (*yah* 68:5/19, 77:12, 89:9, 94:7/12, 102:19, 115:17/18, 118:5/14/17/18/19, 130:3, 135:4, 150:6), FONT OF BEING from the Ziön (*yhwh mitssiyon* 110:2, 128:5, 1343:3, 135:21), FONT OF BEING! Divine One of Israël (*yhwh 'elohey yisra'el* 41;14, 106:48), FONT OF BEING! Divine Sabaöth! (*yhwh 'elohiym tsaba'ot* 59:6, 80:5/20, 84:9), FONT OF BEING! Divine One of the Sabaöth! (*yhwh 'elohey tsaba'ot* 89:9), FONT OF BEING-Adonay (*yhwh 'adonay* 68:21, 109:21, 140:8, 141:8), FONT OF BEING My Rock (*yhwh tsuriy* 19:15, 92:16, 144:1), FONT OF BEING-Sabaöth (*yhwh tsaba'ot* 24:10, 46:8/12, 48:9, 68:7, 84:2/4), FONT OF BEING Who Is Just (*yhwh tsaddiyq* 129:4)

## Psalm Phrases in the Hebrew Bible

**Amos** 3:15 (Ps 114:1), 7:4 (Ps 36:7), 9:8 (Ps 114:1)

**Canticle of Canticles** 1:5 (Ps 120:5)

**Chronicles** 1:21:1 (Ps 109:6), 29:17 (Ps 119:7); 2:6:41 (Ps 132:8), 7:6 (Ps 137:4), 30:27 (Ps 68:6) / **Daniel** 6:19 (40:18)

**Deuteronomy** 4:11 (Ps 97:2), 4:17 (Ps 148:10), 4:43 (Ps 143:10), 5:6 (Ps 81:11), 9:5 (Ps 119:7), 17:1 (Ps 64:6), 23:10 (Ps 64:6), 22:27 (Ps 18:42), 26:15 (Ps 68:6), 28:4/18 (Ps 105:35), 30:3 (Ps 14:7), 33:29 (Ps 128:2)

**Exodus** 15:8 (Ps 78:16), 15:11 (Ps 35:10), 19:3 (Ps 114:1), 20:1 (Ps 81:11)

**Ezekiel** 27:34 (Ps 69:3), 34:12 (Ps 97:2) / **Ezra** 8:21 (Ps 107:7)

**Genesis** 1:11 (Ps 148:9), 1:18 (Ps 136:8), 1:21 (Ps 78:27), 2:19 (Ps 104:11), 20:5/6 (Ps 78:72), 46:27 (Ps 114:1)

**Hosea** 6:4 (Ps 133:3), 6:7 (Ps 82:7), 11:11 (Ps 55:7), 13:3 (Ps 133:3), 13:4 (Ps 18:42), 14:6 (Ps 133:3)

**Isaiah** 2:10 (Ps 36:2), 8:14 (Ps 98:3), 8:17 (Ps 114:1), 10:20 (Ps 114:1), 14:1 (Ps 114:1), 22:9 (Ps 25:19), 25:1 (Ps 30:2), 33:2 (Ps 73:14), 38:11 (Ps 142:6), 40:31 (Ps 103:5), 41:8 (Ps 114:1), 41:15 (Ps 149:6), 42:17 (Ps 106:19), 44:3 (Ps 78:16), 46:3 (Ps 114:1), 47:15 (Ps 18:42), 49:17 (Ps 106:13), 51:10 (Ps 69:15), 53:9 (Ps 10:7), 58:1 (Ps 114:1), 60:8 (Ps 55:7), 61:10 (Ps 19:6), 62:6/7 (Ps 83:2), 63:5 (Ps 22:12)

**Jeremiah** 1:18 (Ps 108:11), 2:4 (Ps 114:1), 5:16 (Ps 5:10), 5:20 (Ps 114:1), 5:28 (Ps 64:6), 10:13 (Ps 135:7), 11:17 (Ps 98:3), 12:9 (Ps 104:11), 13:16 (Ps 23:4), 14:7 (Ps 51:3); 15:8 (Ps 78:27), 17:8 (Ps 1:3), 18:21 (Ps 63:10), 20:3/10 (Ps 31:14), 20:8 (Ps 73:20), 23:28 (Ps 45:5), 24:30 (Ps 68:6), 27:6 (Ps 104:11), 31:9 (Ps 107:7), 46:23 (Ps 25:19), 48:28 (Ps 55:7), 51:16 (Ps 135:7)

**Job** 8:13 (Ps 9:18), 11:5 (Ps 51:17), 15:5 (Ps 144:13), 16:19 (Ps 148:1), 28:13 (Ps 142:6), 33:3 (Ps 119:7), 31:33 (Ps 82:7), 33:14 (Ps 62:12), 34:36 (Ps 49:20), 38:17(Ps 9:14), 38:40 (Ps 104:22), 38:41 (Ps 147:9), 39:6 (Ps 107:34), 39:26 (Ps 78:26), 40:5 (Ps 62:12) / **Joel** 2:2 (Ps 97:2) / **Jonah** 2:9 (Ps 31:7)

**Judges** 9:51 (Ps 61:4), 12:3 (Ps 18:42) / **Joshua** 5:2/3 (Ps 89:44)

**Kings** 1: 9:4 (Ps 78:72), 2: 3:19 (Ps 108:11)

**Lamentations** 1:7 (Ps 44:2), 1:12 (Ps 80:13), 2:15 (Ps 50:20), 2:17 (Ps 44:2), 2:22 (Ps 31:14), 3:23 (Ps 73:14), 5:10 (Ps 11:6)

**Leviticus** 26:45 (Ps 81:11) / **Malachi** 2:6 (Ps 26:12)

**Micah** 2:7 (Ps 114:1), 3:9 (Ps 114:1), 4:2 (Ps 114:1), 6:12 (Ps 120:2/3)

**Nahum** 1:34 (Ps 86:15) / **Obadiah** 1:17/18 (Ps 114:1)

**Proverbs** 4:19 (Ps 146:9), 5:15 (Ps 78:16), 6:17 (Ps 109:2), 7:2 (Ps 17:8), 8:30/34 (Ps 7:2), 12:19 (Ps 109:2), 12:26 (Ps 146:9), 16:25 (Ps 107:7), 16:29 (Ps 36:5), 18:10 (Ps 61:4), 21:6 (Ps 109:2), 21:26 (Ps 106:14), 26:28 (Ps 109:2), 27:4 (Ps 76:8), 30:8 (Ps 58:4), 31:12 (Ps 23:6), 31:14 (Ps 138:6).

**Qohelet** 5:1 (Ps 109:8), 8:3 (Ps 64:6), 10:6 (Ps 148:1), 12:10 (Ps 45:5)

**1 Samuel** 1: 9:9 (Ps 102:26), 11:7 (Ps 36:2), 17:4 (Ps 58:12)

**Zechariah** 2:17 (Ps 68:6), 3:1 (Ps 106:9), 9:15 (Ps 144:12)

**Zephaniah** 1:15 (Ps 97:2)

# Bibliography

ALONSO-SCHÖKEL, Luis.
*Biblia del peregrino* (Bilbao: Mensajero, 1993).

ALTER, Robert Bernard.
*The Book of the Psalms: A Translation with Commentary* (New York and London: W.W. Norton, 2007).

AMBROSE OF MILAN. *Explanatio super Psalmos XII* in Corpus scriptorum ecclesiasticorum latinorum, volume 64 (Wien: F. Tempsky and Leipzig: Freytag, 1919), and in Patrologiae Latinae cursus completus, volume 15 (Paris: J.P. Migne, 1887), pp. 959-1238.

AUGUSTINE OF HIPPO.
*Enarrationes in Psalmos* in Patrologiae Latinae cursus completus, volumes 36 and 37 (Paris: J.P. Migne, 1865); in Corpus Christianorum series latina, volumes 38-40 (Turnhout, Belgique: Brépols, 1956); English translation in Nicene and Post-Nicene Fathers, First Series, Volume VIII (Oxford, 1847; reprinted Grand Rapids, Michigan: Wm. B. Eerdmans).

BEA, Augustin.
*Psalterium* (Roma: Pontifical Institute Press, 1945); reprinted in COLUMGA.

BARDTKE, H., editor.
*Liber psalmorum* in *Biblia Hebraica Stuttgartensia* (Stuttgart: Württembergische Bibelanstalt, 1969).

BROWN, Francis; DRIVER, Samuel Rolles; and BRIGGS, Charles Augustus.
*A Hebrew and English Lexicon of the Old Testament* (Oxford: Clarendon, 1907; corrected reprint 1972).

CASSIODORUS, Magnus Aurelius.
*Expositio Psalmorum I-LXX* in Corpus Christianorum series Latina, volume 97 (Turnhout, Belgique: Brépols, 1958).

COLUMGA, Alberto and TURRADO, Laurentio, eds.
*Biblia Sacra iuxta Vulgatam Clementinam Nova Editio* (fourth edition Madrid: Biblioteca de autores cristianos, 1965).

CONGREGATION FOR DIVINE WORSHIP.
—*Liturgia horarum* (Vatican City: Libreria Editrice Vaticana, 1971; editio typica altera 1985, 1986, 1987).
—*Liturgiam authenticam: Fifth Instruction on Vernacular Translation of the Roman Liturgy* (Vatican City, 28 March 2001; Washington, D.C.: USCCB, Latin text and English translation, November 2001).

DAHOOD, Mitchell.
*Anchor Bible Psalms: A New Translation with Introduction and Commentary* (Garden City, NY: Doubleday, volume one 1966; volume two 1968, 1973; volume three 1970).

EHRLICH, Arnold Bogumil.
*Die Psalmen* (Berlin: Poppelauer, 1905).

ERBACHER, Rhabanus.
*Tonus Peregrinus: Geschichte eines Psalmtons* in *Münsterschwarzacher Studien* Band 12 (Münsterschwarzach: Vier-Türme, 1971).

GUNKEL, Hermann.
*Die Psalmen* in *Handkommentar zum Alten Testament* (Göttingen, 1926), translated by Thomas M. Horner as *The Psalms: A Form-Critical Introduction*, translated by Thomas M. Horner (Philadelphia: Fortress, 1967), and by James D. Nogalski as *Introduction to the Psalms: the Genres of the Religious Lyric of Israel* (Macon, Georgia: Mercer University Press, 1998).

HAIK-VANTOURA, Suzanne.
*Musique de la Bible revelée* (Paris: Dessain et Tolra, 1976, 1978); *Music of the Bible Revealed* (Berkeley CA: BIBAL; San Francisco: King David's Harp, 1991).

HILARY.
*Tractatus super Psalmos*, ed. A. Zingerle in Corpus Scriptorum Ecclesiasticorum Latinorum, volume 22 (Wien: F. Tempsky and Leipzig: Freytag, 1891).

HOFTIJZER, Jacob and JONGELING, K.
*Dictionary of the North-West Semitic Inscriptions* (Leiden: Brill, 1995).

HOLLADAY, William L.
*A Concise Hebrew and Aramaic Lexicon of the Old Testament* (Leiden: Brill, 1971).

INTERPRETER'S BIBLE.
*Volume Four: Psalms and Proverbs* (New York and Nashville: Abingdon, 1951).

JEROME, Eusebius.
*Tractatus in Psalmos* in Corpus Christianorum series Latina, volume 78 (Turnhout, Belgique: Brépols, 1958).

JOÜON, Paul.
*Grammaire de l'hébreu biblique* (Rome: Institut Biblique Pontifical, 1923, 1982).

KRAUS, Hans-Joachim.
*Psalmen* in *Biblischer Kommentar Altes Testament* (1978); translated by Hilton C. Oswald as *Psalms: A Commentary* (Minneapolis: Augsburg, 1988).

KUGEL, James L.
*The Idea of Biblical Poetry: Parallelism and Its History* (New Haven, Connecticut: Yale, 1981).

LISOWSKI, Gerhardt.
*Konkordanz zum hebräischen alten Testament, zweite Auflage* (Stuttgart: Württembergische Bibelanstalt, 1958).

LUNDBERG, Matthias.
*Tonus Peregrinus: The History of a Psalm-Tone and its use in Polyphonic Music* (Farnham, England and Burlington VT: Ashgate, 2011).

MOWINCKLE, Sigmund.
*Offersang og Sangoffer* (Oslo: H. Aschehoug, 1951; translated by D.R. Ap-Thomas as *The Psalms in Israel's Worship* (Oxford: Basil Blackwell, 1962; New York: Abingdon, 1967; Sheffield: Academic Press, 1992).

PRITCHARD, James B., ed.
*Ancient Near Eastern Supplementary Texts and Pictures Relating to the Old Testament* (Princeton: University Press, 1969).

RAHLFS, Alfred.
*Septuaginta Id est Vetus Testamentum graece iuxta LXX interpretes* (Stuttgart: Deutsche Bibelgesellschaft, 1935; ninth edition 1984).

SANDERS, J.A.
*The Psalm Scrolls of Qumran Cave 11 (11QPsᵃ)* in Discoveries in the Judean Desert of Jordan 4 (Oxford: Clarendon, 1965).

SOLESMES EDITIONS.
*Antiphonale monasticum* (Sablé-sur-Sarthe: Abbaye de St Pierre de Solesmes, 2005, 2006, 2007).
*Liber usualis* (Tournai: Desclée, 1928).

WEIL, Gérard E., ed.
*Massorah Gedolah iuxta Codicem Leningradensem* (Roma: Pontifical Institute Press, 1971).

WERNER, Eric.
*The Sacred Bridge: Liturgical Parallels in Synagogue and Early Church* (London: Dobson, 1959).

ZERR, Bonaventure.
*The Psalms: A New Translation* (New York: Paulist, 1979).